The Drive-In

The Drive-In

Outdoor Cinema in 1950s America and the Popular Imagination

GUY BAREFOOT

BLOOMSBURY ACADEMIC
NEW YORK • LONDON • OXFORD • NEW DELHI • SYDNEY

BLOOMSBURY ACADEMIC

Bloomsbury Publishing Inc, 1385 Broadway, New York, NY 10018, USA
Bloomsbury Publishing Plc, 50 Bedford Square, London, WC1B 3DP, UK
Bloomsbury Publishing Ireland, 29 Earlsfort Terrace, Dublin 2, D02 AY28, Ireland

BLOOMSBURY, BLOOMSBURY ACADEMIC and the Diana logo are trademarks of Bloomsbury Publishing Plc

First published in the United States of America 2024
Paperback edition published 2025

Copyright © Guy Barefoot, 2024

For legal purposes the Acknowledgements on p. vii constitute an extension of this copyright page.

Cover design: Eleanor Rose

Cover image: Aerial view of drive-in theater in rural Indiana, ca. 1955 © Kirn Vintage Stock / Corbis / Getty Images)

All rights reserved. No part of this publication may be: i) reproduced or transmitted in any form, electronic or mechanical, including photocopying, recording or by means of any information storage or retrieval system without prior permission in writing from the publishers; or ii) used or reproduced in any way for the training, development or operation of artificial intelligence (AI) technologies, including generative AI technologies. The rights holders expressly reserve this publication from the text and data mining exception as per Article 4(3) of the Digital Single Market Directive (EU) 2019/790.

Bloomsbury Publishing Inc does not have any control over, or responsibility for, any third-party websites referred to or in this book. All internet addresses given in this book were correct at the time of going to press. The author and publisher regret any inconvenience caused if addresses have changed or sites have ceased to exist, but can accept no responsibility for any such changes.

A catalog record for this book is available from the Library of Congress.

Library of Congress Cataloging-in-Publication Data

Names: Barefoot, Guy, 1957- author.
Title: The drive-in : outdoor cinema in 1950s America and the popular imagination / Guy Barefoot.
Description: New York : Bloomsbury Academic, 2024. | Includes bibliographical references and index.
Identifiers: LCCN 2023019762 (print) | LCCN 2023019763 (ebook) | ISBN 9781501365928 (hardback) | ISBN 9781501375019 (paperback) | ISBN 9781501365911 (epub) | ISBN 9781501365904 (pdf) | ISBN 9781501365898 (ebook other)
Subjects: LCSH: Drive-in theaters–United States–History.
Classification: LCC PN1993.5.U6 B2975 2024 (print) | LCC PN1993.5.U6 (ebook) | DDC 791.43/0973–dc23/eng/20230710
LC record available at https://lccn.loc.gov/2023019762
LC ebook record available at https://lccn.loc.gov/2023019763

ISBN: HB: 978-1-5013-6592-8
PB: 978-1-5013-7501-9
ePDF: 978-1-5013-6590-4
eBook: 978-1-5013-6591-1

Typeset by Deanta Global Publishing Services, Chennai, India

For product safety related questions contact productsafety@bloomsbury.com.

To find out more about our authors and books visit www.bloomsbury.com and sign up for our newsletters.

Contents

List of illustrations vi
Acknowledgements vii
Note to the reader ix

Introduction 1

1 Place 21
2 Programme 57
3 People 109
4 Pictures 147

Conclusion: The drive-in and cinema history 181

Notes 189
Archive collections and databases consulted 232
Select bibliography 233
Index 246

Illustrations

Figures

1. The Gratiot Drive-In, Roseville, Michigan 7
2. The Gratiot Drive-In sign and screen tower at dusk 7
3. Photograph of the future site of the Park Drive-In 34
4. From 'Abilene's Newest Drive-in' brochure, 2 42
5. Aerial photograph, 1959, showing Sharpstown before the mall was built and the Southwest Freeway was completed. Loew's Sharpstown Drive-In occupies part of the open space in the middle of the picture 47
6. 'All the Comforts of Home' advertisement for Park Drive-In 53
7. *Orange Leader* advertisement for the Strand and MacArthur Drive-In 68
8. *Chowan Herald* advertisement for the Taylor, Eden and Hi-Way 17 74
9. Advertisement for the Twin Open-Air Drive-In Theatre 80
10. From 'Abilene's Newest Drive-in' brochure, 6–7 115
11. The drive-in as part of 'ugly town' in *Targets* (dir. Peter Bogdanovich, Saticoy Productions/Paramount Pictures, 1968) 149
12. Teenage delinquents at the drive-in in *The Delinquents* (dir. Robert Altman, Imperial Productions/United Artists, 1957) 152
13. Danny (John Travolta) singing 'Sandy' in front of a drive-in snack food advertisement in *Grease* (dir. Randal Kleiser, Paramount Pictures Corporation, 1978) 154
14. Robert Frank, 'Drive-In Movie – Detroit' 172

Tables

1. Highest Box-Office Takings at the Razorback Drive-In 89
2. Highest Box-Office Takings at the Asher Drive-In 90
3. Highest Box-Office Takings at the Pines Drive-In 91
4. Composition of Groups at the Cinema, Indoor and Outdoor 120

Acknowledgements

This project had its origins in a paper I delivered at the 'Researching Past Cinema Audiences: Archives, Memories and Methods' conference, held at Aberystwyth University in 2018. That paper then became an article, 'My Search for "Passion Pits with Pix": Cinema History and 1950s Drive-In Audiences', published in *Participations: Journal of Audience and Reception Studies* in 2019. My thanks therefore go back to Kate Egan and Jamie Terrill for organizing that conference; to Martin Smith, Sam Manning and the late Martin Barker for their help with the article; and to Katie Gallof and Alyssa Jordan at Bloomsbury for being such supportive editors as my article grew into a book.

My initial research for the book was made possible thanks to research leave granted by the University of Leicester. That made it possible for me to visit the Harry Ransom Center, the Austin History Center, the Dallas History and Archives Division of the Dallas Public Library in Texas, the University of Arkansas at Little Rock Center for Arkansas History and Culture, the CALS Main Library in Little Rock and in Los Angeles, the William H. Hannon Library, Loyola Marymount University, the Margaret Herrick Library and the Charles E. Young Research Library at UCLA. My thanks to the librarians and archivists there who helped me during my visit. Other research was made possible by online and digital resources, including the Media History Digital Library, the Internet Archive more generally, the Cinema Treasures website and different digital newspaper platforms: the Chronicling America site for Historical American Newspapers, the NewspaperArchive and Newspapers.com, Proquest Historical Newspapers, the Arizona Memory Project, the Historical Newspaper Collection at Memorial Hall Library, Andover, Massachusetts, the North Carolina Digital Collections and the Portal to Texas History.

Thanks also to the History and Archives Division of the Dallas Public Library for allowing me to reproduce material from the Park Drive-In scrapbook, to the June Leaf and Robert Frank Foundation for permission to use Robert Frank's 'Drive-in – Detroit' photograph, to the Media History Digital Library for being able to reproduce other photographs of the Gratiot Drive-In, to Positive Image for the aerial photograph showing the Sharpstown Drive-In, to Miriam Caldwell for permission to quote from her 'Diary of Vilma' blog, to Carl Weese for permission to quote from his 'Working Pictures' blog, to Wright State University Libraries' Special Collections and Archives for permission to quote from their interview with Glenna Rogers and to the editors of the *Orange Leader* and the *Chowan Herald* for permission to use material from their newspapers. I have also used an image from *El Sol* (Phoenix), but despite my best efforts I was unable to identify a copyright holder for this newspaper.

I received further help from staff at the Historical Society of Western Virginia, the Harry B. Lee Library, Brigham Young University, Utah, the British Library and the BFI Reuben Library in London, the Kimberlin Library at De Montfort University, Leicester, and the Charles Wilson Library at the University of Leicester. Thanks also to James Russell and Jim Whalley for giving me access to their 'Hollywood and the Baby Boom' survey.

I presented provisional findings at panels, seminars and webinars run by History of Art and Film at Leicester, the HoMER network and the Archives and Archival Methods group at BAFTSS. My thanks to the organizers and participants of those events. I am particularly grateful to Kathryn Fuller-Seely for her encouraging comments on my original proposal and the draft manuscript. Thanks also to the other anonymous reviewers of my proposal, to Gozde Naiboglu for her feedback and to other colleagues at Leicester, including James Chapman, Lin Feng, Chris Horn and Claire Jenkins. Finally, thanks to Derek and Pauline Underwood for their hospitality in Dallas and to those who helped me carry on during lockdown, including Dave Watts, Rebecca Styler, Jenny Stewart, Scott Freer, Dave Deverick, Llewella Chapman and Sara Barefoot.

Note to the reader

This is a book about drive-in cinemas. I have spelt this out where necessary; where I have simply referred to 'the drive-in' you should assume that I mean a place designed for watching films in a car, not a drive-in restaurant or other service accessed by car. In the United States places dedicated to showing films are more commonly called theaters or theatres, and throughout this book you will find quotations using those words though also occasions where a distinction is made between theatres and drive-ins. Drive-ins were also known as 'ozoners' and were distinguished from 'hardtop' or 'conventional' cinemas. On occasion, I distinguish between outdoor and indoor cinemas: an outdoor cinema is not necessarily a drive-in but the outdoors were central to the drive-in experience. That drive-ins were also known as 'passion pits' is discussed further in the book.

Introduction

In 1998 the US Postal Service polled the public about topics for stamps to commemorate the different twentieth-century decades. Topping the poll for the 1950s was the drive-in movie, which received 456,176 votes, ahead of *I Love Lucy* (453,903), *The Cat in the Hat* (449,919), rock 'n' roll (415,052), victory over polio (406,251) and topics such as school desegregation (334,045).[1] The stamps themselves were issued in 1999, including one showing rows of cars parked in the dark beside speaker poles and above them the glowing image of a cowboy on horseback, projected onto a drive-in screen.[2]

Two decades earlier, in 1975, *Esquire* had published a collection of 'great American writers on great American things'.[3] Contributions included Joan Didion on 'The Shopping Center', Andy Warhol on 'TV' and William Price Fox on 'The Drive-in Movie'. Evoking a different screen image from the one on the stamp, Fox quoted one exhibitor's comment that 'I can look out some nights on my back row and I won't see a single head. Not one. Everyone's going at it. I could be running black leader.'[4]

As David Church notes, the drive-in is polysemic.[5] The drive-in cinema is remembered in different, even contradictory ways, as a place for young children or teenagers, as a safe or dangerous space, as innocent or disreputable, as somewhere to take the kids and save on the cost of a babysitter or as a place to see Crown-International's 1970 film, *Weekend with the Babysitter* (tagline, 'She came to sit with baby . . . and went away with daddy!'), subsequently included in the 2008 Mill Creek Entertainment DVD collection, *Drive-In Cult Classics, Volume 3*.[6] For Don and Susan Sanders, it belongs with fond memories of growing up in the 1950s, alongside piano and ballet lessons and watching *Ozzie and Harriet* (first shown in 1952) on television, a place where you could play on the swings at the drive-in playground, 'eat hamburgers and hot dogs, drink too many soft drinks, and eat as much popcorn as we could possibly hold', before falling asleep in the back seat of the station wagon while your parents watched the film on the screen.[7] When, three decades later, Hunter S. Thompson went with Maria Khan to see a three o'clock in the morning screening of *Climax!* (1985) at the Sonomarin Adult Drive-In Theater in Northern California, he found that 'The popcorn stand was closed, and when I asked where I could get a cup of coffee, the ticket man said "Nowhere"'.[8]

That this suggests a narrative of decline (not just in the provision of beverages) might explain those votes for the drive-in to represent a lost world of 1950s innocence on a postage stamp though also why even historians of the drive-in have downplayed its significance. In 1992 Kerry Segrave ended his history of the drive-in by speculating that a few might be kept alive as subsidized living museums but concluded that they were 'finished as a part of the American landscape. New one will never be built. It is only a matter of time'.[9] While there has been some drive-in construction in the current century, and the affection for the drive-in remains, so has the sense of decline, stoking the nostalgia in different ways.

The variety of connotations that the drive-in can bring were more recently evident in the 'The Last Picture Show' episode of the Netflix series, *Riverdale* (Season One, 2017). At the episode start, Jughead Jones (Cole Sprouse) describes the closure of the Twilight Drive-In as 'just one more nail in the coffin that is Riverdale. No, forget Riverdale, in the coffin of the American dream'. The Twilight, he insists, 'should mean something for us. People should be trying to save it'. Jughead's friends show little concern. 'In this age of Netflix and VOD do people really want to watch a movie in a car?' asks Veronica Lodge (Camila Mendes). When she adds, 'Who even goes there?' Kevin Keller (Casey Cott) volunteers, 'People who want to buy crack.' *Riverdale* mixes nostalgia and affection for 1950s style with the drive-in's negative and ambivalent associations. The choice of *Rebel Without a Cause* (1955) for the closing screening leads to cries of 'That hair!' from Kevin and 'That jacket!' from Veronica, while in another car her mother (Marisol Nichols) and Fred Andrews (Luke Perry) have differing recollections of their senior year date watching *Candyman* (1992) at the Twilight. In a shot that pans across film reels and posters, the Twilight projection booth becomes a shrine to movie history. The Twilight is a place of class divisions and connections, hetero- and homosexual assignations and undercover business deals. For Kevin, the Sheriff's gay son, it is a place to meet a gang member of the Southside Serpents. For others it is a piece of real estate to be exploited in corrupt business deals. For Jughead it has been where he grew up, his place of work and his home. It is also part of the episode's period mix (a Netflix series originating in the 2010s derived from a comic strip first published in the 1940s and looking back to 1990s horror and 1950s teenage angst). Before he is evicted it is presented as being at the heart of the community and on the margins. After this episode it disappears from the Riverdale narrative.

One core opposition in writing about the drive-in has been between the family and teenage audience. While this can be understood in historical terms, in Gary D. Rhodes' words, 'as the audience demographic shifted from 1950s families to 1960s teenagers', writers have also identified it within the

1950s, in different ways.[10] 'It was the family group that dominated and that produced big profits for operators. Teens were a small minority' in the 1950s, insists Segrave.[11] In their briefer mention of the drive-in's place in US cinema between 1945 and 1960, Kristin Thompson and David Bordwell write that the drive-in was popular because it allowed parents to 'bring their children and avoid the cost of a baby-sitter', adding that there were drive-ins specializing 'in teenpics, and the prospect of sharing a dimly lit front seat for several hours brought many adolescent couples to the local "passion pit"'.[12] Others emphasize the latter. 'Because drive-ins offered bargain-basement prices and double or triple bills, the theaters tended to favour movies that were either second-run or second-rate. Horror films and teenage romance were the order of the night. Pundits often commented that there was a better show in the cars than on the screen', writes Kenneth T. Jackson in his examination of suburban drive-in culture of 1950s and 1960s America.[13] In his account of sex and the American automobile, David L. Lewis similarly writes that drive-in 'patrons generally agreed that there was a better show in the cars than on the screen', while automobile historian James Flink uses almost the same words in his account of how the drive-in's family appeal was overshadowed by its 'passion pit' reputation.[14]

These alternative images and accounts of the drive-in and the 1950s provide my starting point. However, my concern is less to establish whether 1950s drive-ins appealed to families or teenagers than to look beyond the binary oppositions and repeated phrases that have dominated discussions of the drive-in. This book sets out to provide a more detailed and less monolithic account of the 1950s American drive-in and even of its myth.

The drive-in has never been forgotten. Online sites provide detailed information on individual drive-ins.[15] Historical overviews of post-war American cinema make some, if not extensive, reference to the drive-in.[16] Academic publications have examined the drive-in in relation to not only horror and cult cinema but also teenage audiences, B-films, hot rod movies, independent cinema, changes in spectatorship and distribution and exhibition practices, the baby boom generation and the political-economic landscape of the 1950s.[17] In Kerry Segrave's history of the drive-in from 1933 to the 1990s it already has a detailed overview based on an examination of the film industry trade press.

The history of the drive-in remains incomplete, often unclear and contradictory. This book is a work of film history but not a history of the drive-in, and its focus is on the 1950s, not the 1930s or the 1980s. Focusing on one decade allows for exploration below the surface. However, it is neither possible nor productive to separate the 1950s from what came before and after. To understand the topic, it is important to provide a historical perspective to, first, set out key elements of the history that has been told and, second, to identify variations to that history and the questions that it raises, and the questions raised by a focus on the drive-in in the 1950s.

The story of the drive-in, as told so far

Just about every account, from Joe Bob Briggs'[18] 'Why God Created Drive-Ins' to *The Big Book of Car Culture*, notes that the drive-in cinema can be traced back to the cinema Richard Hollingshead Jr opened on 6 June 1933.[19] The date's significance was already established on 6 June 1958 when numerous newspapers marked the drive-in's twenty-fifth birthday.[20] Hollingshead introduced the drive-in as a way of combining three American passions: movies, cars and food. Having conducted a series of experiments in his driveway, he devised a system of ramps that would give people in their cars a clear view of the screen in front of them even if another car was parked in front. Approved in May 1933, the patent gave details of how the ramps would work, how cars would enter and exit the drive-in, even how insects would be eliminated from the path of light from the projector, all allowing customers to watch a film without getting out of their car.[21] By then, construction had already started on the Drive-In Theatre on the Admiral Wilson Boulevard, in the township of Pennsauken, just outside the city limits of Camden, New Jersey. On 16 May, in the Camden *Courier-Press*, Hollingshead set out the benefits of this novel form of cinema. It allowed audiences to smoke, eat and talk as much as they liked. It transformed 'an ordinary motor car into a private theatre box':

> Here the whole family is welcome, regardless of how noisy the children are apt to be and parents are furthermore assured of the children's safety because youngsters remain in the car. The aged and infirm will find the Drive-In a boon because they will not be subjected to inconvenience such as getting up to leave others pass in narrow aisles or the uncertainty of a seat.[22]

These benefits came with problems for a film industry outsider. Segrave reports that 'The opening attraction was the 1932 release *Wife Beware*, starring Adolphe Menjou. It was then in second-run (or later status). . . . This problem of access to first-run films would bedevil drive-ins.'[23]

There were other problems. Hollingshead worked with the (Camden-based) RCA Victor Company to produce 'controlled directional sound', created by three speakers. However, projecting sound from the front to cars spread out across a large area could lead to variations in sound volume, lack of synchronization between sound and image and complaints from neighbours for whom the sound was a nuisance.

Hollingshead and his business partner Willie Warren Smith were new to the film business. Hollingshead's father ran a company that had moved from making saddle soap to a range of 'Whizz' products for cars. Smith, who provided the finance, owned a garage in Gladwyne, across the state border in Pennsylvania.[24] They knew something about cars and car parking but lacked inside knowledge of the film industry.

Treated with suspicion by the Hollywood Majors, the number of drive-ins remained low until the end of the Second World War but grew exponentially after the war. Many indoor cinemas closed in the ten years following the war, but in this period the number of drive-ins increased rapidly across the United States. They became particularly important in the summer months. While some drive-ins in the south stayed open throughout the year, northern drive-ins tended to close for winter, and (longer daylight hours notwithstanding) drive-in business was best between June and September. In July and August 1952 drive-in admissions exceeded admissions to indoor cinemas.[25]

The post-war growth of car ownership provides one clear reason for the growth of the drive-in. It was accompanied by a growth of roadbuilding and took place at a time of decreasing support for trains and other forms of public transport. The end of the Second World War was also followed by the expansion of suburbia. The fact that less people were living, or working or shopping, in the centre of town and that getting in and out of the centre was becoming more difficult made downtown cinemas less attractive. Existing indoor cinema owners were often tied to locations that were seen as less desirable. In addition, the exhibition circuits affiliated to the Hollywood Majors were restricted from opening new cinemas by the anti-trust ruling (the Paramount Decrees) that demanded they reduce their exhibition holdings. Thus, though there was an overall decline in the number of people going to the cinema, there was room for independent operators to open new cinemas in out-of-town locations. The drive-in's relatively low construction cost made this the cheapest way of entering the exhibition business and allowed drive-in operators to charge less than other cinemas.

There were other reasons for the post-war growth of the drive-in. Hollingshead and Smith had not remained exhibitors for long, setting out instead to make money from licensing their patent to other drive-in operators. Some drive-in operators initially complied with the royalty demands of Hollingshead and Smith's Park-In company, others disputed those and some ignored them. On 8 April 1949, the First Circuit Court of Appeals ruled that the Hollingshead patent was invalid. In the 1950s it was no longer something drive-in operators needed to worry about.

There were technological improvements. The tinny sound that came from in-car speakers, developed in 1941 but only introduced into drive-ins from 1946, was less than ideal but provided more consistent sound projection, without the need for fully open car windows, and produced a sound less likely to disturb any neighbours. In-car heaters, and the increasing number of cars with a top, could also make the experience of watching a film on a chilly night a little more comfortable. There were even ways of lessening the mosquito menace.

Provision for food and drink sales was developed; commentators frequently noted that these constituted a much higher proportion of the takings at drive-ins than at indoor cinemas.[26] Free admission for children could make business sense if that led to a rise in sales at the concession stand. Developing Hollingshead's 'the whole family is welcome' approach, drive-ins often provided playgrounds for children, and over time these became increasingly elaborate.[27] 'What started out a few short years ago to be a place to see a movie in the cool of the countryside away from the heat of the town', wrote James P. Cunningham in the mid-1950s, 'has grown to be an amusement center with playgrounds and swimming pools, bowling alleys, golf driving ranges, archery courts, snack bars, cafeterias and smart restaurants, trails for horseback riders, picnic areas, concession stands of fantastic proportions and content'.[28] There were live acts and competitions, as, in Segrave's words, 'More and more drive-ins turned to selling an evening of fun in which the film being screened was only a part – and not necessarily the most important one'.[29]

The drive-ins themselves became more elaborate, imitating picture palaces in their grand towers or creating flamboyant neon displays.[30] Visitors to the Gratiot Drive-In, which opened in 1948 in Roseville, in the Detroit metropolitan area, approached through a private 'hairpin type loop roadway' which gave 'patrons a view of a 115-foot tower with its multi-lighted "living curtain" of waterfalls over three cascades' (see Figures 1 and 2).[31] 'Patrons would come early to stand in front of the screen tower and have the water cascade down in front of them', write Don and Susan Sanders.[32] On the other side of the tower the screen faced a space designed for up to 1,056 cars, while the 'park size' playground came complete with 'swings, slides, teeter totters, free pony rides' and 'trained matrons' in charge.[33]

These developments helped to make the 1950s the 'golden age' of the drive-in. However, problems remained at the drive-in even at the height of their popularity. Films continued to be screened in imperfect conditions: David Church notes that 'Ambient light pollution and the unconventional distance between projector and screen created dim, washed out images'.[34] According to Segrave, innovations such as 3-D and CinemaScope did not work at the drive-in.[35] Drive-ins continued to have problems with Major distributors who

FIGURE 1 *The Gratiot Drive-In, Roseville, Michigan,* Boxoffice, *17 July 1948, 28. Courtesy of the Media History Digital Library.*

FIGURE 2 *The Gratiot Drive-In sign and screen tower at dusk,* Showmen's Trade Review, *5 March 1949, E-8. Courtesy of the Media History Digital Library.*

were reluctant to let them have first-run screenings and sometimes to let them have films at all.[36] The drive-in experience was generally a low-class one, summed up by Eric Mark Kramer as 'lowly technology with lowly patrons and lowly content and lowly food', places where 'The fancy movies limp into the drive-in worn and tattered if at all'.[37]

Drive-in operators found it easier to obtain lower-budget films from independent distributors. In the second half of the 1950s that included the company established in 1954 as American Releasing Corporation and renamed American International Pictures (AIP) the following year. A distinctive feature of AIP was that they targeted their films at teenagers. Thus, drive-ins became associated with two audiences. From Hollingshead's promotion of the drive-in as a place where parents could safely take the children to subsequent provision of playgrounds and emphasis on the drive-in as avoiding the need for babysitters, the drive-in had been linked to married couples with young children. Drive-in operators denied stories that their cinemas were 'passion pits', insisting that their audience consisted of families rather than necking teenagers. Over time, however, the teenage audience became more important at the drive-in.[38]

Younger audiences could delay but not prevent the drive-in's decline. Writing at the beginning of the 1990s, Segrave concluded, 'A significant decline in the early 1960s was followed by a stagnant decade and half. This was followed by a steady decline, which commenced in the late 1970s and continues to the present as the drive-in inexorably follows the path of the dinosaur.'[39] The family audience stagnated and then declined. By the end of the 1960s children's playgrounds were closing as insurance costs rose. As the new system of film classification was introduced, an increasing number of drive-ins were showing 'adult' films. In the 1980s and 1990s the drive-in was celebrated, but either as a nostalgic remnant of a disappearing world or in writings and later television appearances of Joe Bob Briggs and others for whom the drive-in movie meant the exploitation film. That cult of the drive-in grew out of the fact that drive-ins were showing more horror films but even the exploitation and adult market shrunk as films increasingly became available on VHS, later DVD, Blu-Ray and (as Veronica pointed out in *Riverdale*) through streaming.[40]

The growth of the video market was just one of the reasons for the closure of drive-ins. Their period of biggest expansion had occurred when indoor cinemas were closing but from the 1960s exhibition companies began to invest in indoor cinemas again, notably through cinemas in shopping malls. With the multiplex the number of indoor screens multiplied rapidly. By the 1970s and 1980s drive-ins established twenty or thirty years ago were showing their age and their technical facilities were looking and sounding even worse in comparison with the improved facilities at indoor cinemas. Owners had to choose between trying to get by with a deteriorating drive-in, an expensive investment in refurbishment and new equipment (that would still leave their cinemas at a disadvantage), and selling the drive-in to a property developer. The latter became more attractive as land prices rose, and this was particularly significant for drive-ins built on what had been relatively cheap rural land but were now part of the urban environment. Other businesses had operated on leases which came to an end in the 1970s or 1980s. In the 1970s fuel prices rose, challenging the car culture that had driven post-war drive-in expansion. Smaller cars were more evident but less comfortable for watching a drive-in double or triple bill and for those in the car not watching the movie. Changing sexual values and living habits led to a wider range of places couples could go to for greater privacy than the drive-in provided. For Segrave, the very success of the drive-in led to complacency and so contributed to its decline.[41]

Some twentieth-century drive-ins have been built but operators of older drive-ins have been faced with the challenge of the cost of converting to digital projection.[42] Though there were reports that Covid-19 restrictions on indoor cinemas benefitted the drive-in, the overall number has remained small in comparison to the 1950s.[43]

The story of the drive-in, revised

In writing this brief overview I have drawn extensively on Segrave's history because it remains the most important book devoted to the drive-in, because it is based on identified primary sources and because it corrects some assumptions about the importance of the teenage audience in the 1950s. Along with other accounts, however, it leaves questions on points of detail and approach as well as significant gaps.

On a point of detail, the problem with Segrave's identification of *Wife Beware* as the opening drive-in screening is that there is no film with that name, and it is unclear if any feature film was screened on the 6 June opening. A week later, *Variety* reported, 'After the opening, policy was changed from exclusive showing of shorts to that of indie pictures. "Wife Beware" was first with "The Racing Strain" following.'[44] The Tuesday and Wednesday *Courier-Post* advertisements do not identify a specific film. *Wife Beware* was advertised on Thursday and Friday but on Saturday this was corrected to *Wives Beware!* the title used in the United States for the 1932 British film *Two White Arms*. *Motion Picture Herald* listed the film's American release date as June 1933.[45] Hollingshead later claimed, 'The first film at the drive-in was three years old and cost us $400 for four days. The last time the film had run was in a little South Camden movie that paid $20 a week for it.'[46] It was (like *The Racing Strain*) last year's film but new to the United States, and the Friday advertisement at the drive-in claimed it was the first South Jersey showing.[47]

Some (but not all) subsequent accounts have continued to refer to *Wife Beware*, while to my knowledge the only account that identifies other screenings at Hollingshead's Drive-In is Don and Susan Sanders' *The American Drive-In Movie Theatre*, which reproduces a pair of later advertisements.[48] That is a shame as the subsequent programme is relevant to the later history of the drive-in and to debates about the drive-in programme. Hollingshead's difficulties obtaining films from the Major studios (or at least his 'indie pictures' policy) are evident in his drive-in's reliance in its opening year on films such as *Slightly Married* (Invincible Productions, 1932), *Strange Adventure* (Monogram, 1932) and *The Midnight Lady* (Chesterfield, 1932).[49] In August 1933, it did show RKO's *Rockabye* (1932) followed by a few Universal films including *Vanity Fair* (1933) and *Back Street* (1932) but these were exceptions.[50] In 1935, as well as showing double bills of Monogram films such as *The Mystery Man* (1935) and *A Successful Failure* (1934), the films it screened included *Scarface* (Caddo, 1932), *Jack Ahoy* (Gaumont-British, 1935) and two films that had longer runs: *The Road to Ruin* (Willis Kent, 1934), held over for a second week in June, and *Elysia (The Valley of the Nude)* (Elysian Pictures, 1934), which played for over eight weeks, from Sunday 18 August to Monday 7 October.[51] The latter run was by some distance longer than any other drive-in run I have come across, in any decade. What had become known as the Camden Drive-In closed for good on Monday 21 September 1936 with *Spy 77* (originally released as *On Secret Service*, British International Pictures, 1936).[52] It is unclear whether the first example of the American drive-in opened with a British film, but it does seem to have closed with one.

The Road to Ruin is an example of what Eric Schaefer labelled the 'sex hygiene' film.[53] Some cinemas showing it carried a 'Children under 16 [or 18] Not Admitted' notice, perhaps designed to make the film appear more salacious than it was.[54] No such notice appeared when it played at the Camden Drive-In, and the *Courier-Post* merely repeated the distributor's line that 'perhaps never has such a subject dealing with such a delicate topic as sex delinquency been so cleverly handled'.[55] The police seized a copy of *Elysia*, which depicted a California nudist camp, when it was programmed in 1942, 'Adults Only', at the Star Theatre, Camden, but I have not seen similar reports from when it played the Camden Drive-In in 1935.[56] The drive-in's location outside the city limits might have been a factor, though the local paper only reported that there would 'be much to interest the spectator and to make him ponder over this fad that has spread over the world and now has thousands of adherents'.[57]

The screening of these films fits the argument that drive-ins, at least at the beginning, had to rely on films from sources other than the Major studios. However, Hollingshead later said that the man who brought the drive-in from him (and transported it to Union, New Jersey) 'had several indoor theatres in north Jersey, so he could easily get films', and that he sold the first licence for his drive-in patent to a Los Angeles exhibitor who 'owned several indoor theaters, so they didn't have the trouble we did in getting films'.[58] Hollingshead's recollections are not always reliable, but we should not assume that drive-in ownership was necessarily separate from the ownership of indoor cinemas, or that drive-in operators were necessarily new to the film business, or that the films were necessarily shown at drive-ins later than at indoor cinemas (even if they often were). It is also clear that the association between the drive-in and the exploitation film has a longer history than been generally acknowledged.

This has implications for the drive-in audience. As other have pointed out, on the second day of its operation, the drive-in advertisement in neighbouring Philadelphia consisted of a drawing of a large woman trying to sit down in a crowded cinema and to right of this the statement that 'EVEN KATE SMITH would have no trouble getting a seat in the world's first automobile mobile theatre where you see and hear talkies without leaving your car'.[59] Hollingshead's earlier comments about families being able to take children to the drive-in were picked up in a *Variety* report which noted that younger children were barred from Camden's indoor cinemas in the evening.[60] In 1936, Everett H. Mattix, manager of the Camden Drive-In, told *Motion Picture Herald* that attendance was up on the previous year, on account of 'a very good family trade'.[61] Drive-in operators in the post-war years continued this emphasis on the family trade, children and the drive-in providing a place for the otherwise excluded (from the overweight to the underage). One question here is whether the extended runs for *The Road to Ruin* and *Elysia* indicate a divide between claims made by drive-in operators and their actual programming strategy. Another concerns drive-ins' appeal to different audiences.

Was the Camden Drive-In even the first drive-in cinema? Others have traced the drive-in further back in time. For example, in 1921 J. Henry Meloy, looking for ways to publicize his gasoline-powered farm electric lighting plant business, took to touring Shelby County, Indiana, in his Model T Ford roadster on which he had installed a projector, giving outdoor shows of films advertising the lighting plant equipment mixed with agriculture education films. He went on to show religious films, westerns and other fiction films. The subsequent press description of farmers arriving 'with their families as much as two hours before the show time to pick out advantageous spots to park their autos or sit on the grass' resembles an account of a drive-in show.[62]

There were reportedly 'about 50 similar picture operations elsewhere in Indiana and this gradually spread to other states'.[63]

Airdomes had earlier allowed people to watch films in the open in the summer. 'The novel idea seems to please the general public, whether the airdome is operated in a county town or on a vacant lot in a large city', noted *Cyclopedia of Motion Picture Work* in 1911.[64] Airdomes were similar to the drive-in not just in lacking a roof but also as places where 'the refreshment business is so much associated with the motion picture business, and they are so mutually helpful to each other that they usually are run in conjunction'.[65] They provided seats for people rather than spaces for cars, but the plans for an Airdome in Las Cruces, New Mexico, in 1914, included provision for two rows of cars, to allow the occupants to watch a film screening without leaving their car.[66] When the Theatre de Guadalupe opened the following year, it included spaces for 700 seated patrons and 40 cars.[67]

Airdomes remained essentially walk-in rather than drive-in cinemas, and their existence does not cancel the significance of the drive-in on Admiral Boulevard. However, there are further questions worth asking about who went to the post-war drive-in and who did not. The drive-in has been linked to increased car ownership 'among white, middle-class, increasingly suburban households' but it has also been seen as a place that brought different communities together, and that was linked, particularly after the 1960s, to working-class audiences.[68] It has been associated with the heterosexual couple (whether married with children or dating teenagers). This leaves questions about other audiences, from larger mixed or same-sex groups to Hispanic or African American audiences attending segregated, unsegregated or drive-ins dedicated to their own communities, in addition to questions about the overall composition of the drive-in audience in terms of generation, gender, class and ethnicity.

There are further questions about the life of the drive-in after 1960 as well as the number of drive-ins before and after that date, and about the size of drive-in attendance. Segrave's figures for drive-in numbers are taken from US census reports, and his comment on the significant decline in the early 1960s is supported by the fall in those numbers from 4,063 drive-ins in 1958 to 3,502 in 1963 and from 3,805 to 3,375 for those drive-ins with a payroll.[69] However, the census figures also indicate that the receipts of drive-ins with a payroll increased from $230,417,000 in 1958 to $253,766,000 in 1963, at a time when receipts for indoor cinemas declined from $928,128,000 to $803,458,000, while overall car capacity of these drive-ins increased from 1,428,600 in 1958 to 1,652,200 in 1963.[70] The overall number of drive-ins may have been declining, but if these figures are correct the average capacity of drive-ins continued to increase into the 1960s as more became twin screen or multiscreen or simply expanded car capacity.

The census figures are not the only ones and may underestimate numbers. *Film Daily* published figures for the number of drive-ins from 1941 onwards. The initial figure it gave was 95, rising to 300 in 1946, 1,203 in 1949 and 4,587 in 1955.[71] A slight decline to 4,494 in 1956 and 1957 was followed by 4,700 in 1958, 4,768 in 1959, 4,700 in 1960, 6,000 in 1961 and 1962, a drop to 3,550 in 1963 and then a steady rise again up to 4,975 in 1968 before declining to figures between 3,730 and 3,801 between 1969 and 1975.[72] There are reasons to be sceptical at least about some of these figures. Given the number of drive-ins opening and closing each year, it is unlikely that the overall number would be exactly the same as the previous year in both 1956 and 1957 and 1961 and 1962. They were published as estimates, while the 6,000 figure for the latter two years appears to be rounded up or down. It is unclear why there would have been a dramatic fall between 1962 and 1963.

Other figures circulated in the 1950s and 1960s, often with a comment about the difficulty of providing a definitive number. After noting that there was no agreement in the accepted directories, and wide variations in the calculated national total, in 1952 one report estimated 3,835, including not only 'itinerate operations' but also 'operations designed for construction this year'.[73] According to one 1956 trade journal, recent estimates placed 'the number of drive-in theatres in the United States at almost 4,600', a year after another had identified almost 5,000.[74] At the beginning of 1962, the Department of Commerce revised its figure of 4,700, saying 'that drive-in theatres may now number over 5,000'.[75]

A precise, definitive number of drive-ins is not possible and even if achievable such a figure would still be incomplete. In the 1970s, according to Dennis Giles, while the number of drive-ins fell by 17 per cent, at most the number of drive-in screens (as opposed to cinemas) declined by 5 per cent, and regional trends meant that in some locations the number of drive-ins continued to increase.[76] Even Segrave's figures indicate that while drive-in numbers peaked in Texas in 1954, they did not reach their highest point in California until 1967 and in Illinois until 1972.[77] While discussing local drive-in closures, a 1980s report on drive-ins in the Athos-Orange area of Massachusetts quoted one exhibitor as identifying the drive-in's 'golden age' as between 1956 and 1966 and going on to say that the drive-in market rose in the late 1970s and early 1980s with 'slasher' horror films, describing one drive-in as having 'super seasons in 1980 and 1981' and another as having its 'best season in its 30 year history' in 1984.[78] More recently, in one account Church writes of the initial novelty of the drive-in wearing off by the early 1960s, revenues peaking in the mid-1960s, the early 1970s showing a modest upswing in attendance and the construction boom in new screens only slowing by the mid-1970s.[79] In another account he refers to a late 1950s peak and the total number of drive-in screens and attendance 'dipping over the 1960s and recovering in the 1970s, and a long industry collapse over the 1980s'.[80]

Whatever the precise figures, there is evidence here of regional and historical fluctuations within an overall pattern of growth, plateau and decline, the latter only becoming marked in the 1980s. As well as indicating a longer period when drive-ins accounted for a significant portion of the domestic market, this complicates the picture of an industry that grew complacent in a period when the drive-ins were full all the time and thus it did not matter what was on the screen so long as it was inoffensive. While Segrave suggests that 'Anyone who opened an outdoor theater in the 1940s or 1950s made money almost in spite of him – or herself', Blair Davis cites trade press reports on 1957 as 'the worst in years' and 1958 drive-in audiences becoming as choosy as the audiences for indoor cinemas.[81] Not all drive-ins were successful in the ten years following the end of the Second World War: one list of cinemas closed between 1947 and 1952, the period of greatest drive-in expansion, includes a hundred drive-ins.[82]

The drive-in in the 1960s and 1970s cannot be entirely explained in terms of either decline or stagnation, and there are indications that closures during this period were less driven by the declining popularity of this form of cinema than by the rise in property prices, which meant that owners could make quicker and higher returns by selling the land. Drive-ins still existed in the 1980s, but they closed at a more rapid rate. In the 1980s there are also more indications that their programmes had changed.

On 6 June 1983, fifty years after the first public screening at the drive-in on Admiral Wilson, the Camden *Courier-Post* carried advertisements for three drive-ins, the twin-screen Tacony-Palmyra Bridge and ATCO drive-ins and the single-screen Pennsauken.[83] While other cinemas, many now based in shopping malls, were showing a range of films from the PG-rated *Return of the Jedi* (1983) to the R-rated *48 Hrs.* (1982) and the X-rated films showing at the Budco Ritz, all the films showing at drive-ins were R-rated. There was some overlap with indoor cinemas: *Chained Heat* (1983) and *The Man with Two Brains* (1983) were playing indoor and outdoor in and around Camden. There was also a difference between the Tacony Red's double bill of *The Man with Two Brains* and *Cheech and Chong's Nice Dreams* (1981) and the Tacony Blue's triple bill of *Summer Heat* (1982), *The First Time* (1981) and *Voluptuous Graduates* (1980). The ATCO screens were similarly labelled red and blue. However, this was a shift from ten years previously, when the five advertised drive-ins clearly appealed to different audiences.[84] On 6 June 1973, the paper carried advertisements for *Deadly Fathoms* (1973), 'For the Entire Family', accompanied at the Pennsauken Drive-In by the similarly G-rated *American Wilderness* (1970) and the PG-rated *Sometimes a Great Notion* (1971) and at the Black Horse Pike Drive-In by *American Wilderness* and the R-rated *Pat Garrett and Billy the Kid* (1973). The Tacony-Palmyra and the Starlite Drive-Ins were showing a PG triple bill of *Class of '44* (1973), accompanied by *Jenny* (1969) and *Red Sky at Morning* (1971), while the ATCO was showing two R-rated films, *Deep Thrust* (also known as *Lady Whirlwind* (1972)) and *The Savage Seven* (1968), accompanied by the unrated *Conqueror Worm* (released in Britain in 1968 as *Witchfinder General*). The *Courier-Post* advertised more screens on Sunday 6 June 1993 but that was because of the expansion of the multiplexes.[85] There were no longer any advertisements from drive-ins. In the Camden area the drive-in evidently continued to appeal to family and adult audiences in the 1970s, had a narrower, adult market (though one that still had two, colour-coded strands), fewer cinemas but the same number of screens in the 1980s, but had gone by the 1990s.

Other locations will provide variations on an overall pattern in which drive-ins remained in significant numbers in the 1970s and in that decade could still attract a family audience. The final illustration to Mary Morley Cohen's 1996 article on the drive-in is captioned 'The dinosaur lives on: children in a makeshift bed wait for the film to start at the Grayslake Outdoor Theater, Grayslake, IL. 1993'.[86]

As Church warns, 'an accurate history of drive-in theatres must avoid over-emphasising the ratio of exploitation films to mainstream product, as these exhibition sites were not always the contra-Hollywood hotbeds that exploitation fan cultures have often claimed'.[87] There is a similar danger of emphasizing the extent to which a company such as AIP identified itself with the drive-in in the 1950s. A 1958 *Los Angeles Times* profile of the company goes no further than quoting co-head of the company on that August obtaining '5000 bookings out of the possible 14,000-15,000 theaters and drive-ins operating in America'.[88] The association was more evident in the mid-1960s, when a *New York Times* report on the beach party movie referred to the company tailoring 'its product mainly for the teen-age "drive-in" trade', and firmly established by the end of the 1970s, when that paper reported on a Museum of Modern Art season of AIP films under the headline 'Museum Celebrates "Drive-In" Movies'.[89]

The drive-in on Admiral Boulevard showed 'classical exploitation' films in the 1930s but 'drive-in movie' as a synonym for exploitation film was a post-1950s construction. It is commonly traced back to Joe Bob Briggs but effectively existed earlier in the reviews that Edward Kelleher, writing as Edouard Dauphin, wrote for *CREEM* (self-styled as 'America's only Rock 'n' Roll Magazine') from the mid-1970s, in his 'Drive-In Saturday' column (a title taken from the David Bowie song of the same name). A hint of a changing understanding of the term 'drive-in movie' is also evident in a 1973 *Cinefantastique* interview in which horror film director George Romero was asked if he thought *The Crazies* would be 'a "drive-in" movie like *Night of the Living Dead* was, or if it would be an "indoor"?'[90] John Irving Bloom, writing as Joe Bob Briggs, gave the link between the horror and exploitation film and the drive-in greater prominence in 1982 when the *Dallas Times Herald* began publishing his 'Joe Bob Goes to the Drive-In' column.

The meaning of 'drive-in movie' has changed since the 1950s but what it has changed from remains unclear, for another tendency in writing on the 1950s drive-in has been to avoid all but the broadest references to films. After commenting on the opening screening at the Camden Drive-In, Segrave only cites individual film titles in the closing chapters of his book, which focus on the 1960s, 1970s and 1980s. 'The film on the screen was largely irrelevant, as long as it was wholesome', he argues.[91] It has been treated that way, by historians.

While I address that gap in the pages that follow, I will not address the drive-in beyond the United States. The brief history of the drive-in set out earlier omits the drive-ins established in other countries. The 1950s growth in the drive-in in the United States extended to the southern regions of Canada. Ben Goldsmith writes, 'In the 1950s and 1960s, the drive-in became a familiar site throughout urban and rural Australia.'[92] I am writing this in Britain, where drive-ins never really took root, though in 2020, when Covid-19 restrictions forced other cinemas to stay closed, a few drive-ins appeared even here, showing major new releases as well as popular revivals such as *Grease* (1978). Drive-ins in continental Europe have a longer history, as they do in Latin America and parts of Africa and Asia. Segrave's book has a chapter on 'Foreign Drive-Ins' and the Australian and Canadian drive-in has received some attention, but otherwise there has been limited scholarly attention to the drive-in beyond the United States.[93] Others will, hopefully, remedy that.

Outdoor cinema in 1950s America and the popular imagination

A more comprehensive examination of the drive-in cinema would need to address its global history and its twenty-first-century existence, up to the attention it received when, in the spring of 2020, drive-ins were briefly the only functioning cinemas in the United States.[94] However, attempting to cover such wide territory in a single volume would inevitably lack depth. The drive-in after 1960 deserves its own study, as do the drive-ins of countries other than the United States. By adopting a more limited focus I aim for a deeper exploration into the heart of the drive-in cinema. Even revivals and recent representations of the contemporary drive-in often look back to the American 1950s, confident that it is that decade and cultural context that still permeate the drive-in in the popular imagination (and vice versa, as the postal service poll indicated). It is worth raising questions about this, and entirely restricting what follows to the 1950s would not be helpful but focusing on the drive-in in 1950s America allows for a more detailed analysis of that decade (agreed, generally and with good reason, as the height of American drive-in popularity) and what it has meant.

This also explains why I also include the place of the drive-in in the popular imagination. As an example of cinema history, this book uses empirical research to examine where drive-ins were and who owned them, what films they showed and what other attractions they provided, who went to them and what evidence there is about what they did there. Behind this are questions about what the drive-in has meant and how that meaning has varied and shifted. To examine those underlying issues, as well as drive-ins as an exhibition venue with specific locations and histories, I also look at ways in which the drive-in has been imagined and represented, during and after the 1950s.

My overall approach is thematic rather than chronological. In the first of the following chapters I focus on not only place but also property and community: not only where drive-ins were located but also who owned them and more generally the manner and extent to which they belonged to a local and industrial network or were outsiders and outliers, integral to the industry or fighting against the industry. The next chapter, on the programme, examines how this was organized, what films drive-ins showed, what evidence there is on what was popular and what was on the programme as well as films, addressing the widely held perception that they were limited to the substandard. This is followed by a chapter on people, who went to the drive-in and what do we know about their experience, addressing the debate about whether the drive-in was a teenage 'passion pit' or was dominated by families with young children but also whether that debate has neglected other audiences. I go on to examine the picture and meaning the drive-in has taken on film and in song, literature, photography and other still images, examining how images of the drive-in have varied and changed and the extent to which they continue to look back to the 1950s.

These are not discrete themes. Who went to the drive-in was linked to their location, ownership and programme and the different ways in which the drive-in has been imagined. However, a focus on different Texas drive-ins allows for a close examination of the relationship between a drive-in and both its local community and the film industry, a focus on drive-ins in different US states allows for a closer examination of different programming approaches and a focus on audience surveys and reports on the drive-in audience in newspapers and the film industry trade press can illuminate the relationship between place, programme and audience. Looking at different drive-ins in these different chapters can help broaden the overall picture, but I also look at one drive-in, the MacArthur, Orange, Texas, in the chapters on place, programme and people, to illustrate the interrelationship between these different topics and examine the issue of the drive-in and ethnicity in the chapters on place and programme as well as the one on audiences. Finally, a focus on representations of the drive-in on film and song, in literature and still images, allows for an analysis of how images of the drive-in differ in different media and have varied and changed over time, of the extent to which they continue to look back to the 1950s and of the relationship between image and reality.

I have combined different research methods to provide as comprehensive a picture as possible within the limits I have set out. To gain a rounded picture of perceptions of the drive-in, I started out watching films in which they featured, however briefly. In early 2020 I was (just in time) able to visit archives in Austin, Dallas, Little Rock and Los Angeles. Returning to Britain, and now (with the spread of Covid-19) locked down, I was still able to consult newspapers and other digitalized online sources and to do the sort of research that would not have been possible a decade or so earlier. While others researching historical cinema audiences have drawn on the memories of cinemagoers, I have concentrated on printed and archival sources, though I have made some use of memories published online, questionnaire results for a project on 'Hollywood and the Baby Boom' and one diary published online.[95]

All these sources have advantages and limitations. Local newspapers provide a picture of what feature films drive-ins screened; when, where and with what other feature film or films; how the film or experience was sold; and sometimes how much was charged for admission. Some archive collections provide more detailed information on box-office takings, the short programme as well as the feature, what the weather was like or the size of confectionary sales. We can learn something from broader comments on topics ranging from the problems of sound projection at drive-ins to speculations about audience responses to a film or behaviour at the cinema. The latter may tell us more about the person speculating than about the spectators themselves. There are occasions when people wrote of their own experiences at the drive-in, whether to complain or because they wanted advice. This still leaves gaps. For a start, in most cases, we do not know whether someone who went to a drive-in watched the film, if they did how it affected them and if they did not what they did do.

Thus, the material presented here is incomplete. However, it can correct misconceptions, can clarify confusions and can provide a more detailed picture of the drive-in cinema in 1950s America and thus of the drive-in and American popular culture more generally. It is, of course, also reliant on what others have written on the topic and in part serves to bring together important findings from a range of publications, academic and otherwise. It follows examples of what has become known as New Cinema History which address their topic from below rather than above.[96] Film history has traditionally (and unsurprisingly) started with films, examining either the stylistic and thematic detail of a film or patterns across films or films in relation to their creators and producers. It has often focussed on a select group of films or filmmakers. Looking at individual cinemas, and not restricting that look to metropolitan or first-run cinemas, can provide a broader and richer picture of film culture. Histories of the drive-in have correctly (if sometimes misleadingly) emphasized that cinema involves more than watching movies. We should not assume that drive-in audiences did not care what was on the screen but examining the drive-in can reveal how cinemagoing was part of a broader pattern of life.

One way of working from below rather than above is to identify named cinemas and use these as a way of calculating the number of drive-ins in the 1950s. If this is, ultimately, impractical, it is so in a revealing way. At the last count I was able to identify 4,710 drive-ins for which there is evidence that they screened films at some point in the 1950s. That figure is incomplete. While the excellent 'Cinema Treasures' website provides details of the precise opening and closing date of some drive-ins, as well as of what was playing on the opening night and what the drive-in site has subsequently become, and while there are other sources including trade press reports, newspaper listings and individual memories, even combining all available sources will not provide a definitive answer. There are drive-ins for which I have been unable to establish whether they opened after, or closed before, the 1950s. Some drive-ins have left little or no trace. To identify the number of drive-ins that existed in the 1950s is, anyway, different from identifying the number that existed at any one time. Drive-ins continued to open during the decade, some had closed by the decade's end, some with a short life opened and closed in the 1950s. The overall pattern of growth, plateau and eventual decline conceals a more complex and continuously changing picture in which drive-ins were expanding in one location while they declined in another and individual drive-ins changed their names, expanded, in some instances split in two, moved, or where closing for the winter turned into closure for good.

The size of the figure and the range it contains anyway means that the discussion that follows has had to be highly selective. On the one hand this has meant identifying not only common patterns from the evidence of individual cinemas and their audiences but also the networks of production, distribution, exhibition and regulation that controlled the industry as a whole: history from above and below. On the other hand, my use of case studies is designed to reveal individual characteristics. The drive-in has too often been discussed in a series of repeated phrases: children asleep at the back of the car, cars in which the show was better than the one on the screen, even the phrase 'drive-in movie'. By looking at individual examples and a range of sources, this book aims to provide a more detailed and nuanced picture of the drive-in cinema in 1950s America, based on specific examples rather than generalizations, and thus to clarify its place in people's experience, lived and imagined.

1

Place

On 14 March 1950, North Carolina's *Charlotte Observer* reported that a drive-in screening had caused 'one of the city's biggest traffic jams' on the southern limits of Fayetteville, with 'a long line of cars . . . backed up on highway 301 for several blocks, after capacity of the theater had been reached'.[1] A drive-in causing a traffic jam will be familiar to those who know the story of how the career of Herschell Gordon Lewis, and the splatter horror subgenre, took off after police had to turn away the crowds trying to see *Blood Feast* (1963) at the Bellevue Drive-In outside Peoria, Illinois.[2] However, the drivers on the edge of Fayetteville were not trying to get to a horror film but to see Ingrid Bergman in *Stromboli* (1950).

In its own way it remains an arresting image: a traffic jam caused by drivers attempting to drive to a North Carolina drive-in showing the RKO version of an Italian film about post-war displacement starring a Swedish-born Hollywood star. *Stromboli* tells of Karin Bjørnsen (Ingrid Bergman), born in Lithuania, living in Czechoslovakia and Yugoslavia before the war, who at the beginning of the film is stuck in an Italian internment camp from where she hopes to emigrate to Argentina. Denied a visa, she gets out of the camp by marrying a fisherman who takes her to his home on the Mediterranean, volcanic island of Stromboli. The priest who welcomes the newly married couple to the island tells them of how many of the inhabitants have left for other countries. The men brought in to clean their home are just back from America where, one proudly tells Karin, they all had cars. The *Charlotte Observer* report, however, reminds us that cars can be parked in front of a movie screen or, just as Karin is stuck on the seemingly barren island of Stromboli, stuck in traffic.

'Probably no film in history has received as much publicity as *Stromboli*', claimed *Variety*, suggesting that the attraction was not the film but the notoriety of Bergman's extramarital relationship with the film's director, and father of her child, Roberto Rossellini.[3] RKO's version of Rossellini's film received poor reviews in the United States, and many cinemas refused to screen it.[4]

Looking back at the beginning of 1951, *Variety* noted its disappointing 1950 box-office performance, adding, 'Few more bookings are likely outside of drive-ins, where it has been doing strangely well.'[5]

Place and displacement were significant post-war film subjects. Place can be examined through the textual analysis of individual films (Rossellini's films from *Rome, Open City* (1945) are particularly inviting to such readings), through a comparison of different versions of a film (e.g. through a comparison between the RKO and Rossellini edits of *Stromboli*) or in relation to where cinemas are located and the cinema as a place.[6] As Jeffrey Klenotic notes, a 'consequence of film studies' focus on text and textual interpretation has been the suppression or marginalising of the spatiality of the experience of cinema'.[7] When film history did take a spatial turn it was initially to the city. For Giuliana Bruno, 'in order to exist, the cinematic apparatus needs a home – a movie "house." And, housed in the city, since the beginning of the twentieth century . . . the screen . . . became the city square'.[8] However, reflecting on the tendency to link cinema to the city, more specifically to urban mobility as *flânerie*, Doreen Massey noted that 'it is not just city spaces which were "of transit"' and warned against essentializing 'what was a genuine and deep, but historically and geographically grounded, connection into a narrative which separates "cities" off with what, I believe, is an immensely rich field of enquiry: that of the relationship between film and spatiality in general'.[9]

Picking up on this, Klenotic makes the case for a more detailed, and empirically grounded, mapping, exploration and visualization of cinema's spatiality and sociality.[10] For Klenotic:

> Where we watch movies matters. To understand the powerful role that movies play shaping culture and identity, we first need to know where they have been seen. We then need to know how they got there, when, under whose auspices, and in what physical conditions and social contexts they were experienced, discussed, regulated, acted upon, and remembered by diverse audiences.[11]

This is a complex process, for the drive-in no less than other cinemas. Drive-in cinemas do not need a house (though a building at the bottom or back of the screen sometimes served as a home for their operators and their family), could occasionally themselves be mobile or portable and identifying where they were, let alone from where their audience came, is not always easy to determine. The 1950 *Film Daily Year Book* lists only two Fayetteville drive-ins, the Boulevard, identified as one of nineteen 'portable' drive-ins in North Carolina, and the Sky-Vue.[12] According to Hill's 1951 *Fayetteville Directory*, the city had 'four regular theatres and four drive-in theatres', and though it does not name them all it does have an address for the Boulevard Drive-In, but on Bragg Boulevard, which runs into Fayetteville from the north-west.[13] The Jet Drive-In opened in 1953 on Highway 301, on the south side of Fayetteville, on the site of the Cumberland Drive-In, which might have been the drive-in showing *Stromboli*, if it was operating at the beginning of the 1950s (it is not mentioned in the *Fayetteville Directory* or the 1951 *Film Daily Year Book*).[14]

More precise information is available on other drive-ins, but the issue here is not only one of identifying addresses. Leaving aside the question of memory for the time being, this chapter examines not only the location of the 1950s drive-in but also the place of the drive-in within local communities, within a nation increasingly defined in terms of the automobile and roadside development and within the American film industry. Questions of place are also about the relationship between locations: between the city, the city limits and beyond; between where audiences lived, worked or studied and where they watched films; between cinemas and both local communities and those prepared to travel longer distances; and between distributors, censors (who could have more control over what was shown within city limits) and exhibitors. All these were changing in the middle of the twentieth century. While only a few drive-ins were themselves mobile, all appealed to an automobile audience. For Carol Morley Cohen the drive-in 'literalized the cinema's illusion of mobility by addressing its spectators as voyagers. Even the names of many drive-in theatres reinforced this illusion of travel and adventure: El Rancho, Prairie, Go West, The Oasis'.[15] Other drive-ins took their names from the sky (Starlight or Starlite were the most frequent names), from the road on which they were located or from the local town. To discuss the place of the drive-in is to examine their place within a network of roads, distribution and ownership.

This chapter examines that territory by moving from the general to the particular and then out again. In the first section, I refer to drive-ins across the country and comparisons between different states. I go on to focus on the state which had the largest number of drive-ins in the United States in the 1950s: Texas. I next use a series of case studies of Texas drive-ins: the Chief, Seminole and the Hondo, as examples of drive-ins on the outskirts of towns with populations under 10,000; Orange and Abilene, as examples of medium-sized cities which had, in the case of Orange, a single drive-in on its outskirts, at one point seven drive-ins in the case of Abilene; finally, Loew's Sharpstown Drive-In in Sharpstown, a suburb of Houston.

I have selected Texas because of the availability of digital and paper archival resources, because it was central to the post-war drive-in boom, because it contained small communities and major cities and because the state's demographic growth and shifts highlight ways in which the drive-in existed in this broader context of change. However, to balance this focus in this chapter I follow my case studies with a discussion of evidence from other US states and an analysis of what these different examples reveal about the nature and place of the drive-in within post-war exhibition and post-war America.

The national picture

Where were drive-ins? They were, first, in the United States, though some 1950s reports acknowledged that they had also began to appear elsewhere: in 1956 one writer who identified them as flourishing only in the United States and southern Canada added that in South Africa and Australia the drive-in was 'beginning to come into its own'.[16] Initial discussion of the drive-in's American growth often used a rural vocabulary, as in James Cunningham's identification of their origins as 'a place to see a movie in the cool of the countryside away from the heat of the town'.[17] 'Drive-in Business Burns up the Prairies' announced *Life*.[18] 'The Movies Take to the Pastures' reported the *Saturday Evening Post*, arguing that the drive-in market had not yet (in 1950) reached saturation point but was spreading rapidly across the country.[19] Alternatively, they were associated with the urban fringe. In 1951, one regular commentator on the topic suggested that drive-ins were 'usually in an urban area, but away from congested areas'.[20] Subsequent discussions of the spread of drive-in have linked this not only to the growth of suburbia but also to the small town, to the outskirts, the hinterlands and the rural.

'The development of the drive-in was an American phenomenon because of the huge demand for auto-convenient movie exhibition by the millions of new suburbanites from coast to coast', writes Douglas Gomery.[21] Noting that drive-ins catered to a mobile audience, James Russell and Jim Whalley locate the drive-in 'on the edge of small towns and in other rural areas'.[22] They tended to be on the edge of town, where land was cheaper, notes Maggie Valentine, or, according to Cohen, 'at the intersection of rural, urban, and suburban communities'.[23] Jackson includes the drive-in in his history of the suburbanization of the United States but writes that when these 'originally opened, they were typically out in the hinterlands', defined elsewhere as that urban space beyond the city's immediate environment, 'the variegated non-city spaces that are swept into the maelstrom of urbanisation'.[24]

They could move. In 1948 the exhibitor H. D. Hearn claimed that portable drive-ins accounted for around seventy-five of the hundred or so drive-ins in the Charlotte area of North Carolina.[25] These makeshift drive-ins were generally operated by leasing a tract of farmland for between $50 and $100, attaching the screen to a pair of trees and installing their equipment in a small frame booth that might or might not be fireproof. They had no in-car speakers or ramps to allow a clear view of the screen and in wet weather the cars could get bogged down in the muddy fields.[26]

Even for Hearn, while these migrant operations offered some competition to local small-town cinemas, they had little long-term future.[27] There were occasional later reports, along the lines of James Morris's comment that there were 'still "theatres" that consist merely of a couple of old telegraph poles erected in a field with a screen of plywood nailed across them'.[28] Sound came from a speaker nailed to one of the poles, 16mm projection equipment was normally used and there might be fifty cars at the show.[29]

The problem with such reports is the lack of evidence on specific examples.[30] Where the film trade press did refer to individual rural drive-ins, it was to more permanent examples. In 1954 *Motion Picture Exhibitor* reported on how 'even primitive [concession] stands in rural drive-ins can be made attractive and appealing, with a little extra decorating and inexpensive interior set-ups'.[31] As one example it cited the 1000 Islands Drive-In in upstate New York, where the rough wood building 'gives the effect of being rustic, appropriate for its particular environment'.[32] The 1000 Islands was remote as well as rustic, depending on the holiday trade, which meant that the small population of Alexandria Bay expanded in the summer months.

The small number of drive-in operators who contributed to the *Motion Picture Herald* 'What the Picture Did For Me' and the *Boxoffice* 'Exhibitor Has His Say' columns illustrate a variation on the rural drive-in in that they tended to identify themselves with the columns' emphasis on 'small town and rural patronage'. For contributors to these columns, place was not just an address, it was also a community with which they were familiar. 'Bogart still has very good drawing power here', noted Kenneth Clem of the Monocacy Drive-In, Taneytown, Maryland (identified as 'rural patronage'), following a screening of *To Have and Have Not* (1944).[33] At the Homestead Drive-In, North Montpelier, Vermont ('small town and rural patronage'), John C. Coffrin tied *High Noon* (1952) 'with a local "High Noon" radio show and it paid off'.[34] These drive-ins may have been physically on the edge of town, but the published screening reports convey the exhibitors' efforts to link their cinemas to the local community.

At the other extreme there were drive-ins that were more urban than suburban and that were sometimes built within the city limits. Having run the Dearborn Tool and Die Company, the Clark family opened the Ford-Wyoming Drive-In on 19 May 1950. The story that Karen Dybis tells of the efforts to open and maintain the Ford-Wyoming in part illustrates why drive-ins did not tend to be urban. Built within the Dearborn city limits on land zoned as 'Industrial A', it first had to be approved by the Dearborn Zoning Board. While the Board initially approved, the city mayor and a consortium of neighbourhood clubs did not, and the drive-in was only opened after different petitions, demands and rulings. Local zoning ordinances across the United States placed restrictions on buildings in residential, commercial and industrial districts, and in built-up areas local pressure groups often raised objections to drive-in construction, whether because of concerns about noise and traffic or fears about the drive-in's reputation and who it might attract.[35]

Local newspapers carried regular reports on objections to a proposed drive-in. For example, proposals for a drive-in in the Laguna Honda neighbourhood of San Francisco were met with objections from the vice president of the Forest Hills Association, who complained that a drive-in 'would tend to attract undesirable groups into a high-grade residential neighbourhood'.[36] A rezoning application for a drive-in in Tampa, Florida, was turned down in November 1952 after a hearing at which some 'based their arguments against changing the zone from residential to commercial on grounds that it would create traffic hazards and noise, and devaluate their home property'.[37] Such complaints could mask others. The Tampa proposal was for a drive-in for African Americans and despite repeated attempts 'to prevent injection of the racial question . . . about 70 of the protesting property owners of the neighbourhood argued that any mixing of the races would "lead to trouble"'.[38] Objections to the Ford-Wyoming were on the grounds of 'traffic, morality and undesirables'.[39]

The Ford-Wyoming was built on industrial rather than residential land and opened because in this instance there was land available: an unused site next to the Dearborn Tool and Die plant. In general space limitations and property prices made the inner city drive-in impractical. The urban drive-in could succeed if circumstances allowed for a location close enough to densely populated areas or workplaces. Dearborn is close to downtown Detroit, which in 1950 was, with a population of 1,849,568, the fifth largest city in the United States.[40] It was at the centre of Henry Ford's industrial empire. Some of the largest drive-ins were those clustered around the largest cities. When the Ford-Wyoming opened it could accommodate 750 cars, but at its height in the 1990s it was a nine-screen drive-in with space for 3,000 cars.[41] A 1949, *New Yorker* report that began, 'Drive-in movie theatres have been springing up all over the country for the last year or so, the way miniature golf courses did in the late twenties', illustrated what 'all over the country' meant by going on to describe the 850-car capacity Whitestone Bridge Drive-In in the Bronx, identified by Segrave as 'perhaps the most urban drive-in in the country'.[42] The number of drive-ins operating in the 1950s meant that, just as the location of indoor cinemas ranged from small town to big city, there were urban and suburban as well as rural drive-ins.

Urban did not have to mean metropolitan. In a sign of later indoor developments, Walter Reade's downtown Dover Drive-In sat on top of a multi-story car park next to a shopping centre in downtown Dover, New Jersey, which in 1960 had a population of 13,034.[43] In one sense, it defines the limits of urban drive-in expansion. It had a short life at the end of the 1950s, not helped by the fact that the neon signs advertising the shopping centre resulted in a screen image that was indistinct even for a drive-in.[44] Drive-ins could survive in an urban environment but not downtown or in the metropolitan centre where land prices were prohibitively expensive, where the proximity of other buildings made a permanent open-air cinema impractical and where even indoor cinemas struggled in the post-war era. A drive-in was built in the Bronx but not Manhattan, in Dearborn but not downtown Detroit.

Drive-ins were thus absent from the very space with which cinemas have been primarily associated. If, as Robert Allen writes, 'Keeping the metropolitan experience of moviegoing at the center of our historical map of American cinema squashes a complex and dynamic cultural and social geography into a simplistic binary grid of city/country', that is accentuated in the case of the drive-in cinema and can partially account for their relative academic neglect.[45]

In 1950 Alice Hughes wrote that one of the disadvantages of living in New York city was 'lack of space. For one thing, we have no room for drive-in theaters on hot summer evenings. However, a short ride and a bridge toll, and you're in Long Island, Westchester, or New Jersey, where the carpark movies flourish'.[46] The significance of place for cinema is not just the location of the cinema itself but also its catchment area, which was likely to be extended in the case of the drive-in. Rodney Luther's 1949 survey of drive-ins in the Minneapolis-St Paul area indicated that the average patron travelled a fifteen-mile round trip to and from the drive-in.[47] He extended that figure to 17.6 miles in his 1950 survey.[48] The following year Wilfred P. Smith wrote about reports that 'a moviegoer will drive up to ten miles to a conventional theatre to see a first-run picture; but that he will drive up to 30 miles to attend a drive-in theatre!'[49] Six years later, Arthur Steel, manager of the Elmsford Drive-In in New York State, wrote of his concern about competition from neighbouring drive-ins that were better equipped and showed films on earlier runs. These included the Rockland in Monsey, which was 'only about 20 minutes away on the Thruway . . . While the cost of attending these drive-ins for Westchester and New York residents will be the $1.00 bridge toll, I do not think that the extra dollar will mean too much to those who have four or five in the car'.[50] The Bronx is the closest New York County to both Elmsford and Monsey, but it is more than a thirty-mile drive from the Bronx to Monsey.

Steel's desire for additional support to renovate his own operation may have led him to exaggerate the distance people were prepared to drive to the drive-in. As the number of drive-ins grew, the distance people travelled to reach them is likely to have contracted. What is clear is that drive-ins often drew in people from across city limits and county lines, combining the rural with the urban and the suburban. This was not limited to the metropolis and its surroundings. The contributors to the 'Exhibitor Has His Say' column included the Pratt-Mont Drive-In in Prattville, Alabama, around three miles away from Prattville and fourteen miles from the Maxwell Air Force Base on the edge of Montgomery. It listed 'farm, state capital, small-town and air base' as its patronage.[51]

Those making the journey from Montgomery to the Pratt-Mont or from New York to the Rockland were dependent on roads and cars. Along with diners, gas stations and motels, drive-in cinemas were a feature of roadside America. In 1949 the American Association of State Highway Officials calculated that nearly all drive-ins were located outside the limits of towns and cities and 90 per cent of drive-ins were located on major highways, 46 per cent on two-lane highways and 81 per cent on highways carrying more than 3,000 cars a day.[52] The motive behind the report was to reduce congestion and accidents by ensuring that future drive-ins were on secondary roads rather than highways, an aim made more difficult by the tendency of drive-ins to be built outside city limits and therefore outside city jurisdiction (which was one reason they were often built outside city limits).

There were people who lived close enough to be able to walk to the drive-in, and there were drive-ins that provided a seating area, but whether on or just off the main highway, drive-ins had to be accessible for the vast majority who came by car. Expanding car ownership was a key factor in their growth and their location outside the city. The US share of the global motor vehicle market was 76.2 per cent in 1950.[53] While that figure decreased over time, the percentage of American car ownership continued to increase, from 60 per cent of families owning one or more cars and 7 per cent two or more cars in 1950 to 74 per cent owning one or more cars and 15 per cent for two or more in 1959.[54] For James J. Flink the 'Passage of the 1956 Interstate Highway Act ensured the complete triumph of the automobile over mass-transit alternatives in the United States and killed off, except in a few large cities, the vestiges of balanced public transportation systems that remained in 1950s America'.[55] Before that, state and local spending had expanded the road network across the United States, and this construction, and the expectation of future road building, played a fundamental role in drive-in location.[56]

The relationship between cars, roads and drive-ins was scrutinized in contemporary studies, though these indicated that drive-in expansion varied in different states, for a variety of reasons. As outdoor cinemas, climate was self-evidently important for the drive-ins. One question was therefore the extent to which there were more drive-ins in southern states or in drier locations. A 1952 survey by Jack H. Levin Associates looked at the number of drive-ins in different states (excluding Alaska, which at that date had no drive-in, and Washington, DC, which never had one), the number of days they stayed open as well as figures for car registration, road density, temperature and rainfall.[57] It identified a link between the number of drive-ins and car registration numbers and road density and between drive-in season length and higher temperatures but not lower rainfall. However, the figures provided in the *Variety* report on the survey indicate a more complex picture. States with a higher number of drive-ins tended to have a higher number of cars but there were significant variations in the number of cars per drive-in. New Jersey, New York and Maryland had between 32,474 and 36,795 cars per drive-in, while further south West Virginia and North and South Carolina had between 3,398 and 3,587.[58] Other southern or rural states had relatively small numbers of cars per drive-in (Georgia had 5,864, Wyoming 4,136), while more urbanized, northern states tended to have a larger number (22,133 in Connecticut, 28,500 in Rhode Island).[59]

A survey reporting figures up to the end of 1955 identified much smaller numbers of cars per drive-in across the United States. By this date, the figures for New Jersey, New York and Maryland were, respectively, 710, 542 and 451 cars per drive-in, with New York and Maryland now lower than Connecticut (693), Rhode Island (602) and California (667).[60] West Virginia and North and South Carolina had 312, 271 and 251, respectively, while both Georgia and Wyoming had 322 cars per drive-in.[61]

Richard Egerton has examined other data on the number of drive-ins between 1948 and 1954 in individual states and the net decrease of indoor cinema over the same period, as well as state population, the percentage classified as urban and the mean January temperature between 1921 and 1950.[62] The figures reveal the Carolinas and Florida as the states with the highest proportion (over a third) of drive-ins to indoor cinemas and that the proportion of drive-ins to indoor cinemas tended to be higher in the southern states, though the proportion was higher in Vermont, Wyoming and Oregon than it was in Mississippi, Louisiana, California and Nevada.[63]

The relatively low proportion of drive-ins to indoor cinemas in California may seem surprising. It points not only to the relatively high number of indoor cinemas (as well as cars) in the state but also to the relatively late Californian drive-in expansion: in 1954 North Carolina, Pennsylvania and Texas each had more drive-ins than California, where the number of drive-ins did not peak until 1967 and which only overtook Texas as the state with the most drive-ins after 1977.[64] Reports on the Levin survey indicated that precipitation did not have a marked effect on the length of the drive-in season, with drive-ins in the wettest state, Louisiana, tending to stay open throughout the year, but the relatively low proportion of drive-ins to indoor cinemas in Louisiana and Mississippi suggests that this may have been a factor in the number of drive-ins if not how long they stayed open.[65]

The drive-in complicates the picture of cinema closures in the 1950s. While in New Jersey there was an overall loss in the number of cinemas, in some states (such as Nebraska) new drive-ins balanced the closure of indoor cinemas, and in others (such as Georgia) there was an overall 1950s increase in the number of cinemas due to new drive-ins construction.[66] When Dennis Giles looked at the state of the drive-in in 1983, he traced an Appalachian 'drive-in belt', including Oklahoma, Missouri, Tennessee, Kentucky and West Virginia, widening at the centre to include Indiana, Ohio and (probably) Southern Illinois.[67] By 1977, he noted, Texas (despite remaining particularly associated with the drive-in) had a below-average number, accounting for 19 per cent of the state's theatrical receipts, in comparison with a national average of 27 per cent, while there was a higher concentration in Southern California, 'where the urban sprawl included open, undeveloped parcels of land'.[68] The Great Plains and Deep South had large rural populations but relatively few drive-ins but in general the drive-in was hill-country culture and high urbanization had a general but not inevitable negative effect on drive-in strength.[69] There are some continuities here with the 1950s though also some differences. In the 1950s, Texas had more drive-ins than any other state but not the highest proportion of drive-ins to indoor cinemas, car ownership or population.

Texas also points to complications within states. It contained major, rapidly growing cities such as Dallas and Houston but also extensive land outside of the city as well as a significant number of smaller cities and towns. Looking at the material collected by Levin and Egerton is useful for understanding the location of drive-ins across the United States and the factors influencing this in broad terms. For a closer understanding we need to examine the situation within individual states and locations.

Texas

The 1952 Levin report listed Texas as having 339 drive-ins.[70] The Texas figures given by Segrave are 388 in 1954, declining to 382 in 1958 and 315 in 1963.[71] The 1955 *Texas Theatre Guide* lists 420 drive-ins.[72] There is evidence for at least 534 Texas drive-ins that were open at some point in the 1950s, though at no point in the decade would all of these have been in operation. Some only opened towards the end of the decade by when others had already closed.

For example, in 1959 *Motion Picture Exhibitor* reported that F. B. Leathers might not reopen the Chief Drive-In, Paducah, that season 'unless this region receives good rains', noting also that the drive-in had not opened the previous season 'for economic reasons'.[73] On 21 March 1960, *Boxoffice* reported that Leathers was 'dismantling his drive-in, which he has not operated for several years'.[74]

The US state that after Alaska covered the largest land area, Texas, offered the open space needed for drive-in construction while its growing population offered the potential audience. The 1950 US census defined the urban population as those living in cities of 2,500 or more and, for the first time, those living in unincorporated areas with a population of 50,000 or more. For the first time it also identified Texas as more urban than rural (under the old and new definitions), on account not just of those living in suburban areas outside the city limits but also of migration to expanding cities such as Dallas, which grew from 294,734 in 1940 to 434,462 in 1950 and 679,684 in 1960.[75]

Even the smaller Texan towns could have more than one drive-in, though how many more is not always clear. Kermit, forty-five miles west of Odessa and 229 miles east of El Paso, had a population of 6,912 in 1950 and 10,464 in 1960.[76] This small town had three indoor cinemas in the 1950s: the Kermit, the Oasis and the Texas. The 1955 *Film Daily Year Book* also lists three drive-ins: the Lariat, the Tower and the Yellow Jacket.[77] In fact, Kermit had a mere two drive-ins: the Tower was renamed the Yellow Jacket in the early 1950s.[78] Multiple drive-ins surrounded major Texas cities. By the end of the 1950s Dallas (which at the time of writing no longer has a single drive-in), San Antonio and Houston each had at least seventeen, Fort Worth thirteen and El Paso ten drive-ins.

Of the 420 drive-ins listed in the 1955 *Texas Theatre Guide*, 184 were identified as owned by individuals or companies with no other Texas drive-ins. The two names accounting for the largest number of drive-ins were Frontier Theatres (thirty-three) and Rowley United (twenty-seven). The Dallas-based Frontier Theatres chain operated indoor and outdoor cinemas in New Mexico and Texas: by 1961 thirty-three had fallen to twenty-three, though the company was reported as owning approximately eighty-five cinemas in total.[79] Also based in Dallas, in 1950 Robb and Rowley (also known as Rowley United) controlled 146 indoor and outdoor cinemas in Arkansas, Oklahoma and Texas.[80]

Next behind these two was Claude Ezell, accounting for twenty-one Texas drive-ins. Unlike Frontier and Rowley, Ezell's exhibition interests were solely in drive-ins. According to *Variety*, he pioneered the drive-in business in Texas, operating 'a total of 42 ozoners, the largest chain of open-air theatres in the nation'.[81] Following his death in 1961, *Boxoffice* noted that he was 'termed the "father" of the drive-in theatre in Texas'.[82] Having worked in film distribution, for General Film Co., Lewis J. Selznick & Co. and Warner Bros., he moved back to Dallas where, with W. B. Underwood, he had the franchise for distributing Monogram films. With Underwood, in 1940 he moved from distribution to drive-in exhibition. Following Underwood's death in 1948, he set up companies under different names, including Ezell & Associates and Lone Star Theatres. He established the Texas Drive-Ins Theatre Owners' Association and the International Drive-In Theatre Owners' Association, the latter claiming links with countries including Canada, Mexico, Guam, Hawaii, Panama and Australia. His show business career reputedly began when, aged eleven, he joined the circus, and he brought something of the circus to the drive-in, using monkeys, donkeys, mechanical elephants and other attractions alongside film screenings.[83]

While some Texas drive-ins were run as local, small-scale businesses, at least those surrounding major and medium-sized cities were more often part of larger circuits or chains, whether dating back to the early days of the drive-in or earlier. Other studies identify a similar pattern. In Laredo, notes José Carlos Lozano, 'a small US-Mexico border town' where by 1950 Mexican Americans accounted for 86 per cent of 51,910 inhabitants, indoor and outdoor exhibition was dominated by Robb and Rowley, while Texas more generally saw the increased consolidation of the dominant cinema circuits, reduced from ten Texas chains in 1930 to four in 1949.[84] Javier Ramirez calculates that Lone Star Theaters, W. O. Bearden Theaters and Lester O. Dollison Theaters controlled 55 per cent of the El Paso drive-in market, and that from 1955 to 1960 cinema chains owned either all drive-ins or held a majority of the marketplace in the Texas cities of Brownsville, Del Rio, Harlington, Laredo, Pharr and Rio Grande.[85]

There were close relationships between the larger Texas circuits. When Underwood and Ezell established the Buckner Boulevard in Dallas in 1948, it did this by purchasing land from the Interstate Circuit and borrowing half of the estimated $150,000 construction costs from Interstate.[86] When the Buckner Boulevard Corporation went into liquidation in 1952, its assets were distributed to Interstate, which in 1954 sold the Buckner to Ezell & Associates.[87] Interstate shared a half interest with Ezell's companies in other Texas drive-ins in Fort Worth (the Bowie Boulevard, the Hempstead and the Irvington), Waco (the Circle), Haltom City (the Belknap), Dallas (the Northwest Highway) and Houston (the Winkler).[88] Ezell's ownership fluctuated during the 1950s. In 1955 *Motion Picture Daily* announced his sale of drive-ins in Fort Worth, Waco, San Antonio, Brownsville, Houston and Dallas to E. L. Pack's Bordertown Theatres, and two Austin drive-ins to Trans Texas Theatres and one Corpus Christi drive-in to Rowley United, noting that Ezell & Associates would continue to run two Port Arthur drive-ins with the Jefferson Amusement Company and would retain other cinemas both within and outside Texas.[89] The report went on to note that Ezell & Associates would keep hold of other cinemas in Texas towns and outside the state but that Ezell was aiming for less responsibility and more leisure. That aim may not have been realized, for the drive-ins he sold to Bordertown were subsequently brought back by Lone Star Theatres, the company that had previously operated as Ezell & Associates.[90]

In contrast to Ezell, Interstate's position as the most powerful Texas exhibitor was achieved through its indoor cinemas. Established in 1905 as the Interstate Amusement Company, by the mid-1940s it operated over 150 cinemas across the state and Albuquerque, including not only movie palaces such as the Majestic Theatres in Dallas, Houston and San Antonio but also subsequent-run non-metropolitan cinemas operated under the Texas Consolidated name. As a circuit affiliated to Paramount Pictures, Interstate was directly affected by the Supreme Court's Paramount Decree of 1949, which required that the Hollywood Majors divorce their exhibition holdings from their production and distribution operations and decrease the number of those cinemas over a five-year period. However, by the 1950s it was already operating Texas drive-ins through full ownership or in partnership with others. The 1955 Texas Theatre Guide identifies seven drive-ins under Interstate control: the Bowie and the Mansfield in Fort Worth, the Shepherd and the South Main in Houston, the Oleander in Galveston, the Airport in Paris and the Cactus in Pharr. It lists the Park Drive-In in Abilene and the Crest Drive-In in Tyler as run by Texas Consolidated, though the Park Drive-In was identified (and promoted) as an Interstate cinema from before its opening (see Figure 3).

In the 1950s Interstate was restricted in the degree to which it could expand its drive-in operations. In 1958 Jake Lutzner, owner of the Co-Ed Drive-In in Denton, asked Interstate if they were interested in buying his cinema. John Q. Adams of Interstate was sceptical, reporting to his fellow directors, 'I told Jake that most drive-ins today were having a very rough time and that with one or two exceptions, our own drive-ins were running substantially behind 1957. Further, that probably as many as 25 or 30 drive-in theatres had been offered to us within the last year, at prices far below original cost.'[91] He went on to comment: 'even if we could work out some sort of a deal, we had no assurance that the Department of Justice would permit us to acquire the theatre under our consent Decree'.[92] Different factors will have influenced this pessimistic outlook, some local and temporary. Drive-ins were one part of Interstate's holdings, and the circuit continued to explore the possibilities they offered, whether through partnership or full ownership. Individual and small-scape operators were part of the Texas drive-in expansion, but larger cinema circuits and chains remained dominant across the state, in the outdoor as well as the indoor market.

FIGURE 3 *Photograph of the future site of the Park Drive-In, Abilene, Texas, Scrapbook for Park Drive-In, 16 December 1949, 5, Interstate Theatre Collection. From the collections of the Dallas History & Archives Division, Dallas Public Library.*

Seminole and Hondo

The Chief Drive-In, just south of Seminole, and the Hondo Drive-In, on the west of Hondo, will serve here as examples of small-scale operations serving small Texas towns. The West Texas town of Seminole, in Gaines County, had a population of 3,480 in 1950 and 5,737 in 1960.[93] To the west of San Antonio in Medina County, Hondo was closer to the Mexican border. With a population of 4,190, it was a little larger than Seminole in 1950 but smaller (4,992) in 1960.[94] Published figures indicate that the two towns had a different ethnic composition: the 1956–7 *Texas Almanac* lists Gaines County as 97.1 per cent 'Anglo-American', 1.6 per cent 'Latin American' and 1.3 per cent 'Negro'.[95] It lists Medina County as 56.3 per cent 'Latin American', 42.5 per cent 'Anglo-American' and 1.2 per cent 'Negro'.[96] However, other evidence suggests that there was a significant Hispanic audience in the vicinity of both towns.

One individual or one family dominated exhibition in both towns. In Seminole it was W. E. Cox Jr, his wife Fronia, his brother Audrey and Audrey Cox's wife (invariably identified in the press as Mrs Audrey Cox). In Lamesa (forty miles to the east of Seminole), Audrey Cox and his wife owned the Majestic, Palace and Tower indoor cinemas and the Yucca Drive-In (which opened in 1948). They also opened the Palace on Seminole's Main Street in 1936, with W. E. Cox as manager, and with W. E. Cox in 1940 they opened the more comfortably furnished Tower further down the street, at 215 South Main.[97] The Palace and the Tower were indoor cinemas that over time came to cater to different audiences, the Palace showing Spanish-language films (which were not advertised in the *Seminole Sentinel*) while the Tower restricted non-white audiences to the balcony.[98] Opening on 6 June 1950, the Chief Drive-In was the third Seminole cinema, a mile south of Seminole on US 385 towards Andrews and Odessa.[99]

The 1963 *Film Daily Year Book* lists Cox Theatres Inc. as a five cinema business, with Mrs Audrey Cox (her husband having died in 1955) as owner-manager of the Palace and the Yucca Drive-In in Lamesa and Mrs Audrey Cox and W. E. Cox as co-owners of the Palace and Tower as well as the Chief Drive-In in Seminole.[100] Celebrating its third year in 1952, the Chief was promoted as 'West Texas Finest "Little" Drive-In Theatre', equipped with 'the most complete children's playground of any Drive-In Theatre in West Texas', complete with slides, see-saws, swings and a newly installed Merry Widow Whirl and 'the most complete Drive-In Concession in the south, specialising in sandwiches, hot-dogs, french fries, cold drinks, ice cream, peanuts, popcorn, candy, scones and anything you might want to eat'.[101] It remained open for most of the year but was closed either around Christmas or in January. Having closed on 21 December 1957, it did not open again until 7 February 1958, and then initially from Fridays to Mondays, only opening for the full week from 14 March. In July and August that year the Tower moved to opening at 2 pm on Saturdays and Sundays and 7 pm on Fridays and Mondays, remaining closed for the rest of the week. Evidently, small-town owners of multiple cinemas could use different sites either to segregate audiences or to reduce costs by closing the drive-in for some of the winter and one indoor cinema on some summer days.

The Chief was physically out of town but connected to businesses at the town's centre and owned by a family whose business interests were not limited to the cinema. Fronia Cox also operated as a beautician.[102] The Tower Theater building also housed a café, a dress shop and an appliance store.[103] W. E. Cox sold the building in 1947 (while continuing to run the cinema) but in 1959 he opened the Indian Lanes Bowling Alley, adjacent to the Chief Drive-In.[104] Profiling him shortly before the opening of the Tower, the *Seminole Sentinel* noted that he had been active in civic affairs since moving to Seminole 'and at present is the only city commissioner on the hold over from the last term, a director in the Chamber of Commerce and a member of the Rotary

Club'.[105] By the early 1960s he had become one of the directors of the Texas Drive-In Theatre Owners' Association.[106] When her husband died in 1972, Fronia Cox continued his civic work, serving as a Justice of the Peace and from 1979 to 1989 as a City Judge.[107]

At weekends the Chief functioned as an action house, and 30 per cent of the films it advertised in the *Seminole Sentinel* in the 1950s were westerns. During the week its programme spanned a wider range of genres. It did not always show films that had Production Code approval: *The Moon Is Blue* (1953), which United Artists released without the seal of approval from the Hollywood Production Code, played the Chief Sunday to Tuesday at the beginning of November 1953. There were, however, limits to which Cox Theatres would step out of line: in 1950, Aubrey Cox and his wife told the *Lubbock Morning Avalanche* that their cinemas would not be screening *Stromboli*, explaining that if they had done so it would have been a 'disservice to the community' and thanking 'all our friends and clergymen of Lamesa and Dawson County who wrote letters expressing their disfavor for portraying this movie'.[108]

Closer to the Mexican border, forty miles to the west of San Antonio, in some respect Hondo presents a similar picture to Seminole. Ray Jennings dominated local cinema ownership from his arrival in Hondo in 1920. He moved from running a tailor's, a male outfitters and steam laundry, to part ownership of the Colonial Theater, closing that when he opened the Raye in 1938 (which, like the Tower in Seminole, restricted African Americans to the balcony), and going on to open the Park cinema in 1942.[109] Hondo had an outdoor cinema in the 1920s, the Airdome, which the *Hondo Anvil Herald* subsequently described as 'a sort of combination brush arbor and drive-in movie where picture shows were projected on an outside wall as viewers sat on long benches'.[110] In 1950 that paper had reported on Jennings' plans to build an actual drive-in, half a mile east of the city limits, towards San Antonio on Highway 90.[111] The Hondo Drive-In that opened on Thursday 16 August 1951, with a free screening of *Frenchie* (1950), was on that highway, but a mile west of Hondo, and was opened not by Jennings but by Harry Hammill and his wife.[112] Hammill's background was in aviation and the circus business: with Benjamin C. Davenport, he had previously run the Austin Bros Circus and the Dailey Bros Circus.[113]

Hammill stayed in the film business but did not retain the Hondo for long. In 1954 he made a deal with Gidney Talley in which he acquired two indoor cinemas owned by Talley in Mathis, Texas, and Talley acquired the Hondo Drive-In.[114] At and after this time the drive-in's opening and programming policy shifted. It was initially open seven days a week, generally showing a single feature. From January to early March 1954 openings were cut back to Thursdays to Mondays, and mid-week closures returned between November 1954 and June 1955, in 1956 and 1958. In 1955 it began showing Spanish-language films two days a week, as other local cinemas were doing. Immediately after the Second World War Anthony Paiz and Jesus Romanes had established an indoor cinema in Hondo showing Spanish-language films, but this did not last long as it soon had to compete with the Park Theater which started to show Spanish-language films, initially on Sundays, later during the week.[115] Up to the end of 1955, the *Hondo Anvil Herald* also carried advertisements for the Medina Drive-In, about twenty miles south of Hondo: it played Spanish-language films on Tuesdays in November and December 1955.

The fact that the Hondo Drive-In was not owned by a local exhibitor suggests that it was more of an outsider than the Chief. The week it opened the *Hondo Anvil Herald* carried only a brief note that 'Mr and Mrs Hammill announced the opening of the Hondo Drive In Theatre this week' and a longer piece on the following page about the upcoming screening at the Park Theatre of *The Prince of Peace*, the religious film originally released as *The Lawton Story* in 1949 and given roadshow screenings by Kroger Babb, complete with the sale of Bibles and religious pamphlets, in the 1950s.[116] Talley, the man who brought the drive-in from the Hammills, is best known for setting up Social Guidance Enterprises and then (with Kroger Babb, Irwin Joseph and Floyd Lewis) Modern Film Distributors, before selling out his interest in the latter to self-styled 'trash-film king' David Friedman. He set up Social Guidance Enterprises to distribute and promote *The Story of Bob and Sally* (1948), having brought the film from Universal after it had been refused Production Code approval. At screenings of the 'sex hygiene' exploitation film (as at other examples of the subgenre) there were lectures from supposedly renowned sex hygiene experts, 'nurses in attendance' and books on sale to accompany the film.[117] There were separate screenings for men and women at indoor screenings, though when it played the Hondo Drive-In, Thursday, and Friday 7–8 October 1954, it was (as at other drive-ins) advertised as the 'first time shown to male and female audiences together'.[118]

The Hondo Drive-In screening of *The Story of Bob and Sally* was not, however, unusual for either outdoor or neighbourhood indoor cinemas. The films it advertised in the *Hondo Anvil Herald* include less westerns (22 per cent) than the Chief and occasional distinctive strands such as a Humphrey Bogart month in February 1957 but are otherwise similar to the Seminole drive-in. When, in 1956, a new manager, W. McDermott, moved in with his wife and children, Rusty (age two) and Dolores (age one), he told a local reporter that he would be installing a suggestions box 'to find out what patrons like best in movies or general improvements in the snack bar or anything else', continuing the weekly entrance prize and making Thursday evenings 'club night', when '25 percent of all proceeds for the evening will go to some church, school project or civic organisation in Hondo . . . Club night is my way of saying I want to be part of this community'.[119]

On the basis of his research into early twentieth-century film exhibition in North Carolina, Robert Allen noted that what was striking about the social status of small-town cinemas in that state and, he suspected, elsewhere was 'not how removed or obscured they were from what some might call hegemonic culture or how alternative or autonomous they were as public spaces, but rather how tightly woven they were, or aspired to be, into not just the town's social or cultural life but its civic life as well'.[120] The operators of the Chief and Hondo Drive-Ins appear to have had similar aspirations. The Chief was more tightly woven into the social, culture, civic and business life of Seminole but even the Hondo, notwithstanding the fact that for much of the 1950s it was owned by someone now best known as a distributor of exploitation films, aspired to be part of the community.

Orange and Abilene

Orange and Abilene will serve here as examples of medium-sized urban centres. I will say less here about Orange and the MacArthur Drive-In as I will return to that drive-in's programme and its audience in the following two chapters. In discussing Abilene, I examine not just the seven drive-ins that encircled the city by the decade's end but also the city's indoor cinemas, to provide a more comprehensive picture of the place of the drive-in within the city's exhibition network.

At the eastern edge of Texas, the population of Orange fluctuated from 1940. It expanded rapidly during the Second World War, when it became a major shipbuilding centre. Its population declined immediately after the war but then rose from 21,270 in 1950 to 25,610 in 1960 and from 40,567 to 60,357 in Orange County, before slowly declining in subsequent years.[121]

Orange had five downtown cinemas at the beginning of the decade, though only three of these regularly advertised in the *Orange Leader*: the Bengal, the Royal and the Strand, all operated by Julius Gordon's Paramount-affiliated circuit, the Jefferson Amusement Company. In the early 1950s the paper also carried small advertisements for another Jefferson Amusement Company cinema, the Surf Drive-In, twenty miles away in Port Arthur. The 1951 *Film Daily Year Book* also lists two further Orange cinemas, the Dragon (for black audiences) and the Gem (listed in earlier editions as a Jefferson Amusement Company cinema).[122] It lists seventy-four Jefferson Amusement Company cinemas, all in Texas, including a fourth cinema in Orange, the MacArthur

Drive-In, which had opened on 18 August 1950.[123] The 1955 *Texas Theatre Guide* lists nine Jefferson Amusement Company drive-ins, in Baytown, Beaumont, Henderson, Jacksonville, Kilgore, Longview, Lufkin as well as Orange and Port Arthur.[124]

The MacArthur Drive-In was to the north-west of downtown Orange, on Strickland Street off MacArthur Drive, in an area that became residential in the 1950s through the Roselawn housing development.[125] Opening with a firework display and an appearance from Koko the Clown, it initially had a capacity for 600 cars, a snack bar in front of which was a seated 'patio' area and a children's playground in front of the screen.[126] It stayed open throughout the year.

In this corner of Texas, the dominance of the Jefferson Amusement Company lasted throughout the decade, though by the end of the 1950s the *Orange Leader* was only carrying advertisements for the Strand and the MacArthur. Thus, the MacArthur survived while other local cinemas did not but with a status that was secondary to the Strand. In 1958, a teenager interviewed by the *Orange Leader* complained, 'the town would be better off if it had more than one movie. There used to be three downtown theaters but now there is only one'.[127] He went to say, 'Some of the kids drive to Beaumont or Port Arthur to see a movie', before admitting, 'Well, there's a drive-in theater, but it usually shows films which are re-runs.'[128] For some, the drive-in could be (or become) an afterthought, for all its aspirations to be part of the community.

There were more cinemas (outdoor and indoor) in Abilene, where expansion was more rapid and extended. It was already expanding in the 1930s, when the Abilene Chamber of Commerce promoted Abilene as a fast-growing city (having grown from 10,274 inhabitants in 1920 to an estimated 28,000 plus) at the centre of one of the largest farming and cattle raising areas in Texas and the Southwest and an undeveloped oil field with the prospect of being one of the biggest producing fields in Texas.[129] Amusement facilities included four cinemas, 'all showing sound pictures, with a seating capacity of 3,000'.[130] Its expansion gathered pace during the Second World War, when an army training camp was established eleven miles south-west of the city. Camp Barkeley closed in 1945 but the land was later used for the Dyess Air Force Base, established in 1956. Abilene's growth continued during this period, rising from 45,570 in 1950 to 90,368 in 1960.[131] A road building programme in the late 1950s and early 1960s also led to the construction of Loop 322, linking US 83 and US 84 to what was then US 80 and subsequently became Interstate 20.[132]

Cinema ownership was more complicated in Abilene than Orange. In 1937, three of the city's cinemas, the Majestic, the Palace and the Paramount, were part of the Texas Consolidated chain, which with the Interstate Circuit was under the overall control of Karl Hoblitzelle. As well as the independently operated Gem, previously known as the Rex, another Texas Consolidated cinema, the Queen, had closed in 1935 but reopened in 1938, with a policy of 'weekend double-bills and rock bottom prices'.[133] John Blocker opened the Texas Theatre in 1938.[134] Phil Isley (father of Phylis Isley, better known as Jennifer Jones) opened the Bobby Walker Theater in 1940, and Ruth Likins opened the Broadway with her husband George in 1941.[135] Ruth Likins then opened the Grand in 1942: it showed films for African Americans and for a couple of days a week became El Teatro Grande, showing Spanish-language films.[136] Camp Barkeley had its own cinemas (as did Fort Dyess when it opened), though initially the only one that African Americans could attend was an outdoor cinema (presumably walk-in rather than drive-in).[137] By 1943 the Gem had become the Star, under the ownership first of Ike and Abe Levy, then Bob Bourland.[138] At this time, the *Abilene Reporter News* noted, a number of Abilene cinemas were operated by women: as well as Ruth Likins, in 1945 the paper identified 'Mrs John Blocker', 'Mrs Ted Winn' and 'Mrs Clarence Marsh'.[139]

Cinemas continued to change names and hands after 1945. Tom Griffing took over the Texas in 1945, then the Bobby Walker (which was subsequently renamed the Linda) in 1946 and the Metro in 1947, opened the previous year by I. B. Adelman of Tivoli Realty.[140] In 1948 Griffing sold the Texas and Linda to Paul H. Nixon and Clinton St Clair.[141] He closed the Metro but it was reopened in September by Arch Boardman.[142] Two years later R. H. Walner brought the Texas and the Linda and the cinema (having been the Rex, the Gem and the Star) now known as the State.[143] United Paramount's acquisition of full ownership of Interstate Theatres and Texas Consolidated Theatres meant it had to divest itself of seventy-six cinemas to open up competition.[144] In 1954, it sold the Majestic to Trans Texas Theaters, the company run by Louis Novy, former manager of Interstate cinemas in Austin.[145] In 1960 Trans Texas sold the Majestic to Thomas Tucker, who had built but not opened the Metro in 1946.[146]

Some consistency remained during this period. The Hoblitzelle cinema interests, whether known as Interstate or Texas Consolidated, remained at the centre of exhibition, with the circuit's Paramount Theatre on Cypress Street at the heart of the city. It, and other Interstate cinemas, remained under the management of Wally Akin. In other respects, the pattern was one of repeated but not unlimited change. Not all cinemas survived. The Grand closed in 1947, according to Ruth Likins, because the audiences it served were now allowed into other Abilene cinemas, though other reports indicate that even in the late 1950s Interstate had a written policy instructing employees to tell customers the 'the theatre does not cater to Negro patronage at this time'.[147] The closure of Camp Barkeley may have reduced the size of the non-white audience but allowing African Americans to attend cinemas was not the only issue: in 1958 the Abilene-Taylor County Health Department reported on 'a health situation created by the fact that Texas Theatre doesn't provide restrooms for its negro patrons'.[148] By the early 1960s the Broadway, the State and the Texas had also closed (the Metro continued, in part as an art cinema). The post-war opening of the Metro pointed to a trend away from the centre: it was the city's first suburban cinema. Manager I. O. Daniel told the Abilene *Reporter News* that 'one of the outstanding features offered by the Metro will be the adjacent hard-surface parking lot which is well-lighted and is fenced with barbed wire'.[149] Providing indoor cinemas with adjacent parking lots acknowledged the increasing importance of the car, but other cinemas were soon recognizing this in a way that integrated cinema and car park.

Abilene's first drive-in was the Skyline, opened by ex-servicemen Carroll Jones and C. L. Williams. They only ran it for a limited period before it became the Elmwood Skyline, run by Ruth Likins and her husband.[150] Kathryn Kirkeby, her husband Owen Kirkeby and her brother Rudy Erickson opened the Tower Drive-In later in 1947.[151] Interstate opened the Park Drive-In, 'conveniently located' on the northern edge of Abilene in December 1949 (see Figure 4).[152] Rudy Erickson and the Kirkebys then opened a second drive-in, the Crescent, in 1952, converting both cinemas into twin-screen drive-ins.[153] Maurice S. Cole opened the Key City Drive-In the same year, selling it in 1953 to All States Theaters, run by Tom Griffing and E. L. Wilkinson.[154] In 1955 Clarence McNeil opened the Chief Drive-In.[155] In 1956, when Leon Enterprises opened Abilene's seventh drive-in (and third twin), the Town and Country, he told the *Reporter News* that, though this type of theatre was designed for much larger cities, in his view the larger scale was merited by the city's anticipated growth.[156] It boasted capacity for 1,457 cars and a 'Kiddy Land' with an electric Ferris wheel, an electric merry-go-round as well as slides, swings and climbers.[157] The paper also carried reports of an All States drive-in to be called the Flamingo.[158] This had to be abandoned due to the construction of the Abilene bypass, but when the Chief reopened it was under the new ownership of All States.

The Chief seems to have had a short life but for a period towards the end of the 1950s Abilene had more drive-ins than indoor cinemas. They circled the city, the Town and Country and the Park to the north, the Key City to the east, the Crescent to the South and to the west the Chief, the Elmwood Skylight and the Tower.[159] Cinema ownership in the city was no longer dominated by a single chain as it had been in 1937, though that shift had begun in the late 1930s. Some exhibitors restricted their businesses to the drive-in. Ruby Erickson and Owen and Katherine Kirkeby ran drive-ins in Mertzon, Brady and Big Lake as well as Abilene's Crescent and Tower: when they opened the latter in 1947 the *Reporter News* wrote that they had been in the drive-in theatre business for fifteen years, though that seems unlikely as it would mean they predated the drive-in opened in New Jersey in 1933.[160] However,

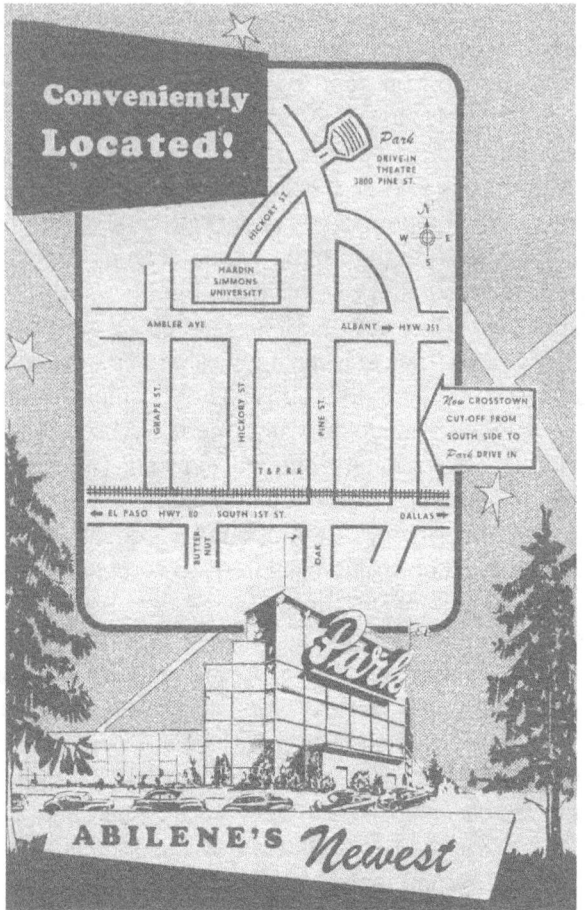

FIGURE 4 *From 'Abilene's Newest Drive-in' brochure, 2, in Scrapbook for Park Drive-In, 16 December 1949, 89, Interstate Theatre Collection. From the collections of the Dallas History & Archives Division, Dallas Public Library.*

Abilene cinema ownership does not indicate a simple split between indoors and outdoors. Interstate dominated the Texas market through its circuit of indoor cinemas but promoted the Park Drive-In alongside the indoor cinemas it operated in Abilene. Promotional devices to launch the Park in 1949 included a model of the drive-in, complete with toy cars, placed in the lobby of the Paramount, trailers in 'all down town theatres' as well as a launch at the drive-in at which fifty gallons of coffee and 1,750 donuts were provided.[161] In order to conform with the Consent Decrees, Interstate subsequently had to sell one of their Abilene cinema: it chose to sell the Majestic and to retain the Park.[162]

Other Abilene exhibitors owned indoor and outdoor cinemas. Ruth Likins brought the Elmwood Skylight having run the Grand and the Broadway and for most of the 1950s ran both the Elmwood and the Broadway. As well as the Town and County Drive-In, C. D. Leon of Leon Enterprises owned not only three Dallas drive-ins as well as drive-ins in Fort Worth, Denison, Sherman and Tyler, but also indoor cinemas in Brownsville and El Paso.[163] The 1963 edition of *Film Daily Year Book* lists All States as owning fifteen cinemas, all drive-ins, in New Mexico and Texas, but before he ran the Key City and the Chief drive-ins in Abilene with his All States Theatres partner E. L. Williamson, Tom Griffing ran the Linda, Texas and Metro indoor cinemas.[164] Tom Griffing's brother Henry was, until he died in a plane crash in 1960, president of Video Independent Theatres, which in 1957 was reported as owning and operating 150 conventional and 60 drive-in cinemas in Oklahoma, New Mexico and Texas.[165] In the 1960s Video Independent (by then part of RKO General) took over the Crescent, the Key City, the New Chief and the Tower drive-ins.

If there is some evidence here to support the image of drive-ins as small-scale, family operations, run by those new to the film industry, that is only true within limits and with complications. Carroll Jones and Chuck Williams, who moved to running the Skyline after serving, respectively, in the 656th tank destroyer battalion and as an air force engineer, fit the image of the industry newcomer but only ran their drive-in for a short period.[166] When Ruth Likins took over the Skyline with her husband (apparently initially projecting films onto a sheet suspended from the tower scaffolding) she did so after a career that included teaching French at Episcopal St Hilda's Hall in Charleston, West Virginia, staging 'community shows' across the country for the Universal Producing Company and selling advertising films to cinemas for her husband's Alexander Film Company.[167] One account notes that George Likin's career included operating several miniature golf courses.[168] However, by the time the couple took over the drive-in they already had years of experience running indoor cinemas in Abilene. Tom Griffing moved into indoor and then outdoor exhibition after 'handling music and other coin operated machines' and operating a drive-in construction business.[169] His, and his brother's, cinema interests were part of a wider interest in new media possibilities: with his business partner E. L. Williamson and his brother Henry he had an interest in Vumore, a cable/pay-per-view television company which later became part of RKO General's Cablecom General.[170] Clarence McNeil opened the Chief Drive-In having run an Abilene children's store, though before that he had apparently 'been in the motion picture business in Oklahoma'.[171] Indoor as well as outdoor cinema owners could be new to the business: Paul Nixon took over the Linda and Texas cinemas after six years' association with 'the Soil Conservation Service at Seymour' and before that time as a schoolteacher and superintendent.

R. H. Walner, who brought the cinemas from him, was a partner with his father in a rig building business.[172]

Drive-ins were often operated by married couples, sometimes by other family groups, though such family businesses varied in size. The important role that women had had in running Abilene cinemas during the Second World War continued after the war. George and Ruth Likins worked together on indoor and outdoor cinemas: I have highlighted the role played by Ruth Likins rather than by her husband in line with contemporary newspaper reports. She continued to operate the Elmwood Skylight from her husband's death in 1959 until she sold the drive-in for redevelopment in 1965. Owen and Katherine Kirkeby owned the Crescent and the Tower with Rudy Erickson, who was Katherine Kirkeby's brother; Katherine Kirkeby then continued to run the Crescent and the Tower after her husband died in 1952, initially with her brother, and when he died in 1959, with her nephew, Duane Gates. The family interests of Tom Griffing, his brother Henry and his son James were (as indicated earlier) more extensive.

The picture was also mixed when it came to the degree to which drive-ins were at the centre or on the periphery of Abilene life. The Paramount Theatre on Cypress Street, with its grand Moorish-style entrance, lobby and foyer, complete with arches, tilework, oil paintings and statuary, remained (and remains) at the cultural heart of the city, while the Park Drive-In was on the city's northern edges but belonged to the same company and (the publicity claimed) the same community.[173] But the notion of community can be used to exclude as well as include. In 1950 the *Abilene News Reporter* quoted Interstate president Karl Hoblitzelle as saying: 'For nearly a century Interstate Theatres have been proud of their slogan, "Dedicated to Community Service"'. This was in response to a story about Roberto Rossellini's *Stromboli*; Hoblitzelle reassured his patrons, 'Without having any desire to act as self-appointed censors, we feel we would be rendering our communities a disservice to exhibit the picture.'[174] None of Abilene's cinemas (indoor or outdoor) screened the film, though it was shown at the Rio Theatre, an indoor cinema in Clyde, fourteen miles to the east of Abilene.[175]

The fact that *Stromboli* was not available within the Abilene city limits can ultimately be attributed to the fact that the City Censor Board decreed that it should not be shown. Eight years later the same board banned the Brigitte Bardot film *And God Created Woman* (1956). Interstate's Wally Akin had initially planned to show the film at the downtown Queen cinema but cancelled this after the Censor Board ruling.[176] Subsequently, the Crescent and the Tower drive-ins also had to abandon planned screenings. However, this was done through state statute rather than city regulations, as though the Tower was within the city limits, the Crescent was not.[177] The two drive-ins showed the

Bardot film in November 1958. According to the *Abilene Reporter News* there was a 'turn-away crowd', though Mrs Erickson told the newspaper that it was not the first time that they had been sold out nor their biggest audience.[178]

The Elmwood Skyline further illustrates the complex relationship between the centre and the periphery. It was started by people new to the film industry and was then operated by a woman whose distinctive career included running cinemas for those otherwise excluded from the cinema. However, when it was sold in 1965, the *Reporter News* noted that a drive-in that had once bordered 'fields and fence rows' was now surrounded by, and about to become, homes and businesses.[179] Owner and operator Ruth Likins was herself an Abilene insider rather than an outsider, a woman who had been brought up in the city and whose retirement in 1965 was front-page news for the local paper.[180] Her memberships, the report noted, included the 'Magna Carta Dames, Americans of Royal Descent, Mayflower Descendants, Colonial Dames of the XVII century, Daughters of American Colonialists (William Norwood Chapter), United Daughters of the Confederacy and U.S. Daughters of 1812', and she was going to celebrate her retirement with a trip across the Atlantic on the *Queen Elizabeth* so that she could attend the 750th anniversary of the signing of the Magna Carta.[181]

Loew's Sharpstown Drive-In, Houston

My final example comes from Texas's biggest city, Houston, which grew from 596,163 in 1950 to 938,219 in 1960, when the population of the urbanized area of Harris Country reached 1,139,678.[182] By the early 1960s it was the only major US city without zoning, though to the south-west of the city it also contained Sharpstown, a planned community identified as the largest project of its kind in the world.[183] Named after the property developer Frank Sharp, Sharpstown, like the drive-in, was based on car ownership and highway infrastructure: Sharp donated part of the land he owned and organized donations from other landowners, to enable the construction of US Highway 59.[184] It was promoted as the 'world's largest residential development', a 'city within a city' spanning 6,500 acres with plans for 25,000 homes (more than the 16,000 at Levittown in Pennsylvania).[185] Announcing the imminent opening of the Houston Music Theater (financed by Sharp) in 1966, the *New York Times* went on to note that Sharpstown 'contains private homes, apartment houses, colleges, public and private elementary and secondary schools, churches, a shopping center, a combined bank and office building, its own industries, three hospitals, a motion-picture house, and an 18-hole golf course'.[186]

The paper's reference to a motion-picture 'house' may be misleading. The cinemas built in Houston in the period up to the Second World War were clustered around the city centre.[187] Interstate had a central position, owning the city's most opulent cinema, the Majestic on Rusk Avenue, and taking over the nearby Kirby and Metropolitan cinemas after the collapse of the Publix chain in the 1930s. By the time the Fulton opened in 1947, they owned eighteen indoor cinemas across the city. The Houston cinemas built after the war were suburban and in the main drive-ins. Interstate operated the Shepherd and the South Main Drive-Ins. They remained on the look out for further sites and were interested in establishing a drive-in in Sharpstown. However, in January 1956, Al Lever of Interstate reported back that Frank Sharp had made a deal giving Loew's Incorporated a twenty-year lease with an option to buy, and that this would involve building a thirty-five- acre 'Florida type Drive In, with a capacity of not less than twelve-hundred cars, plus playground, swimming pool, and beautified by palm trees, gardens, etc.'.[188]

Loew's needed federal approval for the drive-in: due to the Paramount Decrees, the circuit could not acquire new cinemas until it had sold enough of its existing holdings and then only with permission from the courts, which had to be satisfied that the new cinema would not deter competition. Having reduced its number of indoor cinemas by more than the court required, in the second half of the 1950s the company began the selective opening of new drive-ins, including the Sharpstown.[189] Loew's had an existing first-run cinema in Houston, but while the Sharpstown was to be built on a grand scale, it would be a subsequent-run cinema, and as one of Houston's forty-five subsequent-run cinemas it was agreed that this second Loew's cinema in Houston (and the company's fourth US drive-in) would not give the company an unfair advantage.[190]

Like the MacArthur in Orange and the Elmwood Skyline in Abilene, this was a project started out in open space before it became residential, but on a different scale (see Figure 5). A three-page *Boxoffice* report emphasized that this drive-in was aimed at the family, both from 'the burgeoning subdivision that will be larger than Levittown' and US Highway 90 which 'will eventually pass within 300 yards of the Sharpstown Drive-in, and will enable families from other parts of the metropolis to reach' it within a short driving time.[191] The swimming pool was abandoned (the Sharpstown Country Club already had three Olympic-size swimming pools) but other attractions included a miniature train; a zoo with monkeys, cinnamon bears, ducks and miscellaneous domestic animals; a 'dog adoption center'; two large playgrounds; and 'nightly performances of Boffo the clown and his menagerie'.[192] The train was the Sharpstown Flyer, capable of carrying forty-eight adults or seventy-two children, running over 1,650 feet of track, across a desert of cactus plants, around the carousel, through a tunnel in which 36-inch animated elves were at work at

FIGURE 5 *Aerial photograph, 1959, showing Sharpstown before the mall was built and the Southwest Freeway was completed. Loew's Sharpstown Drive-In occupies part of the open space in the middle of the picture. Photographer unknown. Courtesy of The Positive Image.*

their 'secret diamond mine' and past eleven fairy-tale houses designed around subjects from the 'Old Lady in a Shoe' to 'Judge Bean's Courthouse'.[193] As well as the cafeteria, bottle-warming and diaper services, there was a mobile 'foodmobile' to deliver food directly to customers' cars and air-conditioned toilets. Eighty-four tropical plants had been imported, and 'an unusual lighting system' was designed 'to enhance the tropical appearance of the theatre'.[194] The back of the 52- by 122-foot screen (which could accommodate different formats including CinemaScope and VistaVision) was 'a zigzag sawtooth construction' designed to attract the attention of passing motorists.[195] For the local *Bellaire Texan* it was 'a veritable palace in outdoor movie emporiums'.[196] For *Boxoffice* it was 'a veritable children's wonderland'.[197] Designed by John J. McNamara, an architect better known for his renovations of movie palaces in Times Square, New York, the overall eventual cost was $1,200,000.[198]

While coffee and donuts were used to launch Abilene's Park Drive-In, the opening promotion for the Sharpstown Drive-In on 26 February 1958 included a cocktail party at Houston's downtown Shamrock Hotel and contests arranged with three Houston newspapers, one offering prizes for the best colourings of line drawings of the fairy-tale villages, another for a 'name the parrot contest' and another to Houston's 'happiest family'.[199] A 'Miss Sharpstown' was selected by the University of Houston and made appearances on seven radio programmes and three television shows.[200] Each of the Houston papers carried double-spread, two colour advertisements for the cinema, and the *Houston Post* and *Houston Chronicle* published what *Motion Picture Daily* described as 'laudatory editorials welcoming the new venture'.[201] Editors from eighteen Houston High School newspapers were given a preview tour and an opportunity to interview visiting stars Chill Wills and Barbara Lang (newspaper advertisements carried a 'I wish I could be there for the opening, but my agent got me this job in Las Vegas' apology from Jerry Lewis), who went on to appear at the opening (covered by six radio and one television station), along with a 115-piece band, searchlights, a parade of vintage cars led by speedway champion Johnny Parsons and appearances from Houston mayor Lewis Cutrer, 'fabled Texas cattle raiser' R. E. Bob Smith and Frank Sharp.[202]

Within a year the running of the Sharpstown Drive-In had been taken over by Claude Ezell and Associates.[203] After Ezell died in 1961, Lone Star Theatres continued to run the Sharpstown until they were taken over by Stanley Warner who then sold their interest in the Sharpstown to Gulf States Theatres in 1964.[204] The drive-in closed in 1976.[205] In the twenty-first century the Sharpstown Center, opened in 1961 as Houston's first air-conditioned shopping mall, was renamed PlazAmericas, reflecting a demographic shift as the neighbourhood became more Hispanic and diverse.[206] The Sharpstown Drive-In closed before that, probably because its lease expired and the value of its thirty-five suburban acres exceeded that of box-office and concessionary receipts of what may have been a palace of outdoor movie emporiums and a children's wonderland but was still a subsequent-run cinema.

Location, mobility, industry

The Sharpstown is one drive-in that has attracted academic attention. In discussing the context in which cinemas adopted widescreen formats in the

1950s, John Belton cites it as an example of how the 'spatial flexibility' of the drive-in was adapted to different audience needs, through playgrounds, laundry services or more elaborate facilities.[207] His examples include the Florida drive-in where people could fish and watch movies at the same time; the Pennsylvania drive-in with an auction house, a roller-skating rink and a furniture store; and the Sharpstown, which, Belton notes, 'obviously sought to copy the successful formula for participatory amusement pioneered' by Walt Disney.[208]

Picking up on Belton's comments, in his discussion of how American cities have come to represent themed fantasy experiences, John Hannigan cites the Sharpstown as an example of an entertainment complex, 'perhaps inspired by Disney', created around the drive-in.[209] According to Hannigan, the terms of the Paramount Consent Decree had neutralized the major cinema circuits and made a space in the drive-in business for 'local "Mom and Pop" owners': 'With most ozoners existing beyond the reach of corporate ownership and control, this left plenty of room for local initiative and experimentation.'[210] Attractions such as the miniature railway and elves at the Sharpstown 'exhibited a degree of local creative input and control which regrettably disappeared with the ascendency of shopping center multiplexes in the 1970s and 1980s'.[211]

James Hay makes a different connection. In his account of how 'cinema and the city have relied upon and developed through one another', he refers to the growth of drive-ins in 1950s suburban Houston as 'a feature of Raymond Williams' concept of mobile and semi-privatised spaces': for Hay, the Sharpstown Drive-In offered 'a vivid example of Houston suburbia's dependence upon cultural technologies and spaces such as drive-ins as makeshift and mobile markers of "hometown"'.[212]

The link between the Sharpstown Drive-In and Disney is apt. Disneyland, opened in 1955 in Anaheim, California, transformed the American amusement park and was a vital part of a transformation of the Disney corporation and of American leisure habits. In the 1950s, Disney continued to make films, but the company also recognized the importance of television and how its brand gave it the opportunity to exploit a changing market in which outdoor entertainment played a greater role. Belton notes that 'the more time and money spent in outdoor recreation, the less there was left for going to the movies'.[213] However, entrepreneurs had already discovered that the automobile could facilitate a combination of cinema and the outdoors.

In providing playgrounds for children, drive-ins did not offer the controlled experience of Disneyland but what they provided ranged from the slides, see-saws, swings at the Chief on the outskirts of Seminole in West Texas to the zoos and train rides through fantasy landscapes found at the Sharpstown Drive-In on the east of the state. More generally, the drive-in and Disneyland belonged to a longer tradition of American outdoor entertainment. In the 1950s *Billboard*, which identified itself as 'The Amusement Industry's Leading Newsweekly', included sections not just on the film industry (including a 'drivin' round the drive-ins' column) but also on carnivals, circuses, fairs and expos, general outdoor (including state fairs and rodeos), parks, resorts and pools.[214] Drive-in cinemas, and the miniature train rides, zoos and other displays they sometimes included, existed in this outdoor amusement context.

Though the link with Disney is apt, the Sharpstown is the wrong drive-in to use as an example of a business beyond the reach of corporate ownership and control. The clue is in its full title: Loew's Sharpstown Drive-In. It does illustrate some of the complexities of ownership and control, and the interaction between the corporate and the local, at the end of the 1950s. It was set up by one of the Major exhibition circuits at a time when they continued to be restricted by judicial anti-trust oversight, in coordination with a local property developer with political connections who tapped into demographic and transport trends. Its operation quickly passed into the hands of an exhibitor who was in some respects 'independent' but who worked closely with other exhibitors, including the Major circuits.

More generally, the characterization of drive-in cinemas as 'mom and pop' operations is misleading. The consensus in the 1950s was that independent ownership was more evident among drive-in than indoor cinemas, and this has informed histories of the drive-in. Hannigan's source for the higher degree of independence among the drive-ins is Segrave's citation of a 1952 study which identified 28 per cent of drive-ins owned by chains, in comparison with 46.8 per cent of indoor cinemas and 61.8 per cent of the latter's seating capacity.[215] However, according to the same survey, circuit ownership of drive-ins was weighted towards those with capacity for more than 500 cars (54.9 per cent) while non-circuit ownership was weighted towards those with capacity for less than 500 cars (63.6 per cent): in terms of car numbers, the circuits accounted for a higher proportion even in 1952.[216] The report noted that 'most of the earlier drive-ins were constructed by non-circuit operators. However, within the past two years, the circuits have gone into the drive-in business in growing numbers'.[217]

It is unclear to what extent this continued, and the distinction between circuit and non-circuit, or circuit and independent, can be complicated, as can questions of ownership. According to a 1956 report, of what were then 4,600 US drive-ins, 'only 61 are in any way connected with the big indoor circuits currently chaffing under the limitations imposed on them by anti-trust rulings', but this did not include 'leading open-air circuits' such as Smith Management Corp. (forty-two drive-ins in New England and the Mid-West) and Rowley United.[218] As discussed in this chapter, the Interstate Circuit owned some drive-ins but more indoor cinemas, though it had a share in several drive-ins listed as owned by another company. At the other end of the scale, there were family teams such as W. E. and Fronia Cox, operating the Chief Drive-In alongside other business enterprises and the indoor and outdoor cinemas owned by W. E. Cox's brother and sister-in-law.

Hay's reference to Raymond Williams on 'mobile privatisation' needs a little more unpacking. He is not the only writer to apply Williams' term to the drive-in. For W. T. Lhamon, the way that the drive-in 'melded together mass and private experience' was a form of 'mobile privatisation': the combination of 'two apparently paradoxical yet deeply connected tendencies of modern urban industrial living: on the one hand mobility, and on the other hand the apparently self-sufficient family home'.[219] Linking the drive-in to home video, David Church cites Mary Morley Cohen's comparison of drive-in and television spectatorship, 'as the car represented the extension of the private living room into public space – a sort of "mobile privatisation" permitting viewers to disregard rules of etiquette that they would not have to follow at home'.[220] Cohen does not cite Williams herself and her references to the drive-in as an inclusive and interactive space are at odds with the fragmentation and isolation Williams identified but she also discusses the drive-in as a combination of the private and the mobile, placing this in a broader context of post-war suburbanization and car culture, in which the perception of the car 'as an extension of the home and its private space . . . often clashed with Americans' impulse to get out of the house and engage in outdoor entertainment'.[221]

Williams himself used the term 'mobile privatisation' in a discussion of radio and television broadcasting, seeing this as a product of the replacement of an 'earlier period of public technology, best exemplified by the railways and city lighting . . . by a kind of technology for which no satisfactory name has yet been found: that which served an at-once mobile and home centred way of living: a form of *mobile privatisation*'.[222] He later explained that mobile privatization means 'that at most active social levels people are increasingly living as private small-family units, or disrupting even that, as private and deliberately self-enclosed individuals, while at the same time there is a quite unprecedented mobility of such restricted privacies'.[223] He traced the idea back to the account of driving in traffic in his novel *Second Generation* (1964), where 'Looked at from right outside, the traffic flows and their regulation are clearly a social order of a determined kind, yet what is experienced inside them – in the conditioned atmosphere and the determined music of the windowed shell – is movement, choice of direction, the pursuit of self-determined private purposes. All the shells are moving, in comparable ways but for their own different private ends.'[224]

If the mobile privatization of radio and television allowed people to metaphorically travel to distant places without leaving their home, this was different from the drive-in. Drive-in audiences might similarly travel to distant places, from cars equipped, the Park Drive-In claimed in promoting its electric car heaters, with 'All the comforts of home', a point driven home by the illustration of a couple and a child, at home, in front of the flames coming from the domestic hearth (see Figure 6).[225] However, this was only after a car journey to a place maintaining the earlier technology of the cinema: they were outdoor cinemas/car parks but still cinemas. However, as Williams' reference to traffic flows makes clear, mobility, like home, is not only a metaphor. Mobile privatization can refer to literal travel undertaken in small family groups, as couples or individually. Driving to the drive-in was itself a more private experience than taking the bus, train or other forms of public transport to the cinema. Drive-in growth was assisted by post-war subsidies that favoured road building rather than rail, the individual or family car rather than buses, trams and trains. Trains were important for individual drive-ins but as amusement rides rather than ways of getting anywhere.

Place needs to be understood here not only in terms of geographical location but also in relation to travel, communication and distribution networks as well as changes in the built environment and its relationship to nature, and in the relationship between the centre and the periphery. This has been recognized in accounts that link the growth of the drive-in to other post-war developments in the film industry (notably the effect of the anti-trust rulings) and society (notably the growth of car ownership, road building and suburban development). It is important, however, to acknowledge the complexity of these changes and what did not change as well as what did.

The fact that drive-ins and suburbia expanded simultaneously did not necessarily mean that drive-ins were located in suburbia, though some were. As Russell and Whalley point out, they catered to a mobile audience and so could be built miles from where that audience lived, worked or went to school. However, suburbia was itself mobile, as an entity and as a concept. It spread rapidly in the 1950s. 'In 1950, a quarter of Americans lived in suburbs; in 1960, a full third', notes one study.[226] Critiques of suburbia that emerged in and just after the 1950s tended to complain about its homogeneity. For Lewis Mumford it had resulted in

> a multitude of uniform, unidentifiable houses, lined up inflexibly, at uniform distances, on uniform roads, in a treeless communal waste, inhabited by people of the same class, the same income, the same age group, witnessing the same television performances, eating the same tasteless prefabricated foods, from the same freezers, conforming in every outward and inward respect to a common mould, manufactured in the central metropolis.[227]

FIGURE 6 *'All the Comforts of Home' advertisement for Park Drive-In, Abilene, Texas, from Scrapbook for Park Drive-In, 16 December 1949, 51, Interstate Theatre Collection. From the collections of the Dallas History & Archives Division, Dallas Public Library.*

In turn, this critique was itself challenged as being based on an idea rather than evidence, or selective evidence: the assembly-line suburbia of Levittown. New Suburban History has argued for an understanding based more on diversity and contests for power.[228]

Even the planned community of Sharpstown reveals a more complex reality. The Sharpstown Drive-In was built in a suburb that was expanding and changing. Promoted as 'the largest project of its kind in the world', it was initially a predominantly white, upscale, middle-class community. With and after the opening of the Sharpstown Mall in 1961, it shifted 'from a residential enclave to a regional hub of strip commercial developments, fast-food chains, and high-rise office complexes'.[229] In the 1960s, the planned community ideal was dissipated amidst Houston's lack of zoning, which meant that apartment blocks could be built for younger, single occupants.[230] The drive-in had gone by the time Sharpstown had transformed into a more ethnically diverse but majority Hispanic neighbourhood, though as early as 1960 residents included affluent Cubans who had emigrated to the United States after the Cuban Revolution.[231]

In 1960, the Sharpstown Drive-In was suburban but not in the same way that the MacArthur or the Elmwood Skylight came to be suburban. Drive-ins built on the outskirts of urban centres came to be suburban or even urban. Others remained roadside but rural though their number is difficult to measure as it includes those which were portable or genuinely makeshift and others leaving little trace. That might sound like an inconclusive conclusion, but it is important to emphasize differences between drive-ins in different locations, just as 1950s suburbia was not as homogenous as it has sometimes been portrayed.

To this extent, Hannigan may be accurate in identifying a degree of local creative input and control even in drive-ins owned by the larger circuits in comparison with the multiplexes of the 1970s and 1980s. In a discussion of the post-war American suburb, Robert Fishman invoked what Frank Lloyd Wright had called Broadacres, a new form of urban development that was 'everywhere but nowhere', places that had in effect become new cities independent from the old cities, often built along ring roads designed to skirt around the city rather than take traffic into its heart.[232] Yet for Fishman these 'new cities' did not represent, as Wright had hoped, a break up of centralized power. On the contrary:

> The large corporation has adapted so well to the new city that genuine small business is nowhere more at risk than in the outer city. Where Wright had hoped to see a culture and a society based on individuality and independence, there had emerged the heartland of the mass media and the mass produced.[233]

In looking at shopping malls where even small businesses were branches or franchises belonging to a regional or national corporation, Fishman was looking at late-twentieth-century retailing and suburban development. The situation in the 1950s was refreshingly messier to the extent that it is a challenge to provide helpful generalizations about the place of the drive-in in relation to America's built environment and the American film industry's industrial structure.

Two points are clear. One, the drive-in cinema belonged to a trend in the 1950s towards decentralization and a loss of status of downtown areas. Two, in the film industry, though the 1950s was a decade of change and uncertainty, there was not a break away from the existing structure, and this was not just because drive-in operators lacked the power to challenge the Majors but also because many were part of the existing industry hierarchy. The problem with understanding the drive-in as at war with the film industry is that drive-ins in general belonged to that industry and individual drive-ins such as the Park in Abilene and Loew's Sharpstown were opened by exhibition circuits affiliated to the dominant industry powers, the Hollywood Majors.[234]

That provides one explanation for why *Stromboli*, identified by *Variety* as doing 'strangely well' at drive-ins, did not play at any of the drive-ins open at the beginning of the 1950s examined in this chapter. RKO sales staff suggested that the film's overall poor performance 'was due more to theatermen's refusal to book it than customer resistance', while people who 'might feel self-conscious at being seen in or near a regular theatre playing the film' might have 'no compunction about seeing it in the anonymity of a car'.[235] The Park Drive-in did not show the film because it was owned by Interstate, a circuit that decided not to screen the film. Other cinemas, indoor and outdoor, that did not screen *Stromboli* would have done so due to local pressure or demand.

Stromboli did play at the Tower Drive-In in Rocky Mount, North Carolina, a Wilby-Kincy cinema (another company affiliated to Paramount). While Bosley Crowther had dismissed *Stromboli* in the *New York Times* as 'incredibly feeble, inarticulate, uninspiring and painfully banal', when *Stromboli* opened at the Tower on 19 November 1950, the *Rocky Mount Telegram* described it as 'a searching study of a woman's heart' in which 'the Swedish star gives a magnificent performance', adding that 'the remarkable photography and menacing background help to make "Stromboli" the cinematic triumph that it is'.[236] Perhaps Rocky Mount was too far (geographically and culturally) from New York for Crowther's review to have much effect but not too far away from the RKO publicity machine.

Of course, *Stromboli* was not a typical Hollywood release. It played at Rocky Mountain's Tower Drive-In between the Bill Elliot western *The Last Bandit* (1949), on Saturday 18 November, and, on Thursday 22 November, the Dean Martin and Jerry Lewis comedy, *My Friend Irma Goes West* (1950). In the next chapter I examine the extent to which the latter films were more representative of the drive-in programme, though also at variations in that programme, looking not just at Texas drive-ins but also at other drive-ins in North Carolina, Massachusetts, Iowa, Arizona, California and Arkansas.

2

Programme

There might be little point in examining the drive-in programme if, as Kerry Segrave starkly put it, 'Nobody went to the drive-in to see the movie in the fifties and sixties'.[1] Segrave qualified this when he suggested that drive-ins appealed to 1950s parents looking for films 'they felt would not warp little Johnny. With that exception, what film was being screened mattered little (if at all) to patrons'.[2] Others have argued that the film programme was the least of the drive-in's attractions or part of a low-quality experience: in the words of one recent account, 'their technological inefficiency did not matter because the movies did not matter'.[3]

The latter perception can be traced back to contemporary reports. In 1950 John Durant, after listing some of the things the drive-in audience could do without taking their eyes off the screen, including eating a complete meal, getting your car washed and serviced, having your laundry or shopping done or the baby's bottle filled, described the films as 'in the main pretty frightful. Most are third-run pictures, rusty with age'.[4] He added that this did not seem to make much difference to the audience.[5]

From one perspective, the 'drive-in movie' can appeal precisely because of its lowly status. Associating the drive-in with companies, genres and films that in the 1950s lacked status has provided a basis for its subsequent cult status. In his autobiography, American International Pictures (AIP) co-founder and producer Samuel Z. Arkoff writes of how the running gag about drive-ins in the 1950s was that 'They play last-run movies, right after drug stores. The major studios never really considered them reputable.'[6] In Arkoff's account, AIP turned to the drive-ins when the newly established company had difficulty getting film bookings at downtown cinemas, transforming 'the last-run "ozoners" into first-run venues' for AIP films.[7] In his autobiography, Roger Corman identifies AIP's 1955 release of *The Day the World Ended* with *The Phantom from 10,000 Leagues* as a pioneering strategy, 'two low-budget films from the same genre on a double bill', that 'was designed in large part to lure teenagers and young adults to drive-ins. It became a standard AIP approach once it proved to be commercially profitable'.[8]

Commentators have gone on to link teenagers and what was showing at the drive-in in the 1950s through different film genres and cycle, notably through the science-fiction or horror film.[9] According to Phil Hardy:

> By the mid-fifties, the distribution and exhibition patterns of Science Fiction films, with the exception of the big budget extravaganzas of the period – *War of the Worlds* (1953), *1984* (1956) – were targeted almost exclusively at the youth audience. By all accounts more Science Fiction films were played in drive-in cinemas (the growth of which in the fifties coincided directly with the Science Fiction boom) than were films of any other genre.[10]

Made in 1983, Hardy's comment is cited unchallenged in more recent studies, if alongside other statements that indicate a broader generic range, in the words of Peter Lev, 'from Westerns and comedies to the more youth-orientated horror, science fiction and teen films'.[11]

The clear, consistent point across these different comments has been that the drive-in programme consisted of films that were old, cheap or made outside the Hollywood studio system. A problem is that they tend to be based on other secondary sources, and that the most extensive history of the drive-in is uninterested in the pre-1960 film programme. There have been accounts that pay more attention to what was showing at the drive-in, but their focus tends to be on the period after the 1950s. The comment that Mike Walsh, Richard Maltby and Dylan Walker make of 1960s Australian cinema holds also for the United States in the 1950s: 'While we are used to generalizations that drive-ins programmed either for families, or for teens receptive to exploitation films, little of this is based on empirical research into programming policies.'[12]

Attempting to move beyond this, in what follows I approach the drive-in programme from different angles. First, I examine broad questions of American film distribution and exhibition in the 1950s and the place of the drive-in within this. This involves clarifying what a first-run or a third-run release meant and its relationship to the terms under which films were made available to cinemas and cinema chains, the pressure for change during the decade and the extent of actual change. Second, in looking at what individual cinemas screened I start with the MacArthur Drive-In, on the outskirts of Orange on the south-eastern edge of Texas. I have details of most but not all MacArthur screenings from the 1950s. To give a picture from across the United States, from drive-ins in which I have full programming details for the decade, I move to four further examples, two from the east (the North Reading Drive-In, Massachusetts, and the Hi-Way 17 outside Edenton, North Carolina), one from the Midwest (the Dubuque Drive-In, outside Dubuque, Iowa) and one from Phoenix, Arizona, in the Southwest. This last example opened as the Twin Drive-In with separate north and south screens before dividing into the Acres of Fun Drive-In and the Peso Drive-In, the latter showing Spanish-language films. The programmes of these drive-ins thus range from the WASP suburbia of New England to the urban racial mix of the Southwest and from the fast-growing city to suburban Massachusetts and rural North Carolina. Moving further west, I also examine box-office reports from the Airport Drive-In, near Santa Barbara, California, before going back inland to assess box-office reports from three Robb and Rowley drive-ins in Little Rock, Arkansas. In examining drive-ins in Texas, Massachusetts, North Carolina, Iowa and Arizona, I look at the programme across the decade. My focus on the California and Arkansas drive-ins is narrower, but here the box-office data allows for a closer analysis of box-office takings. To balance and supplement this with more detail, I also draw on the contributions from drive-in exhibitors to the *Motion Picture Herald* 'What the Picture Did For Me' column but mainly from the *Boxoffice* 'Exhibitor Has His Say' column, in which independent exhibitors (usually identifying themselves as catering to a 'small-town' audience) reported on screenings of individual films.

Post-war exhibition: Runs and rentals

The vertically integrated structure of the American film industry had remained remarkably stable during the Great Depression and the Second World War. Throughout this period five corporations (the 'Big Five') dominated US production, distribution and exhibition. They produced almost all the most profitable films, dominated film distribution and owned the majority of first-run cinemas. Films were distributed and exhibited on a hierarchical system of runs, clearances and zones. As Douglas Gomery notes:

> All major city picture palace first-runs were followed by a period of time (the clearance) of seven to thirty days before the film could play second-run – all within certain geographical limits (the zone). Then the film would play second-run. A clearance would follow before the third-run, and so on down the line.[13]

First-run cinemas situated in metropolitan centres charged the highest prices and took the most money. Each cinema had a fixed run-clearance-zone status, keeping distributors' bargaining and negotiation costs to a minimum.[14] Most cinemas were independently operated, but most of these were subsequent-run cinemas and thus only able to screen major films months after their initial release. In addition, the practice of block booking limited choice, forcing many independents to rent groups of films rather than select individual films. The industrial framework governed the nature of films as well as their production, distribution and exhibition. Cinemas affiliated to the Majors would only show films that had a Production Code seal of approval, issued by the Majors' own trade body, the Motion Picture Producers' and Distributors of America (the MPPDA, later the Motion Picture Association of America, or MPAA).

The situation was not entirely static. The double bill became prevalent in the 1930s, with the result that exhibitors needed more films, initially expanding the space for low-budget, independent production, particularly in subsequent-run cinemas. However, this space contracted when the Majors created their own B-production units, designed to supply relatively low-cost material for the bottom half of the double bill. Beyond this, exploitation films were made without Production Code approval as they could be shown not only at dedicated 'grindhouse' cinemas but also at subsequent-run 'neighborhood cinemas' on an irregular basis.

The 1949 Federal Supreme Court ruling that the existing industry structure constituted a restrictive practice led to greater but not complete change. The court outlawed block booking and ordered the separation of the Big Five's exhibition circuits from their production and distribution operations (divorcement) and that those circuits should reduce their number of cinemas (disbursement). They could only open new cinemas if the courts were satisfied that these would not create unfair competition. While these restrictions helped open a space for new, independent operators, they were entering a destabilized market that was still based on the existing system in which the out-of-town cinemas tended to be at the end of the run.

Different factors contributed to this changing structure. The Big Five no longer had a direct interest in exhibition, leading to complaints that they were producing less films for which they could then charge higher prices and demand longer first runs. Abandoning block booking gave exhibitors greater choice, but the move to competitive bidding for the right to screen films added to uncertainty. After the steady increase in cinema attendance during the war, attendance started to decline. In an age of television and a wider range of leisure pursuits, cinemagoing no longer seemed unassailable.

Some drive-in exhibitors saw opportunities for first-run status in this changing market. In the 1950s the highest profile of these was David E. Milgram, who in 1949 opened the Boulevard Drive-In on the US 22 leading into Allentown, Pennsylvania. Aiming to make the Boulevard a high-end cinema showing first-run films, Milgram successfully sued the Major distributors when they would not allow him to bid for first-run screenings or, in some instances, sell him their films at all.[15] It was, in Segrave's words, a hollow victory: as he points out, the right to bid for first-run status was not the same as achieving first-run status.[16] Rather than a flat rental it involved paying a percentage of the box-office takings to the distributor, a percentage that increased for the more sought-after films. Earlier runs for prestige films might increase the box-office take but also meant that more of that take went to the distributor. In addition, while the law forbade discrimination against drive-ins, distributors continued to favour the cinemas that they judged to be more prestigious.

Many in the industry looked down on drive-ins even as they as they grew in numbers. Distributors often insisted that their primary loyalty was to their long-standing customers who operated indoor cinemas (including the divorced circuits which still dominated the box office). In 1950, Andy W. Smith, 20th Century Fox vice president in charge of sales, listed five contributions his company could make to the welfare of exhibitors, one of which was 'the refusal to negotiate for "drive-in first-run" in any community for the protection of regular first-runs, but, in cases where the company is "forced" to give drive-in an earlier clearance, it will consent, where the situations warrant, to commit drive-ins to compete or buy on the same availability as the first neighborhood-run'.[17] Concern about the growth of the drive-in persisted throughout and beyond the 1950s. One 1965 trade press report directed readers to 'consider the plight of the well-operated long established indoor house' asked to compete with a drive-in. 'No one can object to a drive-in as such', it continued, before listing reasons for objecting: they were limited to after-dark screenings and most of them operated on a seasonal, double-feature basis and admitted children for free.[18] The report ended with the rhetorical question: 'What distributor would want to operate a fine first-run house in the centre of town in similar conditions?'[19]

This did not mean that there was a simple divide between drive-in operators and the dominant forces in the film industry. Individual examples, such as the Elmsford Drive-In in New York State, present a more complex picture. Opened in 1950, it was run by the Star Theatres Drive-In Corporation: its owners included Steve Broidy, founder of Allied Artists, and Allied Artist producers Harold and Walter Mirisch. Just before the opening, the drive-in manager Arthur J. Steel reported to Broidy that the estimated final costs of opening the drive-in would be slightly in excess of $300,000, that is, more than the $256,884.55 that W. D. Phillips reports Milgram spent on his 'quality' Boulevard Drive-In.[20] Like Milgram, it filed a successful anti-trust suit (which 'would, of course, exclude Allied Artists').[21] However, it did not do this until the 1960s, when it also moved into the first-run market as one of twelve 'Premier

Showcase' cinemas in the New York metropolitan area giving simultaneous release to United Artists films. In 1963 Steel wrote to Broidy:

> We have had some exceptional results on some of the pictures we have played in the last few months on the Premiere Showcase and Golden Showcase programs. THE LONGEST DAY, TOYS IN THE ATTIC, IRMA LA DOUCE, and currently THE CARETAKERS have really been outstanding. We have had a few flops such as MARILYN. However, on balance, I think we have been pursuing the right policy.[22]

More generally, in the early 1960s drive-in playdates could be equivalent to playdates at indoor cinemas. On the drive-in's thirtieth birthday (6 June 1963) the Camden *Courier-Post* listed screenings for fourteen drive-ins. Of the twenty-two films these were screening, seven were also playing at indoor cinemas, four (*Come Fly with Me* (1963), *Miracle of the White Stallions* (1963), *Mill of the Stone Women* (1960) and *Trauma* (1962)) at suburban cinemas and three 1963 releases (*The Birds*, *Call Me Bwana*, advertised as a 'First Run Showing', and *Hud*) at downtown cinemas.[23] Indoor and outdoor cinemas were playing many of the same films, the principal difference being that drive-ins offered double or triple bills. Even the 6 June 1953 edition of the *Courier-Post* listed weekend screenings of *Call Me Madam* (1953) and *City Beneath the Sea* (1953) at the Garden State and the Starlite as well as at local indoor cinemas, if also older films playing at the Bridgeton Drive-In.[24]

In the 1950s there were other drive-in operators who accused dominant players in the industry not just of looking down on them but also of actively working against them. When Guy William Meek appeared before the US Senate Select Committee on Small Businesses on 2 April 1953, he introduced himself as the owner of the Palo Alto Drive-In, with an interest in two further Northern California drive-ins and as the buyer and booker for a further two.[25] Having returned to the film business after a twenty-year gap when he was released from the Navy in 1946, in 1949 he had served as the interim president of the newly established National Association of Drive-In Theatres.[26] He had already attracted attention in 1952 when he travelled to Washington with, *Motion Picture Daily* reported, 'considerable evidence of possible violations of the consent decree and the anti-trust laws'.[27] Listing his complaints to the Senate Select Committee convened in Los Angeles the following year, he accused distributors of practices that included charging him higher rates even for films he received later than the larger circuits, changing the terms on which he could play films after those terms had been agreed, penalizing him for being selective in the films he brought, refusing to allow him to bid for films and insisting on higher prices for 'road show pictures'.[28] According to Meek, the affiliated circuits were also trying to drive him out of the business by setting up a rival drive-in close to his own.[29]

On behalf of the distributors, Benjamin Melniker replied that they had investigated Meek's accusations and found them to be without merit. It was, they claimed, Meek who had attempted to change the terms after they had been agreed, in addition to under-reporting box-office figures, while Metro had sold films to the affiliated circuit's drive-in after or simultaneously with Meek's drive-in on the same terms.[30]

While Meek was distinctive in alleging a deliberate attempt to drive his drive-in out of the business, there were widespread complaints about terms and availability. A 1951 survey of 3,000 drive-in operators identified 88 per cent in favour of better runs and just 12 per cent satisfied with the current situation.[31] The latter included Edward Fessler, from Mobile, Alabama, who commented, 'We opened a year ago with first runs and have been playing them ever since . . . We compete with town houses, and, as you can judge, outgross them.'[32] Fessler, however, acknowledged that his situation was unusual.[33] Others, including another Alabama operator, J. W. Gaylard, complained about distributors restricting first runs to conventional cinemas and charging higher rentals for the drive-ins.[34]

Some of these complaints resurfaced at further hearings of the Small Business Select Committee in 1956, set up in response to 'complaints from exhibitors dealing with a wide variety of topics such as film shortage, price of film rentals, arbitration, block booking, and competitive bidding'.[35] In one case, David C. Forbes, owner of the Ozark Drive-In, Crocker, Missouri, complained that Major film companies refused to sell him films at terms he could afford to play and held back films scheduled for the nearby (indoor) Crocker Theater, even though it was currently closed.[36] The response of the local Universal branch manager was to cast aspersions on the condition of the Ozark (which apparently suffered from a surface of sawdust and wood shavings rather than gravel or asphalt), to object that Forbes was seeking the committee's assistance to stop selling its films to a small independent cinema and to insist that Universal had sold films to the Ozark on both flat rental and percentage rates and had not withheld their films from the drive-in.[37] Universal, he stated, was prepared to license him *To Hell and Back* (1955), *All That Heaven Allows* (1955), *The Benny Goodman Story* (1956) and *World in My Corner* (1956), 'all top grossing products' on which they had not heard back from Forbes.[38] Insisting that their selling practices had 'consistently been fair and equitable, taking into account the needs of the exhibitors and their business problems', the Paramount representative reported that the Ozark had brought five of their films in the 1954–5 season and all of their films in the 1955–6 season while the Crocker had brought only eleven films since 1954, stressing, 'During the current 1955-56 season, all of our product have thus far been sold to the drive-in . . . since 1954 only 11 pictures were sold to the conventional theater.'[39] Paramount had sold Forbes *The Greatest Show on Earth* (1952) on a 50 per cent basis but 'practically all' of their films for under $20: 'in the current season *Trail of the Lonesome Pine* [1936], *Shepherd of the Hills* [1941], *Trouble with Harry* [1955], and *Desperate Hours* [1955] were sold for $15; *Court Jester* [1955], *Lucy Gallant* [1955], *Ulysses* [1954], and *The Girl Rush* [1955] were sold for $17.50; and, *Anything Goes* [1956], *Rose Tattoo* [1955] and *Artists and Models* [1955] were sold for $20'.[40]

Other independent exhibitors complained about different disputes with distributors, though these included complaints about rather than from competing drive-ins. Thus W. E. Horsefield, who operated indoor cinemas in Kentucky, listed the different distributors demanding 50 per cent deals, noting, for example, that 'with drive-in opposition in Morganfield and Marion, Universal has failed to call on me, even at my request, and even though these drive-ins are closed, from 4 to 5 months of the year, and still further, even though one of my situations outgrosses the drive-in when it is open'.[41] In response, the manager of the Indianapolis branch of Universal exchanges described the Morganfield cinema as 'a rundown smalltown theater on which Mr Horsefield had not spent any money in an effort to make it presentable' and called the terms for which he was asking as 'not justified businesswise'.[42] He went on say that Universal had licenced its films, first run, to the Sunset Drive-In, five miles from Morganfield, when it opened in 1952, 'and we then split our product first run' between the Sunset and the Broadview Drive-In, Morganfield, when the latter opened in 1953, and sold its product to the drive-in that opened in Marion when that opened in 1954.[43] The representative from Warner testified that they had granted the Broadview 'a competitive opportunity to obtain Warner pictures on first-run', but they had been informed that Horsefield and the Broadview operator had agreed to split all the distributors' films, and under this agreement Warner films had been allotted to the drive-in.[44]

Whatever the truth of these and other conflicting accounts, they indicate just how local 'first run' could be (in 1950 Morganfield had a population of 3,257).[45] In this sense drive-ins did play Major first-run films, but that did not put them on a par with downtown metropolitan cinemas. Distributors could use a cinema's status (a surface of wood shavings rather than asphalt or a lack of upkeep) in determining who received films and the prices they demanded. Local factors were important (above all, competing cinemas) as well as federal action and national trends. These and other examples demonstrate that the efforts of drive-in operators to obtain better films at earlier dates existed in the context of a wider chorus of complaints from independent exhibitors in general, indoor and outdoor.

One persistent complaint at both hearings, and in the trade press across the 1950s, was that the Majors were not making enough films. Abram F. Myers, chairman of Allied States Association of Motion Pictures, told the 1956 committee that film companies were 'obsessed with the idea that they can make more money by supplying a few pictures to the big city key theaters for exhibition for extended engagements at high admission prices than by producing a lot of pictures to play shorter runs in a large number of theaters at normal admission prices'.[46] Throughout the 1930s the Majors produced over 300 films annually, reaching a peak of 408 in 1937 that approached the even larger numbers released annually in the silent era. Independent distributors released a similar annual number. Numbers fell during the Second World War, and though they were back at 320 in 1951 they fell again later in the 1950s to the extent that in 1959 the Majors released only 189 films. Releases from independent distributors had themselves fallen to 179 in 1955 but increased to some extent later in the decade, with the result that, if overseas imports are included, they outnumbered releases from the Majors. Of the 439 films released in the United States in 1959, 250 were from independent distributors.[47]

A cinema that played double bills and made regular changes to their programme needed a regular supply of films. This often applied to the drive-ins, where concession sales were proportionally higher and where the break between features, therefore, took on greater importance.[48] If films from the Hollywood Majors were difficult to obtain, expensive or simply less plentiful, cinemas had to look elsewhere, and that prospect could become more attractive if independent distributors offered better terms or earlier availability. Thus, if the drive-in was, as Arkoff wrote, crucial for the success of the newly established American International Pictures in the second half of the 1950s, studios such as an AIP were a valuable additional film source for many drive-ins.[49] However, AIP was just one independent distributor. Others included United Artists, Allied Artists, Filmmakers, Distributors Corporation of America, HOWCO and Lippert. These companies mainly distributed low-budget American films but also a small but increasing number of films from overseas.

The Major and the independent distributors supplied an exhibition system that was becoming increasingly fragmented. Peter Lev has identified, by the late 1950s, 'at least four distinctive (though at times over-lapping) film audiences in the United States': one, those attending '"Road-show attractions", played in elaborate downtown theaters'; two, 'the traditional first-run/second-run audience for Hollywood pictures . . . attracted by popular stars, high production values, and often a well-known source'; three, 'the big city and university town spectators who favored art movies' and who had 'a strong interest in films with frank and adult sexual content'; and four, 'the working class, small town, and teenage spectators who had traditionally supported action films and low-budget comedies'.[50] These were distinctions of place and product as well as audience: in Lev's account, this fourth category included the drive-in, which 'attracted the family trade (because of convenience and price) but were even more attractive to teenage audiences. So drive-in programming ranged from Westerns and comedies to the more youth-oriented horror, science fiction and teen films'.[51]

'Range' is an appropriate word, though as we will see, the programme range at the drive-in stretched to each of Lev's four categories.

The MacArthur, Texas

The Jefferson Amusement Company's MacArthur Drive-In opened on Friday 18 October 1950 with a policy of four changes a week, with new shows on Sunday and Tuesdays, a double feature on Thursdays and another double feature on Fridays and Saturdays.[52] Initially, Sunday to Wednesday programmes tended to consist of a single feature, but from 1952 there were also double bills on Tuesdays and Wednesdays and from 1954 on Sundays and Mondays. There were also midnight screenings and, in the second half of the decade, dusk-to-dawn screenings. As well as films there were firework displays on 4 July and other dates, Easter Egg Hunts, occasional screenings of boxing fights and personal appearances. Captain Earl MacDonald, high fire diver, featured on 24 and 25 September 1950; Daisy and Violet Hilton, 'The 8th Wonder of the World, The Siamese Twins', accompanied a screening of their film *Chained for Life* (1952) on 20 and 21 May 1954; and on 23 January 1955 visitors could see Mezeppa, advertised as 'the largest reptile in captivity'.

Most films played for two days. Three-day runs became more common in 1959, and there were four-day, Sunday to Wednesday runs for *From Here to Eternity* (1953) from 23 May 1954, *On the Waterfront* (1954) from 3 April 1955, *Giant* (1956) from 18 August 1957, *Bernardine* (1957) from 13 October 1957 and *Rio Bravo* (1959) from 5 April 1959, as well as a Friday-to-Monday run for Disney's *The Shaggy Dog* (1959) from 1 May 1959. Other films came back for one-off screenings: in 1953 *My Darling Clementine* (1946) played the MacArthur 12 November and 22 and 23 December, again on 1 July 1954 and again on 7 and 8 February 1956.

Teenpics became more evident at the MacArthur towards the end of the decade. Screenings in March to June, 1959, included *Hot Rod Gang* (1958) on 20 and 21 March; *Motorcycle Gang* (1957), 26 March; *The Party Crashers* (1958), 31 March to 1 April; *The Astounding She Monster* (1958), 2 April; *High School Hellcats* (1958), 10 and 11 April; *Dino* (1957) on the Saturday late show, 16–17 May; *The Cry Baby Killer* (1958), 21 May; *Attack of the 50 Ft. Woman* (1958) on the late show, 23–24 May; *Teenage Cave Man* (1958), *Reform School Girl* (1957), *Crime in the Streets* (1956) and *Rock Around the World*

(1957) at the dusk-to-dawn moviethon starting Saturday 30 May; *Life Begins at 17* (1958) and *Juke Box Rhythm* (1959), 2 and 3 June.[53] Overall, however, such films constituted a small proportion of the films shown at the MacArthur and tended to reach the drive-in after they had played the Jefferson Amusement's Strand Theatre in downtown Orange. *Rock Around the Clock* (1956), for example, which played at the MacArthur on 4 November 1958, had opened at the Strand on 15 May 1956.

MacArthur screenings included major science-fiction productions such as *Forbidden Planet* (1956) (part of a quadruple bill, 11–12 October 1957 and again on a six-film moviethon on Saturday 14 March 1959) as well AIP films such as *Invasion of the Saucer Men* (1957) which played on Thursday 7 May 1959. However, AIP double bills were as likely to play downtown at the Strand: for example, on 13 August 1959, the Strand was showing *Killer Shrews* (1959) and *The Giant Gila Monster* (1959), with a midnight screening of *The Beat Generation* (1959), while the MacArthur was showing *The Vikings* (1958) and *Snowfire* (1957) (see Figure 7). The MacArthur showed many more westerns. The issues of the *Orange Leader* that I have seen list 34 science-fiction films, a further 44 horror films and 494 westerns.[54] The MacArthur ended the decade with a screening of *Go, Johnny, Go!* (1959), featuring Alan Freed on a talent search for a new rock 'n' roll star. However, the twenty-five films screened at the drive-in in December 1959 included *The Hangman* (1959), 3–5 December; *Day of the Outlaw* (1959), 10–12 December; *The Gunfighter* (1950), 15 December; and *Santa Fe* (1951), 17 December. On 25 and 26 December the MacArthur showed John Ford's *The Horse Soldiers* (1959), starring John Wayne, a film that the American Film Institute lists as a drama rather than a western.

In 1953 Anthony Downs had distinguished between drive-ins that 'show only first-class pictures as part of the second-run group of theaters' and those that 'specialise in action shows', though suggested that 'the majority combine both kinds of cinema in a weekly schedule calling for three picture changes' a week, usually with 'a high-class' starting Sunday, a midweek 'better-class show to attract business during these rather dull days' and at the weekend 'an action film to attract the modest-income customers'.[55] A variation on this mixed programming policy was evident at the MacArthur. Alongside its reliance on the western and other forms of action cinema, the MacArthur held weekday screenings of at least six of the Academy Award Best Picture winners in the 1950s: *All About Eve* (1950), 30 and 31 October 1951; *An American in Paris* (1951), 23 and 24 March 1954; *Marty* (1955), 15 and 16 April 1956; and *Gigi* (1958), 20 and 21 October 1959, as well as *From Here to Eternity*. It screened films directed by Roger Corman, including *Five Guns West* (1955), 5 and 6 February 1956; *It Conquered the World* (1956), 1 and 2 January 1957;

FIGURE 7 Orange Leader *advertisement for the Strand and MacArthur Drive-In, 13 August 1959, 14. Courtesy of* Orange Leader, *Orange, Texas.*

The Undead (1957), 23 January 1958; *Rock All Night* (1957) in a dusk-to-dawn show starting 5 September 1959; *Viking Women* (1958) on 'family night', 19 March 1959; *Carnival Rock* (1957), 16 February 1958; *Machine Gun Kelly* (1958), 30 April 1959; and *Teenage Cave Man* and *I, Mobster* (1959), 13 and 14 October 1959. However, it appears to have screened at least as many films directed by Douglas Sirk, including *No Room for the Groom* (1952), 21 and 22 September 1952; *Has Anyone Seen My Gal* (1952), 10 and 11 April 1953; *Take Me to Town* (1953), 5 and 6 February 1954; *All I Desire* (1953), 7 and 8 January 1955; *Taza, Son of Cochise* (1954), 17 and 18 December 1954; *Magnificent Obsession* (1954), 18 and 19 January 1955; *All That Heaven Allows*, 8 and 9 May 1956; *Written on the Wind* (1957), 9 and 10 July 1957; *The Tarnished Angels* (1958), 2 and 3 November 1958; and *Interlude* (1957), 10 and 11 March 1959. Perhaps more surprising is that it showed at least ten British films directed by Terence Fisher: *Man Bait* (British title *The Last Page*, 1952), 11 December 1952; *Stolen Face* (1952), 28 and 29 September 1952; *The Black Glove* (British title *Face the Music*, 1954), 9 December 1954; *Blackout* (British title *Murder by Proxy*, 1954), 20 January 1955; *Spaceways* (1953), 3 March 1955; *The Last Man to Hang* (1956), 26 and 27 February 1957; *Kill Me Tomorrow* (1957), 16 January 1958; *The Horror of Dracula* (British title *Dracula*, 1958), 16 and 17 August 1959; *The Revenge of Frankenstein* (1958), 27 and 28 March 1959; and *The Hound of the Baskervilles* (1959), 6 and 7 December 1959. These include not only the horror films that one might expect to find at a drive-in but also earlier crime films.

Lippert Pictures provides one explanation for the latter. Robert Lippert was an exhibitor who built up a portfolio of drive-in cinemas but who also moved into production and distribution after he set up Screen Guild Productions in 1945, changing the name to Lippert Pictures in 1948. In the 1950s Lippert Pictures worked with the British company Exclusive (which went on to set up Hammer Studios) to co-produce films made in Britain but featuring American actors and released in Britain and the United States. While the vast majority of the films shown at the MacArthur were American, of the remainder, the largest number were British. These ranged from Gabriel Pascal's 1945 *Caesar and Cleopatra* (21 and 22 April 1953) to the 1959 British New Wave film, *Room at the Top*, given a midnight, 'adults only' screening, 20–21 June 1959. Across the decade the MacArthur showed at least ninety-three British films, in addition to fourteen from Italy, eight from France and others from Greece, Japan, Mexico, the Philippines, the Soviet Union, Switzerland, Sweden and West Germany. In part these offered exploitation potential: as well as the 'adults-only' screening of *Room at the Top*, the films programmed at the drive-in included *The Queen of Sheba* (31 January 1957, originally released in Italy as *La regina di Saba*, 1952) and *One Summer of Happiness*, released in Sweden as *Hon dansade en sommar* (1951) and promoted at the MacArthur as 'The Picture that made all France blush!' (12–13 October 1954). The drive-in programme ranged not only from westerns, comedies, science fiction and horror but also encroached on the territory of cinemas appealing to the demand for popular stars, high production values and familiar sources, the art cinema and cinemas catering to the exploitation market. It screened not only (24 September 1957) *Paris Does Strange Things*, the US release title of Jean Renoir's *Elena et les hommes* (1956), starring Ingrid Bergman, but also (14 and 15 April 1953) *Hitler's Strange Love Life* (1948), a Dwain Esper compilation (also known under other titles, including *Will It Happen Again?*) of pre-war and wartime footage, accompanied by *Passion's Payment* (also known as *Nuremberg Trials*, 1946), a Soviet film co-directed by Elizaveta Svilova, the wife of Dziga Vertov. In 1953 (13 and 14 January) it promoted *The Story of Bob and Sally* ('It's Boldly Frank! It's Humanly True! It's More Than Just a Story! It's Life Itself!') promising nurses in attendance.

The MacArthur needed films in quantity. It stayed open throughout the year, played double bills and changed its programme three or four times a week. In 1954, a year when Major distributors released 225 films and independent distributors released 202, the MacArthur played 388 films.[56] It needed to programme films from the Majors but even if it had taken all those films it would have needed more to fill its schedule.

Of course, the films that the MacArthur screened in 1954 did not all date from 1954. Only seventy-one did, a further 181 were first released in 1953: the remainder included some relatively recent films that slowly made their way to the MacArthur (*An American in Paris*), older B-westerns (*Guns A'Blazing*, a reissue of *Law and Order* (1932), shown 2 December), classics such as *Casablanca* (1943), shown 21 and 22 March, and a double bill of *Little Caesar* (1931) and *Public Enemy* (1931), 5 and 6 October. It did not show major Hollywood studio films first run but this did not mean that it did not screen films from the major Hollywood studios. Nor was this simply a case of the drive-in owner being unable to bid for an earlier run since the Jefferson Amusement Company did screen films earlier at the Strand in downtown Orange. The Strand and the MacArthur shared the same manager.[57]

The North Reading, Massachusetts

Located in what is now Greater Boston, the North Reading Drive-In (which later appears to have become the Starlight) was close to the town of Reading, an example of what James C. O'Connell describes as upscale,

WASP suburbanization, with a traditional, historic core that mitigated against the sense of placelessness surrounded by new residential subdivisions and commercial strips.[58] The North Reading Drive-In opened on 30 June 1950, with a reported capacity for 1,000 cars.[59] It was one of a small number of drive-ins built by Stephen Minasian, Philip Scuderi and Robert Bersamian, who ran the Route 114 Drive-In, Middleton, Massachusetts, but leased the North Reading to the American Theatres Corporation.[60] The latter was formed in 1949 on the break-up of Paramount subsidiary Mullins & Pinanski.[61] By 1954 American Theatres were operating six drive-ins, though their overall number of cinemas decreased.[62]

It showed less films than the MacArthur as it was only open for around half a year and programmed fewer weekly changes. Thus in 1951 it reopened on 31 March and closed in early October. It generally changed the programme twice a week and, in some instances, played films for the full week, either on a double or single bill. The latter was the case with *The Greatest Show on Earth* from 30 July 1952, *The Bridge on the River Kwai* (1957) from 31 July 1958, *Around the World in 80 Days* (1956) from 16 July 1959 and *The Ten Commandments* (1956) from 23 July 1959. Double bills that played a week included *Shane* (1953) and *The Farmer Takes a Wife* (1953) from 5 July 1953, *Loving You* (1957) and *Apache Warrior* (1957) from 16 July 1957, *Peyton Place* (1957) and *Ambush at Cimarron Pass* (1958) from 24 April 1958 and in 1959, *Imitation of Life* (1959) and *Wild Heritage* (1958) from 29 May, *Some Like It Hot* (1959) and *Guns, Girls and Gangsters* (1958) from 9 July and *A Hole in the Head* (1959) and *Escort West* (1959) from 24 September.

The North Reading showed films earlier than the MacArthur. *All About Eve* (1950), accompanied by *An American Guerrilla in the Philippines* (1950), played the North Reading 3–5 May 1952 and the MacArthur 13–14 November that year, *Gidget* (1959) played the North Reading 23–25 April 1959 and the MacArthur 5–7 November 1959. The North Reading could also show films earlier than the Andover Playhouse, an indoor cinema that also advertised in the *Andover Townsman*: for example, it played *High Noon* (1952) on 31 August 1952, two months before it played at the Playhouse. It only occasionally showed films more than a year after their initial release. In 1954 the *Andover Townsman* carried advertisements for eighty-one features at the North Reading. Fifty-nine of those were first released that year, sixteen in 1953, two Disney films (*Blackbeard the Pirate* and *The Story of Robin Hood*) date from 1952 and there were a small number of westerns or action films from the late 1940s: *Sands of Iwo Jima* (1949), *She Wore a Yellow Ribbon* (1949), *Wake of the Red Witch* (1948) and *The Angel and the Badman* (1947).

The importance of the family audience to the drive-in is evident in the programme and advertisements that highlight events such as a 'doll cart and carriage parade' a 'Kiddies Redhead Contest' and a 'Kiddies "Freckle-Face" Contest'.[63] Older films screened at the drive-in across the decade included the equine drama *Stormy* (1935, accompanying *20,000 Leagues Under the Sea* (1954), 23–25 June 1955) and the Disney films *Bambi* (1942), 25–28 August 1957; *Snow White and the Seven Dwarfs* (1937), 13–16 April 1958; and *Song of the South* (1946), 15–17 April 1956. Like other drive-ins, the North Reading screened a mix of major releases and films associated with small-town audiences. The 1954 programme included *From Here to Eternity* (from 7 April), *Roman Holiday* (1953) (from 11 April), *Magnificent Obsession* (from 9 September), *Rear Window* (1954) (from 12 October) as well as *Ma and Pa Kettle at Home* (1954) (from 23 May). About 21 per cent of the films it screened across the decade were westerns, while horror and science-fiction films accounted for 5 per cent.

Films with youth appeal included *Love Me Tender* (1956, screened 28 March 1957), *Rock Pretty Baby* (1956, screened from 18 April 1957) and a double bill of *Dragstrip Girl* (1957) and *Rock All Night* (1957) from 16 June 1957. In 1954 almost all the films it advertised were American and from the Majors: the only non-US films that year were British films (all dating from 1953) with Hollywood leads: Alan Ladd in *Paratrooper* (25–28 April), Louis Hayward in *The Saint's Girl Friday* (17–19 June), Wendell Corey in *Laughing Ann* (accompanying *The Wild One* (1953), 20–23 June) and Van Heflin in *The Golden Mask* (19–21 August). Later in the decade its programme included an 8–11 September 1957 double bill of *The Curse of Frankenstein* (1957) and *X. . . . The Unknown* (1957) as well as a series of re-edited versions of Japanese science-fiction films: *Half-Human* (1955, screened 26–29 May 1957), *Rodan* (1956, 10–13 August 1958), *Gigantis, the Fire Monster* (a re-edited version of *Godzilla Rides Again*, 1955, screened 18–20 June 1959), *H-Man* (1958, 25 and 26 June 1959) and *The Mysterians* (1957, 9–12 August 1959). It also attracted some trade press attention when in 1955 it was one of five New England cinemas (and the only drive-in) to broadcast the Rocky Marciano-Don Cockell world heavyweight fight on closed-circuit television.[64]

The Hi-Way 17, North Carolina

The 1959 Edenton City Directory noted that in 1950 the US census gave the coastal town of Edenton a population of 4,468 and that the current local estimate was 5,000.[65] The 1950 figure included 1,680 identified as 'colored'.[66] The population would have expanded to an extent in the summer: according to the City Directory, 'Edenton's town and country homes are nationally known for their colonial authenticity and fine state of preservation', and there were 'four modern motels and a centrally located hotel'.[67] Half a mile north of Edenton on the Edenton-Hertford Highway, the Hi-Way 17 Drive-In opened on 9 May 1950. It was a segregated drive-in: reporting on the opening, the local paper described the new drive-in as 'modern in every respect. In-car speakers are provided, with a snack-bar in operation and modern restrooms. A section will also be reserved for colored people'.[68]

The Hi-Way 17 was operated by the Taylor Theatre Company, initially run by Mr and Mrs S. W. Taylor, then by Jim Earnhardt, who also owned the town's downtown indoor theatres, the Taylor (established in 1928) and the Eden.[69] The Eden closed around 1957, but in that year the Taylor Theatre Company also took over the Plymouth Theatre and the Plymouth Drive-In, on the other side of the Albemarle Sound.[70] Like the drive-in, the downtown Taylor Theatre was segregated, with African Americans restricted to the balcony. This led to an NAACP picketing campaign in 1962.[71]

Like the North Reading, it tended to open late March or early April, but it generally closed at the end of November. It remained open on weekends for the 1956/7 and 1957/8 winters but in 1959 it only appears to have shown films Fridays to Mondays, from early April to early November. The programme generally changed Fridays, Sundays, Mondays and Wednesdays, though *The Greatest Show on Earth* played four days from 1 July 1953, and there were equivalent runs for *A King and Four Queens* (1956) from 25 September 1957 and *No Time for Sergeants* (1958) from 17 October 1958. It played two nightly screenings of a single feature or (less often) Fridays and Saturday double bills. The drive-in is associated with the double or triple bill, but the latter was more evident after the 1950s while during the 1950s the smaller drive-in programme could consist of a single feature. The Chief in Seminole, Texas, was another drive-in that mainly remained restricted to single feature shows, and the Midway Drive-In on the Edenton-Winsor Highway was also advertising a single feature a night in 1950. One occasion when the Hi-Way 17 did programme a double bill (though with a combined running time of only a little over two hours) was on Wednesday and Thursday, 27 and 28 July 1955, when *I Led Two Lives* (1953) played with the 'vice film' *Escort Girl* (1941), with an adults-only recommendation. *I Led Two Lives* was directed by Edward D. Wood Jr and is better known as *Glen or Glenda*.

Like the MacArthur, the Hi-Way 17 often showed new releases a year after their initial screening. In 1954 Edenton's *Chowan Herald* carried advertisements for 154 films at the Hi-Way 17. Of those, only seventeen had had their first release that year, while eighty-eight dated from 1953, seventeen from 1952 and the remaining fourteen from the 1940s. Most of these were films from the Hollywood Majors (thirty were from MGM, while the six from United

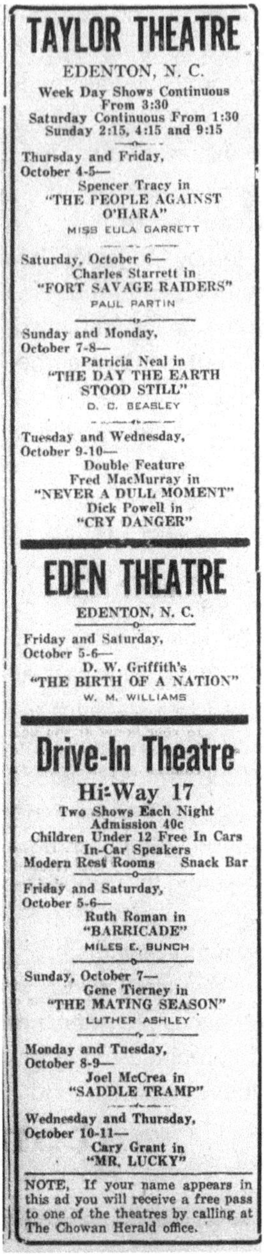

TAYLOR THEATRE
EDENTON, N. C.
Week Day Shows Continuous
From 3:30
Saturday Continuous From 1:30
Sunday 2:15, 4:15 and 9:15

Thursday and Friday,
October 4-5—
Spencer Tracy in
"THE PEOPLE AGAINST
O'HARA"
MISS EULA GARRETT

Saturday, October 6—
Charles Starrett in
"FORT SAVAGE RAIDERS"
PAUL PARTIN

Sunday and Monday,
October 7-8—
Patricia Neal in
"THE DAY THE EARTH
STOOD STILL"
D. C. BEASLEY

Tuesday and Wednesday,
October 9-10—
Double Feature
Fred MacMurray in
"NEVER A DULL MOMENT"
Dick Powell in
"CRY DANGER"

EDEN THEATRE
EDENTON, N. C.

Friday and Saturday,
October 5-6—
D. W. Griffith's
"THE BIRTH OF A NATION"
W. M. WILLIAMS

Drive-In Theatre
Hi-Way 17
Two Shows Each Night
Admission 40c
Children Under 12 Free In Cars
In-Car Speakers
Modern Rest Rooms   Snack Bar

Friday and Saturday,
October 5-6—
Ruth Roman in
"BARRICADE"
MILES E. BUNCH

Sunday, October 7—
Gene Tierney in
"THE MATING SEASON"
LUTHER ASHLEY

Monday and Tuesday,
October 8-9—
Joel McCrea in
"SADDLE TRAMP"

Wednesday and Thursday,
October 10-11—
Cary Grant in
"MR. LUCKY"

NOTE. If your name appears in this ad you will receive a free pass to one of the theatres by calling at The Chowan Herald office.

FIGURE 8 Chowan Herald *advertisement for the Taylor, Eden and Hi-Way 17, Edenton, North Carolina, 4 October 1951, 9. Courtesy of the* Chowan Herald, *Edenton, North Carolina.*

Artists included *The Moon Is Blue*). They were all American except for *The Ivory Hunter* (1951, known in Britain as *Where No Vultures Dare*, shown 26 and 27 November) and possibly the 'adults-only' film *I Want a Baby*, shown 22 and 23 November, which Eric Schaefer suggests may be a retitled version of the 1949 Danish sex hygiene film, *We Want a Child*.[72]

Later in the decade it screened *Rock Around the Clock*, 24 and 25 October 1956; *Don't Knock the Rock* (1957), 15 and 16 May 1957; and *Shake Rattle and Rock!* (1956), 31 March to 1 April 1958. It showed no AIP films, and the few science-fiction films it screened were at the higher budget end of the genre, for example, *The Day the Earth Stood Still* (1951, shown 21 and 22 May 1952) and *Forbidden Planet* (shown 31 May to 1 June 1957). Horror and science-fiction films account for just 2 per cent of the films, while westerns accounted for 23 per cent. On rare occasions it showed films with an African American cast or that addressed issues of racism: *Carmen Jones* (1955) played on 3 June 1956, *Night of the Quarter Moon* (1959, featuring Julie London as a mixed-race woman with a white husband) on 13 September 1959. Downtown, *The Birth of a Nation* (1915) had played at the Eden Theatre on 5 and 6 October 1951 (see Figure 8).

The Dubuque, Iowa

Dubuque is on the western side of the Mississippi, in Iowa but close to both Illinois and Wisconsin. It differed from Edenton in size and ethnicity. Its population increased from 49,670 in 1950 to 56,610 in 1960 and was largely white: according to later accounts, in the 1940s and 1950s there were no more than five black families in the city, and 'police advised blacks who stepped off the train to move on to the next town'.[73] The Dubuque Drive-In opened on 11 August 1949, just under four miles north of Dubuque city centre, on a steep slope with two terraces above the main field that prompted reporters to describe it as the first drive-in with a balcony.[74] 'In the rear of balcony, outdoor stoves, tables and a children's playground provides family atmosphere prior to showtime', noted *Billboard*, which identified it as a Tri-States cinema.[75] It was later owned by Central States Theatres of Des Moines, Iowa.[76] United Paramount Theatres had held an interest in both Central States and Tri-States Theatres but in 1950 sold its interest in Central States to that company's new president, Myron Blank, and brought out Myron Blank's stock in Tri-States Theatres; Myron Blank's father, A. H. Blank, resigned as president of Central States but remained president of Tri-States.[77] According to Myron Blank's obituary, in 'the 1950s he was the largest operator of Drive-In Theatres in the country'.[78]

In 1954 it opened in late February, an 'extra early' sign of spring, with an announcement from manager Richard Davis: 'As in other years, the bill will change three times weekly – on Sunday, Wednesday, and Friday . . . Thursday will be family night, with all the occupants of one car admitted for a single, set price.'[79] It was usually open from March or early April till October or early November, while the programme structure changed across the decade. In 1950 it advertised double bills for Tuesday and Wednesday but single features on other days. The double bills switched to Fridays and Saturdays in 1951, and from 11 August that year Saturdays included an additional horror film, starting with *The Ghost of Frankenstein* (1942). In 1953 it was playing double bills across the week and triple bills some nights. In 1957 it changed its programme Sundays, Tuesdays and Thursdays. In 1959 this was reduced to changes on Sundays and Thursdays.

The double bill of *Karamoja* (1954), an exploitation 'exotic' filmed in Uganda, and *Half Way to Hell* (1953), a film featuring wartime and concentration camp footage, ran for a week from 3 September 1954. No other films played that many days at the Dubuque Drive-In in the 1950s. It advertised 258 feature films in 1954. The relatively high number is explained partly by the regular programme changes, partly by the additional Saturday and sometimes Friday night screenings, which ranged from *Dracula* (1931) on 13 March to John Garfield in *He Ran All the Way* (1951) on 29 and 30 October. Only 9 of those 258 films were first released in 1954. A total of 108 dated from 1953, 57 from 1952, 23 from 1951, 5 from 1950, 42 from the 1940s and 13 from the 1930s.

New releases tended to reach the Dubuque late. For example, the Charlton Heston western *Arrowhead* (1953) played the North Reading from 3 September 1953 and in 1954 at the Hi-Way 17 from 21 May, the MacArthur from 9 July, only reaching the Dubuque on 10 September. In addition, it played a smaller proportion of new releases from the Majors, relying on older westerns, crime and horror films and distributors such as Allied Artists, Lippert and Republic. Across the decade, horror and science-fiction films still accounted for only 5 per cent of feature films in comparison with 22 per cent of westerns. However, looking at the decade as a whole can flatten out shifts. *Rock Around the Clock* played the Strand in downtown Dubuque from 1 May 1956. The film did not reach the Dubuque Drive-In till it played on a double bill with *Rebel Without a Cause* on 1 August 1957, but that year did see the drive-in's programming place a particular emphasis on rock 'n' roll and youth-orientated films more generally. Screenings in 1957 included *The Girl Can't Help It* (1956), 28 and 29 July; *Love Me Tender*, 16 and 17 July; *Rock Pretty Baby*, 22–24 August; and *Rock All Night*, 12–14 September. On Saturday 18 May 1957 it offered not just a triple bill of *The Red Pony* (1949), *Seven Angry Men* (1955) and *The Catman of Paris* (1946) but also a 'Rock n Roll Review Show' with band leaders Artie Shaw and Ralph Materie.[80] It followed this with a series of two-reel musical shorts from Universal: *Rhythms with Rusty Draper* (1956) accompanied *Oklahoma Kid* (1939) and *Badmen of Missouri* (1941) on Friday 24 May; *Bright and Breezy* (1956), with Charlie Barnet and his Orchestra and the King Sisters, and *Mr Black Magic* (1956), with Billy 'Mr Black Magic' Daniels, accompanied *The Searchers* (1956) and *A Strange Adventure* (1956) on 31 May; and on 7 June *Around the World Review* (1956) and *The Bills Brothers on Parade* (1956) accompanied *Runaway Daughters* (1956) and *Shake, Rattle and Roll*. The 1958 programme included the Thursday to Saturday triple bill of *Bundle of Joy* (1956), *Rebel Without a Cause* and *Don't Knock the Rock*, 8 to 10 May, and a 10–12 July quadruple bill of *The Girl Can't Help It*, this time with *Tender Trap* (1956), *A Cry in the Night* (1956) and *Dino* (1957).

The Dubuque highlighted the short programme as well as the feature in a way that indicates the importance of the preteen as well as the teenage audience. A 21 and 22 July 1950 screening of the horse drama *Black Gold* (1947) was accompanied by a 'cartoon carnival', two midweek days, 13 and 14 August 1951, were devoted entirely to 'comedy cartoon shorts' and there were further 'nothing but cartoons' midweek days on 10 and 11 June 1952. The same year ten cartoons accompanied the Bowery Boys comedy *Master Minds* (1949) on 15 and 16 July. In 1953 it showed Abbott and Costello's *In Society* (1944) plus a 'Big Cartoon Carnival' on Friday 8 July, also with a late-night screening of the Universal mystery *Nightmare* (1942) on the Saturday, as well as a one-night 'all cartoon show' on 5 August. A 'Walt Disney cartoon carnival' accompanied the western *The Lion and the Horse* (1952), 20 and 21 July 1954, a 'Walt Disney all cartoon festival' accompanied the 1954 stop-motion version of *Hansel and Gretel* on 12 July 1955 and there was a 'Free cartoon show' for the 11 March 1957 reopening, though there were no further references to cartoons in advertisements later in the decade.

Another shift was the move from 'owl screenings' of old Universal horror films to more recent science-fiction films. In 1959 its programme included late screenings of *I Married a Monster from Outer Space* (1958), 5 and 6 June, *Attack of the Crab Monsters* (1957), 4 July, and *Fiend without a Face* (1958), 8 August. But these films existed in the context of a broad programming policy including a mix of genres but a still regular number of westerns alongside other films with exploitation potential. The 1958 season opened on 13 March with *The Violent Men* (1955) and *The Way to the Gold* (1957) and closed with a short run of *Gun Glory* (1957) and *Four Girls in Town* (1957) starting Friday 10 October with a late screening of the UA distributed horror film *The Vampire* (1957) accompanying the Saturday programme.

The Twin, Acres of Fun, New Acres and Peso, Phoenix, Arizona

The population of Phoenix, Arizona, grew fourfold from 106,818 in 1950 to 439,170 in 1960.[81] It also expanded geographically. Having been little more than ten square miles in 1930, by 1960 it covered 290 square miles, a result, Andrew Needham writes, of the aggressive annexation policy pursued by city officials concerned to maintain control of the fiscal benefits of metropolitan growth and prevent the decay of the city's core.[82] Overall population density thus did not increase at the same rate as population growth, though it did increase in some areas and for some ethnic groups. 'As subdivisions sprawled northwards', notes Needham, 'racial inequality assumed a new spatial scale', with the 1960 census showing 90 per cent of Phoenix's African Americans living in nine of the city's 108 census tracts, which also contained one-third of the city's residents with 'Spanish surnames'.[83] Those nine tracts were south of Van Buren Street, within the city's 1930 limits, characterized into the mid-1960s by 'unpaved streets, unconnected sewers and inadequate public utilities' and few white inhabitants.[84] 'The new landscapes north of Van Buren developed between 1950 and 1960 formed a stark' and, notes Needham, almost exclusively white, 'counterpoint to southern Phoenix'.[85] Along Van Buren itself, an increasing number of motels were established in the 1930s, the 1940s and the 1950s; according to Douglas Towne, the street 'reached its zenith as a tourist strip by the early 1960s'.[86]

It was also along this divide, on 3600 East Van Buren Street, that Phoenix's first drive-in opened in 1940, according to contemporary reports, by Seth Perkins, who also ran the San-Val Drive-In Burbank, California.[87] Another drive-in, the Twin Drive-In, or Twin Open Air, opened on 3700 West Van Buren in early 1951. Described by *Exhibitor* as the largest drive-in in Arizona, with a capacity of 1,500 cars and a construction cost of $390,000, it initially showed westerns and action films on the North Screen and a 'Variety' programme on the South Screen. Before long, its border line location was reflected in the divide between the two screens, one devoted to English-language films, the other to Spanish-language films.

The South Screen's double bill of *Life with Father* (1947) and *Margie* (1946) on 12 and 13 February was followed by one of *Wing and a Prayer* (1944) and *Submarine Patrol* (1938).[88] The double bill that followed on 18 February, pairing two exploitation films, *Street Corner* (1948) and *A Modern Marriage* (1950), played for a week on both screens, with the announcement that 'No segregated audiences here!': the reference was not to racial segregation and was explained by the statement that this was 'Requested by married couples who should see this presentation together in the privacy of their own cars', indoor screenings for such films being either women only or men only.[89] There was also a 'Midnight Show', 29–30 June, featuring 'Zorina', 'the world's most perfectly formed woman and her gorgeous girls' and the short film, *Maid in the Hay*.[90] The latter may have been the 'film with naked women in the cast' which the *Arizona Republic* reported had been seized by the police, though if it is the film described in the *Exhibitor* in 1953 it tells a story of how a woman's unsuccessful attempt to find fame in the movies is followed by 'some nude modelling (not shown)' and 'a warning to girls not to come to Hollywood'.[91] From 31 May 1951, the North Screen began to combine English- and Spanish-language films, and from June advertisements in Phoenix's Spanish-language *El Sol* promoted the Twin Open-Air Drive-In Theatre as a place where its readers could dress as they wanted, smoke and talk (see Figure 9). It moved to an exclusively Spanish-language programme in August.

The Twin temporarily closed at the end of July. The South Screen ('Newly Oiled! No More Dust!') reopened on 10 August with a double bill of *Ma and Pa Kettle Back on the Farm* (1951) and *The Fat Man* (1951). The North Screen reopened the following week with *Yo Quiero se Hombre* (1950) and *La Carne Manda* (1948). The drive-in announced an 'indefinite' closure in January 1952. By this time it was identified as a 'MacCormack-Nace enterprise'.[92] The following April the South Screen reopened as the Acres of Fun Drive-In, now owned by Fred Crockett and Harry Nace.[93] In July the North Screen reopened as the Peso, showing Spanish-language films.[94] In October 1954 what had been the Acres of Fun began advertising as the New Acres. However, *Boxoffice* still referred to the earlier name when in 1956 it announced the sale of the Northern, Phoenix, Silver Dollar, Peso and Acres of Fun drive-ins to Southwest Drive-Ins Theatres Inc., in a deal that brought out Crockett.[95]

Southwest Drive-Ins Theatres was run by Harry L. Nace Jr and W. R. Foreman. Harry Nace Sr had been the dominant figure in film exhibition in Phoenix until he took his own life in 1953. 'Mr Nace's career spanned the entertainment field from vaudeville to video', noted the *Arizona Republic*, also reporting that he had arrived in Phoenix in 1909 as a circus acrobat, moved to film exhibition when he had taken over the Airdome, subsequently 'built or helped to build every theater in Phoenix with the exception of the Fox'.[96] 'His was the first drive-in here', claimed the newspaper, and at the time of his death 'he owned 40 movie houses and drive-ins'.[97] In 1949 the holdings of Paramount Nace Theaters and Harry L. Nace Theaters included the two Phoenix drive-ins, the Phoenix Drive-In on 3600 East Van Buren Street and the Indian Drive-In, before he and his son resigned 'in connection with a split of interest in accordance with the Paramount consent decree'.[98] The split led to Paramount taking

FIGURE 9 *Advertisement for the Twin Open-Air Drive-In Theatre, Phoenix,* El Sol, *15 June 1951, 3.*

over the Phoenix and Indian drive-ins, though Harry L. Nace Jr followed his father in operating indoor and outdoor cinemas.[99]

W. R. Foreman was president of Pacific Drive-In Corp., and, according to Arkoff, the man who, as much as any exhibitor, 'recognized how important AIP was to his theaters, particularly the drive-ins'.[100] In reporting on the 1956 deal, *Boxoffice* described Pacific as 'the largest drive-in chain in the world' and noted that the Acres' new booking policy would be determined in the next two weeks.[101] In fact, a shift in policy had already emerged. It consistently screened double bills, while the Twin South Screen initially changed the programme twice a week, moving after its August 1951 reopening to three changes a week, on Fridays, Sundays and Tuesdays. That policy initially continued when it reopened as the Acres of Fun, before a return to two weekly changes but with an additional western or action film on Fridays and Saturdays from August 1952. By September 1953 that additional film was no longer advertised. A double bill of *Mister Scoutmaster* (1953) and *City of Bad Men* (1953) played a week from 8 November 1953, and from 7 February 1954 week-long runs became the norm.

There were variations. In 1954 some weeks still saw two programme changes while some films ran longer than a week. Following the installation of a new, wide screen, on 25 May 1954, *The Robe* (1953) played twelve days, accompanied by two CinemaScope shorts rather than a second feature. Programmes changed on different days of the week, meaning the films had runs of varying lengths, though by June 1956 Wednesday had become the standard changeover date. A further change is evident in 1959, as more films were given longer runs, including two-week runs for double bills of *The House on Haunted Hill* (1959) and *From Hell It Came* (1957) from 1 April, *Rio Bravo* (1959) and *The Black Orchid* (1958) from 22 April, *The Shaggy Dog* and *Tom Thumb* (1958) from 6 May, *Pork Chop Hill* (1959), the first week, from 27 May, with *The Mugger* (1958) and the second week with *Alias Jesse James* (1958), and *Around the World in 80 Days* (1956), from 17 June, single billed.

When it operated as the Twin South Screen, the drive-in programme still included films from the 1940s or even earlier. It opened on 1 February 1951 with a double bill of *Homestretch* (1947) and *South of St Louis* (1949) and followed this with a mix of last year's and older films such as the double bill of *The Flame and the Arrow* (1950) and *Stanley and Livingstone* (1939), playing 25–27 February. The older films had largely disappeared by 1954. Of the 113 feature films Acres of Fun advertised that year, 55 were first released in 1954 and the same number in 1953. The only older films were *Quo Vadis* (1951), single billed 14–20 February; *Pinocchio* (1940), double billed with *The Rocket Man* (1954), 24–27 September; and *The Egg and I* (1947), double billed with *Francis Joins the WACs* (1954), 6–9 October. In 1954 the North Reading screened a higher proportion of films first released that year, but this was because it did not open until April. The Acres showed some titles after the North Reading (e.g. *Elephant Walk* (1954), which played the North Reading from 3 June and the Acres from 22 August) and some titles before (*Roman Holiday* played the Acres from 10 January 1954 and the North Reading from 11 April).

In 1952, writing on Phoenix's Park Drive-In, which subsequently became another Southwest Drive-In, Al Hine noted that the films 'were not first first-run, but new enough so that you'd find them at your neighborhood movie house'.[102] The Acres was similarly not a first-run cinema, even though it occasionally announced a screening as first Phoenix run or first Phoenix drive-in run. However, by the end of the decade it was showing films relatively close to their release date. *Up Periscope*, released at the beginning of February

1959, reached the North Reading on 26 April, the Hi-Way 17 on 16 August, the Dubuque on 20 August and the MacArthur on 4 October. It played at the Acres for a week starting 18 February, with another February 1959 release, *City of Fear*. It was followed at the Acres by another double bill of new releases, *Tank Commandos* and *Operation Dames* (which reached the North Reading on 12 April), and the following week by a pair of late 1958 releases, *Geisha Boy* and *Houseboat* (the North Reading played the former 10 May, the latter on 20 September, the MacArthur on 9 July and 25 May).

One clear distinction between the Acres and the other drive-ins discussed earlier lies in the proximity and extent of the competition. For example, on 25 October 1959, the *Orange Leader* carried advertisements for three cinemas – the MacArthur (showing *Horrors of the Black Museum* (1959) and *The Sheriff of Fractured Jaw* (1958)), the Strand in downtown Orange (showing *The FBI Story* (1959)) and the Bridge (showing Silvana Mangano and Van Heflin in *Tempest* (1958)) in Bridge City, between Orange and Port Arthur. On the same date, the *Arizona Republic* carried listings and advertisements for six Phoenix indoor cinemas, nine drive-ins (including the Acres and the Peso) and a further eight 'Valley Theatres', including two drive-ins, from the neighbouring suburbs. The films at other cinemas ranged from *South Pacific* (1958), in its '9th record breaking month!' at the downtown Vista, to *Five Gates to Hell* (1959) given sensationalist prominence at the Cinema Park Drive-In, while the Kiva in Scottsdale was showing Ingmar Bergman's *Wild Strawberries* (1957). That week, the Acres was playing an older film, *Mogambo* (1953), but in a double bill with the relatively recent *The Big Circus* (1959). If it was appealing to audiences travelling to indoor and drive-in cinemas across the Phoenix area, programme changes within the week would make less sense while the competitive market would make screenings as soon as possible after first release even more important unless a film retained a longer-lasting appeal.

The screening of AIP double bills was part of this move towards earlier runs. The war-themed *Tank Commandos* and *Operation Dames* was one AIP double bill, following on from Acres screenings of double bills including *I Was a Teenage Werewolf* and *Invasion of the Saucer Men* (from 31 July), *Motorcycle Gang* and *Sorority Girl* (from 27 November), *I Was a Teenage Frankenstein* and *Blood of Dracula* in 1957 (from 25 December) and including *High School Hellcats* and *Hot Rod Gang* (from 23 July) and *How to Make a Monster* and *Teenage Cave Man* (from 27 August) in 1958.[103] It operated across genres, including science-fiction and horror films which are evident also in other Acres screenings towards the end of the 1950s (e.g. *The House on Haunted Hill* and *From Hell It Came* double bill mentioned earlier). Across the decade, science fiction and horror still accounted for only 7 per cent of the films screened at the Acres in comparison with westerns, which accounted for 20 per cent.

These figures remain similar to the other drive-ins examined here, though at the Acres science fiction became more evident towards the end of the decade.

Exploitation films and other films that could be exploited for their sensational content accounted for another strand of programming at the Acres. In the 1950s it screened eight of the films listed in Eric Schaefer's exploitation filmography: as well as *Street Corner* (accompanied by *Modern Marriage*, a 'sex hygiene' film not listed by Schaefer), in 1958 it showed *Mom and Dad* (1945) and *She Shoulda Said No* (1949), 22–28 February; *Adam and Eve* (1956, alongside Diana Dors in *The Unholy Wife* (1957)), 9–22 April; *The Mating Urge* (1958, accompanied by Lita Milan in *Naked in the Sun* (1957)), 25–31 June; *Mixed Up Women* (1950, also known as *One Too Many*, accompanying a screening of Harriet Andersson in *Monika*, the US version of Ingmar Bergman's *Summer with Monika* (1953)), 7–13 September; and *Liane, Jungle Goddess* (1958, accompanied by Agnes Laurent in *Mademoiselle Striptease* (1957)), 10–18 December. In 1959 it showed *Bewildered Youth* (1958, also known in the United States as *The Third Sex*), Veit Harland's film about the perils of homosexuality and electronic music, with Sophia Loren and Vittorio De Sica in *Too Bad She's Bad* (1954), 2–8 December.[104]

Other non-US films it screened included the British double bill of *The Curse of Frankenstein* ('Not recommended for people of nervous disposition. Please try not to faint') and *X. . . . the Unknown* (1956), 17–23 July 1957; the Anglo-German double bill of Sylvia Syms as Anna Neagle's daughter in *Teenage Bad Girl* (1956, also known as *My Teenage Daughter*) and Horst Buchholz and Karin Baal in *Teenage Wolfpack* (1956), 31 December to 6 January 1958; and the French film *The Case of Doctor Laurent* (1956), 7–13 January 1958. The Acres' appeal to youth and sensationalism existed as part of an appeal to different audiences. Throughout the decade, the drive-in continued to promote itself as 'the family theatre', showing Disney films including, in 1957, *Cinderella* (1950), one week from 24 July, *Bambi* (1942), two weeks from 28 August, and *Perri* (1957), one week from 18 December, *Old Yeller* (1958), one week from 26 March 1958, and *Darby O'Gill and the Little People* (1959), one week from 26 August 1959, as well as mainstream studio releases.

The Peso was different. It maintained a policy of programme changes during the week throughout the 1950s, alternating between two and three changes a week. Double bills were standard. It showed Mexican films, the occasional film from Argentina and a smaller number from Spain, Chile, Cuba, Venezuela, France, Italy and even the United States (Walt Disney's *The Littlest Outlaw* (1955), starring Pedro Almendariz and screened as *El Cabarro de mi general* on 7–10 October 1959). Films almost always arrived at the cinema at least a year after their initial release in their country of origin. According to my calculations, of the 194 films screened at the Peso in 1954, 4 were first released that year, 17 in 1953, 42 in 1952, 30 in 1951, 42 in 1950, 24 in 1949, 12 in 1948, 22 earlier in the 1940s and 1 in 1938. When it reopened on 18 July 1952 it was with a double bill of *Tres Huastecos* (1948) and *Mas Alla Del Amor* (1946). On the same date in 1959 it was playing *La Venganza de Villabobos* (1955) and *Primavera en el Corazon* (1956). Films often returned at a still later date. Of the 1,161 films shown at the North Twin and Peso in the 1950s, 535 returned for at least one repeat screening.

The Peso regularly played films featuring *ranchera* star Pedro Infante, most of which received multiple screenings. For example, *Ahi viene Martin Corona* (1952) first played the Peso 22 August 1953, returning on 7 August 1955, again on 12 June 1957 and again on 23 May 1958. This fits the broader pattern, described by Rogelio Agrasánchez, of the star's popularity increasing during his career and (to an even greater extent) following his death in 1957: in Agrasánchez's words, 'Pedro Infante belonged to the screen of every theater catering to Hispanic audiences.'[105] With one exception, the Peso also showed all the Mexican films directed by Luis Buñuel up to 1955 from *Los Olvidados* (1950), 4–5 February 1954, to *El Gran Calavera* (1949), 23–24 April 1958. The exception was *Las aventuras de Robinson Crusoe* (1954), which with *Adam and Eve* (1956, screened at the Acres 15 November 1956) was the only Mexican film from this time shown alongside English-language films and which in Phoenix played at the Palms Theatre in June 1954 and in July at the Strand and Indian Drive-In.[106]

This examination of programming of cinemas in Texas, Massachusetts, North Carolina, Iowa and Arizona has revealed common practices as well as differences. As it has been limited to an examination of what films (and largely what feature films) were playing at individual drive-ins, it has not established the comparative box-office draw of the films on the screen beyond the indication that films played for a longer than usual number of days would have been expected to have attracted larger audience numbers. Box-office figures are less readily available than film listings, and I have not seen these for any cinema for the 1950s as a whole. However, in what follows I examine weekly box-office figures for the Airport Drive-In, in Goleta, California, for the period between March 1955 and May 1956, and then daily figures for three drive-ins in Little Rock, Arkansas, in 1958.

The Airport, California

The Airport Drive-In, close to the Santa Barbara Municipal Airport in Goleta, opened on 3 April 1951, with capacity for 900 cars.[107] The Goleta airport had served as a Marine Corp. training base during the Second World War before returning to Santa Barbara County in 1947. The drive-in was owned by Jay Sutton, Sherrill C. Corwin and E. Graybill.[108] When he died in 1980, the *Los Angeles Times* described Corwin as 'the motion picture exhibitor who reaped the success of Los Angeles' palatial movie theatres during the 1920s and '30s and then kept them open when bad times befell the industry', noting that the man who was 'Probably the best known theater owner in downtown Los Angeles' combined film screenings with live acts between 1933 and 1949, and 'when vaudeville and big bands no longer sold tickets, Corwin introduced closed-circuit television to Los Angeles sports fans in the 1950s and '60s, using his downtown theaters', and converted the downtown Orpheum and Million Dollar to cinemas showing Spanish-language films.[109] His involvement in the Airport Drive-In demonstrates that his interest in the changing nature of the exhibition market was not limited to downtown.

By 1955, the Airport Drive-In had installed a new screen for CinemaScope.[110] It remained open through the year, though its quietest week was the one ending 27 December, which saw only 840 admissions and gross takings of $604.08.[111] That compares with figures between the weeks ending 26 July and 6 September, which saw weekly admission numbers of 4,026, 3,091, 3,093, 2,411, 5,660, 4,371 and 4,055 and takings between $1,848.26 and $4,060.56. All programmes were double bills, generally with programme changes on Tuesdays and Fridays. There were week-long runs for *20,000 Leagues Under the Sea* (1954) and *The Bob Mathis Story* (1954) the week ending 22 March, *Mister Roberts* (1955) and *The Cobweb* (1955) the week ending 23 August, while *The Caine Mutiny* and *On the Waterfront* (1954) played 6–16 April. *Mister Roberts* also returned for a repeat engagement 8–10 April 1956, in a double bill with *Rebel Without a Cause*.

The *Mister Roberts/The Cobweb* double bill brought the highest admissions and takings though not the greatest profits. It was followed by a week in which the first half offered *The Lady and the Tramp* (1955) paired with the Bowery Boys in *High Society* (1955) and the second half *Davy Crockett: King of the Wild Frontier* (1955) paired with *Abbott and Costello Meet the Mummy* (1955). Attendance for the latter week was 4,371 and box-office takings were $3,176.40, but concession sales of $625.98 led to a profit of $1,363.23, in comparison with a $872.08 profit for the week when the *Mister Roberts/The Cobweb* double bill played, when concession sales were only $344.65.

The figures confirm that even drive-ins open throughout the year did better business in the summer, with the highest attendance in August. Attendance also increased in the two weeks leading up to Easter Sunday, in 1955 and 1956. However, weekly fluctuations suggest that other factors were also important. Attendance may have been affected by the weather or other competing attractions, but the fact that in the week ending 16 August 1955 there were 2,411 admissions to see double bills of *City Across the River* (1949) and *Girls in the Night* (1953) plus *The Prodigal* (1955) and *An Annapolis Story* (1955), plus a Saturday 'Midnight Show', while the following week more than twice as many (5,660) paid to see the double bill of *Mister Roberts* and *The Cobweb*, suggests that what was on the screen did matter.

Films reached the Airport Drive-In relatively early in comparison with the other drive-ins discussed here: of the eighty films shown at the Airport in this period that the Acres also screened, fifty-four were shown earlier at the Airport. *Rock Around the Clock* played at the Airport on 22–24 April 1956, the Hi-Way 17 in October, the Dubuque in August 1957 and the MacArthur on 4 November 1958. Like other drive-ins, the Airport screened a mix of films. Westerns accounted for 18 per cent. In 1955, the Airport screened not only non-metropolitan favourites such as *Ma and Pa Kettle at Waikiki* (1955), 8–11 June; *Abbott and Costello Meet the Mummy* (1955), 28–30 August 1955; and *Francis in the Navy* (1955), 9–12 November 1955 but also Alec Guinness in *The Detective* (released in Britain as *Father Brown*, 1954), 23–26 March 1954. It is the only drive-in I have examined that screened a Shakespeare adaptation: *Julius Caesar* (1953) played 13–15 March 1955, accompanied by the Korean War air drama, *Battle Taxi* (1955).

The Asher, Pines and Razorback, Arkansas

With a population in 1950 of 102,213, Little Rock was around the same size as Phoenix, though it was a significantly smaller city in 1960, with a population of 107,813.[112] The city attracted international attention in 1957 when nine African American students were initially prevented from enrolling at the then all-white Little Rock Central High School. The fight for desegregation at Little Rock has attracted a considerable body of literature. Less attention has been paid to other aspects of the city's segregation, though John A. Kirk reports that segregation continued to exist in Little Rock into the early 1960s, 'at lunch counters, movie theaters, golf courses, parks, swimming pools, and a whole range of other public and private facilities'.[113] It was only in 1963 that *Boxoffice* reported on a 'quiet' integration that included the city's drive-ins.[114]

At the beginning of the 1950s those movie theatres included two downtown cinemas operated by Robb and Rowley (the Arkansas and the Capitol), five other indoor Robb and Rowley cinemas (the Center, the Heights, the Lee, the Prospect and the Roxy) and two Robb and Rowley drive-ins (the Asher and the Pines). Overall, Robb and Rowley operated 161 cinemas at that time.[115]

Based in Dallas, the majority of the company's cinemas were in Texas, the remainder in Oklahoma and Arkansas. Its Little Rock cinemas were supervised by City Manager James A. Carbery for the company's subsidiary, Arkansas Amusement Corporation.[116] The Asher Drive-In had opened in August 1948 and the Pines Drive-In in August 1951.[117] In September 1952, the company opened a further Little Rock drive-in, the Razorback, named after the University of Arkansas athletics team, the Arkansas Razorbacks.[118] In 1954 it brought the Riverside Drive-In, which in 1962 became the Razorback Twin after the closure of the original Razorback.[119]

The records of the Arkansas Amusement Corporation include daily box-office reports for 1958 for the Asher, Pines and Razorback. They list cartoon shorts as well as features, distributors and weather conditions. An examination of the reports for the Razorback across 1958 as a whole reveals that takings were highest in August.[120] This is unsurprising: drive-ins are associated with the summer, and in broad terms the figures for the Razorback confirm this, with the period between the beginning of May and the end of September bringing the highest takings. However, a closer examination reveals a more complex picture. After August ($8,653.10), the highest box-office receipts were in May ($7,847.05), which brought in significantly higher takings than June ($5,729.00), with March ($5,071.65) and November ($4,919.80) not far behind. This is a variation from the overall pattern of drive-in admissions increasing each month up to August and then decreasing for the remaining months of the year, identified by Sindlinger & Company in the first half of the 1950s, indicating that the national trend was varied in the case of individual cinemas due (at least in part) to the films they played.[121]

Programme changes were often on Sundays and Thursdays, and variations in the receipts for programmes on different days give an indication of the higher weekend attendance, with Saturdays tending to be busiest, followed by Fridays and Sundays in third place though there could be different patterns in the summer. The double bill of *Bombers B52* (1957) and *Yaqui Drums* (1956) took $68.40 on Thursday 9 January, $194 on the following Friday and $284.40 on the Saturday. *Slaughter on 10th Avenue* (1957) and *Joe Dakota* (1957) followed, taking $125.40 on the Sunday, $23.40 on Monday and $40.80 on Tuesday. *Fort Dobbs* (1958) and *Damn Citizen* (1958) brought in takings of $93, $265.50 and $287.40 on Thursday, Friday and Saturday, 10–12 April, followed by $193.80 and $68.40 for *Night Passage* (1957) and *All That Heaven Allows* on the following Sunday and Monday. In the summer months takings could be highest on the Friday: the combination of *Vertigo* (1958) with the Dean Martin and Jerry Lewis comedy *Jumping Jacks* (1952) brought in $257.50 when it first played on Thursday 7 August, $410 on Friday and $379.40 on Saturday. *Peyton Place* (1957) had an eight-day, single-feature run, bringing in $288.60 on Friday

2 May, and on the following days $780, $454.80, $185.40, $214.20, $180.60, $154.80 and closing with $162.60 on Friday 9 May. The eight-day run for *The Bridge on the River Kwai* (1957) was even more successful. When it opened on Thursday 29 May it took $499.50. On the following days it took $615.50, $507.70, $439.20, $234.60, $235.80, $178.20 and $153.50. In the weekend that followed, the triple bill of *Baby Face Killers* (1954), *Kronos* (1957) and *Gunmen on the Loose* (also known as *Crashout*, 1955) took only $103.30 on Friday and $127.30 on Saturday.

Different factors influenced box-office takings. As well as the time of the year and the day of the week, school, college and public holidays would have been important, and competing attractions. The fact that the reports list the weather confirms the particular importance of this for drive-in operators, even if poor weather did not necessarily deter customers. The highest taking for *Old Yeller* ($351.15) was on a rainy 22 March. The double bill of *The Wayward Girl* (1957) and *Eighteen and Anxious* (1957) brought in $229.20 on Saturday 15 February, significantly more than $63.60 the day before, when it was snowing, though that was up on Thursday's $31.80, which was simply listed as 'cold'. The year ended with a rainy Wednesday Hitchcock triple bill of *To Catch a Thief* (1955), *The Man Who Knew Too Much* (1956) and *Strangers on a Train* (1951) that brought in $199.30, up on the previous night's $121.80 for the same programme.

Box-office receipts ranged from $16.80 for the remake of *My Man Godfrey* (1957) paired with *Run of the Arrow* (1957) on a cold Monday 10 February to $780.00 for *Peyton Place* (1957) on a cloudy Saturday 3 May. Table 1 lists the five programmes with the highest box-office receipts at the Razorback in 1958.

The average nightly takings of the third, fourth and fifth programmes in this list were higher than those of the first and second, but they all played only Thursday, Friday and Saturday. Had they also played Monday, Tuesday and Wednesday, it is likely that their average nightly takings would have been lower.

The films indicate a varied programme. *The Bridge on the River Kwai* was Columbia's most commercially successful film of the 1950s, bringing in higher US and Canadian box-office returns than any other film released in 1957.[122] It won seven Academy Awards. Released in Britain in October 1957 and first released in the United States in December 1957, it reached the Razorback two months after the Academy Awards but relatively early in relation to the other drive-ins discussed here: it opened at the North Reading on 31 July 1958, the Dubuque in August and the Hi-Way 17 on 15 May 1959. It was one of a series of films about the Second World War that played at the Razorback, the Asher and the Pines. *Peyton Place* was also a major box-office success following its

Table 1 Highest Box-Office Takings at the Razorback Drive-In, Little Rock, 1958

Feature(s)	Nights Played	From	Total Box Office
The Bridge on the River Kwai (1957)	8	29 September	$2,864
Peyton Place (1957)	8	2 May	$2,361
King Creole (1958)/Stake Out on Dope Street (1958)	3	21 August	$1,609.20
God's Little Acre (1958)/Decision at Sundown (1957)	3	24 July	$1,514.30
Snowfire (1957)/The Littlest Hobo (1958)	3	28 August	$1,323.80

Source: Arkansas Amusement Corporation Papers, Center for Arkansas History and Culture, University of Arkansas at Little Rock, Box 5, Folders 2–5.

December 1957 release.[123] While not at the very top of the year's box office, *King Creole* was a commercially successful Elvis Presley film, and its pairing with *Stake Out on Dope Street* is a sign of the importance of the youth market for the Little Rock drive-in. *God's Little Acre* (1958) was another relative box-office success that reached the Razorback earlier than other drive-ins. Like *Peyton Place*, it was based on a controversial, bestselling novel: the *Independent Film Bulletin* described it as 'A Natural for SEXploitation'.[124] It played the Razorback with a Randolph Scott/Budd Boetticher western. *Snowfire* and *The Littlest Hobo* (1958) are family-friendly animal films, the former about a white stallion, the latter about a German shepherd. Most of these were Hollywood Major films, though United Artists distributed *God's Little Acre*, Allied Artists *Snowfire* and *The Littlest Hobo*. Of the 291 feature films screened at the Razorback in 1958, the reports identify forty-six as from 20th Century Fox, forty-two from Universal, thirty-five from MGM, thirty-five from Paramount, thirty-three from Columbia, twenty-six from Warners, twenty from United Artists, seventeen from Allied Artists, eleven from Republic, seven from HOWCO, six from Buena Vista, three from NTA, two from Rank, while there were eight AIP films listed as from 'Colnl', 'Colo' or 'Colon'. Of the short films listed (almost all of which were cartoons) forty-one were from Paramount, twenty-seven from Warner, thirty-three from MGM, sixteen from Universal, thirteen from Buena Vista, five from Columbia and five from Fox. The 'were identified' is necessary here because there may be places where the distributor has been incorrectly identified: Kingsley International distributed *And God Created Woman* in the United States but for the film's screening at the Pines it is listed as distributed by HOWCO.[125] What is clear is that most films screened at the Razorback (and the Pines and the Asher) were distributed by Hollywood Majors.

The equivalent figures for the Asher (but just for the period between 1 January and 30 September 1958) are lower, in part because no films played there more than three nights, though takings at the Asher were generally lower than at the Razorback. The Asher ran Saturday night dusk-to-dawn screenings, and its highest take for a single night was on Saturday 28 June, when it took $648.90 for a programme of *The Beast with a Million Eyes* (1955), *The French Line* (1953), *The Silver Lode* (1954) and *The Day the World Ended* (1955), almost matched by the Friday 26 July screening of *Tammy and the Batchelor* (1957), *Teenage Monster* (1957), *River's Edge* (1957), *The Incredible Shrinking Man* (1957) and *Affair in Havana* (1957).[126] Its lowest take ($9) was on Monday 17 February, for a pairing of *Sea Wife* (1957) and *Huk!* (1956). The films with the highest overall receipts at the Asher in the period are listed in Table 2.

Armored Attack! was a version of *The North Star* (1943), a Lillian Hellman-scripted film about Ukrainian resistance during the Second World War. It was reissued in 1957, minus scenes of Soviet collective farming and with an added reference to the 1956 Hungarian uprising, with *Battle Stripe*, itself a retitled version of *The Men* (1950), in which Marlon Brando plays a paraplegic war veteran. When the double bill played at the Asher, the second night fell on Friday 4 July, and that night accounted for $633 of the programme's take. The other films include six westerns, two music films and one Jerry Lewis comedy.

Table 2 Highest Box-Office Takings at the Asher Drive-In, Little Rock, 1 January–30 September 1958

Feature(s)	Nights Played	From	Total Box Office
Armored Attack! (1943) and *Battle Strike* (1950)	3	3 July	$1,119.60
Cowboy (1958)/*Jamboree* (1957)	3	25 September	$1,002.10
The Tall T (1957)/*Country Music Holiday* (1958)	3	14 August	$993.10
Comanche (1956)/*Canyon River* (1956)/*The First Texan* (1956)/*At Gunpoint* (1955)	2	29 August	$923.60
The Sad Sack (1957)/*The Gunslinger* (1955)	3	4 September	$922.70

Source: Arkansas Amusement Corporation Papers, Center for Arkansas History and Culture, University of Arkansas at Little Rock, Box 1, Folders 5–7.

Overall, the Asher played a higher number of westerns than the Pines and the Razorback. Like the Razorback, it showed *Peyton Place*, but four months later, initially on a late Saturday screening immediately following *The Sad Sack* and *The Gunslinger* and then on Sunday and Monday, 7 and 8 September, when it took a combined total of $417.60.

At the Pines, in the period between 11 April and 13 September, three films that played for between one and two weeks had significantly higher box-office takings. The top five programmes in this period are listed in Table 3:

When *And God Created Woman* opened at the Pines on a warm Saturday 24 May the receipts were $1,392.30, far higher than any other single night for these drive-ins during this period. Ticket prices were 90c per person, which would come to 1,547 full-price admissions: the programme was advertised as 'ADULTS ONLY! No one under 18 Admitted Unless Accompanied by Parents'. The six-minute Casper cartoon, *Dutch Treat* (1956), accompanied the ninety-minute feature on the first night, the seven-minute Chuck Jones cartoon, *Boyhood Daze* (1957), on other nights. This allowed for three screenings. Takings declined over the subsequent days and were below $300 a night for the final Monday to Thursday period but were still higher than any other takings at the drive-in between early April and late June. *Liane, The Jungle Goddess* (1956) and the Brian Keith western *Sierra Baron* (1958) opened on a hot Tuesday 5 August, at the same time as it opened at another Robb and Rowley cinema, the New Theatre on Main Street, in downtown Little Rock. In this instance it attracted higher admissions on the Tuesday and Wednesday screenings than on Friday, Saturday or Sunday.

The Pines charged higher prices for *The Ten Commandments*: $1.25 with prices of 50 cents for children between six and twelve.[127] The film's premiere

Table 3 Highest Box-Office Takings at the Pines Drive-In, Little Rock, 11 April–13 September 1958

Feature(s)	Nights Played	From	Total Box Office
And God Created Woman (1956)	13	24 May	$6,992.10
The Ten Commandments (1956)	14	14 August	$6,338.91
Liane, Jungle Goddess (1956)/*Sierra Baron* (1958)	7	5 August	$2,054.40
The Young Lions (1958)	3	10 July	$718.10
Peyton Place (1957)	3	3 July	$612.90

Source: Arkansas Amusement Corporation Papers, Center for Arkansas History and Culture, University of Arkansas at Little Rock, Box 4, Folders 8, Box 5, Folder 1.

dated back to 8 November 1956, but regular 'pre-release' engagements did not begin until 19 March 1958 and it did not go into general release until 1959.[128] It opened at the Pines on Thursday 14 August (when the weather was hot, though over the next two weeks it was also warm, fair and cloudy), accompanied by the six-minute Famous Studios cartoon, *Possum Pearl* (1957), with a single, nightly screening for the 220-minute film. It took $1,027.75 on its opening night and $1,126.75 on its first Friday screening. Takings then declined, and at its final screening on Wednesday 27 August it took an unspectacular $149.75.

And God Created Woman had opened in France as *Et Die . . . créa la femme* in 1956, reaching the United States towards the end of 1957. It played at arthouse cinemas including New York's Paris Theatre, where it ran for thirty-eight weeks, reaching a far wider audience in 1958. Local attempts to ban the film (e.g. in Abilene) and condemnation from the Legion of Decency for its 'open violation of Christian and traditional morality' restricted exhibition in some locations but more generally helped the publicity.[129] According to *Variety*, some exhibition chains (large and small) were keeping 'the C-rated pix out of their key houses, but are booking them in their secondary situations'.[130] In Little Rock, it may have come to the Pines because the drive-in was outside the city limits: that is what happened in 1954 when the Little Rock censor board and the Legion of Decency asked for cuts to *The French Line*.[131]

'As it began to play in commercial circuits', notes Charles Drazin, 'there were alarmed reports that it was outgrossing Cecil B. De Mille's *The Ten Commandments*.'[132] This happened in Little Rock. Its box-office success points to a clear pattern, evident also at other drive-ins and other American cinemas in the late 1950s. It played slightly earlier at the Acres, for a week starting 30 April, paired with Robert Mitchum in *Second Chance* (1953), and at the North Reading, for a week beginning 15 May, alongside the Stewart Grainger western *Gun Glory* (1957). It played three nights from 11 November at the MacArthur, accompanied by Diana Dors in *The Unholy Wife*, and was presumably sufficiently successful to justify the further two nights, 10 and 11 November 1959, this time with the teenage crime drama, *The Young Captives* (1959). A different programming policy for drive-ins is evident in listings for Chicago published on Saturday 19 April 1958 which included advertisements for *And God Created Woman* screenings at the Sky-Hi Drive-In in Villa Park, the North Avenue Drive-In in River Grove, the Sunset Drive-In in Stokie and the South Screen at the Bel-Air Drive-In in Cicero.[133] Each of these showed the Bardot film as part of a multi-film package, at the Sky-Hi alongside the James Cagney-directed *Short Cut to Hell* (1957), *Armored Attack!* and *Battle Stripe*; at the North Avenue and the Sunset with *Short Cut to Hell* and *Damn Citizen*; and at the Bel-Air with *Short Cut to Hell*, *Damn Citizen* and *The Wayward Girl*. There were no 'Adults Only' notices at these drive-ins, only a 'Children Free, Kiddie Playground' reminder at the Bel-Air.

Following the box-office success of *And God Created Woman*, there were drive-in screenings of other films in which Brigitte Bardot appeared. *The Girl in the Bikini* (originally released as *Manina, la fille sans voile*, 1952) played the Acres 21–27 January 1959 and 13–15 August at the Dubuque. The Dubuque's 13 August 1959 advertisement announced 'The PIXIE of PARIS and the NIFTY of NAPLES in the Pounding Programme that'll Pop the Pulse of Every Red-Blooded American!' and with a sexist mock fight promoter approach introduced 'in this corner at 110 pounds and 39-24-39 Brigitte Bardot just the way you like her! in *The Girl in the Bikini*' and in the other corner 'wearing the black leotards . . . Gina Lollobrigida a tasty antipasto to say the least! in *Flesh and the Woman* [1954]'.[134] The Dubuque also played *Doctor at Sea* (1954), 9–11 July 1959, presumably because of Bardot's supporting role in the second entry in the British comedy series, and ended the year on 12 October with Bardot in *That Naughty Girl* (originally released as *Cette Sacrée Gamine*, 1956). The MacArthur played *La Parisienne* (1957), 21 and 22 April 1959, and *Love Is My Profession* (originally released as *En cas de malheur*, 1958), 29 and 30 November that year, while the Hi-Way 17 played Roger Vadim's follow-up Bardot film, *The Night Heaven Fell* (*Les bijouteries du claire du lune*, 1958), 11 and 12 September 1959. In addition, Bardot was invoked in the promotion of films starring other European women. The *Arizona Democrat* advertisement for *Liane* identified Marion Michaels (who featured as the jungle goddess) as 'Germany's answer to Brigitte Bardot'.[135]

The fact that *And God Created Woman* and *The Ten Commandments* were by some distance the films with the highest takings at Robb and Rowley drive-ins in 1958 indicates the wide-ranging but divided nature of drive-in programming. As Sheldon Hall notes, by the end of the 1950s, drive-ins had established themselves as a mainstay of the film industry.[136] Big roadshow releases were one aspect of the market still denied them but following the 1956 release of *The Ten Commandments* and 'nearly 1,000 domestic roadshow engagements in its first year', the most expensive Hollywood film to that date was released for limited runs in small groups of cinemas, including drive-ins, within given territories.[137] The Pines was one of the cinemas screening the film for two weeks in 1958, charging higher than normal prices. Other drive-ins played the film for shorter runs the following year: having played at the Strand in downtown Dubuque in 1957 it reached the drive-in on 2 August 1959, and a similar pattern was evident in Edenton, North Carolina (where it opened at the downtown Taylor on 31 December 1957, returning 3–6 April 1959 before reaching the drive-in on 31 July), the North Reading (which played the film for a week from 23 July 1959) and the MacArthur (where it played 19–22 July 1959).

Not all exhibitors were happy with the way that *The Ten Commandments* was released. Objections raised in *Harrison's Reports* initially centred on the length of time independent cinemas had to wait before they could show the film, then on the terms Paramount demanded. Thus, in July 1958 it reported on five Massachusetts drive-ins that had agreed to show the film for two weeks 'under reported terms that called for royalty payments of 68c for adults and 30c for children for the first week, and 57c for adults and 25c for the second week', meaning that 'the theatres were required to charge $1.25 for adults and 50c for children'.[138] When the 1,800 car-capacity Medford Twin Drive-In on the outskirts of Boston wanted to drop the second week due to lower than expected box-office receipts for screenings on both its screens, Paramount insisted that they keep to the contract and, concerned about adverse trade publicity, highlighted first-week takings of around $8,110.[139] In response, president of the Independent Exhibitors of New England Edward W. Lider argued, 'It is very common for Boston drive-ins to gross $8,110 in four days and in excess of $12,000 for a week. Several theatres in the Boston area smaller than the Twin gross these figures on many occasions at regular prices, children free, with resultant higher concession business.'[140] According to Lider, the running length of *The Ten Commandments* also meant that the drive-in had to operate until 1.30 am and thus an increased payroll, and the 60 per cent rental cost left a below-average net profit and the prospect of a second-week loss at the busiest time of the year.[141]

Behind this was a wider complaint that though distributors were forbidden from demanding set admission charges, they were using 'royalty payments' as a way of forcing exhibitors to raise their prices, for children as well as adults. This was a particular issue for drive-ins where the standard practice was to allow free admission for children. The complaint from distributors was that free admission for children, as well as the practice adopted at some drive-ins of charging admission by carload rather than individual at least on one night of the week (often 'buck night'), was a way of avoiding paying the full rental percentage on the basis of the money the drive-in received from concession sales.

The issue led to friction between drive-in operators and the Disney corporation. At the 1953 US Senate Hearings, Ruben Shor, operator of the Twin Drive-In in Cincinnati, Ohio, told the committee of a telegram he had received from Disney, threatening action if he did not change his policy of not charging for children when screening *Peter Pan* (1953).[142] Shor's complaint was that this amounted to price fixing by the film companies, in contravention of the federal anti-trust ruling. For RKO (then distributing Disney films), William Zimmerman countered that Shor was using free admission for children 'as a lure, without compensation for Disney of any kind, to attract children into Mr Shor's Twin

Drive-In Theaters so that he could make a killing in candy, popcorn, and other concession sales'.[143] The issue remained a sore one at the end of the decade: when the Hi-Way 17 outside Edenton screened Disney's *The Shaggy Dog* from 7 August 1959, it charged adults 50 cents, students 40 cents and children 20 cents, adding 'Disney demand in contract' in its advertisement.[144] The drive-in does not appear to have raised its prices for *The Ten Commandments* when it played the previous week, as by that date Paramount had apparently changed the wording of its contracts for *The Ten Commandments* so that they required a royalty payment for each adult and for each child '*if the Exhibitor shall charge an admission price for children*'.[145]

'What the Picture Did For Me' and 'Exhibitor Has His Say'

The Asher, the Pines and the Razorback belonged to a circuit operating cinemas in different states, indoor and outdoor. Aside from the Hi-Way 17, the other drive-ins I have examined also belonged to concerns of significant size. As such, they do not fit perceptions of the drive-in as dominated by small-scale, independent operators. I did not select them on that basis and their existence indicates that drive-ins were less marginal than is sometimes assumed. It is, though, worth looking also at drive-ins operated on a smaller scale through the 'What the Picture Did For Me' (WTPDFM) column carried in *Motion Picture Herald* and 'Exhibitor Has His Say' (EHHS) column in *Boxoffice*. These reports from exhibitors provided opinionated responses to films and their dealings with distributors. They mostly concerned indoor cinemas, but regular contributors included James H. Hamilton, of Pine-Hill Drive-In Theatre, Picayune, Mississippi, and other drive-in operators. In line with other contributions to the column, these exhibitors mostly identified their drive-ins as 'small town and rural patronage', though Arden A. Richards of Craigsville Drive-In, West Virginia, listed 'coalmining, farming and lumber patronage' while George Yarborough of Washington Shores Drive-In, Orlando, Florida, identified his drive-in as appealing to 'negro patronage'.

In her examination of the WTPDFM column before the Second World War (i.e. before the column included drive-in operators), Kathryn Fuller-Seeley notes that contributors tended to attribute a film's success to the extent to which it included 'significant elements of action, broad comedy, a fast-paced plot, scenic locations, and an American setting. Correspondents claimed that small-town audiences preferred what exhibitors called "real" characters, not high society fogs, or exotic sirens swathed in elaborate historical costumes'.[146]

The comments that I have looked at do not indicate that American settings were essential ('Apparently my patrons will come to see any film having a background remotely suggestive of Africa', wrote James H. Hamilton) though westerns were popular and in general similar criteria were invoked by drive-in operators in the 1950s.[147]

'I am convinced that good action pictures are hard to beat for drive-ins', wrote Robert B. Tuttle, of Sky Drive-In Theatre, Adrian, Michigan, following a successful pairing of *Back to Bataan* (1945) and *Marine Raiders* (1944).[148] He was still making the point five years later, insisting: 'For drive-ins, give us Action! Action! Action!'[149] 'Good story, good action picture for drive-in situations', wrote George R. Armstrong of Arroyo Drive-In Theatre, Cortez, Colorado.[150] 'This one has been kicked around for some time but it is one of the best western boxoffice attractions we have played on Saturday in many months', wrote D. H. Haymans, of Candler Drive-In, Metter, Georgia, of Monogram's *Son of Belle Star* (1953).[151] 'It has several ingredients which we have found to be sure box-office', quipped Hamilton of *Jesse James' Women* (1954): '1) Technicolor; 2) a western; 3) sex (it was banned in Memphis), and 4) Jesse James in the title. Also, it contains the best female fight since "Destry Rides Again [1939]".'[152] For Olin Evans of Starlite Drive-In, Florala, Alabama, films had 'to have horses, boots and saddles in these parts'.[153]

Popular comedies included *Francis Covers the Big Town* (1953) ('Too bad more of our big stars don't have big ears', commented Hamilton of the talking mule series), *Ma and Pa Kettle Go to Town* (1950) ('This type of film draws everyone out', wrote George R. Cobern of Pratt-Mont Drive-In Theatre, Prattville, Alabama) and *Hit the Ice* (1943) (twinning this with *Twilight in the Sierras* (1950), prompted Rene L. Garneau of Midway Drive-In, Ascutney, Vermont, to report that 'A Roy Rogers-Abbott and Costello combination gave us the highest gross of the season').[154] For Charles Townsend, of Wagon Wheel Drive-In, Spearman, Texas, *Timberjack* (1955) 'is a very fine picture and has some fine scenery and a good story'.[155] In contrast, having screened the Fred Astaire musical *Funny Face* (1957), O. M. Shannon, of Portland Drive-In, Portland, Texas, warned: 'Small towns do not touch. Might have been good in New York, but my people do not seem to agree with the reviewers.'[156] Arden Richards described *The Red Shoes* (1948) as 'far too snooty for more than 1 per cent of our people. Personally, I liked it, but that doesn't pay the bills'.[157]

John Wayne, Gary Cooper and Randolph Scott were among the stars identified as popular. While westerns were a reliable attraction, opinion on musicals was divided. 'Musicals just die at the drive-in', wrote W. E. Seaver Jr, of Beacon Hill Drive-in, Bristol, Tennessee.[158] For Hamilton, the Esther Williams films were 'the only musicals that I am never afraid to play', and *Singin' in the Rain* (1952) 'was one of the best musicals I have ever seen.

Everything about it is mammoth, except my boxoffice', but while his patrons did not like either Doris Day or musicals, even the customers who shied away from musicals liked the musical western, *Calamity Jane* (1953).[159] Horror films could appeal: Pearce Parkhurst, of Lansing Drive-In, Michigan (who specialized in elaborate promotions, particularly for exploitation films), thought *The Mummy's Hand* (1940) 'Good and spooky. Try horror pictures for a Saturday night attraction after the regular show and you may be surprised at the results'.[160] There were also a small number of (not necessarily enthusiastic) comments on science-fiction films. *This Island Earth* (1955) brought George Tatar, of Lockport Drive-In Theatre, Gasport, New York, 'my poorest Labor Day Sunday and Monday in years. I do not believe my clientele cares too much for science pictures or it was due to my competition showing "Strategic Air Command" [1955]'.[161]

Drive-in exhibitors regularly cited colour as important. For Billy W. Wright, of Wayne Theatres, Drive-In, Whitesburg, Kentucky, *County Fair* (1950) was 'the finest yet of the color series to be produced by Monogram. It is excellent for any Drive-In – not too long, good story, excellent color, and best of all, reasonable rental!'[162] 'Good color, good acting, good western, good business' was how John C. Coffrin Jr, of Homestead Drive-In Theatre, North Montpelier, Vermont, summed up *Bend of the River* (1952), while for Major I. Jay Sadow, of Starlite Drive-In Theatre, Rossville, Georgia, *The Wild Blue Yonder* (1951) received a 'Poor response. If this had been in color we could have done much more business'.[163] However, as the comments on *County Fair* and *Bend of the River* indicate, the mere fact that a film was in colour was not necessarily itself sufficient. For George R. Armstrong, *Flat Top* (1952) was a 'Good wartime action picture and okay for drive-ins on a dark night. Color not clear on the print we used'.[164]

The drive-in's relative lack of darkness made colour and print quality of particular importance, accentuating the problem brought by older films. The print Hamilton received of *Gentleman's Agreement* (1947) 'was faded looking in spots. Sound not up to par'.[165] This could also be a problem with more recent films. 'The exchange sent us a very poor print which was streaked and ruined the picture in many places. Insist on a good print if you play' *High Noon* (1952) advised George Armstrong.[166] After a screening of *Fort Apache* (1948), he wrote, 'Although this picture is five-year-old, John Ford's direction still drags 'em in. Good in outdoor situations on a dark night.'[167] Going further back, when James Tuttle doubled *Somebody Loves Me* (1952) with *Cleopatra* (1934) the 'telephone calls concerned "Cleopatra" and what time it started', though he added, 'We missed the color in "Cleopatra" – present day spectacles are usually rainbowed.'[168] Hamilton even described the 1918 version of *Uncle Tom's Cabin* as the 'Biggest Thursday-Friday since September when we played "The

Moon is Blue." After all these years the film is still good entertainment. Print good. Only a handful walked out. Boxoffice 247 per cent'.[169]

It is generally acknowledged that many of the films shown at drive-ins in the 1950s were, to varying degrees, old. However, the complaints in the WPDFM and EHHS columns tend to focus on the price asked for more recent films. For Hamilton, MGM prices were a particular problem. 'Metro prices, even second run, are steep for me', he wrote after screening *Singin' in the Rain*, while *Pat and Mike* (1952) prompted him to complain that 'MGM has very little to offer the small-town. Not that their pictures do not draw but that the rental is much too high.'[170] In contrast, while he was unenthusiastic about United Artists' *Actors and Sin* (1952), he also noted, 'Because of the low price, I more than paid expenses – had a small profit.'[171] 'Some of you folks in small situations try these oldies. They are very good. They outdrew WB newest Randolph Scott picture by nearly one third. Price is also right', commented O. M. Shannon after playing *Station West* (1948), ten years after its initial release.[172]

These columns served as a forum for exhibitors to voice their views on more powerful forces in the film industry. In October 1954, Arden Richards complained that Fox was withholding CinemaScope films from his drive-in to please a local indoor house.[173] However, in other instances complaints were about the distributor's price rather than film availability. Contributors also wrote positive comments on their suppliers. For George Yarborough, *Horizons West* (1952) was 'Another good Technicolor U-I western. I like this company. I haven't played a bad picture from them yet. They seem to know just what we need'.[174]

They also used the columns to reflect more generally on the problems of running a drive-in and the strategies they adopted to make a profit. Commenting on poor weekday takings, Robert Tuttle wrote: 'We're earning our living two days a week. If the film companies get too hungry on weekends, we'll really have to do some belt-tightening.'[175] On Saturdays, 'Usually a Dead End Kids or hillbilly type of film sends us scurrying around the lot to find parking spaces. The critics should come to the theatre to see some of the pictures the public like to pay to see.'[176]

Different exhibitors outlined different strategies. While comments were often about the different double bill components, in September 1950 Tuttle reported that his 'new "three-shorts-with-a-single-feature" policy' did better than average business.[177] He also did better than average business at a screening of *Rome, Open City* (1945), using the 'sexiness line' in one advert and omitting to mention that it was a foreign-language film, though he added, 'I doubt if we would consider playing any more foreign language films'.[178] Other publicity ranged from Bentley B. Davis, of Pelican Drive-In Theatre, Jennings, Louisiana, promoting *Take Care of My Little Girl* (1951) with a note saying, 'If you have gone to college or have a child in college, you can't miss this one', adding, 'I had to turn them away both nights', to Tuttle's screening of *Karamoja* which involves a $700 advertising budget, sending out 14,000 heralds, saturation radio coverage for two days and an additional 140 inches of newspaper space.[179]

They also listed the external factors with which drive-ins had to deal. Different contributors identified rain as a particular problem. *Call of the Wild* (1935) was a reissue that gave Hamilton 'one of the best Sunday nights we have had. Took a nose dive Monday but that was caused by continuous rain, almost death for drive-ins'.[180] Others listed films screened by neighbouring cinemas, local basketball or football games, the county fair, carnival or Grand Ole Opry tent show, a Baptist revival meeting, a local PTA meeting, the hunting season and a coalminers' strike affecting the amount of money people had to spend on entertainment. Outside of these columns there were others who identified other factors. According to *Movie Market Trends*, the television broadcast of *The Wizard of Oz* (1939) on Saturday November 3, 1956, 'directly cost the nation's theatres and drive-ins $2,000,000', mostly in the Mid-West, the Northwest and the South: 'Drive-Ins were hardest hit.'[181]

The WTPDFM and EHHS comments indicate the distinctive nature of the drive-in. 'I believe that the people who go to drive-in theatres are not the same people who go to the indoor houses', wrote Kenneth Clem (Monocacy Drive-In Theatre, Taneytown, Maryland), after showing a double bill of *Fancy Pants* (1950) and *Let's Go Navy* (1951).[182] Drive-in managers had to deal with particular problems, as Parkhurst highlighted when he warned following a screening of *Elephant Stampede* (1951):

> Be careful, if you also welcome dogs to your theatre, that the animal noises don't set off an area full of barking dogs. At our family drive-in we advertise: 'If there is room in your car, "Fido" is always welcome here at the Lansing Drive-In.' In fact we present a large size dog biscuit free to every car containing a dog. It's a daily feature here and works well except on extremely noisy animal pictures when we have to watch our step.[183]

'The drive-in manager has a decided disadvantage in that it is difficult to get comments from the audience', wrote Hamilton.[184] Yet drive-in managers (Hamilton included) regularly passed on audience comments. 'We have had more comments on this picture and it was liked by everyone', reported Paul Wood, of Escambia Drive-In, Century, Florida, on *Sitting Pretty* (1948), while, following a screening of *The Greatest Show on Earth*, Coffrin reported that the 'Only bad comments were on the length'.[185] There were different ways of judging audience response. 'From comments, and not forgetting boxoffice, this is certainly what my patrons want', reported Hamilton of *The City of Bad Men*, while *Invaders from Mars* (1953) prompted Mrs J. Files, of Starlite Drive-In Theatre, Grand Junction, Colorado, to write, 'There was not ONE favorable comment and more drive-outs during the show than we have ever had.'[186] These exhibitors emphasized their familiarity with their customers, noting which films brought in new faces, which drew favourable comment and which did not. 'Some haven't stopped yet. . . . This one will be hard to live down', reported J. Bye Coverston, of Big Sombrero Drive-In, Sulphur Springs, Arkansas, after a well-attended but poorly received screening of *What Price Glory?* (1952).[187]

The entertainment to which these comments refer was not limited to film: 'If we hadn't had the personal appearance of a western band, things would have been really tough', noted Coffrin in his report on *The Marrying Kind* (1952), adding that he would not recommend the film to 'small-towners'.[188] Complaining about a well-attended but too costly screening of *Pat and Mike*, Hamilton commented, 'The only consolation is that the larger the crowd, the more concession sales – but it's a shame that pictures have to become the secondary business of an exhibitor.'[189] However, while the films reported on were often old, cheaply made and could be in poor condition, for these exhibitors they remained primary. In her discussion of the pre-war WTPDFM column, Fuller-Seeley identifies one exhibitor's 'They came from the rural district through deep mud to see *Man from Dakota* (1940)' as possibly 'the highest praise a film could garner'.[190] The 1950s variation on that came from Harry Ziegler, of the Drive-In Theatre, Thorntown, Indiana, who reported:

> They drove through cornfields to come to see 'Shane'. Over one-lane gravel by-roads, through 'cricks' and sticks and fields, they came to see 'Shane' as the best western they ever saw. We showed it to capacity crowds every night although the highway on which our drive-in theatre is located is closed for reconstruction.[191]

A mixed programme

Previous accounts of the 1950s drive-in programme are correct on some points. Drive-ins often screened films months, sometimes years, after their initial release. In the second half of the decade, they did screen films made with a teenage or young adult audience in mind, including AIP science-fiction double bills. The film was not the only attraction of the drive-in. Drive-ins were understood as different from other cinemas. Ultimately, however, that difference did not rest in film titles.

The image of the drive-ins as at war with the film industry hides a more complex picture. The growth of the drive-in brought in new people and companies into the industry. Many drive-in operators identified themselves as independent exhibitors. They could be treated with suspicion by established forces within the film industry and could be in conflict with neighbouring cinemas and the Major distribution companies. But battles with Major distributors were fought by smaller businesses in general, indoor and outdoor. In some instances, cinemas were denied access to individual films, but disputes were more common over the terms under which films were made available. When a drive-in screened an older or less prestigious film it could be because the price at which it was available made it a more commercial proposition or because of a perception that last year's *Ma and Pa Kettle* film was still likely to bring in a sizeable audience.

Drive-ins were not all independent or part of small-scale operations. In the 1950s there were drive-ins operated by Major circuits and others in which Major circuits had an interest. The term 'independent' was used to include small, medium and large businesses. The MacArthur, the North Reading, the Hi-Way 17, the Dubuque, the Acres, the Peso, the Airport, the Asher, the Pines, the Razorback: none of these were lone enterprises. The fact that tracing patterns of ownership has in the main led me to companies operating across different states illustrates how 1950s drive-ins were integral to the film industry rather than outsiders. A smaller company operated the Hi-Way 17 but even this example fits a pattern of a concentration of (outdoor and indoor) cinema ownership within individual localities. If a drive-in showed films later than neighbouring indoor cinemas that could be because the owners had decided to adopt that strategy for their different cinemas.

Some drive-ins were lone enterprises. Harry Ziegler, the exhibitor who wrote to *Boxoffice* about showing *Shane* to capacity audiences, opened his drive-in between Lebanon and Frankfort, Indiana, in 1946, apparently initially using a 16mm projector and a chicken coop for the projection booth.[192] He sold the drive-in (which up to that date seems to have had room for between 100 and 150 cars) in 1972 but (at the time of writing) it is still operating, now as the M.E.L.S. at the Starlite Drive-In.[193] Differences between programming at outdoor and indoor cinemas can be overstated but more attention could be paid to differences between drive-ins. Even independent drive-ins varied considerably. Ziegler's drive-in contrasts with the Medford Twin, which could accommodate more than ten times as many cars and where the receipts of over $8,000 for a week of *The Ten Commandments* were apparently a disappointment.

Rather than discuss the drive-in in general and monolithic terms, my aim in this chapter has been to examine different specific examples. It is an approach that reveals patterns across differences. It indicates that Major studio releases were not the exception but were part of the regular drive-in programme. Columbia, MGM, Paramount, 20th Century Fox, United Artists, Universal and Warners together distributed 237 of the 291 (over 80 per cent) feature films screened in 1958 at the Razorback, Little Rock. The Chief in Seminole, Texas, operated a programme that was closer to the 'action house', but the last advertisement I have seen for the cinema in the *Seminole Sentinel* announced a mixed programme: a Friday and Saturday (2–3 May 1958) double bill of the war film *Under Fire* (1957) (distributed by 20th Century Fox) and the Universal crime film *Criss Cross* (1949), a Sunday and Monday screening of Gene Kelly in George Cukor's MGM musical *Les Girls* (1957) and on Tuesday to Thursday, James Cagney in the MGM western, *Tribute to a Bad Man* (1956). That broadly fits the strategy that Downs outlined in 1953 of three programme changes a week, with a midweek, 'high-class', show included. There were variations to this, but I have yet to discover a drive-in limited to B-films or films from independent distributors.

Of the films that the *Seminole Sentinel* advertised as showing at the Chief in the 1950s, 30 per cent were westerns. That is a higher proportion than other programmes I examined, though all those I examined across the decade consisted of at least 20 per cent westerns. If any single genre dominated the drive-in in the 1950s, it was the western, not the science-fiction film, which accounted for relatively small numbers. Gary R. Boye and Michael P. Thomason outline a similar situation in their respective accounts of the Sky-Vue Drive-In, Watauga Country, North Carolina, and the Mesa Drive-In, Pueblo, Colorado. Boye calculates that in the period when the Sky-Vue was open (1950–67) only 2 per cent of the screenings were science-fiction or horror films; of the genres accounting for at least 10 per cent of screenings, the western accounted for 22 per cent.[194] The picture was similar at the neighbouring indoor cinema, the Appalachian in Tennessee, though the equivalent figures there was 4 per cent science fiction and horror and 18 per cent westerns.[195] Thomason calculates that in the 1951–9 period the Mesa Drive-In showed 1,712 films, of which 362 (21 per cent) were westerns and 98 (6 per cent) were science-fiction or horror films.[196] However, the situation that Thomason outlines changed after the 1950s, as the proportion of westerns at the Pueblo drive-in declined to 8 per cent in the 1960s, 3 per cent in the 1970s and none in the 1980s, while science fiction and horror increased to 15 per cent in the 1960s, 22 per cent in the 1970s and 24 per cent in the 1980s.[197] There are signs of a more general shift towards the end of the 1950s though drive-ins were still showing westerns on a regular basis in 1959. In the 1950s some drive-ins did periodically run 'spookathons', 'all-nite' or 'dusk-to-dawn' shows which often included horror films, whether from the 1930s, 1940s or 1950s, and on occasion these attracted press attention and alarm.[198] However, such screenings were the exception rather than the norm.

The prevalence of the western lends weight to the idea that while drive-ins showed a range of films, they concentrated on action films. Individual contributors to the 'What the Picture Did For Me' and 'Exhibitor Has His Say' columns said as much. However, drive-ins were not out of step with cinemas in general in this respect. Edward Buscombe has estimated that 34 per cent of the US feature films produced in 1950 were westerns.[199] According to his figures the proportion had declined to 21 per cent in 1959, and there are other figures that suggest 27 per cent in 1950 and 18 per cent in 1953.[200] The overall picture remains clear: in the 1950s westerns continued to be made in large numbers on the perception that there was a significant market for them in rural, small town and neighbourhood cinemas and more generally for young audiences, indoor and outdoor. Drive-in programming reflected a larger trend.

War films were also made and watched in significant numbers. In films such as *From Here to Eternity*, *The Bridges at Toko-Ri* (1954), or the less commercially successful *Paths of Glory* (1957), Hollywood drew on the First, most frequently the Second World War but also the Korean War. Examining the programmes and where available box-office returns of individual drive-ins reveals how this operated at a local level. While war is a persistent theme, it is evident in different ways. The largest audience at the Airport Drive-In was in the week when it showed the military comedy, *Mister Roberts*. In 1958, the film with the highest box-office gross at the Razorback in Little Rock was the British-made Oscar-winner, *The Bridge on the River Kwai*. At the nearby Asher Drive-In, the highest gross for period I examined was for the three days when *Armored Attack!* and *Battle Strike* were playing, a package that revised and retitled films originally issued in 1943 and 1950. The Korean War drama *Pork Chop Hill* (1959) was one of the small number of films that played two weeks at the Acres in Phoenix. For drive-in exhibitor Robert B. Tuttle, *Strategic Air Command* was the film that 'gave the finest business of any picture we have run this year. We played it second run, single bill with Disney's "Siam" [a 1954 32-minute featurette about what is now Thailand] to round out the programme'. Through the pairing of *Tank Commandos* and *Operation Dames*, the war film was even evident in the AIP double bill. While discussion of American cinema in the 1950s has often linked it to anxieties about science and the future, at the drive-in the war film and the western were more evident than science fiction.

As at cinemas in general, not even single-billed films were shown unaccompanied at the drive-in. Even the lengthy *The Ten Commandments* was accompanied by a few minutes of *Possum Pearl* when it played the Pines in

Little Rock. Strictly speaking, drive-ins showed more cartoons than any other type of film. Most of these were only a few minutes long, though Disney features were important for the family audience and some drive-ins advertised cartoon festivals or cartoon carnivals. The double bill remained dominant (but not universal) at the drive-in, no doubt in part because the break between films helped concession sales. The fact that it often combined two quite different films could be a subject of complaint in the 1950s as it had been in the 1930s. In 1955 a letter to the *El Paso Herald Post*, complaining about 'the low-class, degenerate, "bad girl" type movies that seem to have taken over' the drive-ins, provoked columnist Ann Carroll to recount of how her recent visit to the drive-in to see *The Glenn Miller Story* (1954) was spoilt because her party 'got there too late for the good one and decided to sit through the cheap one. We left before that one was halfway through. I have not in a long life seen as many prominent bosoms or wiggling hips, on blondes with blank faces, or heard as many shots fired or groans from stabbings as in that picture'.[201]

Three decades on 'the cheap one' might have prompted a more celebratory response. In 1955 it led Tommy Boggs of the Trail Drive-In to respond, insisting that 'drive-in theaters show good pictures and do not always tack on a picture which you class as trash': that month the Trail, Boggs protested, was playing *Daddy Long Legs* (1955) with a western, *20,000 Leagues Under the Sea* (1954) with *The Silver Chalice* (1954), *A Man Called Peter* (1955) with a drama, 'along with several other good programs, all of which are suitable for the entire family'.[202]

The double bill policy may not have been to combine quality with trash but often combined films from different genres, from *A Letter to Three Wives* (1949) shown with the western *Massacre River* (1949) at the North Reading in 1950 to *The Hound of the Baskervilles* (1959) shown with *A Streetcar Named Desire* (1951) at the MacArthur in 1959. It may of course have meant that some people did what Ann Carroll had intended to do: watch one film and not the other. There were also single-genre double bills. This is evident in the first half of the decade: a nice example is the MacArthur's combination in 1954 of the two 1949 westerns, *Hellfire* and *Brimstone*. It became more evident in the second half, when the Acres in Phoenix was one of the cinemas adopting the policy of screening AIP double bills such as *The Killer Shrews* and *The Giant Gila Monster* and programmes such as *Teenage Bad Girl* (1956) combined with *Teenage Wolf Pack* (1956). The drive-in has come to be particularly associated with this type programming, though, as Arkoff noted, it was a strategy not limited to the drive-in.[203] At the end of the decade combining films from different genres remained the standard practice. The last double bill of the decade for which I have a record at the MacArthur paired *Goliath and the Barbarians* (1959, peplum) with *The Big Circus* (1959, circus drama), at the North Reading it was *John Paul Jones* (1959, historical drama) and the British-made *Tarzan's Greatest Adventure* (1959, action-adventure), at the Dubuque *Some Like It Hot* (1959, comedy) and *Fort Massacre* (1958, western) and at the Acres *Lil Abner* (1959, musical comedy) and *The Jayhawkers!* (1959, western).

More generally, the overall programmes of individual drive-ins were remarkable for their diversity. In discussing distinct 1950s US audiences, Peter Lev cites *Windjammer* (1958), *South Pacific* (1958), *This Is Cinerama* (1952), *The Bridge on the River Kwai* and *Around the World in 80 Days* as roadshow attractions that were playing in first-run Broadway cinemas mid-1958.[204] As examples of films appealing to the 'traditional first-run/second-run audience', he cites *Imitation of Life*, *A Summer Place* (1959), *Rebel Without a Cause* and *Blue Denim* (1959).[205] Acknowledging some overlap between first-run and art-house exhibition, as examples of the art film, he notes that on 1 October 1958, midtown Manhattan's art cinemas were playing French imports including *La Parisienne* and *Le Rouge et le Noir* (1954), while the Little Carnegie was showing *The Matchmaker* (1958) and the Fine Arts was showing *Me and the Colonel* (1958). What is remarkable is how many of these played at the drive-ins I have examined, if sometimes years later. Despite the CineMiracle and Cinerama processes being essentially unsuitable for drive-ins, the Super 50 Drive-In in New York played *Windjammer* in 1960 and Pacific's Century Drive-In in Inglewood, California, played *This Is Cinerama* in 1964, the year in which *South Pacific* was rereleased in indoor and outdoor cinemas.[206] *Bridge on the River Kwai* reached the Razorback on 29 May 1958, the North Reading on 31 July, the Dubuque on 26 August and the Hi-Way 17 on 15 May 1959. *Around the World in 80 Days* played the Acres from 17 June 1959. *Imitation of Life* played the North Reading from 28 May 1959, the Hi-Way 17 on 9 October and the MacArthur on 15 November. *A Summer Place* played at the Acres from 25 December 1959. *Rebel Without a Cause* played the Acres from 5 April 1956, the MacArthur 4 May, the Dubuque 1 August 1957 and the Hi-Way 17 14 September 1958. *Blue Denim* played the North Reading from 8 October 1959 and the MacArthur from 17 December. None of the drive-ins I have examined in detail played *Le Rouge et le Noir* or *The Matchmaker*, though the latter did play at drive-ins (in the Philadelphia area in September 1958 it was playing at eleven indoor cinemas and the Airport and MacDade drive-ins).[207] *La Parisienne* played the Acres from 22 October 1958 and the MacArthur from 21 April 1959. The MacArthur played *Me and the Colonel* from 26 May that year.

As Lev says, drive-in programming ranged from westerns and comedies to more youth-orientated films.[208] But by the end of the 1950s it was also taking in roadshows, high- and medium-budget Hollywood films and the art films as well as exploitation films, the latter ranging from those that could be sold as art films to *The Story of Bob and Sally* shows that were still doing the rounds a decade after they were made. There were drive-ins such as the Medina Valley in south central Texas which varied its emphasis on comedies, westerns and other action films with titles such as *An American in Paris*, the occasional Spanish-language film and, from 'the outer limits of the exploitation film in its classical phase', burlesque films such as *Teaserama* (1955) and *Varietease* (1954).[209] *Salt of the Earth* (1954), the film made by blacklisted filmmakers that was denied a general release in the 1950s and which addressed issues of ethnicity, gender and class avoided in Hollywood films of the time, played six nights at the Silver Sky-Vue Drive-In in New Mexico, to capacity audiences.[210] There were other drive-ins devoted to Spanish-language films and that thus offered a programme that was completely different from most cinemas but like other indoor cinemas that catered to Hispanic audiences.

The drive-in programme indicates the importance of the film at the drive-in, but the programme was not limited to film. The MacArthur was not alone in scheduling live acts. Continuing a career that went back to early-twentieth-century carnival and vaudeville shows, conjoined twins Daisy and Violet Hilton sisters made personal appearances at drive-in screenings of *Chained for Life*, as well as indoor burlesque and floor shows, up to the early 1960s, when the agent who had promised further drive-in dates went off with their takings, abandoning them at the New Monroe Drive-In in North Carolina.[211]

Drive-ins also served as music venues. 'Most early performances took place in schoolhouses and the occasional theater, with flatbed trailers and the roofs of drive-in movie refreshment stands serving as stages in the summer months', writes David W. Johnson of the Stanley Brothers.[212] The Foggy Mountain Boys would similarly perform on the flat roof of the drive-in concession stand, their microphones plugged into the sound system so that they could be heard through the in-car speakers: 'Patrons would honk their car horns at the end of each song rather than applaud.'[213] It was from the Winchester Drive-In concession stand roof in 1961, in the break between *King of the Wild Horses* (1947) and *Young Jesse James* (1960), that Patsy Cline, dressed in her cowgirl regalia, fled in tears when hostile members of the audience honked their horns and booed.[214]

The box-office success of *The Ten Commandments* and *And God Created Woman* at the Pines, Little Rock, reveals the importance of timing. A drive-in could increase its audience when it screened an in-demand film before its immediate competitors, and this commercial value could (but did not necessarily) outweigh the likely higher rental charges. Those two films are also evidence of contrasting though related trends within late 1950s film programming.

The Ten Commandments, made by an American whose directing career went back to the beginnings of Hollywood, is a biblical epic that used traditional Hollywood storytelling and performance as well as more recent technological developments and was promoted with an appeal to established religious groups.[215] The feature debut of a French director in his twenties, the contemporary-set *And God Created Woman* received a 'Condemned' rating from the Legion of Decency, had at its centre a character who wilfully broke moral commandments and was an early taste of the French new wave. In their different ways, both films depended on the spectacle of colour, the big screen and the suggestion of sex, and for American audiences a combination of distance and the present. Through Cecil B. De Mille's on-screen introduction, which defines the film as 'the story of the birth of freedom' and insists that the battle between mankind being 'the property of the state or free souls under God' is one that 'continues throughout the world today', *The Ten Commandments* linked the film's biblical narrative to contemporary, Cold War America. In showing Saint-Tropez and Brigitte Bardot, *And God Created Woman* director Roger Vadim gave Americans a glimpse of a different world. For Ginette Vincendeau, 'part of Bardot's French specificity' was that while 'the archetypes of American teenage rebel were James Dean and Jack Kerouac, France offered a more feminized version of youth rebellion'.[216] It was, however, a version seen by millions of Americans, in different contexts: alongside a western at the North Reading Drive-In, a Diana Dors film at the MacArthur, but sufficient on its own to attract repeated full crowds at the Pines Drive-In in Little Rock.

These two films were successful at the American box office, not just at the drive-in box office. The significance of what was shown and what attracted the largest audiences at drive-ins is not limited to outdoor cinema. Drive-in programming was distinct in some respects, but it also reflected broader patterns in its shifting mix of films from the Hollywood Majors, independent American studios and occasional (and occasionally very successful) films from overseas. The programme was not homogeneous at individual drive-in and varied between drive-ins. Audiences (the subject of the next chapter) will also have responded in different ways to individual films, on account of the nature of those film and the context in which they were screened.

3

People

According to Sindlinger & Company, of the 82.3 million Americans who went to the cinema in the week ending 1 August 1959, 30.2 million (36.7 per cent) went to 'a movie theatre', while 52.1 million (63.3 per cent) went to a drive-in.[1] In 1959 as a whole, according to the *Film Daily Year Book*, there were 1,094,740,000 paid admissions to US indoor cinemas, 722,655,000 paid admissions to outdoor cinemas and 364,189,000 admissions of children and adults who did not pay.[2] Indoor cinemas still accounted for the majority of cinema admissions and, given that these included the downtown, first-run cinemas that charged the highest prices, the bulk of box-office takings. However, if it is true that a significant proportion of the drive-in audience consisted of children, it would appear that, in terms of audience numbers, by the end of the 1950s cinema attendance in the United States was not that much higher indoor than outdoor, and in some summer weeks the cinema was almost twice as likely to be experienced outdoors as indoors.

Going to the drive-in continued to be treated as a joke, as it had been almost from the start. From speculation in 1933 about 'what fun Young America could have in a coupe under the added stimulation of a sophisticated Hollywood romance!' to late twentieth-century studies that repeat the story that the show was better in the cars than on the screen, its audience's apparent lack of interest in what was on the screen has often attracted more interest than its programme.[3] That was as true in the 1950s as in other decades. Newspapers regularly published humour such as 'Definition of a drive-in movie – A movie where the actors on the screen stop to look at what's going on in the audience' or 'A very good girl is Agatha Jones, a most unusual creature. She went to a drive-in movie and, she actually saw the feature.'[4] The George Hughes illustration used on the *Saturday Evening Post* cover for 19 August 1961 continued the tradition into the 1960s, with its image of a dating couple looking towards the drive-in screen who are themselves watched by three grinning boys looking away from the screen, at the couple in the car.[5] By this time, drive-in jokes had been integrated into stand-up comedy: when *Variety* reviewed Larry K. Nixon's live act in 1959 it described him as 'a fairly tired stand-up comic who runs through standard routines about mothers-in-law, drive-in theaters and marriage'.[6]

The jokes did point to an aspect of cinemagoing that scholarship has tended to ignore. The fact that a negative view of film audiences emerged so soon after the birth of cinema may well be explained, Ian Christie suggests, by

> a combination of elitist distaste for the labouring masses of the turn of the century, and the easily ignored fact that film shows were the first popular entertainment to take place in darkness, with a proportion of those attending almost certainly not there for the movies, or easily distracted from the screen. Warmth, comfort, somewhere to sleep or pass the time; a chance to meet friends and to make new ones; a place for 'a date' – all of these were, and have remained, important reasons for cinemagoing, even if they are rarely acknowledged in film scholarship.[7]

Like early cinema audiences, the view of drive-in audiences has often been a negative one, and drive-in cinemas provided not only darkness but also a degree of privacy (as well as a playground). That did not necessarily mean that drive-in audiences were uninterested in the film, but an examination of the drive-in audience needs to take account of the different reasons people were there, and not just the drive-in's playground facilities but its reputation as a 'passion pit' and how it gained that reputation.

I therefore begin this chapter with a look at the 'passion pit' label. I move on to examine evidence that gives a different picture, based on the drive-in's appeal to parents with babies and children. I then examine different source material: first, surveys undertaken from the late 1940s to the early 1960s; second, newspaper reports and columns, as well as other documents from this period; third, memories and brief entries from a diary written in 1952. I follow this with a discussion of two, conflicting views of the 1950s drive-in, one based on diversity and inclusion, the other on segregation and exclusion. Behind this is a concern to examine the range of the drive-in audience, as individual people as well as numbers in a chart.

'A "passion pit with pix" as some call it'

The phrase 'passion pit' could be used as slang for the drive-in or as a comment on what happened at the drive-in. While Kristin Thompson and David Bordwell simply referred to drive-ins specializing in teenpics as bringing 'many adolescent couples to the local "passion pit"', according to Thomas Doherty, 'among 1950s teenagers, the back rows of any drive-in lot had a deserved reputation as a "passion pit"'.[8] The reputation, and the argument that it was deserved, lived on. 'Even after 50 years, bucket seats, the sexual revolution, and the Playboy Channel, drive-ins are still "passion pits"', wrote Ellen Meloy in 1994.[9] The advice for the amorous remained clear: 'Deter snoopers by parking far from the snack bar. Steam up those windows. Rock that Volvo.'[10]

'Passion pit' existed as a comment on what went on at the drive-in, as an expression of moral panic about what was imagined took place at the drive-in, but also as an ironic comment on that panic. The label was widely used in the 1950s in and beyond the United States. 'Drive-in cinemas, where you watch movies from parked cars, are being denounced by Church groups as "passion pits"', announced the British newspaper, the *Daily Mail*, in 1948, in one of the first times the phrase was used this way in print.[11] In 1959, another British newspaper report, on a visit to a Massachusetts drive-in, was titled simply 'Drive-In: Passion Pit', though it described a variety of behaviours including children asleep in the back of a sedan and teenagers having a 'beer party' while listening to rock 'n' roll on the radio.[12] The term was used by moral campaigners and for blatant sensationalism. In 1957, the trend towards all-night drive-in shows led assistant county prosecutor Harold B. LeCrone to tell the Ohio general assembly: 'Illegitimate births among teen-agers are increasing because the youngsters have turned dusk-to-dawn theaters into "passion pits"'.[13] LeCrone's comment was picked up not only in the film industry trade press but also in a feature in the 'true crime' magazine *Crime Exposé*, in an article purporting to expose 'The shocking truth about drive-in movies, the teen-agers' "passion pits"'.[14]

The trade press repeatedly traced it back to *Variety*. In 1958 Arthur Mayer insisted that drive-ins were 'no longer what *Variety* once called "passion pits with pix" but highly respectable family institutions doing a rushing business in hot dogs, pop. and pizza-pie'.[15] In September 1949 *International Projectionist* reprinted a *Time* article which noted, 'The drive-ins are also popular with young neckers, but exhibitors deny that their places are, in *Variety*'s phrase, "passion pits with pix" . . . nothing happens that doesn't go on in a balcony.'[16] *Variety* itself published similar denials, at least for the contemporary drive-in. A 1959 article about how drive-ins were attracting a family audience came with the subtitle, 'Passion pits with pix? No!'[17] In 1958 it mentioned 'passion pits' but as a term used in a church journal article on 'Drive-Ins and Morality' and 'seldom used nowadays in the trade itself'.[18] 'Drive-In theatres, once known as "passion pits", now obtain 85% of their biz from the family trade' was the *Variety* verdict in 1957, echoing their 1952 report that 'Drive-Ins, once labelled "passion pits with pix", are no longer being looked on by Hollywood as industry stepchildren'.[19] The earliest use of the phrase 'passion pit with pix' that I have been able to discover is in a 1949 *Variety* report. The trade paper noted that the exhibitor had 'at least three adults to a vehicle as his goal. Thus, he can offset charges that his spot is a camouflaged lover's lane . . . a "passion pit with pix" as some call it'.[20]

Those 'some' were not identified. The 'with pix' suffix was a *Variety* invention, but this was not the first time that drive-ins had been called 'passion pits' in print. The first instance I have discovered appeared two days before the *Daily Mail* reference to church leaders denouncing drive-ins as passion pits, when *Time* noted, 'The nation's youth were necking in drive-in movies instead of in shady lanes; teenagers in Indianapolis referred to them as "passion pits".'[21]

At this date, the word 'teenager' had only recently come into common use. The notion of the teenager has a longer history, but it was from the mid-1940s that the idea of the years after twelve and before twenty as a distinct phase of life, and market, came to attract increasing attention. Press interest in this as a new phenomenon examined teenage habits and language. In August 1948, in one of a series of features on the American teenager later published as *Profile of Youth*, *Ladies Home Journal* discussed young habits and slang in York, Pennsylvania, noting:

> They may drive to a hamburger joint on the edge of town for a 'French poodle' (hot dog) and doughnuts with gobs of peanut butter in the hole, play miniature golf, enjoy a fast game of shuttleboard on outdoor courts, head for the 'passion pit' (drive-in movie) or join the 2000 fellas and girls who jam the Teen Age Club on weekends for dancing and table tennis. On big nights couples go to parties sponsored by teen clubs and held in a rented barn equipped with a juke box stocked with Perry Como and Jo Stafford records, and piles of hay convenient for 'schmotzing' – necking.[22]

According to a 1951 *Newsweek* article on teenage slang it was Seattle teenagers who called drive-ins 'passion pits'.[23] 'Since the outdoor movies are largely patronized by young people', claimed Louise M. Ackerman in 1957, 'the language takes on youthful flavour. The official name of an outdoor movie theatre may be Starview, but the patrons will likely refer to it, because of the lovers attending, as the *passion pit*'.[24]

The passion pit label was thus not limited to a description of what took place at the drive-in or alarm at what was supposedly taking place. It also functioned as identity formation, the way in which one generation distinguished itself from another through its language. It was, in the latter sense, not to be taken literally, and when *Ladies Home Journal* returned to survey teenage life and thoughts in 1960, it quoted one teenager's annoyance 'that so many parents are against drive-in movies. Could it be because we call them "passion pits"? We can forget how literal minded parents can be, and that they are in such a sweat about anything that even *sounds* like sex'.[25] The earlier *Ladies Home Journal* report more innocently aligned the drive-in as passion pit with Donuts and table tennis, as if the schmotzing took place elsewhere.

The drive-in as passion pit started out in print as teenage slang. However, similar terms, with a common alliteration, had been published earlier. In 1940, *Motion Picture Herald* reported on the objections of independent indoor cinema operators to 'the see-it-through-a-windshield enterprise being constructed' in Milwaukie by Mid-West Drive-In Theatres, Inc. Harry Perlowitz, business manager of the independent organization, was quoted as saying, 'They're nothing more than licenced petting parks', to which 'practically everybody agreed'.[26] In 1947, Montgomery County in Maryland introduced a $1,000 licence fee and an 11 pm curfew for drive-ins, following 'complaints that Drive-Ins are "licensed petting places", voiced in connection with the building here by Sidney Lust of an auto theater'.[27] In 1948 Jack Jackson anticipated later denials, arguing, 'The concentrated campaigns directed to families and rural groups has pretty well dispersed the once prevalent stigma that Drive-Ins were glorified petting places.'[28]

The first *Motion Picture Herald* report on the Camden Drive-In indicates that the reputation preceded any activity. Associations between sex and cinema, cars and courtship, were established early in the twentieth century.[29] Over time that reputation was augmented, whether by what happened at the drive-in, fears about what was happening at the drive-in or by those exploiting or dismissing those fears for their own interests. Referring to drive-ins as passion pits was as much a play on that reputation as it was an expression of moral concern or panic, though once the name had stuck it could feed into adult concerns and in turn be fed back to teenagers. Thus, the points for study and discussion in a course on 'Adolescents and the Automobile' included questions on 'What safeguards can you help your teen-ager to develop against excesses in unsupervised car dates? Do your adolescents know why drive-in movies are popularly called "passion pits"? Would your daughter know what to do if a boy started to get fresh with her in his car?'[30] The use of the term 'passion pit' in the film industry trade press tended to be as a denial, an insistence that drive-ins were not, or at least were no longer, passion pits. 'Passion pit' did not necessarily mean drive-in: when Professors Towers and Watts (Irwin Berke and John Carradine) invite their new academic colleague Dr West (Mamie van Doren) to 'The Passion Pit' in *Sex Kittens Go To College* (1960), they are not inviting her to the drive-in but the local nightclub. The dominant narrative in the 1950s trade press, a narrative evident also in publications such as *Saturday Evening Post*, was that drive-ins were for families with babies or young children.

Families, children and babies

From the statements that Richard Hollingshead made in May 1933 and others echoed before, during and after the 1950s, commentators emphasized the importance of the family audience and stressed that their cinemas were places to take children and babies. In 1947 Conrad P. Harness claimed that at the drive-in necking youngsters had made way for the 'burb and bottle crowd'.[31] For John Durant in 1950:

> what disproves the cheap gags more than anything else is the type of audience that fills the drive-ins today. It is by far a family audience, with a probable 75 per cent of the cars containing children who, incidentally, are let in free by most drive-ins if they are under twelve. This is the main reason the ozoners have been so successful – their appeal to the family group. They are the answer to parents who want to take in the movies, but can't leave their children alone at home. No baby sitters needed. And the kids are no bother to anyone in the audience.[32]

The point about babysitters was one of the most common and enduring arguments for the drive-in. In 1947, visitors to the Aurora Motor-Inn Theatre in Seattle had to pass pickets carrying placards such as 'DOWN WITH DRIVE-INN'S [sic] MORE WORK for BABY SITTERS' and 'patronize downtown movies MAKE JOBS FOR BABY SITTERS'.[33] It was a drive-in operator's publicity stunt but still evidence that saving on the cost of the babysitter was already familiar as a reason for going to the drive-in. The brochure produced for the opening of Abilene's Park Drive-In was following a widespread trend in emphasizing its appeal to families, the fact that it cost less than hiring a babysitter and the free bottle-warming service (Figure 10).

It was sometimes used as evidence that an important drive-in audience was that of, as Durant put it, 'moderate-income families who bring the kids to save money on baby-sitters'.[34] This understanding did not die out with the 1950s: a *Variety* report that 72 per cent of those attending Pacific Theaters' drive-ins 'were classified as young married couples with two or more children who couldn't afford to go out and pay for a babysitter' dates from 1983.[35]

Emphasizing the audience of married couples with children in part served to counter the drive-in's 'passion pit' association. However, drive-in operators went beyond this, designing and pricing their drive-ins with parents, children

FIGURE 10 *From 'Abilene's Newest Drive-in' brochure, 6–7, in Scrapbook for Park Drive-In, 16 December 1949, 89, Interstate Theatre Collection. From the collections of the Dallas History & Archives Division, Dallas Public Library.*

and babies in mind. 'And the children', Harvey Elliot, manager of the Whitestone Bridge Drive-In in the Bronx, told the *New Yorker* in 1949, 'why hire a baby-sitter for them when they can sleep in the back of the car. We encourage family trade. It accounts for eighty-six per cent of our business. Children under twelve are admitted free, and we've got a bottle warming service for babies'.[36] The bottle-warming service was most frequently cited in reports on the drive-in in the late 1940s, but references continued in the 1950s. In 1953 the *Exhibitor* noted that the Capitol Drive-In, Des Moines, Iowa, 'not only provides bottle warming facilities for babies, but also supplies the tots with free homogenized milk', while in 1955 another Des Moines exhibitor, Art Farrell of Southeast 14th Street Drive-In, told the MGM's ticket selling workshop that 'everything he does is pointed at the family trade, his drive-in having a playground for the kiddies, provision for bottle warming, free gum and free potato chips, etc.'.[37]

Some drive-ins had an admission charge for children over five years old, and some distributors (notably, RKO and Buena Vista for Disney features) insisted on a children's admission charge. In most cases, however, the family audience was encouraged by free admission for everyone under twelve. However, the playground provides the clearest evidence of the importance of the younger audiences at the drive-in. Introduced during the Second World War, they ranged from the swings, slides and merry-go-rounds at the Chief, Seminole, to the elaborate rides available at the Sharpstown. By 1951, the large Pacific Drive-In chain had 'established playgrounds for the youngers at each of its neighborhood theatres'.[38] *Motion Picture Herald* carried regular reports on drive-in playgrounds, noting in 1954 that they had 'grown steadily over the years in becoming an integral part of the general outdoor operation' and in 1956 that an estimated 90 per cent of drive-ins either had a playground or were planning to install one.[39]

For the author of the 1954 *Motion Picture Herald* report the drive-in playground was important, first, for the youngsters who used it, second, for allowing parents to relax (one operator was quoted as saying, 'The active entertainment tires the youngster sufficiently, so that after the cartoon they go to sleep on the backseat of the car and let the grownups enjoy the show') and, third, for the drive-in operator, as it meant that some cars arrived earlier and stimulated 'the appetites of the children for the goodies to be had at the refreshment stand'.[40]

Throughout and beyond the 1950s, exhibitors sold the drive-in as a place for the family. This was not only done through free admission policies and what was provided at the drive-ins. 'Santa Claus who made his temporary headquarters here in Cameron Park got over 200 letters dropped in his park mailbox', reported the *Sunbury Daily Item* at the very end of the decade. Apparently, the 'biggest item asked for was a drive-in movie, a new toy on the market this year'.[41] The Remco Movieland Drive-In Theater came with a battery-powered projector, six filmstrips (Have Gun Will Travel, Heckle & Jeckle, Dinky Duck, Mighty Mouse, Farmer Alfalfa and Captain Kangaroo), six miniature cars and a marque to hang one of three miniature 'coming attractions' posters. 'Every boy wants a Remco toy', insists the boy demonstrating the Remco drive-in at the end of the toy's 1959 commercial, to which the girl (Patty Duke) adds, 'and so do girls'.[42] The 'Snoopy Drive-In Theater' was a 1970s variation.[43]

In identifying the drive-in's primary market as the family, exhibitors and commentators sometimes put a figure on this: 86 per cent according to the manager of the Whitestone Bridge Drive-In, 75 per cent of cars estimated by John Durant for drive-ins more generally. It is difficult to determine the accuracy of such numbers. However, the time immediately following the Second World War was a period when market research took on new importance for a film industry increasingly concerned about declining audiences numbers and changing recreational habits. Surveys of the drive-in audience were part of this trend and can provide some more precise if still partial data.

Surveys and statistics

The first detailed survey of the drive-in audience was conducted by Rodney Luther in 1949 in the Minneapolis-St Paul area. Luther followed with a second survey in the same area the next year.[44] His comments about his findings, and his positive view of the drive-in, fed into the debate about the importance of the family audience and continue to be drawn on in histories of the drive-in.[45] He echoed other accounts in writing that drive-ins appealed to 'parents who ordinarily face the costly and troublesome problem of employing a babysitter, and the aged and handicapped', also mentioning wage earners, farm labourers who liked the informality, pet owners, 'novelty seekers and polio-avoiders, etc.'.[46] The exhibitors, he noted, 'vehemently object to *Variety*'s description of drive-ins as "passion pits with pix", insisting that their largest patronage is the family trade, that patrons' activities are closely watched, and that nothing happens that does not happen in conventional theaters'.[47] Writing of his first survey, he found the drive-in different from indoor cinemas in its appeal not only to the family group but also to older audiences: at the drive-in 'almost 40 per cent of all adults were estimated to be over 30 years of age' but there was 'evidence that attendance at conventional theaters by adults drops off sharply after age 25 had been reached'.[48] *Variety* jumped on this, reporting on Luther's findings under the headline: 'OZONERS LURE "OVER-30" PAYEES'.[49]

The longer-term trend was different, and the more detailed information in his report on the 1950 survey indicates a more complex picture. In both surveys a little over half the cars contained family groups with children (55 per cent in 1949, 54 per cent in 1950).[50] Of those over twelve, in 1949 10.4 per cent were estimated to be age twenty or younger, 48.2 per cent to be in the twenty-one to thirty age range and 41.4 per cent to be over thirty.[51] In the 1950 survey, the equivalent figures were 19.3 per cent, 45.1 per cent and 35.6 per cent.[52] That is, the proportion of 'adults' (understood here as including anyone over twelve) in the twelve to twenty range had almost doubled. The bulk of these, Luther reported, were in the upper third of this category: the absolute number of patrons in the other age groups had not decreased but there was a much greater increase in the number of persons in the seventeen to twenty age group.[53] This group was less evident at weekends and at first performances, but there was a weekday, second performance breakdown of 41 per cent in the twelve to twenty group, 34.2 per cent in the twenty-one to thirty group, 18 per cent in the thirty-one to forty group and 6.8 per cent over forty.[54]

There are a range of possible explanations for this increase. It could indicate a seasonal variation, though the surveys were conducted at a similar time of the year (August and September in 1949, July and August in 1950). It could be because, as Luther claimed, the 1950 survey was 'even more comprehensive'; he notes that customers in over 2,000 cars were selected at random 'on all days of the week, all weeks of the month, and for all performances', while reporting on the 1949 survey he referred only to 1,624 interviews, not which showings or days.[55] Though the surveys were only a year apart, given that this was a time of rapid drive-in expansion, it could indicate a shift towards a younger audience. But whatever the explanation it seems clear that even Luther's research, notwithstanding his emphasis on the family and an older audience, indicated a significant teenage audience, concentrated in later, weekday screenings.

Interpreting other surveys can be difficult for various reasons. Around the same time that Luther was detailing his findings, the *Exhibitor* reported on a different survey for the Gallup-affiliated Audience Research Corp., which apparently revealed that 'More women sold tickets than men, with the age brackets greatest from 18 to 30 and least from 12-17'.[56] As this seems to compare an age bracket covering thirteen years with one covering less than half that period, it raises more questions than it answers. Unfortunately, in this instance, without further details about the survey it is impossible to establish the significance of its findings. It at least points to the complications of making a distinction between a teenage audience and an audience of young married couples with children and the potential problem of discussing teenagers as a single entity.

The broader context to this is of a country in which those aged between fifteen and nineteen made up a relatively small proportion of the population in 1950 but increased during the decade. This increase was not a consequence of the post-war baby boom, which in the 1950s led to an increase in children aged fourteen or under, but which only had an impact on the number of older teenagers in the 1960s. US census figures identified 10,616,598 people aged between fifteen and nineteen in 1950, a smaller number than any other five-year age band below the forties.[57] However, by 1960 that figure had increased to 13,219,243, which was still a smaller number than the lower-age bands (the number for those aged four or younger had increased to 20,320,901) but which was now a larger number than any older five-year age band.[58] In 1960 11.3 per cent of the US population was under five years old, 31.1 per cent was under fifteen years old and 35.8 per cent was under eighteen years old.[59] In successive subsequent decades, each of those percentages declined.[60]

While the broad trend since the 1950s has been towards an older population in the United States, in the 1950s it was towards a younger population. In the 1950s there was also a trend towards younger marriages and younger parents. The median age at which women married declined to 20.3 in 1950 and reached a historic low of 20.1 in 1956.[61] In the words of Landon Y. Jones, eventually 'one of every two first-time brides in the United States was still in her teens, and more than half of them had babies before they turned 20'.[62] The teenager and the married couple with children were not necessarily different audiences.

Given that they used a twelve to twenty age band, Luther's surveys come close to identifying a teenage audience, though in his comments on those between seventeen and twenty he acknowledged important differences between those in the lower and upper ranges in this band. If the Audience Research Corp. survey did indicate increased attendance in the eighteen to thirty range that could still indicate a significant audience of older teens. Later surveys used slightly different age distinctions.

In 1957, the Opinion Research Corporation carried out a survey of cinema attendance (indoor and outdoor) for the Motion Picture Association of America, which they titled *The Public Appraises Movies* (hereafter PAM). Based on 5,021 personal interviews between 13 June and 15 July, this distinguished between those aged nine or younger, ten to fourteen, fifteen to nineteen, twenty to twenty-nine, thirty to thirty-nine, forty to forty-nine, fifty to fifty-nine and sixty or over, helpfully also providing figures for the percentage of the total US population falling into these bands.[63] It does not separate indoor and outdoor attendance for these bands but does this for teenage-only groups (including those in the fifteen to nineteen range attending with a date, friend or another couple, with the qualification that some of these might not have been within the same age range), adult children groups (including those over twenty who said they went with a child and all teenagers who said they went with a parent or relative), husband and wife only groups and other adult groups (including all adults who said they went with a date, friend or relative, and married couples who went with other couples).[64]

The primary conclusion of the PAM survey was made clear at the beginning of the published report: 'The motion picture audience is predominantly a young one.'[65] Young did not necessarily mean teenage but included teenage: 72 per cent of admissions were accounted for by those under thirty (where that age group accounted for 50 per cent of the national population), 52 per cent by those under twenty (38 per cent of the national population) and 31 per cent by those under fifteen (roughly equivalent to the national percentage).[66] However, this was for the cinema audience as a whole, not just for the drive-in audience. According to the report, 'drive-ins are most popular with people in their twenties and those who have children under 15'.[67]

Again, the data itself gives a more complex if incomplete picture. The information it gives on drive-ins is clearest on group attendance. Those surveyed were asked 'The last time you went to the movies, did you go by yourself or with someone else?' and if with someone else to identify with how

Table 4 Composition of Groups at the Cinema, Indoor and Outdoor, June and July 1957

	Total	Regular Admissions	Drive-In Admissions
Teenage-only groups	26%	25%	30%
Adult children groups	22%	15%	34%
Husband and wife only groups	13%	14%	12%
Other adult-only groups	25%	26%	22%
Men who went alone	7%	11%	0%
Teenagers who went alone	4%	4%	2%
Women who went alone	2%	4%	–
Not reported	1%	1%	0

Source: *The Public Appraises Movies*, National Association of Theatre Owners Collection, MSS 1446 Box 9, Folder 10, L. Tom Perry Special Collections Library, Harold B. Lee Library, Brigham Young University, Provo, Utah, 13.

many and their relationship to them. In reporting the responses, the figures for drive-in attendance were distinguished from 'regular' (indoor) attendance (see Table 4).[68]

That adult-child groups were more evident at the drive-in confirms their family appeal. However, the survey also indicated a higher-than-average drive-in attendance from teenage-only groups, and if that figure is added to the small number of teenagers attending on their own it suggests three, roughly even groups: teenage-only groups, adult-child groups and adult-only groups, the latter including married couples attending without children. If anything, the point about the youth of the cinema audience was more evident at the drive-in than elsewhere, given that 55 per cent of the 'regular' audience consisted of adult-only groups or lone adults. The equivalent figure for the drive-in was 36 per cent.

'Most people go to the movies with someone', concluded the survey, above all at the drive-in, where only 2 per cent of admissions were accounted for by lone visitors, almost all of whom were teenagers.[69] This did not necessarily mean people went in pairs: the 98 per cent who last went to a drive-in with someone was made up of 34 per cent who went with one other person, 12 per cent who went with two, 29 per cent with three, 16 per cent with four or more and 7 per cent who could not remember how many were in their group.[70] The equivalent figures for other cinemas were 47 per cent with one other, 15 per cent with two, 10 per cent with three, 7 per cent with four or more and 2 per cent who could not recall how many.[71] Luther similarly identified a tendency for cars to contain more than two people: an average of 2.34

adults per car in 1949 and 2.48 in 1950, an average of .94 children per car in 1949 and .97 in 1950.[72] This can partly but not entirely be accounted for by the presence of parents with children: Luther noted the 1950 increase in the average number of adults in a car 'resulted almost entirely from an increase in the number of cars containing either three or four adults', adding that many of those in the seventeen to twenty age group 'attend in groups of three or four to a car'.[73] Leo Handel's research also indicated that drive-ins were attended in large groups, most frequently in groups of four, while couples were more common in conventional cinemas.[74]

Subsequently, the newly established Theatre-screen Advertising Bureau conducted two surveys. A report on its 1958 survey identified its most surprising statistic as that 'almost 80 per cent of the typical drive-in audience is composed of married couples. Only 18.9 per cent of the drive-in audience were single and 0.9 per cent either divorced, separated or widowed'.[75] This highlights a problem with this and other surveys: they exclude children even while making the case that children attended drive-ins in significant numbers. The survey also identified three age ranges as 'over represented' at the drive-in: those fifteen to twenty-four accounted for 'approximately a fourth of the Summer drive-in audience but only 16.5 per cent of the national population', those twenty-five to thirty-four accounted for 35.1 per cent of the audience but only 19.3 per cent of the population and those thirty-five to forty-four, 22.3 per cent of the audience and 18.6 per cent of the population.[76] This broadly tallies with the PAM survey's point about drive-ins being popular with those in their twenties while indicating a significant older (in this instance up to the mid-forties) and younger adult audience.

The Advertising Bureau's 1959 survey was based on mailed questionnaire returned from 2,683 families (9,629 individuals) from across the United States and used age bands for those under ten, between ten and nineteen, twenty and thirty-four, thirty-five and fifty-four and fifty-five and over: that is, bands of varying length.[77] In reporting on this survey, Steuart Henderson Britt noted that 'most of the drive-in theater-going was in family groups', almost half of American families had attended a drive-in in the previous six months and 66 per cent of those over fifteen were married.[78] Echoing the comments that Luther made a decade earlier, a Bureau spokesperson commented that while 'many people have looked to the drive-in theatre as trysting place for juveniles, those who have been close to the drive-in have watched this audience become a stable, family market' (though this emphasis on the family may not be surprising in a survey based on questionnaires sent to 2,683 families).[79] It indicated a range of ages among those who had been to the drive-in in the last six months, 22 per cent of whom were under ten, 21 per cent between ten and nineteen, 27 per cent between twenty and thirty-four, 22 per cent between thirty-five and fifty-four and 8 per cent fifty-five or over.[80] The picture was different for those who attended most regularly. For those who had been thirteen times or more to the drive-in in the past six months, the breakdown was 13 per cent under ten, 34 per cent between ten and nineteen, 38 per cent between twenty and thirty-four, 12 per cent between thirty-five and fifty-four and 3 per cent fifty-five or over.[81] The younger audience were more likely to be regular attenders but the most regular were those in their twenties or early thirties. More than 80 per cent of those questioned reported three or more people in the car on their last visit to the drive-in.

Each of these surveys examined generation. They paid less attention to gender. The PAM report estimated 27.9 million weekly male admissions and 26.3 weekly female admissions, with slightly higher figures for women in the fifteen to nineteen (5.7 million as opposed to 5.5 million) and twenty to twenty-nine (5.6 million as opposed to 5.4 million) age bands.[82] However, these figures cover indoor and outdoor attendance. The issues of Sindlinger & Company's *Movie Market Activity* that I have seen (for selected autumn and winter weeks in 1956 and 1958) indicate higher overall male rather than female drive-in attendance, with some regional variations. According to this source, in the week ending 29 November 1958 there were 13,453,000 total paid male admissions (indoor and outdoor but excluding children) and 11,152,000 female admissions, the figures for drive-in admissions were 3,736,000 male and 2,606,000 female but in the Eastern and Mid-West states more women (341,000 and 584,000, respectively) attended the drive-in than men (280,000 and 490,000), while in the south the equivalent (and larger) figures were (2,259,000 men and 1,112,000 women).[83] Britt's report on the Advertising Bureau survey identifies those in the twenty to thirty-four age band as the most frequent drive-in attenders: 38 per cent of those attending thirteen times or more between April and September 1959 were in that band, compared with 34 per cent in the ten to nineteen band.[84] However, 41 per cent of the most regular female attenders were in the ten to nineteen age band as opposed to 28 per cent in the twenty to thirty-four age band.[85] More men than women may have attended the drive-in, but the teenage drive-in audience may have been more female than male.

Overall, despite the comments of Luther and *Variety* at the beginning of the decade about drive-ins attracting an older audience, surveys indicate that in the 1950s most of the drive-in audience (and the cinema audience in general) was under thirty. The largest of the surveys indicates that more than half the cinema audience was under twenty. That applied to indoor as well as outdoor cinemas. The teenage audience was not in a majority and was not necessarily attracted to the drive-in rather than the indoor cinema, but it did make up a significant minority of the drive-in audience.

The surveys also examined other questions without providing definitive answers. While Anthony Downs wrote in 1953 of drive-ins' appeal to the 'action house' audience of 'workers who don't want to get dressed up, people who cannot afford the higher prices of first-run or second-run theaters, and balcony-minded young couples', and the argument about saving on the cost a babysitter suggested families with limited funds, Britt interpreted the findings of the 1959 Advertising Bureau survey as revealing that the drive-in audience 'generally had better jobs, higher income, more education, more children, more home ownership, more cars, more major appliances, and more conveniences'.[86] None of the surveys have anything to say on audience ethnicity.

They each leave questions and are open to different interpretations, points illustrated by looking at a much smaller-scale survey taken just after the 1950s. In 1961 Dick Wommack conducted a survey of the audience at the 71 Drive-In, Fayetteville, Arkansas, which he operated for the Commonwealth Circuit. This was not, he acknowledged, professional market research, though he added that 'the statistic instructors of the University of Arkansas did offer criticisms and suggestions which were then followed'.[87] Survey forms were given for each paid admission, with a complimentary ticket for each completed form. The questions included 'What type of movie do you like best?' (westerns were most popular), 'What do you like best about the drive-in?' ('Privacy in car' came top) and 'Which age group are you in?'[88] The answers to the latter were: 0.6 per cent, twelve to sixteen; 31.7 per cent, sixteen to twenty; 25.7 per cent, twenty to twenty-five; 19.0 per cent, twenty-five to thirty; 16.4 per cent, thirty to forty; 3.4 per cent, forty to fifty; 3.2 per cent, over fifty.[89] Of these, 60 per cent were married, and of those who were married 77 per cent had children.[90] Writing that this showed that almost 70 per cent of the drive-in patrons were over twenty years of age, Wommack described the results as 'a squelching argument to the charges of "passion pit" and "legalised parking spot" cracks'.[91]

It was nothing of the kind. The survey displays some of the same problems as other surveys, but the issue was less that some of the age bands overlapped but that those who did not pay for their admission, which meant almost everyone under sixteen, were absent from the survey. In fact, though that absence might have included some of those who were sixteen or over, what is striking about Wommack's survey seems not that almost 70 per cent of those completing the survey were twenty or older (or perhaps over twenty) but that almost a third of those who had completed the survey fell into the narrow age range between sixteen and twenty. The 71 Drive-In may not have been a literal passion pit, but at this drive-in, just after the 1950s, the best-represented adult group seemed to be the older teenager. This might have been an indication of future developments as the drive-in moved into the 1960s but also has implications for the 1950s.

Teenagers and young adults would still have been in a minority. Wommack's survey does not reveal the size of the under-sixteen audience, but we know about the importance of this audience from another article he wrote about the 71 Drive-In, later the same year. Here Wommack argued for the importance of the drive-in:

> because nowhere in the motion picture industry do you get a greater cross-section of the American population. From the young couple on their first date to the grandparents who are treating their grandchildren to a 'night out', from the family who drives a beat-up pickup to those who drive a Cadillac, all are included in the masses which are entertained at the drive-in theatre.[92]

Wommack's vision of cross-class, intergenerational drive-in entertainment was not based on the movies but on showmanship and activities such as horseshoes for dad and basketball for teenagers and the younger dads (it was a narrower vision when it came to gender). However, his main emphasis was the drive-in's 'Kids Funderland', whose attractions included a merry-go-round, a forty-foot miniature train, a miniature stagecoach and a lollipop tree, all based on 'the approach and theory of Disneyland'.[93] In establishing and promoting his Kids Funderland he was following in a tradition widespread in the previous decade just as he was following in a tradition in emphasizing the audience of over twenties in his survey even as the data itself suggested a more complex picture.

Newspapers and other documents

In 1950, Bill Beeney did a feature on Joe Fiegel and his wife, and mother of two children, for the *Rochdale Democrat and Chronicle* in New York State. He described Betty Fiegel as:

> A good-looking, trim, friendly, active young woman with an appreciation for family life and the social obligations that go with making a house a home, she is a good cook ('apple pies her speciality'), is fond of picnics, and believes that the outdoor drive-in theater is the greatest entertainment boom to people with young children since the invention of the ice cream cone.[94]

In 1951 the *New-Herald*, Marshfield, Wisconsin, carried a shorter and sadder report on another mother of two, Dolores Woodward. Woodward (age twenty) had died in the hospital to which she had been taken after an accident in which she had grasped her police officer husband's gun by its muzzle and discharged it. The coroner 'said she was trying to clear the back seat so that the two young Woodward children could sleep while the parents went to a drive-in movie'.[95]

Statistics can tell us something about the overall composition of the drive-in audience but not as individuals. Local newspapers provide a further perspective, if only in a snapshot. They can confirm images found elsewhere of the drive-in as a place to take young children but even when they do that can differ in their associations, from apple pie and ice cream to fatal gun accidents and teenage pregnancies. They point to individual stories behind the numbers.

Newspapers reported on drive-in audiences for different reasons. They reported on police warnings, police action and suspected criminal activity at or in the vicinity of drive-ins. In 1953 Sheriff Tom Reilly warned drive-ins in the Des Moines area that they would have to stop midnight shows if they could not control the teenagers who attended them, saying, 'he'd had complaints that youngsters stayed out till early morning at the midnight shows and drank beer and held petting parties in cars parked at the drive-ins'.[96] In July 1956, the *Miami Daily Herald* in Oklahoma reported on the arrest of twenty-two teenagers for rowdy behaviour at the drive-in north of Tulsa, after the teenagers had bullied their way into the drive-in without paying.[97] In July 1959, a gang dispute between the Glendale Angels and the Peoria Devils at the Rancho Drive-In, Phoenix, Arizona, led to five injured teenagers and another youth giving himself up for firing an automatic rifle from outside the cinema fence.[98]

Drive-ins featured also in allegations of crimes committed elsewhere. In 1950 the *Johnson City Press* in Tennessee reported on assault charges from a girl who said that 'two youths picked her up as she was on her way to church. They took her to a drive-in movie, then to a lonely spot', where she said one of them attacked her.[99] In 1952, sixteen-year-old John Schult of Milwaukie, Wisconsin, was apparently told by his mother that he could not use the family car. He shot and killed his ten-year-old brother, his six-year-old sister, then his mother, took the car and went with a friend to a basketball game at Pulaski High School and then to a drive-in movie.[100] Different papers reported on the murder of Phyllis Meltzer by Cary Jon Johannesson, in 1958. Meltzer (fifteen) and Johannesson (eighteen) watched *Snow White and the Seven Dwarfs* (1937) at the Sepulveda Drive-In before driving to a 'lover's lane' off Mulholland Drive in the Santa Monica Mountains. After they quarrelled, Johannesson strangled Meltzer. The following morning, he called the police, confessed to the murder and directed them to his car, which contained Meltzer's dead body.[101]

Even younger was the fourteen-year-old girl who, in 1954, shot her sixteen-year-old drive-in companion. The *Progress Index* from Petersburg, Virginia, reported, 'She said the boy handed her the pistol – a miniature gun used for firing blank cartridges – and told her to pull the trigger.'[102] She did and later said she initially thought that he was only pretending to be shot but after about half an hour went to the projection room and told attendants what had happened.[103] In 1956, the *Daily News Telegram*, Sulphur Springs, Texas, reported the death of three boys (aged thirteen, eleven and six), hit by a car when they were cycling home from a Harris County drive-in cinema.[104] The eighteen-year-old driver of the car 'wasn't injured, but suffered from shock and hysteria'.[105]

There were reports of crimes allegedly committed by older men. In December 1950, *Johnson City Press* in Tennessee reported on charges against a forty-year-old man: he was accused of visiting the home of a fifteen-year-old girl 'and on the pretence of taking her to visit a neighbour, took her instead to the State Line Drive-In Movie, where he allegedly raped her'.[106] The charge was later changed to violation of the age of consent law.[107] In February 1957, the *Miami News* reported on a man who had been charged with befriending two boys, taking them to a drive-in and assaulting them.[108]

Not all news reports on drive-ins involved attacks, accidents or assaults. Newspapers also noted the celebrations of local inhabitants, revealing glimpses of how drive-ins were woven into everyday life. In 1953 the *Watauga Democrat*, Boone, North Caroline, reported:

> Mrs Claude Gragg was honored on her birthday Sunday June 14 with a bar-b-que supper at Aunt Emma's Sandwich Shop on the By-Pass by her mother, Mrs Ella Penley . . . sliced bar-b-que potato salad, rolls, sliced tomatoes, coffee, birthday cake and ice-cream were served to Mrs Gragg and the following members of her family: Mrs Penley, Mr Fred Penley, Mrs Elise Hollars and son George, Mr Leo Brasswell, Mr and Mrs Boyd Cooke and little daughter, Annie.[109]

Following the supper, those present attended the drive-in theater in Boone, as guests of the Cookes.[110]

Such outings could be cross-generational but the new interest in the teenager meant that some papers introduced gossip columns written by and for local teenagers, in which drive-ins feature. Thus on 27 August 1950, in the 'Teen-Talk' column she had recently started for the *Orange Leader*, Claudia Poutra wrote of Gayle Jackson's guest from Delaware, Martha Jean Broyles, noting that 'Martha and Gayle went shopping to Houston, fishing at the jetties, swimming in Galveston, to the San Jacinto battleground and to the grand opening of the MacArthur Drive-in theatre', adding that 'Bonnie Watson and

Gerry Gilbeaux were at the Drive-in', while 'Patty Smith and Gayle Hogg, Geneva Pollard and Carl May Fogleman couldn't get in at the drive-in opening, so came back to a show in town'.[111] She chronicled further drive-in visits and dates from fellow Lutcher Stark High School students in subsequent columns. Entries include 'Double-dating last week were Wanda Elmore and Tim Howard, Sara Covington and Bryan Tallafferro. The foursome went to the drive-in and afterwards to Sara's home and played records and had refreshments' and a description of how to celebrate Sherry Ramsey's sixteenth birthday, 'Sherry and Garry Schultz, Claudia Poutra and Jimmy Bland, double-dated to the drive-in and afterwards the girls spent the night at Sherry's. Also at the drive-in were Billy Czeech and Wayne Seals.'[112]

Poutra's last reference to the drive-in was October 1952: it lists four couples at the drive-in as well as others at the Strand in downtown Orange.[113] In 1953 another teenager took over the column and either the MacArthur fell out of fashion as a dating venue or the new columnist had other concerns. However, similar columns in other newspapers include references to drive-in outings and dates later in the decade. 'To climax the senior weekend, Jean Gallagher had a party at her cottage on the Alleghany River, near Freeport. The teens danced, ate, threw Mary Sheehe in the river, and went to a drive-in that night', wrote Judy Frantz in 1958 in her 'Town Teen Talk' column for the Pennsylvania *Indiana Evening Gazette*.[114] The 'Teen Talk' column published in the Kansas *Salina Journal* tells of mixed but also single-sex groups at the drive-in. In August 1953, 'The girls hiked around and ate chicken. Then, to top it off, they swiped a patrol boat and went for a swim. The later evening was spent at a drive-in, after which they retired to Felten's for the night.'[115] In July the following year, Janet Falcher helped Janice Peters celebrate her birthday by presenting her 'with various gifts and by eating a mountain of food. They spent the remainder of the evening at a drive-in movie'.[116] The following week a 'special event took place in Sally Anderson's back yard. Dozens of guys and gals met there for a real feast. Chicken potato chips and cold drinks kept them occupied for some time, then after driving a few buckets of balls they headed for the drive-in movie. Some finished the evening with a quick midnight swim!'[117] Having taken over the column by April 1956, Shelley Meitler and Rosie Austin announced that 'This is good drive-in movie weather', listing those who 'gathered at Bette Smith's house to surprise her on her birthday. This accomplished, they all trooped to the drive-in.'[118] The columns I have seen were all female authored but not necessarily female centred. In August 1959, 'A crowded but enjoyable evening was spent by Keith Cushman, Herb Bassett, Mike Loop, Jerry Driscott, Breen Mitchell, Bob Murphy, Bill Carson, Danny Pinkham, Spering Kresge and Wally Sisler. The boys attended a drive-in movie.'[119]

The 'Snooper' column in another Texas paper, the *Rusk Cherokeean*, initially reported on visits to one of the two drive-ins thirty miles away in Palestine, along the lines of 'Believe Victor attended the drive-in in Palestine Sunday night. Who was with you, Victor?????'[120] It subsequently reported on visits to the Chief Drive-In when it opened, twelve and a half miles away in Jacksonville. The comments continued to be pointed, with similarities to the jokes that could appear elsewhere in 1950s newspapers: 'Bob White and his steady, Gail Bagley, were one of those couples at the Drive-in Saturday night. How was the movie???'; 'Kent Miller, Maxine Hassell and Foster Webb, Patricia Persons were seen at the Chief Drive-In Saturday night. They had quite an audience; and from all reports, the performance was very interesting'; 'The drive-in seems to be pretty popular with the younger set. Tommy Lee and Charles took it in Saturday nite. Wonder Why??'; 'Kenny and Maxine and Saudra and Ikey enjoyed the Drive-in Saturday night. I wonder if any of these could tell us what was showing???'; 'Cordelia Johnson and R.C. Hassell surely did enjoy the Drive-in Sunday night. They couldn't tell us the name of it, but we are sure they enjoyed it anyway'; 'The drive-in was really filled with Rusk couples Saturday night . . . What were you kids doing at the drive-in Saturday night? Seems as though Ann McKellar and Rayburn Britton enjoyed the movie, or was it the movie kids????'; 'Kenny Gayle is one boy that rates!!!! He got Maxine Haskell's car to take her to the drive-in Saturday night!!! I wonder if he could tell us about the movie???'; 'Since when does it take two girls to escort Leon Booker to a drive-in movie? What about this, Sue Banks, and Patricia Persons?'; 'Robert Watson and Martha Coker were at the drive-in Saturday night. Seems like they can see better from the back seat.'[121]

Accounts of the drive-in date often discuss it as taking place in the dark, at the back of the drive-in, in the hidden corners of the car. That was the picture that William Mooring, film and television editor for *Catholic Tidings*, gave in 1955 to the US Senate subcommittee investigating juvenile delinquency. He complained that Californian drive-ins had taken to booking what he described as the 'crime and violence and sex picture' but also that some drive-ins:

> not only show pictures that are calculated to provide emotional excitement for some young people, but that they condone and even to a degree encourage behaviour that obviously appeals for some police action. The general technique, as I understand it, is that an eye is blinked at certain cars which are diverted to certain parts of the amphitheatre, and the understanding young patrons take along with them is they need not be overly concerned with the entertainment quality of the picture, that there will be no police patrol passing by and no interference from the manager.[122]

Mooring's 'as I understand it' indicates speculation rather than evidence but there are other reports with a firmer basis, illustrating how for those in the car the problem could be that the drive-in's reputation was as both a private and public place. In 1946, Mae Bell Kirkwood visited an East Baton Rouge drive-in with James McFarland. Kirkwood (a minor over the age of eighteen) later testified in court that while there McFarland (also over eighteen) repeatedly tried to rape her, succeeding on the fourth attempt after he had hit her over the head and rendered her unconscious. Medical evidence backed up her story, but McFarland was acquitted at the original trial and the appeal on the grounds that the sex was consensual. One reason for this decision was that, in the words of the Appeal Judge, this took place 'in a Drive-In Theatre, with other cars parked all around her, and it would have been a simple matter for her to have stepped out of McFarland's car and advised her neighbors of what he was trying to do, or at least, to have called out for help'.[123] The public nature of the drive-in was used against Kirkwood to signify consent.

In the teen-authored columns in local newspapers the drive-in date (though also the larger group) did become a public activity. As Wini Breines argues, 'the post-war dating system in which dates were commodities that validated the individual's worth was based on display, on being seen, since unseen, one's value could not be measured'.[124] For Beth L. Bailey, 'Dating moved courtship into the public world, relocating it from family parlors and community events to restaurants, theaters and dance halls.'[125] This 'lessened parental control and gave young men and women more freedom', but it 'also shifted power from women to men . . . Dating moved courtship out of the home and into man's sphere – the world outside the home'.[126]

The drive-in date was caught up in a power struggle, across generations and genders. This is evident in another part of the newspaper in which the drive-in repeatedly featured: the advice column. Letter writers included wives dissatisfied with married life. When 'Hopeful Jill' wrote to Molly Mayfield she allowed that 'husbands do need a little time to themselves' but went on to ask, 'But what about us wives?' and complained, 'when I ask him occasionally to go to a drive-in movie, he can't go – fight on TV!'[127] 'Also Stuck at Home' got to go to the drive-in once a month, but wrote, 'I don't even get out of the car. I struggle with an 18-month old girl and try to keep two boys, 3 and 9 years old, quiet. My husband doesn't help – he sleeps through the whole show!'[128] Similarly, 'Burned-Up Wife' complained, 'When we go to a drive-in for a double-feature and take the children with us, I am busy all during the first feature wrestling with a baby and trying to get her asleep, while my husband enjoys the show.'[129] In this instance, 'Husband of Burned-Up Wife' chipped in, protesting, 'I have offered to watch the baby through the first show, but no, she says she'd rather do it – and then I get blamed for not doing it!'[130]

There were more frequent letters from or about teenagers and drive-ins. 'Each year when the weather is warm I receive many letters from teenagers and parents, too, about drive-in theaters', wrote Dorothy Ricker in another column, in response to a sixteen-year-old girl whose parents would not allow her to go to the drive-in with her seventeen-year-old date.[131] 'I am well aware that drive-ins are called "passion pits" and various other names by teen-agers', Ricker continued, adding that a 'boy or girl who is really trustworthy can be trusted equally as well at a drive-in, church party or school game'.[132]

Permission to go to the drive-in was a recurring issue. When a boy wrote to Ann Landers complaining that every time he asked his sixteen-year-old date to the drive-in, she said she had to ask her mother, Landers reply was, 'From what I have heard of the "goings-on" at drive-in movies, I think the girl's mother is no dummy.'[133] Sheila John Daly (the younger sister of Maureen Daly, editor of the *Profile of Youth* collection for *Ladies Home Journal* and author of the bestselling novel, *Seventeenth Summer* (1942)) adopted a more permissive stance. One girl wrote for advice, complaining:

> My mother doesn't like me to go to drive-in movies, yet it's one of the favorite activities of our crowd. She seems to think that no one does anything but neck at drive-in movies. She says it would harm my reputation to go. Actually, we go because the drive-ins are cheap and different. But I don't know how to convince her.[134]

'Why not talk with your mother', suggested Daly, 'letting her know that your crowd is more interested in watching Tab Hunter and Piper Laurie than in pitching a little woo yourself'.[135] 'Confused' wrote that her mother thought that 'when you go to a drive-in it's just to neck. Do you think it's because she doesn't trust me?'[136] In reply, Eleanor Hart suggested that her mother might consent to a drive-in date once she got to know the boy, and in the meantime 'The indoor movie house still offers some pretty exciting film fare'.[137]

Access to a car, and the different expectations for boys and girls when it came to driving, was another recurring issue. 'My father will never let me use the family car, even though I passed my driver's test several months ago', complained one writer to Sheila John Daly:

> He says that he doesn't think a girl should be allowed to traipse all over the country side in an automobile; he insists that things would be different if I were a boy and really needed the car for dates. But occasionally it's fun to get a group of girls together and go for a ride or to a drive-in movie; how can I make my father see my point of view?[138]

In another letter to Daly, a boy wrote, 'A drive-in movie has just opened in our town, and it's the big date activity for all the high school crowd. But I've never been able to take my girl, because I don't own a car and my father doesn't have a car.'[139] His girlfriend's father had offered to lend him his car but he'd 'hate to have people think I was dating Sue for her father's car, instead of for herself'.[140] Jane Palmer's mailbag included a letter from a girl who wrote, 'A boy I like very much has asked me to go to the drive-in movie with him – but in my car as he doesn't have one. I don't think that would be right, so I asked him if we couldn't just go to a downtown movie instead. He said he couldn't relax or talk freely in a movie theater.'[141]

Other questions were about what happened in the car. 'Disgusted' wrote to Molly Mayfield about the wonderful guy with whom she was very much in love but who, at a drive-in movie, just as she was getting cosy, 'turned on the radio to see what the score was. It wouldn't have been so bad if he had turned it off after the game was finished. But no, he listened for half an hour longer'.[142]

There were more questions about necking. 'The girls in our crowd understand that an invitation to a drive-in movie means a girl is expected to neck with her date', began one letter to Sheila John Daly.[143] 'I don't approve. If I want to kiss a boy, I'm the one who is going to decide when and where. But I don't know how to avoid it without being considered a wet blanket.'[144] A twenty-year-old wrote to the Beatrice Fairfax column about taking his date to a drive-in where 'she definitely made it clear to me that we were there to see the movie and the movie alone. Now, from a man's point of view, if you go to a drive-in and just sit, the evening is pretty dull, but then I realized that this was a girl who had pride and valued her reputation, so I admired her attitude and felt it was worth a full evening'.[145] He remained worried whether his date cared for him. A seventeen-year-old wrote to Dorothy Ricker after his drive-in date, who he had thought was a 'nice girl' began to make 'unlady-like proposals to me'.[146] 'What am I to do?' he asked; 'I like her but do not want to get seriously involved with her.'[147] In another letter, signed 'Drive-In Cats', two girls (thirteen and sixteen) wrote that they 'go to a drive-in movie on Saturday nights and we usually meet boys who ask us to sit in their cars'.[148] They wanted to know if they were right in turning them down, as doing that meant 'they don't pay any more attention to us so we always end up by ourselves'.[149]

The drive-in's reputation when it came to teenagers is clear. The extent to which it lived up to or beyond that reputation varied. Other newspaper columns occasionally told of a clash between this and other drive-in audiences. 'Have you ever noticed the necking parties at drive-in theaters?' asked columnist Ann Carroll in the *El Paso Herald Post*.[150] 'At the last one I attended with friends, the husbands in the car, bored to loud cries of "Let's go," drew attention to all in the car to a teenage couple in the next car. The shouts of laughter brought the boy up for air from a long kiss. He moved the car, no doubt to a darker, "quieter" place.'[151] Dr George W. Crane's syndicated 'Worry Clinic' column included the comments of the male partner of Alicia, a bisexual woman living with a jealous, 'masculine woman': 'If we go to a drive-in movie, this masculine female tries to park behind us and watch our behaviour; for she resents my kissing Alicia.'[152] There are limits to what newspapers from this era reveal. Writers could discuss heterosexual sex but rarely mentioned same-sex relations, and only as a pathological condition.

Memories and a diary

Another approach to historical film audiences has been to draw on the memories of those audiences through interviews or questionnaires. The fact that 'memories of cinema have revolved far more around the social act of cinemagoing than around the films they saw' fits the 1950s drive-in, conceived as it has often been as a form of cinemagoing where the films are secondary.[153] Memories of the drive-in do not even have to involve going to the cinema. One local resident remembered the illuminated waterfall that cascaded down the back of the Gratiot tower in Roseville, Detroit, long before visits to the drive-in itself.[154] My own initial encounter with the drive-in came not from going to one but from travelling across the United States by Greyhound Bus in 1980, sometimes overnight, and catching glimpses through the window of roadside screens lit up with flickering images.

Memory has been central to non-academic interest in the drive-in. This is evident in nostalgic books that combine historical overviews with old photographs and individual memories, in the entries to the Cinema Treasures website, where details of location, capacity, opening and closing dates and what a drive-in has become since closure are often accompanied by recollections from those who visited or worked at the drive-in, and in social media discussions where the mention of a drive-in can set off a stream of reminiscences.[155] Memories of the MacArthur range from the 'Remembering the MacArthur Drive-In Theatre in Orange, Texas' Facebook site to *Penny Record* columnist Nancy Manning's recollection, inspired by driving past where the drive-in used to be, of families parking in the front rows and the management patrolling the back rows where the teenagers gravitated.[156]

Discussing responses to their online survey of the 'baby boom' generation, James Russell and Jim Whalley note that for some 'the drive-in formed a primal cinema memory'.[157] Films form only one part of such memories. The first cinema memory for one respondent was going to see *Elephant Walk* (1954) at the drive-in, when 'My parents took us all hoping we would sleep in the car while they watched the movie'.[158] For another, 'Almost all my childhood family movie experiences involved drive-in movies. The main thing I remember from these is playing with other kids on the playground beneath the screen, most of us in our pajamas.'[159]

Such memories were not confined to the 1950s. 'I'm not one to look back but this has made me do so', said Brad Pitt when he was awarded Best Supporting Actor at the 2020 Academy Awards. 'And I think of my folks taking me to the drive-in to see *Butch [Cassidy] and [the] Sundance [Kid* (1969)]'.[160] The three respondents to Russell and Whalley's survey who recalled being in the back of the family station wagon on a trip to the drive-in were all (like Pitt) born in the 1960s.[161] Another, born in 1962, remembered *The Bushbaby* (1969) as the first film seen at the drive-in, while, of those born in 1969, one recalled seeing *Jaws* (1975) (adding, 'The crowd reactions were memorable'), another *Star Wars* (1977), both at the drive-in.[162] 'It was a blast when dad and mom took us to the drive in movie theater', remembered one respondent, born in 1961. 'But we always had our pillows and blankets.'[163] Another, born in the mid-1940s, mentioned going to the drive-in, but as a parent rather than a child: 'They were cheaper, we didn't have to pay a sitter, and if one of the kids got tired, they could go to sleep in the car.'[164] Such responses confirm that people continued to take their children to the drive-in in the 1960s and 1970s.

Cinema memories are not limited to childhood. In her study of British cinemagoing memories of the 1930s, Annette Kuhn noted that the men surveyed tended to offer 'memories from childhood rather than adolescence' while women had 'relatively little to say about their preadolescent cinemagoing', instead offering memories of 'growing up'.[165] However, she goes on to write that 'while the back row of the cinema and the "courting" that took place there are legendary in popular memory, romance and sex do not figure very prominently in 1930s cinemagoers' memories of their adolescence'.[166] Because they are writing about the baby boom generation who entered the teens after the 1950s it is understandable that Russell and Whalley's discussion of the 1950s drive-in emphasized childhood memories, though their survey did receive one response from a woman born in 1940 who replied that during her teen years she 'watched movies weekly, usually at a theater or drive-in, with boy friend or girl friends'.[167]

Girlfriends or boyfriends can feature in memories that go back further than adolescence. Steven Spielberg has told of how, when he was in the fifth grade, 'My father took me to a drive-in movie with a little girlfriend of mine. This girl had her head on my arm . . . Next day, my parents lectured me about being promiscuous at an early age.'[168] The crowded car features in other memories of dates at a later age. Glenna Rogers recalled rarely going on dates or to the cinema while she was at high school, but having graduated in 1953, she went to the drive-in ('because it was cheap') with girlfriends at college: she did not remember any of them having a car or how they got to the drive-in and laughed when she told her interviewer, 'I guess one person had a date and we'd all go along . . . She probably only had one date.'[169] Memories of those who would have been older in the 1950s are more difficult to locate, though discussing memories of cinemagoing in Laredo, close to the Mexican border, José Carlos Lozano noted how those questioned 'contrasted in their memories the dual and flexible bilingual preferences of English and Spanish-language films (especially in the case of women) with the almost exclusive preference for Mexican and Spanish-language films amongst their older relatives (parents and grandparents)'.[170] This was not specific to the drive-in but raises the possibility that the El Rancho on the edge of Laredo, as well as other drive-ins that showed Spanish-language films, attracted a higher proportion of older viewers.

Another source goes a little further than one-line recollections that echo, or are echoed by, popular images. Miriam Caldwell's online blog is based around the diary written by her mother, Vilma, which moves from her Catholic upbringing to her work as a 'camera girl' at Clifton's Cafeteria in downtown Los Angeles and eventual marriage.[171] Vilma's dates include different visits to the drive-in. On Thursday 3 January 1952 she wrote:

> I went out with Dick tonight and his '49 Ford Convertible to a drive-in movie and saw some crummy pictures. I don't like him anymore. Talk about being a mad lover, well he isn't it. When I go to a drive-in I like to neck & really go to town, but all he did was hug me and bore me stiff. I think he kissed me all in all three whole times and he is a bum necker anyway. He says he is going to come around on Saturday but he's living in a pipe dream if he thinks I am going to go out with him again.[172]

On Sunday 1 June she wrote of a triple date at a drive-in showing *When in Rome* (1952) 'and some other pictures', though this time she found that her date 'wasn't very cute so I didn't let him kiss me at the drive-in'.[173] She had a different experience with Bill from the San Diego Naval base. On 8 June Vilma wrote:

> Tonight Bill took me to a drive-in, but I sure didn't see much of it. He told me that he loved me tonight and he kept calling me 'darling'. I guess I got him terribly heated with French kissing him and rubbing him and all. I felt him about all over, except for the main part of course, and I sure shouldn't have done any of that. God darn I like him so much.[174]

However, when he asked her to go steady, she replied, 'NO, at this rate you'll make me in a week. You're just going farther and farther and its only two dates since we've known each other.'[175]

Vilma then went with Bill and his friend Glenn to the El Monte Drive-In on 21 June but had a row with him.[176] On Friday 18 July she wrote:

> Bill took me out tonight to a drive in movie. Boy I sure feel like breaking up, he says so many things, he'll be good, he'll be this and that and he just keeps on nevertheless. He tried his damn-dest to fool around tonight but I wouldn't let him and that is the most aggravating thing is when a guy keeps on trying to paw you and keeps on.[177]

In her more succinct entry for Tuesday 5 August, she simply wrote: 'Bill took me to a drive-in and we saw "Jumping Jacks". HATE HIM!'[178] Following her eighteenth birthday on 7 August, on Monday 25 August, she wrote: 'Bill took me to a drive-in tonight and we saw "Smoky Canyon" [1952] and "She's Working Her Way Through College" [1952]. They were pretty good.'[179]

The extent to which Vilma's experiences and attitudes are representative is unclear but they go beyond confirming the existence of necking (and French kissing) teenagers at the drive-in in the 1950s, providing insight into what that meant in terms of one young woman looking for a partner and exploring the possibilities of the drive-in date while doing her best to remain in control and, at least some of the time, watch the film.

The diverse and inclusive drive-in

That drive-in audiences consisted of dating couples as well as parents with young children fits Mary Morley Cohen's discussion of drive-ins as heterotopia, '"spaces apart" or "counter-sites" within which established social rules are mixed, inverted or contested'.[180] They brought together different audiences, and though audiences had, as Hollingshead put it in 1933, their own private box, they also provided spaces (notably the concession stand) and activities that brought those audiences together. What took place in that private box could itself be a contest, one that could lead to violence, dissatisfaction, pleasure or the establishment of boundaries. In the words of Dudley Andrew:

> many Americans were initiated sexually and alcoholically at the drive-in. But in those early years, and even today, the drive-in served other needs and desires. Some spectators relished the spectacle of cinema under the stars

and would lie on the hoods of their cars in the summer breeze, glancing up from the screen to the canopy of the Milky Way. Others, and I count myself amount these, would freely criticize the film and discuss its effects with fellow cinephiles inside the private screening room of our station wagon. One could talk at the drive-in.[181]

Cohen's argument is based on the understanding that the drive-in audience 'cut across class and social lines', drawing on 'a mixture of people from rural, urban and social locations' and those who would not normally attend the cinema, including not only teenagers and parents with children but also people with disabilities.[182] Noting that the overwhelming majority of journalistic articles she came across 'talk about drive-in theatres as special sites of mixing', she cites RCA employee Charles R. Underhill's account of how:

To the amazement of even the drive-in theater owners, in came a type of patronage rarely seen even at indoor theaters; the physically handicapped, invalids, convalescents, the aged, deaf people, expectant mothers, parents with infants and small children – whole families, dressed as they pleased in the privacy and comfort of their own domain on wheels. They are continuing to come in increasing numbers from rural, suburban and city areas – a new clientele representing a long neglected but highly important segment of some 30,000,000 people of the 'Forgotten Audience'.[183]

Underhill delivered his comments at a Society of Motion Picture Theater Engineers (SMPTE) meeting in June 1949 and published them in the SMPTE journal in February 1950. At first sight he seems to be discussing post-war developments, though in his paper he refers to how 'Experience gained previous to the war pointed the way to successful drive-in theater construction, equipment and management'.[184] In fact, very similar words were used in an earlier RCA booklet published during the war, commenting on how:

Contrary to what many anticipated when the first drive-in theatres were opened . . . the drive-in audience was made up largely of a clientele which had not been in the habit of attending the motion picture theatre in the past. This clientele included mothers with small children; laborers and factory workers who, coming from a hard day's work in old clothes, did not want to go to the bother of dressing but wanted to relax in the open air; stout people who found the average theatre chairs uncomfortable; elderly people; people in ill-health; cripples and other shut-ins. It was found that the drive-in theatre also appealed to many young people who had not been in the habit of going to the movies in the past.[185]

This suggests that Underhill's account was less an observation of post-war developments than a modified restatement of what was supposed to have been the situation in the 1930s. Despite the 'contrary to what many anticipated' in the wartime booklet, these comments in effect restate the comments that Richard Hollingshead made, just before he opened his drive-in in 1933, about welcoming the whole family, including parents and children, the aged and the infirm.

Was the image of the drive-in as an inclusive space, welcoming the film industry's 'forgotten audience', more than an image? Was it simply a way of promoting the drive-in and suggesting that it was not a threat to the film industry because it appealed to people who would not normally go to indoor cinemas? Cohen notes that, while drive-in cinemas actively solicited the obese and people with disabilities, 'it is not clear to what extent this potential audience actually attended'.[186] Contemporary surveys asked questions about age, marital status, gender and economic status but not about disabilities.

There is a logic to at least some of the claims made for the drive-in attracting a more diverse audience. The 1973 Rehabilitation Act extended civil rights to people with disabilities. The 1990 Disabilities Act subsequently made provision of facilities for people with disabilities into a statutory obligation for places of public accommodation. Before these dates, cinemas were under no obligation to make any provision for disabilities and it is difficult to find evidence that they did. In this context, the drive-in was a potential improvement. Someone who had to use a wheelchair did not, if they visited a drive-in, have to negotiate steps or stairs. The drive-in audience did not have to fit into the seats provided by the cinema. Drive-ins equipped with individual speakers with volume control were a potential boon to the hard of hearing, while a companion accompanying a deaf or blind person to the drive-in could provide an individual audio description without disturbing those watching the film in other cars.

When interviewed in 1965, Hollingshead spoke of one man who came nearly every week to the drive-in from Elizabeth (more than eighty miles away): he had, Hollingshead said, never seen a movie before, his disability having prevented him from visiting indoor cinemas.[187] Other evidence that I have seen from the 1950s is similarly limited to individual people or cinemas. 'Television and the drive-in movie have widened the scope of interests she may enjoy', reported the *Suffolk News Herald* on one polio victim in 1951.[188] In 1952, in a feature on a man paralysed following an accident, one newspaper noted that friends would stop by and take him to a drive-in movie, while another reported on a boy who had been trying out his crutches, 'and they have already been able to take in a drive-in movie'.[189]

In 1945 the president of Park-In Theatres wrote that the drive-in audience consisted largely of those who had not been in the habit of going to the cinema, including

> mothers with small children (about 80 per cent); labourers and factory workers who, coming from a hard day's work in old clothes, did not want to go to the bother of dressing but wanted to relax in the open air; stout people who found the average theatres chair uncomfortable; elderly people; people in ill-health; cripples and other shut-ins.[190]

Similarly, in August 1948 *Boxoffice* reported, 'Shuts-ins, family groups and many people who do not want to go to the trouble of dressing and of parking their cars have been big factors in current drive-in development.'[191] The advertisement for the opening of the MacArthur in 1950 entreated readers of the *Orange Leader* to 'BRING THE SHUT-INS, THE OLD FOLKS, THE YOUNG FOLKS AND THE BABIES!'[192]

References to 'shut-ins' at drive-in film performances mainly predate the 1950s. In Detroit in 1938, Alden Smith invited 'Shut-ins who are unable to attend ordinary theatres' on specific guest nights.[193] Similarly, in 1942 Carl Zack 'announced a series of guest nights for shut-ins and under-privileged children' at his Indianapolis drive-in, and in 1948 'Bernard Dudgeon, West Dodge Drive-In manager, was host to fifty "shut-ins"' in Omaha, Nebraska.[194] In the 1950s there were also trade press reports of 'shut-ins' at the drive-in, but these tended to be at Sunday morning church services at the drive-in (a change of venue adopted by a number of churches). For instance, in 1952 *Motion Picture Herald* reported on Billy Graham's service at the Trail Drive-In, Houston, 'for the benefit of the sick and the infirm', promoted by the Trail's manager 'for the aged and shut-ins who couldn't battle the crowds or make their way to regular theatre seats'.[195]

In the 1920s, notes Bill Kirkpatrick, the catch-all term 'shut-ins' was widely used 'to refer to those who by illness or injury were consigned to a life of hospitalization or home-bound infirmity' but who could be reached and restored by the new technology of radio.[196] The discourse of the shut-in was more generally important for three reasons. The shut-in was 'the perfect passive listener justifying one-to-many broadcasting' at a time when radio was discarding its association with amateurs who had used it as a two-way medium.[197] The shut-ins' 'need for radio entertainment helped allay concerns about mass consumer culture by assuring observers and policymakers that even the often frivolous (as critics saw it) content of radio could serve a noble social purpose'.[198] Third, invocations of the shut-in were most often connected to support for a particular (and particularly contentious) form of radio: high-powered, professional, commercial broadcasting . . . Thus, the promise of re-abling persons with disabilities through radio, although physically exclusionary, was also culturally inclusionary, contributing in a small but important way to the ongoing process of imagining persons with disabilities as full cultural citizens.[199]

Kirkpatrick's account concerns a different time and a different technology. He argues that 'by the 1930s, the discourse of the shut-in had all but died out'.[200] While radio could be presented as bringing the world to a bed-bound or home-bound listener, cinema was a place audiences had to go to even if they might be metaphorically transported once they were there. In post-war America, television could seem the technology closer to radio in that its programmes were received at home and in the way it connected audiences to a national network. It is clear, however, that traces of the language of the 'shut-in' lingered on in the 1930s, the 1940s and the 1950s: in 1958 the Family Drive-In in Jasper, Indiana, still advertised itself as offering 'convenient recreation for shut-ins'.[201]

In part these images of bringing shut-ins to the drive-in, along with the emphasis on the drive-in as a place where parents could take the baby, served to promote the drive-ins as something other than a passion pit. Thus, using a different vocabulary but making a similar point, in 1952 *Motion Picture Herald* reported:

> In a series of 'good-will' promotions aimed to win new patrons, Ray Crane of the Cranston Auto theatre, installed 'bottle warmers' so parents of infants could dispense with baby-sitting, appealed to the hard-of-hearing by emphasising the advantages of individual speakers in cars, and 'sold' the aged and infirm on the idea that they, too could attend the movies, in the comfort and privacy of automobiles. All these gestures have had a good effect on boxoffice figures.[202]

They may have done more than that and through those individual speakers have given members of the audience a degree of control that they had not had before. The extent to which this was the case is difficult to calculate.

The segregated, excluding or welcoming drive-in

Another claim was that drive-ins were more ethnically diverse than indoor cinemas. In August 1949 *Variety* reported, 'In many sections of the South where segregation in regular houses is strictly enforced, the rule is not applied to ozoners. Because of this, Negroes flock to the open-air theatres which are attractive de-luxe affairs compared to the second-rate flickeries generally available to them.'[203] The following year, listing the advantages of the drive-in, Rodney Luther wrote that most 'practice non-segregation'.[204] Cohen, while sceptical about the claim that African Americans flocked to drive-ins, writes, 'Because the private space of one's car already segregated audience members from one another, many drive-ins over-looked Jim Crow laws. Articles on the Southern drive-ins suggest that they were completely desegregated.'[205] Thomas Doherty, however, writes, 'Jim Crow soon closed the loophole. By the end of the decade, drive-ins in the Deep South were as segregated as the hardtops and no less vehement about staying that way.'[206]

Doherty is correct to point to the extent to which discrimination could be practised at outdoor as well as indoor cinemas: as late as 1963, a policeman told Vivian Malone, one of the first black students to enrol at the University of Alabama, that it was unlawful in Alabama for her to attend a 'white drive-in'.[207] However, the issue was not state legislation. Legislation prescribed segregation for educational institutions and means of transport in a number of states, but as Pauli Murray noted in 1950, 'Few southern states have legislated extensively with reference to segregation in amusements.'[208] Virginia was alone in requiring segregation in the form of separate seating in 'any public hall, theatre, opera house, motion picture show or any place of public entertainment or public assemblage'.[209] Other states had legislation requiring segregation of billiard halls and pool rooms (Georgia and South Carolina), public parks (Missouri and South Carolina), fishing, boating and bathing (Oklahoma), racetracks (Arkansas) and circus and tent shows (Louisiana).[210] The only other states with legislation related to segregation at the cinema were those such as New Jersey, which had a law *against* discrimination in 'any auditorium, meeting place or public hall, any theatre, or other place of public amusement, motion picture house, music hall'.[211]

The point is not that segregation did not exist, since it clearly did, but that, as Murray noted, it was 'generally achieved through local ordinances or through custom'.[212] Her *States' Laws on Race and Color* also listed selected city ordinances, including the Birmingham, Alabama, ordinance that required separate entrances and seating or standing areas for 'every room, hall, theatre, picture house, auditorium, yard, court, ball park, or other indoor or outdoor place'.[213] However, if this points to the limits of Jim Crow legislation what that tells us is that cinemas did not segregate or exclude audiences because that was a legal requirement but because the law allowed it. They did so because they could, chose to do so or because of the consequences of not doing so: in 1958 the *Charlotte Observer* reported that a list of bombings in Charlotte, North Carolina, 'included the bombing of a marquee at a drive-in movie used by both Negroes and whites'.[214]

It is difficult to provide a clear overall picture of the extent to which African Americans had access to drive-ins in the 1950s or of the nature of that access. One means of access existed through the 'negro theatres' that catered specifically for an African American audience and which grew in numbers up to the 1940s, and in the 1950s in the case of drive-ins. In 1949 *Variety* referred to the imminent opening of the Skyline in Compton, Los Angeles, 'an all-colored autotheatre, believed to be the first in the U.S.'.[215] Of the 953 such cinemas identified in the *Film Daily Year Book* on 1 January 1950, only five are identified as drive-ins: the 80, Tuskegee, Alabama; the Alamo, San Antonio, Texas; the Broadway Open-Air, Richmond, Virginia; the Brookdale, Charlotte, North Carolina; and the Sky View, Jacksonville, Florida.[216] The 1952 *Film Daily Year Book* lists a further nine, the 1953 edition a further ten.[217] There were others but local newspapers did not tend to list their programmes or even mention them. Cinemas catering to a Spanish-speaking audience had a more visible presence. Restrictions on attendance also tended to be implicit rather than explicit. As Robert Allen put it when discussing early twentieth-century indoor cinemas in North Carolina: 'the Jim Crow's segregation was so deeply embedded in these communities that its explicit articulation – in discourse – was not necessary'.[218] The point still held for mid-twentieth-century outdoor cinemas.

Some drive-ins segregated audiences, providing a separate entrance and a separate parking area equivalent to the segregated balcony at indoor cinemas. In North Carolina, as well as the Hi-Way 17 (discussed in the previous chapter), the Tower Drive-In outside Raleigh was segregated: in 1956 it advertised in the African American newspaper, the *Carolinian*, that it had become 'the only drive in theatre in the Raleigh area with accommodations for coloreds'.[219] A report next to the advertisement advised that 'Colored patrons should enter the theater from the Stewart's Lake Road, just east of the movie grounds, and turn left where they will find the ticket box. Pop corn, candy and cigarettes will be available for race patrons.'[220] The implication is clear: in this region, most drive-ins (up to this date, all local drive-ins) did not segregate black audiences, they excluded them. Segregation could mean divisions within a drive-in, or it could mean divisions between drive-ins. Thus, when another North Carolina drive-in reopened on 11 April 1952 as the Mid-Way Drive-In it announced itself as 'Winston-Salem's newest "White" Family Drive-In Theatre'.[221] The explicit identification of a drive-in as 'white' was unusual. It is probably explained by the fact that when it had first opened on 22 March 1951 as the Park-Vue it had served a black audience.[222]

The situation varied between states but also within states, into the 1960s. In 1961 the Kentucky Commission on Human Rights reported that, of the 87 out of 106 drive-ins that replied to its questionnaire, 26 did not admit African Americans and 61 did, with 11 of the latter reporting 'some segregation of facilities' or limited parking areas and most desegregated drive-ins saying that their policy dated back to their opening.[223] The discrimination was more prevalent in Western Kentucky than Eastern Kentucky.[224] In North Carolina, the Flamingo and the Winston-Salem drive-ins held out against desegregation into the 1960s. Reporting on a 'park-in' campaign in which protestors drove their cars up to the cashier's window knowing they would be refused admission, in 1962 the *Exhibitor* noted that no drive-in the city of Winston-Salem or Forsyth County admitted African Americans, 'although one in nearby Walnut Cove and another in Pilot Mountain, also close by, admit Negro patrons on an unsegregated basis'.[225] The following year an article on an agreement to desegregate the Winston-Salem drive-in noted the lack of a start date for this process and that one drive-in that was admitting African Americans did so 'with a suggestion that they remain in their automobiles to avoid any possible unpleasantness during the interim period'.[226]

As Douglas Gomery has noted of cinemas in general, where segregation was illegal, de facto segregation by neighbourhood could continue, in the north as well as the south. Examples of more explicit segregation varied.[227] The Bellwood, Richmond, Virginia, had different entrances, rest rooms, concessions and parking areas and a wall dividing the back of the drive-in.[228] The owners of the Martin Theatre in Thompson, Georgia, also ran the local Melody Drive-In: indoor and outdoor cinemas 'catered for both white and colored, with a 25c tilt for admission prices for the white adults' (perhaps indicating different levels of facilities for the two sections).[229] The Brooksville Drive-In, Florida, had 'a back addition for Negroes' while the Stock Auto-Torium outside Williamsburg, Virginia, had separate entrances and restrooms but parking lots that were next to each other (rather than one behind the other) and a snack bar that served both black and white customers from opposite ends, 'BUT . . . we all went to the same concession stand. And we could hear them, and they could hear us', recollected Doris Crump Rainey, one of the drive-in's black customers.[230]

Interracial mixing at the drive-in could be treated with alarm. In 1959, Sergeant George Agard, based at Hunter Airforce Base in Georgia, went with Norma K. Rikeman to a bar and then to what the *Indiana Evening Gazette* in Pennsylvania described as a local 'white drive-in theater'.[231] Agard was fined $100 for being in the company of a white woman. The newspaper reported that he 'appeared white but police testified Friday that his driver's license listed him as a Negro'.[232] Rikeman's attorney argued that Georgia attorney general had recently ruled that 'it was not contrary to state law for a white person to be associated with a Negro in a public place', to which County Police Court Judge Lawrence J. Dwyer apparently replied, 'I'm overruling you and I'm overruling the attorney general.'[233]

The case was another example of an explicit reference to a 'white drive-in'. It points to the absence of legislation as much to its presence. As a report on the south from outside the south it implies a difference of practice, and in quoting a County Police Court Judge saying he was overruling his attorney general it looks towards the desegregation that was to follow. It also indicates a continued enforcement of racial separation and exclusion at the end of the 1950s, at the drive-in as elsewhere, and thus the limits to drive-in diversity.

There are other accounts of different experiences that lend some support to claims that drive-ins could allow a more diverse audience than indoor cinemas. A 1955 report on desegregation in Missouri noted that cinemas had been slow to change from a policy of exclusion or segregation but that 'Drive-in theaters have always welcomed the patronage of all citizens'.[234] Looking back to his experience as a black migrant farm worker in the 1950s and 1960s, Bill Maxwell recalled rarely being 'welcomed in the indoor theatres. But the drive-ins were different. Each Saturday or Sunday night, no matter where we were – Hastings, Fla., Raleigh, N.C., Exmore, Va., Dover, Del., Long Island, N.Y. – we found a Sunset or a Starlite or a Sky-Vue or some other named drive-in'.[235] For Maxwell, 'the cherry Cokes, the hot dogs and burgers, the candy bars, the popcorn and other treats made us feel as if we were part of the human race after all', and the concession stand 'gave us our one real opportunity to mingle with the local residents'.[236]

A mixed but divided audience

Discussion of the drive-in audience in the 1950s has often focused on whether this was primarily a teenage or a family audience. Throughout its history, emphasis on the drive-in as a place where parents took babies and young children has challenged the image of the drive-in as a shady location for youthful romance or sex. While the association between drive-ins and wayward teenagers was difficult to shake off, exhibitors and commentators pointed to the reasons why drive-ins appealed to families and to surveys that supported this. That argument is itself supported by the near ubiquity of the drive-in playground and memories of family, drive-in outings. That drive-ins were popular with families in the 1950s is undeniable. However, simply to replace one image with another oversimplifies and overlooks sections of the drive-in audience.

There were other audiences. The 1957 PAM survey indicated that less adult-only groups went to drive-ins than to indoor cinemas, but that even at the drive-in that audience accounted for 34 per cent of the total, the same proportion as adult-child groups and slightly more than teenager-only groups. It is important not to overstate the size of the teenage audience, but Segrave's insistence that in the 1950s 'Teens were a small minority' downplays the increasing importance of the teenage market in an era when, according to the PAM survey, those between fifteen and nineteen accounted for 7 per cent of the population but 21 per cent of overall cinema admissions.[237] It also overlooks married couples who went to the drive-in without accompanying children and other adult groups. It is understandable that the latter drive-in audience received less attention in the 1950s, given that it was slightly less evident at the drive-in than at indoor cinemas (though the PAM survey identified a bigger gap for adults who went to the cinema on their own, which accounted for 15 per cent of indoor audience but registered as zero for drive-ins). It is also unclear who belonged to the adult-only group audience, beyond the PAM calculation that husband and wife only groups accounted for 12 per cent of the total and the remainder included all adults who said they went with a date, friend, acquaintance or relative, as well as husbands and wives who went with other couples. Some of these will have been only slightly older than the older teenagers who attended in groups of two or more. Some will have belonged to that forgotten audience who did not or could not go to indoor cinemas. Some will have been no different from other cinema audiences, given that drive-ins tended to show the same films as other cinemas. Of course, the PAM statistics are not definitive, but they are likely to be more representative than the percentages volunteered by individual drive-in operators.

Establishing the relative percentages of adults, teenagers and children is not the only issue. Treating the teenage drive-in audience as a single entity is itself an oversimplification. The 'teenage' label is problematic in this context. It combines junior high school students with those who had graduated from high school while missing those at the young end of the twenties (the 'young adults' who, in the words of Roger Corman, were, along with teenagers, the intended audience of AIP double bills).[238] It is divided by the age which in most states was the minimum driving age (sixteen), though when *Ladies Home Journal* looked at the American teenager it suggested that 'the majority of boys learn to drive around twelve or thirteen'.[239] Teenagers were, of course, different in other ways, including gender, ethnicity and class. They did not all have access to a car. When teenagers went to the drive-in it was not necessarily on a date and often in groups of more than two. Dates themselves took different forms and different levels of seriousness. They did not necessarily preclude watching the movie: on a date with Bill, Vilma was still able to appreciate the Durango Kid western, *Smoky Canyon*, and the relationship between

Virginia Mayo's burlesque dancer and Ronald Reagan's college professor in the musical *She's Working Her Way Through College*.

The date itself existed as a set of changing public conventions and codes of conduct. While the 1959–60 handbook of the Mary Washington College decreed that 'The Drive-In Theater in Fredericksburg is out-of-bounds for a student *with* her date', in the 1960–1 edition this was changed to 'The Drive-In Theatre in Fredericksburg is out-of-bounds for a student *without* a date'.[240] The young woman at a drive-in without a date could be seen as more of a problem than the woman with a date. The date was also a more private and personal struggle over the limits of sexual exploration. It was not a hidden aspects of 1950s America, though public discussion ranged from moral prescription to joking inuendo. What remains largely hidden is the difference between what people published and what people did.

In examining the 1950s drive-in audience I have inevitably relied mainly on published sources. These can give different perspectives and within limits could allow for different voices. Individual, personal experiences are largely unrecorded. My account also leaves significant broader gaps. The extent to which the drive-in audience included people with disabilities remains unclear. One survey indicated that the drive-in audience tended to have a higher-than-average income, others indicated the opposite: overall the emphasis on the drive-in as low-cost entertainment suggests it appealed to those with limited means, though that could include teenagers in general. In this and other ways, the picture will have varied between cinemas. Drive-in audiences, like drive-ins, were not homogenous, though the extent to which different audiences interacted at the drive-in is difficult to judge. Luther's second drive-in survey indicated how audiences could differ between surveys, on different days of the week and between the early and the late show.

In his historical directory of African American cinema buildings, Eric Ledell Smith notes the existence of African American drive-ins in the South, only to say that 'Virtually nothing is known about these theaters except that they existed. African American film books have no information on them, and recent scholarship on drive-ins is likewise silent.'[241] Some historians have subsequently looked at segregation at the drive-in (we do know that the architecture of some drive-ins was designed to prevent mixing), but the African American drive-in experience remains largely unexplored. Drive-ins catering to Hispanic audiences were more widespread and more visible but remain a subject for further research.

While commentary on the drive-in, scholarly or otherwise, has acknowledged that people did not only go there for the movies, there is room to go further in examining the place of the drive-in in people's lives. The drive-in could be entertainment, education or struggle. While not an issue for many, even getting to the drive-in could be a battle. For some black audiences, access to the drive-in was restricted or allowed only on a segregated basis. Younger audiences had to deal with parental concerns, social norms, economic practicalities as well as the behaviour of others in the car. The relative privacy of the drive-in was part of its appeal but brought its own challenges. The drive-in was also part of a pattern of recreation and socialization. Questions about the drive-in audience are not just questions about the size of different audiences but also about the meaning of the experience.

4

Pictures

In *Adam at Six A.M.* (1970), Adam Gaines (Michael Douglas), newly qualified Assistant Professor of Semantics, takes his bright red Porsche and leaves his California university, well-to-do family and seemingly active but unfulfilling sex life to go to the funeral of his great-aunt in rural Missouri. At the reception following the funeral, Mrs Hopper (Louise Latham) introduces him to her daughter, Jerri-Jo (Lee Purcell). Adam takes Jerri-Jo to the local drive-in. He is out of place and blatantly starred at, and when he meets Mrs Hopper the next day he tells her he is 'not too high on drive-in movies'. 'Well, good for you', she replies. 'I'm so glad to hear it. To sit in uncomfortable cars with all those rowdy people.' Next time they go on a date, she tells him, she will take him and Jerri-Jo 'to a nice theatre in Kansas City'.

Drive-ins had (in some instances have) a location, a programme and an audience. They also had a reputation, a place in the hierarchy of taste, and existed and exist in the imagination and as places presented and represented on film, in visual images, words and stories, as well as in a wider historical and cultural context. The distinction that Mrs Hopper explicitly makes between the 'rowdy people' at the drive-in and the 'nice theatre in Kansas City', and that Adam implicitly makes between himself and the drive-in, belonged to a wider set of distinctions evident and addressed in the film about him.

The film makes this explicit in a confrontation Adam has with another guest at the funeral reception (Dana Elcar), who asks the young Californian academic to explain what he does, to explain semantics. Adam says that it is the study of meanings . . . meanings of words . . . how meanings change. When the other man insists that 'Words are what they are', Adam counters that 'What means one thing to one person may not mean the same to the person he is talking to'. 'Meanings, huh', shrugs the other guest. 'Well maybe you could just set this man's mind right then and tell me what in the hell is the meaning of those depressing and pervert-type movies that you people make out in California?' The conversation becomes an argument about film taste. The film's initial scenes in California have already established Adam as a cinephile, with a copy of *Agee on Film* by his bed, a W. C. Fields poster on his wall and *The Maltese Falcon* (1941) playing on the television. Asked what films he likes he replies all kinds of films but when pressed singles out Michelangelo Antonioni's *Blow-Up* (1967). 'Oh my God', exclaims the other man, who likes musicals and Julie Andrews and tells Adam that he demanded his money back when he and he and his wife accidently saw *Blow-Up* in Kansas City. Illustrating the point that what means one thing to one person may not mean the same thing to another, he complains: 'how in the hell was I supposed to tell from that title that that wasn't an action war movie'.

The *New York Times* reviewer Vincent Canby accused *Adam at Six A.M.* of being 'a movie full of mid-cult opinions about the vacuity of mid-cult American life', in the way in which it 'knows – and assumes that we agree – that anyone who likes Antonioni must be alright, and that anyone who likes Julie Andrews must be a card-carrying, right-wing, war-mongering, all-American jerk'.[1] Canby was himself later accused of condescension in describing the audience for films such as *Smokey and the Bandit* (1977) as people 'who see most of their movies in drive-ins and respond (I suspect) to the non-stop action (which is often just movement), to the colorful, heightened vulgarity of the language and who feel most at home in the country movie's principal setting: the automobile'.[2] For Derek Nystrom, this highlighted 'the critics' notion that this other spectator is a considerably less sophisticated one'.[3] Or, as David Church (quoting Nystrom) put it, urban film critics assumed that the drive-in audience for 'redneck movies' 'were viscerally moved by vulgar exploitation elements to the extent that their working-class bodies became threateningly unmanageable'.[4]

The drive-in in *Adam at Six A.M.* fits awkwardly in these different oppositions. The Andrews or Antonioni choice is more relevant to that nice theatre in Kansas City, but the drive-in is not showing vulgar exploitation but a double bill that ends with Steve McQueen in *The Reivers* (1969). That can partly be accounted for by the fact that McQueen's Solar Productions produced *Adam at Six A.M.* but it is also true to the drive-in programming of the time which was often devoted to the recent Hollywood studio releases.[5]

Fiction films function as documentaries on their time as well as providing a particular perspective. The New Hollywood trend to which *Adam at Six A.M.* belonged was notable not only for going out on location, producing road movies that showed aspects of America previously rarely seen on American screens, but also for an ambivalent attitude towards popular culture. That is evident in Adam Gaines' journey back to his Missouri roots, the way his encounter with the small-town respectability of Mrs Hopper and her daughter as well as 'those rowdy people at the drive-in' is mixed with

FIGURE 11 *The drive-in as part of 'ugly town' in* Targets *(dir. Peter Bogdanovich, Saticoy Productions/Paramount Pictures, 1968).*

consciousness that he does not fit in either world. Other New Hollywood films recorded the contemporary drive-in in ways that were ambivalent or unsympathetic.

Released a year before *Adam at Six A.M.* (to much greater acclaim and box-office success), *Midnight Cowboy* (1969) opens with a reverse zoom that reveals the blank screen of the Big Tex Drive-In in Big Springs, Texas, seen in daylight, deserted except for a few horses and a lone child on a rocking horse, suggesting a sign of the emptiness of the New West. A year earlier, *Targets* (1968) emphasized the negative connotations of the drive-in through the meeting of its two narrative strands. In one strand, Bobby Thompson (Tim O'Kelly) goes on a shooting spree after murdering his wife and parents which eventually takes him to the Los Angeles-area Reseda Drive-In. In the other, ageing and disillusioned horror star Byron Orlok (Boris Karloff) reluctantly agrees to make a personal appearance at the same drive-in (Figure 11). 'God what an ugly town this has become', says Orlok as he approaches the Reseda, and his view is confirmed when, on arrival, he is dismayed not to hear any response from the audience. With the public sealed off in their cars, the negative view of the drive-in is established even before it becomes clear that it is a death trap. The film's director, Peter Bogdanovich, spelt this out in his comments on the film. He told Paul McClusky:

> I hate the whole idea of seeing a movie in a drive-in. That's almost as alienating as seeing it on television. You're closed off in a car, with a

horrible screen you can't see very well. Awful sound in that tinny little speaker. Sitting with two other people. It's as bad as being at home with television. It's true that you go out, but you never have to get out of your car. Horrible.[6]

The words come from someone known for his love of American cinema and who achieved much greater commercial and critical success with his next film, *The Last Picture Show* (1971), a film that looks back with nostalgia to the 1950s and to the cinema building itself, and the experience of going out but inside to see a film as part of a disappearing communal tradition.

The hint of a more nostalgic view of the 1950s drive-in is already evident in *The Happy Ending* (1969). The film begins with Mary (Jean Simmons) and Fred (John Forsyth) on a date, driving past an indoor downtown cinema showing *From Here to Eternity* to a drive-in showing Linda Darnell, Tab Hunter and Donald Gray in *Island of Desire* (1952), followed by a newsreel report on the coronation of Elizabeth II. The opening to the otherwise downbeat *The Happy Ending* belongs to a brief, happy prologue, before the film jumps forward to 1969 and the disintegration of the couple's marriage.

As indicated at the beginning of this book, the drive-in brought with it a cluster of connotations. At the risk of sounding like Adam Gaines (an all but forgotten, New Hollywood motiveless hero who seems unconvinced by his own academic discipline), this chapter uses film, lyrics, literature and still images to explore what the drive-in has meant and how its meaning has changed and varied in different media, from New Hollywood ambivalence about the drive-in as a sign of the contemporary American roadside to different forms of nostalgia. The connotations of the drive-in could be negative but even within the confines of New Hollywood representation varied and changed. *Targets* is built around a screening of *The Terror* at the Reseda, and *Hollywood Boulevard* (1976) uses the same film-within-the-film to different effect in a scene set at a drive-in with the emphasis on affectionate, knowingly broad comedy rather than horror or commentary. Bogdanovich himself had mellowed by the time he made *The Thing Called Love* (1993), which features a more romantic scene at a Nashville drive-in showing John Ford's *The Man Who Shot Liberty Valance* (1962). As Church notes, drive-ins occasionally appear in exploitation films (including *Targets* and *Hollywood Boulevard*).[7] They also appear in Disney films such as *That Darn Cat!* (1965) and *Herbie Rides Again* (1974), documentaries including *The Hellstrom Chronicle* (1971) and *The Thin Blue Line* (1988) and hardcore pornography (*Passion Pit* (1985)). Drive-ins have been evoked in song, in novels written for adults and children and in innumerable photographs of couples at the drive-in or abandoned drive-ins.

The drive-in on screen

Near the beginning of *White Heat* (1949), Cody Jarrett (James Cagney), his wife Verna (Virginia Mayo) and his mother (Margaret Witcherley) escape from the law by turning off into the San-Val Drive-In, Burbank, California. There are smart, uniformed attendants, at the box office, selling popcorn and attaching speakers to cars. Allowing for studio self-promotion (*Task Force* (1949), another Warner Bros. film, is playing on the screen), plot and character exposition (at the drive-in it is possible to shut off the sound of the film and talk), the scene in *White Heat* was also a sign that Hollywood was moving out of the studio to show the modern cityscape, here illustrated through the drive-in.

White Heat was the first Hollywood feature to feature a drive-in cinema. While the number of drive-ins grew rapidly in the 1950s, they only occasionally appeared in 1950s films. For all the extensive press attention paid to couples taking the baby to the drive-in, *The First Time* (1952) is an isolated example showing Joe (Robert Cummings) watching a cartoon on the drive-in screen while his wife Betsy (Barbara Hale) struggles with their crying baby in the back before she manages a brief look and laugh at the screen. *He's a Cockeyed Wonder* (1950) introduces the drive-in date when Freddie (Mickey Rooney) hides in the car boot (another recurring feature of drive-in memories) when his rival Ralph (Ross Ford) takes Judy (Terri Moore) to the drive-in. It was the first of several films to use Burbank's Pickwick Drive-In and one of a small group of 1950s films that used Los Angeles-area drive-ins. In *The Marrying Kind* (1952) the exterior of Inglewood's Century Drive-In stands in for the Long Island drive-in where Florence (Judy Holliday) and Chet (Aldo Ray) join their friends on a double date, before the narrative moves on to dwell on their subsequent marital problems. *Crime of Passion* (1956) is set in suburban Los Angeles, and the tower of Culver City's Studio Drive-In looms in the background in brief scenes, a faintly disturbing sign of the changing landscape to which the characters in the film never refer. In *Attack of the Puppet People* (directed by Bert I. Gordon for AIP in 1958), Bob Westley (John Agar) and Sally Reynolds (June Kenney) go on a drive-in date to watch Bert I. Gordon's 1957 AIP film, *The Amazing Colossal Man* (1957). Adult extramarital drive-in dates feature in two films released in 1960. In adapting John O'Hara 1958 novel, *From the Terrace*, 20th Century Fox inserted a scene in which David Eaton (Paul Newman) meets Natalie Benzinger (Ina Balin) at the drive-in outside town. 'We're the only two people watching the movie', he quips, before he and Natalie stop watching the movie. The mid-life affair between Larry Gilbert (Bob Hope) and Kitty Weaver (Lucille Ball) in *The Facts of Life*, and their assignation at a drive-in, comes from their boredom after years of married life.

FIGURE 12 *Teenage delinquents at the drive-in in* The Delinquents *(dir. Robert Altman, Imperial Productions/United Artists, 1957).*

The emphasis in these films is on post-teenage relationships but two independently produced films from this period link teenage misbehaviour to the drive-in.[8] Near the beginning of Robert Altman's debut, *The Delinquents* (1957), a young delinquent group cause mayhem at a drive-in in Kansas City, Missouri (Figure 12). The frosty trade press reception given to *The Delinquents* provides one explanation for the rarity of such a film scene: one reviewer complained that 'a sequence in a drive-in theatre that is obviously managed extremely poorly can do the industry much harm', another that the sequence was 'reprehensible' and 'should be resented by every theatre owner'.[9] The drive-in plays a more substantial role in *Too Soon to Love* (1960), a low-budget teenage pregnancy melodrama directed by Richard Rush, and part written by Francis Ford Coppola, that Universal picked up for distribution. In the film, shown in Britain as *Teenage Lovers*, high school student Jim Mills (Richard Evans) works at the drive-in concession stand, where he meets up with his girlfriend Cathy Taylor (Jennifer West) and where Cathy has to fend off the back seat advances of Buddy (Jack Nicholson), leading to a drive-in fight between Jim and Buddy. The drive-in in *Too Soon to Love* is a teen-dominated place, introduced by Cathy's female friend with a paracinematic, 'Back at the passion pit. Ain't it awful.'[10]

The drive-in in exploitation filmmaker Jerry Gross's *Teenage Mother* (1967) is showing Gross's *Girl on a Chain Gang* (1966). However, in the 1960s and early 1970s the association between drive-ins and sex was not limited to the exploitation film. In 20th Century Fox's *Our Man Flint* (1966) the female 'playmates' of special agent Derek Flint (James Coburn) are taken to the headquarters of GALAXY, where they are conditioned to serve as 'Pleasure Units', until Flint rescues them, from go-go dancing, a massage parlour, and an indoor drive-in cinema. The army of Volkswagen Beetles that comes to the rescue at the end of *Herbie Rides Again* includes one from a drive-in, complete with couple in the backseat. *The Hellstrom Chronicle*, winner of the 1972 Academy Award for best documentary, illustrates a discussion on human mating habits with shots of a drive-in.

The drive-in's on-screen presence becomes more evident in films from the late 1960s to the 1980s. It is evident in the number of feature films showing a drive-in on the screen and in films in which a drive-in is central to the narrative, the latter including *Targets, Drive-In* (1975), *Drive-In Massacre* (1976), *Ruby* (1977), *Swap Meet* (1979), *American Drive-In* (1985) and the Australian *Dead-End Drive-In* (1985). *Ruby* is the only one of these set in the 1950s or indeed in the past. In the 1970s the drive-in continued to appear in films as a feature of contemporary, roadside America, whether in the rural Tennessee of *I Walk the Line* (1970) or the Los Angeles cityscape of *The Black Fist* (1976). *Drive-In* (1976) is Texan and contemporary, though while distinguishing his film from the nostalgia of *American Graffiti* (1973) and *The Last Picture Show*, director Rod Amateau acknowledged that 'the small-town setting might seem to create a nostalgic feeling'.[11] It begins with the introduction of the pointedly named Alamo Drive-In to the sound of the Statler Brothers singing 'Whatever happened to Randolph Scott'. The film repeats the song as cars arrive for the evening show and again over the closing credits, emphasizing the implication that the drive-in is at the heart of a cultural divide, offering uncomplicated entertainment not films for which, in the Statlers' words, 'You gotta take your analyst along to see if it's fit to see'.

The teenage period film with drive-in scene arrived in 1974 with *Buster and Billie* and *The Lords of Flatbush*. Set in rural Georgia in 1948, the title characters in the former are a pair of high school students (Jan-Michael Vincent and Joan Goodfellow) who fall in love, swim naked together and go to the drive-in where the socially excluded Billie is enraptured by her first experience of cinemagoing, the screen image of Johnny Weissmuller's Tarzan diving into water linking the film to their earlier swim. Atypically, this drive-in provides a moment of moviegoing pleasure, before a rape-revenge narrative takes over the film. Set in Brooklyn in 1957, *The Lords of Flatbush* points more clearly to the identification of the drive-in as a greaser hangout and the scene of 1950s teenage, interrupted lovemaking. When Chico Tyrell (Perry King) and Jane Bradshaw (Susan Blakely) go to a drive-in screening of *From Here to*

Eternity, the waves on the beach and sexual passion on the screen contrast with the frustration in the car.

Teenpics set in the 1950s that followed in the second half of the 1970s include *Grease* (1978), *Slumber Party '57* (1976) and *Sweater Girls* (1978), each containing a drive-in scene. The drive-in is introduced in *Grease* with a trailer for *The Blob* (1958); the scene closes with Danny (John Travolta) sitting on the drive-in playground swings, cartoon junk food advertisements playing on the screen behind him (Figure 13). The context for this was a broad and multifaceted youth-orientated return to the 1950s that emerged at the end of the 1960s and moved into the mainstream in the 1970s, in which *Grease* played (and was identified as playing) a central but changing role in its different versions.[12] ShaNaNa, whose 1969 Woodstock appearance singing 'At the Hop' (1957) in 1950s dress was, in Vera Dika's words, an 'active parody of a now discarded past', went on to play Johnny Casino and the Gamblers in the film version of *Grease*.[13] When *Grease* first appeared on stage in Chicago in 1971, 'With expletive-riddled dialogue, acerbic humour and references to Chicago landmarks', it was billed 'as a "not-so-fond" revisiting of styles, attitudes and beliefs.'[14] Sometimes, write Oliver Gruner and Peter Krämer, *Grease* 'was declared to have single-handedly galvanised America's obsession with all things fifties': in 1977 Patricia Ann Luchak of the *San Francisco Chronicle* called it the 'musical that launched the nostalgia craze'.[15] However, while in 1972 *New York Times* critic Harris Green welcomed the stage musical as an 'unsentimental' contrast to 'that mad delight in the insipid past that has permitted nostalgia to rage like a plague on Broadway', critics were more likely to identify the film as an example of that nostalgia.[16] Reviewing

FIGURE 13 *Danny (John Travolta) singing 'Sandy' in front of a drive-in snack food advertisement in* Grease *(dir. Randal Kleiser, Paramount Pictures Corporation, 1978).*

the film for the British publication, *Monthly Film Bulletin*, Jan Dawson complained:

> Even in these days of blanket nostalgia, when cinema fashions have all but eclipsed the present tense, *Grease* arguably achieves a new low in retro styles. Spiritual homelessness for a vanished past (real or imagined) is usually despairing enough; but the loving recreation of a style perceived as hideous appears . . . to mark something of a perverse first in backward-looking movies.[17]

Travolta's Danny singing 'Stranded at the drive-in, branded a fool/What will they say Monday at school' is a cleaner variation of the stage version's 'Gee, it's no fun/ . . . At the passion pit wanting you'. The film presented a sunnier, Californian picture of the 1950s, one identified by Michael Ryan and Douglas Kellner as 'a nostalgic return to simpler times'.[18] Its nostalgia can still be understood as multidimensional. For Beth Carroll, '"Sandy" sets up an audiovisual disconnect between the authenticity of Danny's song and the ongoing animated antics of the drive-in screen's advertisements'.[19] *Grease* could be seen as nostalgia for the hideous, as constructing a distinction between authenticity and inauthenticity, or those advertisements as central to the film's celebration of the discarded and disposable traces of growing up.

Through its box-office success and continuing appeal, *Grease* was itself influential in linking the drive-in to the 1950s, teenagers and low-budget science-fiction films even as it acknowledged what else might be on the drive-in programme (the trailers for a western and a Dean Martin and Jerry Lewis comedy also glimpsed in the scene). The drive-in's period associations remained mixed. Of the Hollywood films made in the decade after 1978, only *Mischief* (1985) squarely locates the drive-in (showing *Rebel Without a Cause*) in a 1950s teenage world. In the following decade, Lou Arkoff (son of Samuel Z. Arkoff) produced *Rebel Highway*, a series of feature-length television versions of 1950s AIP films: among them, the Joe Dante-directed *Runaway Daughters* (1994) opens at a drive-in double date (*I Was a Teenage Werewolf* is playing) and later has private detective Roy Farrell (Dick Miller) say, 'Ah, they don't make 'em like they used to', while looking at a drive-in poster of the 1956 version of *Runaway Daughters*. There is no drive-in in *Attack of the 50 Ft. Woman* (1958), but the fifty-foot Nancy Archer attacks a drive-in in the 1993 remake. However, the clearest 1990s link between the drive-in and the 1950s comes not in an American film but in the Australian *Love in Limbo* (1993), which emphasizes 1950s style throughout and in which a drive-in screening of *The Girl Can't Help It* leads to the audience Lindy hopping to the rock 'n' roll on the drive-in screen.

Other films, and television shows, look back to the 1950s indirectly, look back to a different (but sometimes visually similar) decade or use the drive-in because it has come to signify the lost and remembered. Set mainly in the 1970s, *Christine* (1983) revolves around a 1957 Plymouth Fury motorcar that turns murderous during a date at the drive-in. *The Outsiders* (1983) has a 1950s look but a 1960s setting: *Beach Blanket Bingo* (1965) and *Muscle Beach Party* (1964) are playing at the drive-in. The abandoned drive-in in the micro-budget *The Sore Losers* (1997) is part of the film's self-conscious concern with a retro, 1950s, trash aesthetic. Drive-ins in period films are located in the 1940s in *The Cider House Rules* (1999), in the 1950s in *The One and Only* (2009), in the 1960s in films from *Our Winning Season* (1977) to *Brokeback Mountain* (2005) and *Once Upon a Time in Hollywood* (2019), in the 1970s in *Frankenstein and Me* (1996), in the 1980s in *Cold in July* (2014) and in the 1990s in *Hot Summer Nights* (2017). The latter films look not only to the existence of functioning drive-ins beyond the 1950s but also its association with the personal past, often memories of childhood or coming-of-age narratives. Nostalgia or a relationship between present and past can be hinted at through the film showing on the drive-in screen: *Casablanca* (1942) in *Electric Dreams* (1984) in which the drive-in couple's kiss echoes the one on the screen, *Bullitt* (1968) in *The Need for Speed* (2014), *The Town That Dreaded Sundown* (1976) in *The Town That Dreaded Sundown* (2014). It can be developed through a thematic concern with memory. Joel's (Jim Carrey) uncertain memory in *The Eternal Sunshine of the Spotless Mind* (2004) includes watching movies (and ad-libbing invented dialogue) just outside the drive-in. In *Cake* (2014), Claire (Jennifer Aniston) visits 'one of the last operating drive-in theaters' after seeing a television news item about the cinema and the passing of the drive-in which, the announcer tells us, was 'once a popular symbol of youth culture'.

From the 1980s, as the number of drive-in closures increased, films increasingly depict the passing of the drive-in. The drive-in was still showing films in *Swap Meet* but, like actual drive-ins, also serving as a swap meet. In *Red Dawn* (1984), the drive-in is used as an internment camp by the invading Soviet forces. In *Spies Like Us* (1985) the American intelligence agency operates beneath an abandoned drive-in. At the end of the 1980s the abandoned drive-in starts to appear as an element of the filmic landscape of contemporary roadside America. Shortly after the final closure of the Roper Drive-In in Nevada it featured in two 1989 films: *Pink Cadillac* and *The Wizard*. In the latter it is a stopping place in a journey to a Las Vegas video games competition, and the film combines the view of the abandoned screen tower with shots of discarded celluloid: the drive-in, and cinema more generally, features as old media, now displaced by the new, video media. A drive-in appears in *Lone Star* (1995) in a flashback to the 1970s and as a contemporary abandoned ruin at the end of the film. In ideological contrast to the Alamo Drive-In in *Drive-In* (1975), the final words in John Sayles' reflection on racism and the changing ethnicity of late twentieth-century Texas are 'Forget the Alamo', spoken in front of the decaying drive-in screen. In *Jawbreaker* (1999), a deserted drive-in (the recently closed Studio Drive-In) has become a place to escape from the cruelties of high school and watch the sunset. With an abandoned drive-in serving as a makeshift home on the Texas/Oklahoma border, *Angels in Stardust* (2014) provides a more regretful view of the changing west than *Lone Star*. The technophobia in *Cell* (2016) is evident at the drive-in, advertising digital projection but already abandoned, providing temporary shelter for the characters escaping from those turned into killers by their mobile phones.

Drive-in nostalgia is not limited to the United States. It is evident also in the destruction of the drive-in (and home of Aboriginal boy Pete (Cameron Wallaby)) in the Australian film *Satellite Boy* (2012) and in the Brazilian *O ultimo cine drive-in* (2014). The out-of-season drive-in can be less homely. In the Canadian *Weirdsville* (2006), Dexter (Scott Speedman) and Royce (Wes Bentley) think that Mattie (Taryn Manning) has died from a drug overdose and plan to bury her at the drive-in, closed for the winter though unknown to them in use by the local Satanists. 'Were we in hell?' asks a revived Mattie after she has escaped from the Satanists. Royce replies, 'No, we were at the drive-in', as if it might be easy to mistake one location for the other.

Whether looking back to the past or not, what most films showing operational drive-ins have in common, from *Auto-Mates* (1978) to *Stuart Little 2* (2002), is an association between the drive-in and the heterosexual date and/or sex. The experimental *Auto-Mates* was filmed entirely from within the car in which a bickering couple find that they are unable to escape; they continue to drive, aimlessly, at one point into a drive-in showing a 'dirty movie'. The woman invites the man to the back seat but when the couple wake the following morning at the drive-in, she is in the back seat, he is still at the front. In *Stuart Little 2*, Stuart the mouse sits in a toy car next to Margalo the canary, who leans against him as, on the television screen in front of them, Scottie kisses Madeleine in *Vertigo* (1958), here masquerading as a romantic movie. Even though dates are common in on-screen drive-in scenes they do not tend to lead to fulfilment, leaving characters alone at the drive-in (*Grease*) or walking home from the drive-in (*Grease*, *Our Winning Season*).

An on-screen scene at the drive-in does not have to involve romance or sex. Films tend to present drive-ins as attended by white couples, but in *One Potato, Two Potato* (1964), Frank Richards (Bernie Hamilton) can express his anger at racial discrimination, shouting 'Kill the white man' while sitting alone in his car, watching a western at a drive-in. In the Terrence Malick-scripted *Deadhead Miles* (1972) long-distance truck driver Cooper (Alan Arkin) shares his thoughts about Jesus with a hitchhiker he has picked up, while mute images from *Samson and Delilah* (1949) play on a drive-in screen in the background. On-screen drive-ins have mixed genre associations. *The Facts of Life* is one of several films containing a scene at a drive-in showing a western. Near the beginning of *My Girl* (1991), Shelly DeVoto (Jamie Lee Curtis) recalls with pleasure watching films such as *Love Story* (1970) at the drive-in. 'We're here for the early show', Leeroy Fisk (Richard Lawson) tells the victim he has taken to an empty drive-in in *Black Fist*, along with *Heat* (1995) and *Blue Thunder* (1983), one of several crime films that make use of the operational drive-in in daylight. There are drive-ins in biker films (*Northville Cemetery Massacre* (1976)), musicals (*Grease*), family films (*Beethoven's 2nd* (1993)) and varieties of comedy from Frank Tashlin's *The First Time* to the Farrelly brothers' *Stuck on You* (2003). Outside the United States they appeared in films from Michael Haneke's *The Piano Teacher* (2001) to the science-fiction anime, *Cowboy Bebop: The Movie* (2001), where a version of *High Noon* (1952) is playing at a multi-storey drive-in. They are particularly associated with the teenpic (itself a particularly hybrid genre) and the horror genre.

The drive-in/horror association was developed in the 1960s and 1970s through films including a drive-in showing a horror film (*Lolita* (1962), *Targets, Hollywood Boulevard, Twister* (1996)) and horror films containing a scene (or more) at a drive-in (*The Gruesome Twosome* (1967), *Night of the Lepus* (1972), *Dead of Night* (1974), *Drive-in Massacre, Kiss of the Tarantula* (1976), *Ruby*). *The Other Side of the Wind*, Orson Welles' 1970s film that was only completed and distributed in 2018, ends at a drive-in, but what a drive-in means has already been indicated by a shot of the Sepulveda Drive-In advertising a Jerry Gross double bill of *I Drink Your Blood* (1970) and *I Eat Your Skin* (1971).

The trend continued in the 1980s, which brought drive-in scenes in films including *Motel Hell* (1980), *New Year's Evil* (1980), *The Being* (1983), for a moment of father–son bonding in *Monster Squad* (1987) and axe murder in *Blood Rage* (1987). By the 1990s films were looking back to the post-1950s horror film at the drive-in. *Night of the Living Dead* is on the drive-in screen in *Frankenstein and Me*, Hallmark Television's *Flamingo Rising* (2002) and *Cold in July*, while in *Bikini Drive-In* (1995) a woman who inherits a failing drive-in sets out to save it from developers by dropping the family movies and going back to trashy horror and female nudity.

The context for this was the increasing prominence of the horror genre in the 1970s and 1980s, through a small number of major productions that did well at the box office and the American distribution of a larger number of low-budget films (American and non-American), a few of which themselves went on to achieve significant commercial success. Not only through their distribution on the drive-in circuit but also through the cult celebration, including the writings and appearances of Joe Bob Briggs, these lower-budget, more visceral films came increasingly to be known as 'drive-in movies'. As outdoor cinemas closed and more people came to watch films on video (on VHS, then DVD, Blu-Ray and streaming), horror movies and other forms of exploitation cinema were repackaged as 'drive-in classics', while a more diverse cult of the drive-in developed in different ways. As Church notes, the 'drive-in movie' became detached from the drive-in, allowing viewers from different generations and socio-economic classes to embrace different nostalgias for the drive-in experience, regardless of whether they attended the same cinemas or even attended drive-ins at all, and regardless of whether such films were representative of what was screened across the history of the drive-in.[20]

The multiple, overlapping nostalgias of the exploitation film fan existed alongside other nostalgias, evoked on- as well as off-screen. The low-budget anthology, *Drive-In Horror Show* (2009), uses a decaying drive-in operated by the living dead as a framing device, while in *Cars* (2006) the end credits play out against scenes at the Radiator Springs Drive-In, where rows of cars watch parodies of Pixar films (*Toy Car Story*, *Monster Trucks Inc.*, *A Bug's Life*), once again combining children's toys and American car culture and providing another opportunity for studio self-promotion. A scene in which a T-Rex goes on the rampage at a drive-in was filmed for *Jurassic World Dominion* (2022) but not included in the version released in cinemas, leading to complaints that 'The drive-in version of Dominion doesn't even have the drive-in scene', suggesting the drive-in as both mainstream and marginalized.[21]

The drive-in in song

The relative scarcity of on-screen drive-ins before 1960, and their proliferation as the number of drive-ins declined, could suggest a mythology that develops only as what it depicts begins to wane. However, drive-ins were invoked in song lyrics from the 1950s and 1960s. 'Drive-in Show' (Eddie Cochran, 1957), 'Wake Up Little Susie' (Everly Brothers, 1957), 'Rockin' at the Drive-in' (The Beavers, 1958), 'Kissin' at the Drive-in' (Troy Shondell, 1958) and 'Drive-in' (Aquatones, 1958) were followed by songs such as 'Drive-in Movie' (The Strings, 1960), 'Jivin' at the Drive-in' (Mark Valentino, 1963) and 'The Drive-In' (The Beach Boys, 1964).

Songs repeated familiar jokes about drive-ins. In 'You Bug Me, Baby' (1957), Larry Williams sang, 'When we go dating to a drive-in show/The picture playing we never know'. 'Yeah, we'll hop in a jalopy to a drive-in movie and never look at the show', sang Connie Francis in 'Vacation' (1962) while

'You'll see more kissing in the car than on the screen' according to Nat King Cole's 'Those Lazy, Hazy, Crazy Days of Summer' (1963). Drive-in songs were also often about the pleasures of summer and/or romance. In 'Here Comes Summer' (1959), Jerry Keller sang of 'Drive-in movies every night', as did the Fantastic Baggies in 'Summer Means Fun' (1964). The list of 'things he loves' includes 'Drive-ins on Friday night' in 'Popsicles and Icicles' (The Murmaids, 1964). 'Take my girl dating at the drive-in' sang The Reflections in '(Just Like) Romeo and Juliet' (1964).

These different performers sang of the drive-in in the present tense. The Beach Boys were not looking back when singing 'We love the drive-in' but invoking a contemporary world in which the drive-in was one part of youthful Californian pleasure and consumerism. However, the line 'The drive-in movies where we used to go' was already in the Four Lads' 1955 hit, 'Moments to Remember', along with 'And somehow I never watched the show'. The association between drive-in and youth meant that even in the 1950s songs could invoke the drive-in for an audience looking back to a youth already lost.

In 'Don't It Make You Want to Go Home' (1969), Joe South regretted the 'drive-in show where the meadow used to grow'. Yet in later songs it is the drive-in that has been supplanted. Over time the personal nostalgia for early romantic/sexual experience became the social nostalgia for small-town America, or a combination of the two. The personal remained dominant when in 'Old Days' (1975), Chicago sang of 'Drive-in movies/Comic books and blue jeans', when the Steve Miller Band recollected a first kiss at 'the drive-in movie show' in 'Circle of Love' (1981) and when, in 'Casablanca' (1982), Bertie Higgins sang of falling in love watching that film in the 'Back row of the drive-in show in the flickering light'. Similarly, in 'Summer of '69' (1984), Bryan Adams met his girl 'down at the drive-in'. The past tense is more evident in songs of the 1980s, for instance in country music band Alabama's drive-in 'where you and I/Shared our first kiss' ('Cruisin', 1986).

A further shift is evident when Mark Collie, in 'She's Never Coming Back' (1985), declared 'Like the drive-in picture show, she's never coming back', invoking an image of social change for personal purposes. In 'Old Coyote Town' (1987) Don Williams sang of how 'Waist high weeds hide a "For Sale" sign at the drive-in where my innocence died'. In 'Small World' (1990) Andrew Belew looked back to an age 'Of drive-in movies and luxury trains', and in 'The Boy Back Home' (1992), Linda Davis sang of a woman driving home to find 'the drive-in's gone/And her heart longs'. The destruction of the drive-in in Chris LeDoux's 'The Last Drive-in' (1991) means 'a piece of history hit the ground'.

The image of the drive-in supplanted by new developments continued in the 1990s. In John Michael Montgomery's 'High School Heart' (1995) the closure of the old drive-in meant 'They made a shopping mall out of our make-out spot', in the Doobie Brothers' 'Wild Ride' (1996) near 'the old abandoned drive-in' there was 'a brand new Motel 6', in Lonestar's 'Everything's Changed' (1998), the 'ol' drive-in' had become 'a New Wal Mart', while in 'Lee Van Cleef' (Primus, 2011) the Hill-Top drive-in had become an Auto-Mall. 'A Real Country Song' (Dale Watson, 1996) mourned the passing of country legends, along with 'the drive-in picture/Shows and Mom and Pop stores'. In 'Popcorn Box' (2003) Edwin McCain sang of 'The old ways of the drive-in picture show'. 'The drive-in picture show's been closed for years' mourned Buddy Jewell in 'Dyess, Arkansas' (2005), and in 'Summertime' (2006), Josh Rouse remembered 'drive-ins, soap operas, fireworks and country fairs'.

Lending itself easily to rhyme, the drive-in has served as stock vocabulary, not as frequently invoked as moonlight or starlight but a reliable sign of young romance. Its nostalgic connotations can look back to the make-out spot, the small town or the family. Jim Henry's 'Drive-in Movie Picture Show' (1999) looks back to an eight-in-the-car, childhood 'double feature and a playground' visit to the drive-in. Drawing on its more disreputable reputation, in 'Talk Dirty to Me' (1987) Poison sang of being 'At the drive-in/In the old man's Ford', lines subsequently used for the name of the band, At the Drive-In. Asked about their band's name, Passion Pit's Ian Hultquist replied that they had liked the alliteration, 'And I guess we really liked the whole story about the drive-ins, too.'[22]

Novels and short stories

In John Cheever's short story, 'The Cure', first published in the *New Yorker* in 1952, the narrator watches double features at the drive-in, on his own, as 'a kind of anaesthesia' after his wife has left him.[23] In Walker Percy's *The Moviegoer* (published in 1961, set in 1959), Jack 'Binx' Bolling's moviegoing includes a visit to the Moonlite Drive-In in Louisiana, to see *Fort Dobbs* (1958). He is accompanied by his secretary, and current girlfriend, Sharon Kincaid, and by the children of his mother's second marriage: Therese, Mathilde and the wheelchair-bound Lonnie. '*Fort Dobbs* is good', Jack notes. 'The Moonlite Drive-in is itself very fine. It does not seem too successful and has the look of the lonesome pine country behind the Coast. Gnats swim in the projection light and the screen shimmers in the sweet heavy air. But in the movie we are in the desert.'[24]

> Lonnie is happy (he looks around at me with the liveliest sense of a secret between us; the secret is that Sharon is not and never will be onto the little touches we see in movies and, in the seeing, know that the other

sees – as when Clint Walker tells the saddle tramp in the softest easiest Virginian voice: 'Mister, I don't believe I'd do that if I was you', Lonnie is beside himself, doesn't know whether to watch Clint Walker or me).[25]

The Moviegoer provides a further illustration of how looks between members of the drive-in audience can be as significant as the looks at the screen. Short stories and novels have the potential to go further than song lyrics or films in exploring personal relations or their absence and their relationship to environment, whether in the context of the sweet heavy Louisiana air or the New England suburban ennui to which the drive-in belongs in 'The Cure'. In short stories and novels, the drive-in still often signified sex.

'There's a "Passion Pit" just where this comes out on 95', Ernie Cureo, cab driver and undercover Pinkerton operator, tells his passenger in Ian Fleming's *Diamonds Are Forever* (1956).[26] 'Drive-In Movie', he quickly translates for James Bond (and any reader unfamiliar with American slang).[27] Cureo and Bond are being chased just as Cody Jarrett, his wife and mother were chased in *White Heat*, but in Fleming's novel the Las Vegas drive-in which serves as a temporary hideout is indeed also a passion pit, if not only that. Bond looks 'down the lanes of metal standards, like parking meters, from which speakers could be connected with your car to pick up the sound', and glances at the neighbouring cars – 'Two faces glued together. A shapeless huddle on a back seat. Two prim, rapt, elderly faces, starring upwards. The glint of light on an upturned bottle.'[28]

The sexual connotations of the drive-in are more extensively exploited in the paperback sleaze of *Drive-In Girl* (1961), in which Fran Allen gets a job at the Tropical Nites Drive-In in West Los Angeles, which she discovers is run as part of a prostitution racket. 'She was included in the Price of a Ticket', announces the cover, inaccurately.[29] Outlining the business model, the manager explains:

> The studios are producing fewer and fewer pictures every year. Each theater has to draw fifteen hundred paid admissions a week just to break even. With fewer pictures and fewer good double features to offer and the competition of old movies on television, we started to lose business a few years ago . . . Now we can run the same old movies three weeks in a row and the audience don't care.[30]

Even here, however, some still watch the movies. Fran notes, 'It was funny the way she could go to a car, strip and make out with a man while maybe four feet away, in another car, was a family enjoying the movie and never tumbling what was going on right next to them.'[31]

The drive-in as a venue for sex, and a place at the crossroads, is evident in *The Crossroads* (1959), where John D. MacDonald wrote of how:

> At the Crossroads Drive-In Theater, just beyond the Bowladrome, in a pink-and-blue DeSoto in the fifth rank of cars, while a monstrous suffering face of Gregory Peck filled the wide-angle screen, the high school sophomore daughter of Joe Varadi lost the ultimate long-precarious fragment of her innocence, whined with pain, wept, and could not be consoled at all until the cartoon feature began.[32]

In *No Down Payment* (1957), John McPartland's novel of suburban unhappiness, Isabelle Flagg remembers how she and her husband would sometimes 'go to a drive-in movie, with thousands of people around them in the other cars in the darkness. God, what wonderful months, not worrying about anything with the jelly and the diaphragm'.[33] The Moonlite Drive-In in Massachusetts in John Cheever's *The Wapshot Scandal* (1964) is where Emile Cranmer goes on a double date, sitting in the back seat with Louise Meeker, while Charles Putney and Doris Pierce are in the front: 'They were all drinking whisky out of paper cups, and they were all in various states of undress'.[34]

The title character in John Updike's short story, 'The Deacon' (published by the *New Yorker* in 1970), goes to drive-in movies with his wife, where they 'sit in a sea of fornication'.[35] In Philip Roth's *I Married a Communist* (1998), Nathan Zuckerberg tells of how he first got laid at a Pennsylvania drive-in showing an Abbott and Costello movie, his underwear somehow managing to wind itself around the car brake handle and his ankle.[36] In John Irving's *The Cider House Rules* (1985), Homer Wells remembers his introduction to the Cape Kenneth Drive-In in 1940s Maine, which lacks a snack bar and restrooms but has numerous mosquitoes.[37] Unlike Jack in *The Moviegoer*, Homer is perplexed by movie storytelling and what he initially understands as the ultimate purpose of the drive-in: 'losing control of oneself in the back seats of cars'.[38] This is subsequently qualified by the question: 'Wasn't it to tease oneself and one's date into a state of sexual frenzy – which neither of you were allowed to act upon?'[39]

Frenzy is also one of the words used in Allen Hannay's 1982 Texas-set novel, *Love and Other Natural Disasters* (filmed, in 1988, as *A Tiger's Tale*), when Bubber and Rose get a distant view of the Starlight Drive-In. The 1976 version of *King Kong* is playing on the screen but 'the cars were more interesting. Hardly any heads were visible. The whole parking lot seemed engaged in a springtime mating frenzy. Occasionally a boy would run back to the men's room, where he'd emerge in a moment tearing a prophylactic package open with his teeth'.[40] The sex is on the screen in Oliver Bleeck's 1972 crime novel

The Procane Chronicle (filmed as *St. Ives* (1976)), at the drive-in showing a 'Triple XXX feature': *Take Me Naked*, *The Daisy Chain* and *Unsatisfied*.[41]

Bleek's description of the surrounding fence and the cinder-blocked building housing the projection booth and the refreshment stand emphasizes its non-descript nature.[42] In contrast, Thomas McGuane was more lyrical when he wrote (in an essay on fishing for *Sports Illustrated*):

> When you are at the drive-in movie in Key West, watching Adult Fare with all the other sweating neckers, the columns of light from the projectionist's booth is feverish with tropical insects blurring the breasts and buttocks on their way to the screen. If it is a low tide, you smell the mangroves and exposed tidal flats nearby and you are within a mile of sharks that could eat you like a junkie. When the movie is over and you have hung the speaker back on its post and are driving home, palmetto bugs and land crabs pop under the tires.[43]

The Montana drive-in McGuane describes in his novel *Something to be Desired* (1984) is 'a fine old concrete thing that stood in front of the great mountains of wilderness, playing to an amazingly small parking area on a spring night'.[44] However, in the novel that drive-in sees Lucien and Dee sitting at opposite ends of the seat, Lucien discouraged having learnt that Dee is having her period, Dee not a little disgusted by his squeamishness.[45]

In literature as in other media the drive-in sex scene often occurs in period dress/undress or as a coming-of-age recollection. Thus, the 1950s was revisited and revised in the 1970s in the novel as well as on-screen. Ruth Doan MacDougall's *The Cheerleader* (1973) is set in 1950s New Hampshire, where Henrietta Snow ('Snowy'), Tom and their friends visit the drive-in, watch some of the film before 'Little Starched Snowy' ends the evening by giving Tom a blowjob.[46] Lisa Alther's *Kinflicks* (1976) is set slightly later but includes early scenes in which Tennessee cheerleader Ginny Babcock is taken, in the truck of the car, to the Family Drive-In.[47] Biblical epics are on the screen in both novels: *The Silver Chalice* (1954) in *The Cheerleader*, while in *Kinflicks* the sound of dialogue from *The Ten Commandments* is 'mixed with various sighs and gasps and sucking sounds from the front seat, and blasts from car horns throughout the parking area as, in keeping with Hullsport High tradition, couples signalled they had gone all the way'.[48]

There is another minor literary tradition which combined the drive-in date with the fight and the gang. In *The Outsiders* (1967), teenage novelist S. E. Hinton wrote:

> There are lots of drive-ins in town – the Socs go to The Way Out, and to Rusty's, and the greasers go to The Dingo and to Jay's. The Dingo is a

pretty rough hangout; there's always a fight going on there and once a girl got shot. We walked around talking to all the greasers and hoods we knew, leaning in car windows or hopping into the back seats, and getting in on who was running away, and who was in jail, and who was going with who, and who could whip who, and who stole what and when and why. We knew about everybody there. There was a pretty good fight while we were there between a big twenty-three year-old greaser and a Mexican hitchhiker. We left when the switchblades came out, because the cops would be coming soon and nobody in his right mind wants to be around when the fuzz shows.[49]

In a *New York Times* article published the same year, Hinton complained that romance and 'a-horse-and-the-girl-who-loved-it' stories still dominated teenage fiction: 'Nowhere is the drive-in social jungle mentioned. . . . Most kids nowadays date for status. There are cliques and classes and you date so you can say you had a date with so-and-so, the president of the student social council.'[50] For Hinton, 'violence is a part of teen-agers' lives. If it's not on television or in the movies, it's a beating up at a local drive-in'.[51]

Alice Hoffman's first published story was 'At the Drive-In', in which the unnamed seventeen-year-old narrator watches *The Wild Angels* (1966) one more time with local gang leader McKay: the relationship and the drive-in scene feature also in her 1977 debut novel, *Property Of*.[52] She went on to write her own *New York Times* article on the drive-in, singling out Cape Cod's South Wellfleet Drive-In as 'a place sacred to disjointed universes: young love and family togetherness, upscale couples and fishmen's children' and a time of 'summers lost'.[53]

In 'Drive-In Date', Joe Lansdale took the drive-in date in a darker direction: its two speaking characters live in a world of misogyny, racism, murder and necrophilia.[54] Lansdale's dark fantasy novel, *The Drive-In: A B-Movie with Blood and Popcorn, Made in Texas* (1988), takes its lead from the Joe Bob Briggs version of the drive-in movie, with its story of characters trapped at the Orbit Drive-In as it repeatedly shows the quintuple bill of *I Dismember Mama* (1972), *The Evil Dead* (1981), *Night of the Living Dead* (1968), *The Toolbox Murders* (1978) and *The Texas Chainsaw Massacre* (1974).[55] Similar influences are behind the 1996 anthology, *It Came From the Drive-In*, this time with story titles that transformed film titles from 1950s low culture: 'I Was a Teenage Boycrazy Bob', 'Plan 10 from Inner Space'.[56]

In the late twentieth century, the shrinking number of actual drive-ins existed alongside an increased fictional presence that took different forms. One trend was from sex to romance. The Silhouette Desire novel *Dream within a Dream* (1984) includes a scene at a drive-in, when Reid Dillon takes Callie

Foster to a Laurel and Hardy drive-in double bill. Reid has memories of drive-in nights watching *Gidget* (1959) in his brother's white Chevy convertible. Callie has been to a drive-in only once before, with her parents, but she had taken a study unit with her students on the movies (as she explains, how they 'reflect the attitudes of our nation and their times, how they copy reality and when they go beyond what we perceive to be reality and become fantasy'), and on route to the drive-in she reads aloud from a newspaper article on the history of the drive-in ('Let's see, in the decade from 1948 to 1958 the number of drive-in theaters increased to nearly four thousand. And it says here that thirty to forty percent of the gross receipts came from the concessions').[57]

Two Harlequin Romances, Roseanne Williams' *Seeing Red* (1993) and Peg Sutherland's *Queen of the Dixie Drive-In* (1996), tell of the reopening of a drive-in. The latter is set in Sweetbranch, Alabama, where, as a fourteen-year-old, Carson Delaney used to steal into the drive-in and lose herself in temporary fantasy.[58] Returning ten years later, she once again encounters the now respectable Tony de Fuentes and learns about his plans to reopen the drive-in as part of a strategy to promote 'Sweetbranch as a destination for those who wanted to recapture bygone days'.[59] In *Seeing Red*, red-headed Larinda Outlaw inherits the Moonglow Drive-In in Northern California. Her plans to sell the property are complicated by single-parent Cash Bowman, who runs a flea market on the property, drives a red '57 Chevy convertible and who, when Larinda decides she wants to revive the drive-in, joins forces with the local property developer to oppose this. The local authorities initially deny Larinda permission to reopen the Moonglow, despite support from Eva Maycomb, the town's leading preservationist and historian, who argues that drive-ins are 'as American as Big-Macs, baseball, and the Liberty Bell. They're not only entertainment American-style, they're *family* entertainment'.[60] Property developer Cleve Davis claims that drive-ins bring only traffic, noise and light pollution, while Cash suggests that drive-ins are 'passion pits' showing X-rated films that can be seen from neighbouring windows ('If anything', thought Larinda, '*he* was the one who'd helped the term "passion pit" flourish in his teenage years').[61] The decision is reversed after Cash discovers that the development plans would disturb the local fox population. As Eva Maycomb says, it is the town's 'civic responsibility to preserve its fox habitat *and* its outdoor drive-in'.[62]

Children of drive-in operators narrate two 1997 novels, Larry Baker's *The Flamingo Rising* and Marjorie Reynolds' *The Starlite Drive-In*.[63] In Baker's novel the narrator is the Korean-born adopted son of the owner of the Flamingo Drive-In, opened in Florida in 1953. The novel focuses on 1967 and 1968 (the Hallmark Television adaptation has an exclusively 1960s setting), when the narrator has his sixteenth birthday and loses his virginity and when the drive-in screens films such as *The Graduate* (1967), *The Green Berets* (1968) and the invented classical exploitation film, *The Birth of Triplets*. The Flamingo is promoted as the largest drive-in in the world and given to grand firework displays. While *Flamingo Rising*, told from a male perspective, emphasizes size, spectacle and relatively overt, late 1960s sexuality, *The Starlite Drive-In*, told from a female perspective, is a story of isolation, relative poverty, furtive sexuality and hidden violence. The narrator is a movie-obsessed, thirteen-year-old girl, the setting is rural Indiana in the summer of 1956, framed by the contemporary beginning and ending, and the Starlite of the title belongs to a small circuit offering a mixed programme including *Fire Maidens from Outer Space* (1956), *The African Queen* (1951) and *To Catch a Thief*.

Reynolds' *The Starlite Drive-In* was winner of the American Library Association 1998 Young Adult Novel Award. Notwithstanding its 1970s and 1980s association with 'adult movies', when the drive-in appeared in late twentieth and early twenty-first-century literature it was often in novels for young adults or children, often as a form of children's 1950s gothic, with the drive-in standing in for the haunted house or associated with old horror films. *The Starlite Drive-In* starts with the discovery of a body in the grounds of the old Starlite. Part of the 'Strange Matter' series, Marty M. Engle's *Creature Features*, provides a young reader's variation of Lansdale's *The Drive-In*, with its blurring of the lines between the real and reel worlds, beginning not with *I Dismember Mama* on the screen but with an abandoned drive-in and references to *Dr Cyclops* (1940) and *Invasion of the Saucer Men* (1957).[64] When Nancy is sent on a mission to the Hi-Point Drive-In, in the Nancy Drew mystery, *Fatal Attraction* (1988), she is warned that it has been abandoned for years. When she goes there anyway, she finds that 'it seemed to echo with the soundtracks of all the old horror films she had ever seen'.[65]

This strand of fiction tends to have a contemporary setting but sometimes looks back to the 1950s. The 'Wishbone novel', *Drive-In of Doom* (1998), starts on 'Fabulous Fifties Day', which includes the reopening of the Moonlight Drive-In Theatre, and the 1950s experience is emphasized with a 3-D screening of *The House of Wax* (1953).[66] Wanda from the Oaxdale Historical Society explains that once there were more than 4,000 drive-ins, one in almost every town. At the reopening the appeal of the drive-in becomes apparent: 'The warm summer air, the large, bright screen (even if it was streaked in places with dust and grime), and the dark, star-sprinkled sky all made the experience very different from watching an indoor movie or television. It was almost magical. In the car they could talk without disturbing anyone else.'[67] Unfortunately, a takeover by Mega-Mall threatens the Moonlight. In *The Ghost at the Drive-In Movie* (2009), the threat to the Diamond Drive-In comes from Brink's Auto Dealer. 'There used to be hundreds of them all over the country', explains the Boxcar children's grandfather. 'There were dozens right here in Connecticut, back in the old days. Now there are only a few.'⁶⁸ *Island of the Horses* is on the programme rather than a horror film and a planned Halloween event ultimately explains the ghost of the title.

Cheryl and Tweed, the main characters in the two 'Wiggins Weird' novels, are even more devoted to the drive-in, the 1950s and old horror movies. Brought up by their grandfather, 'the sole owner/projectionist/concessions manager/ticket-taker at the Starlight Paradise' Drive-In, and raised 'on a steady diet of movies viewed through the windshield', the twelve-year-old identical twins but cousins rather than sisters have discovered that this is the only way to watch films.⁶⁹ When they are given the responsibility of programming the drive-in in *How to Curse in Hieroglyphics* (2013), they start with a triple bill of *The Creature from the Black Lagoon* (1954) and its two sequels. At the beginning of *The Haunting of Heck House* (2014) they have opted for 'the truly timeless fare for their double-bill: the classic haunted house picture *The Haunting of Maison de Case House*, followed by the horror-comedy masterpiece, *Ding, Dong, You're Dead!* . . . both available in 3-D!'⁷⁰ Sitting 'in Pop's pickup truck at the back of the Starlight Paradise's (full to capacity, thanks to their excellent choices) drive-in movie lot, the girls revelled in the squeals of gleeful terror that occasionally drifted from the other cars parked in the lot'.⁷¹

In Garrison Keillor and Jenny Lind Nilsson's young adult novel, *The Sandy Bottom Orchestra* (1996), Scott invites fourteen-year-old Rachel to a drive-in date. Here greater emphasis is placed on parental anxieties: when Rachel answers her father's question about how late she will stay out with a 'By dawn's early light', he groans, 'Please. No humor. I'm not in the mood' and insists on midnight.⁷² At the drive-in, in Scott's convertible with the top down, they watch a horror film called *Squash*. It concerns an old lady whose hatred of young men leads her to cultivate a carnivorous and aggressive variety of squash plant, and the tactile nature of the tentacles of the plant synchronizes with Rachel and Scott's embrace and kiss.⁷³

The developing literary connection between the drive-in and horror or the gothic is partly explained by the presence of horror films at the drive-in, partly by the cult of the 'drive-in movie' as horror film and partly by the increasing association of the drive-in with the past. In Stephen King's writings, drive-ins run from his 1979 Richard Bachman novel, *The Long Walk*, in which the central character talks of sex 'at the drive-in with the smell of cowshit coming in through the car window from the next pasture'.⁷⁴ In the 1980s King provided the introduction to *Joe Bob Goes to the Drive-In*.⁷⁵ In the 1990s, in the 'uncut' version of *The Stand*, he described a world in which 'all the drive-ins were kaput' (along with the Hell's Angels and good old American International Picture), though the novel also features a scene where a character wakes thinking, initially, that she is in hell and hell was 'whiteness . . . white, ivory, bleached-out nothingness'.[76] She then realizes that the whiteness comes from 'a huge blank drive-in movie screen against a background of white late afternoon rainy sky'.[77] More recently, in his time travel novel, *11/22/63*, the central character passes the time at the Hi-Hat Drive-In in Maine, where he watches *The Long, Hot Summer* (1958) with several other walk-ins, 'mostly elderly people who knew each other and chatted companionly', leaving just as *Vertigo* (1958) starts, when the air turns chilly.[78] In King's fiction drive-ins could be associated with sex, the past, the other worldly but also everyday rural life.

The drive-in's sexual connotations persisted in novels and short stories while as in other media these increasingly became accounts of remembered relationships. Increasingly, the drive-in became associated with the past, whether in fiction with a period setting, an emphasis on period style, stories about a drive-in closed or threatened with closure or plans to revive a drive-in. In his short story 'Eyesores' (2003), Eric Shade describes the mixed feelings of those paid by the owner, Selfridge, to knock down the local drive-in in the fictional Pennsylvania town of Windfall:

> All of us remembered good times at the drive-in and we wanted it to outlive us. Like the bowling alley parking lot, and the semicircle of picnic-table benches under the football bleachers, we'd done our best drinking and groping there, and we hated ourselves for wanting the money, and we hated Selfridge for paying us to tear the place down. But we also wanted some pieces off the screen and the lumber from the supports.[79]

In 'Eyesores', similarities with songs about the death of the drive-in are complicated by the narrator's ambivalence and complicity.

Photography and art

Three iconic photographs, taken by J. R. Eyerman, O. Winston Link and Robert Frank, illustrate different connotations of the drive-in in the latter half of the 1950s. In 1949 Eyerman had taken a series of photographs for *Life* showing embracing couples at a Los Angeles drive-in, though these were never published in the magazine.[80] His photograph of the Oak Hills Drive-In outside Salt Lake City, Utah, appeared in *Life* in December 1958, as part of a special issue devoted to the 'spectacular flowering of U.S. entertainment', due, the magazine explained, to both the growth of prosperity and technology.[81] Sixteen pages followed on 'the biggest, brassiest, lushest, most extravagant midway the world has ever seen', with an emphasis on the outdoors, 'water shows, drive-in movies, fairy-tale amusement parks – for not since the days of ancient Greece and Rome has a nation assembled so much alfresco entertainment'.[82]

The caption for the movies announced: 'Colossal! On gigantic screens with encircling sound, in drive-ins and theaters, the movies are still the main stop on the American midway. At Oak Hills, near Salt Lake City, jets etch the evening sky, Moses in *The Ten Commandments* casts his biblical wrath down at the packed cars.'[83] In the centre of the top half of the double page, colour spread, the drive-in screen shows Charlton Heston in *The Ten Commandments* (1956), his arms outstretched in front of a white and blue sky, at the moment when Moses parts the Red Sea. In front of him, the bulk of the photograph is dark but light enough to reveal rows of cars. Behind the screen we see the lights of Salt Lake City, the silhouette of the mountains in the distance and beyond them the sky still glowing from the setting sun.

There is a mismatch here. The parting of the Red Sea appears around three hours into *The Ten Commandments* and so would not have been seen by a drive-in audience shortly after sunset. The picture is a careful combination of two photographs. Students from nearby Brigham Young University were invited to a free screening, though apparently of *And God Created Woman* rather than the Cecil B. De Mille epic. Eyerman then combined the photograph of that audience watching Brigitte Bardot as the sun set with another shot in which Heston as Moses was projected on the screen.[84] The published image replaced European hedonism with a setting, film and drive-in that all appear to belong to the same epic, biblical and American narrative.

O. Winston Link's 'Hot Shot Eastbound' was another carefully constructed combination of two images but was different in genesis and effect. Link took it on 2 August 1956 at the Iaeger Drive-In in West Virginia. Link is known for his photographs of steam trains, and this picture (or at least the most famous version of it) juxtaposes train, plane and automobile. To the top right of the picture, against the black night sky a steam train passes by the drive-in showing the Korean War aviation drama, *Battle Taxi* (1955). In the foreground a couple sit in a convertible, close together (as in Eyerman's 1949 photographs), watching the plane shown on the drive-in screen. Link apparently gave the couple $10 to sit in Link's Buick, while the remarkable black-and-white clarity of the cars, the train and the couple was achieved by perfectly timed flash photography, though as the light washed out the image on the screen Link had to insert a separate image he had taken of *Battle Taxi* projected onto the screen.[85]

Link took five additional photographs of the drive-in screen and in the photograph initially published, in the 1957 Norfolk and Western Railway pamphlet *'Night Trick' on the Norfolk and Western Railway*, the drive-in is showing a different moment from *Battle Taxi*: not a plane but Captain Russ Edwards (Sterling Hayden) as he gives a talk about the helicopter rescue unit he commands.[86]

'A 74 locomotive adds its tremendous push at the end of a long coal train eastbound in West Virginia', says the caption in the 1957 pamphlet. 'The couple watching the drive-in movie near the town of Iaeger seems impervious to power on the move.'[87] Like the 1958 *Life* photograph, the emphasis of the initial photograph was on power, and Link's subsequent insertion of a moment from the film showing a jet plane accentuated this. However, from the beginning his subject was different: not a Hollywood epic screened in the epic Utah landscape and cityscape but a pair of lovers watching a minor movie at a small-town drive-in. The Iaeger Drive-In could only take 142 cars, and at this point the population of Iaeger was itself around 1,500, shrinking to about 320 in 2005.[88] When Link took the photograph the steam engine was still in use but on its way out. The steam train was an antique by the time the photograph became more widely known as 'Hot Shot Eastbound', following its 1983 exhibition in the United States and the United Kingdom. In the 1950s the drive-in was a relatively new arrival on the American scene but when Vivian Raynor discussed the photographs displayed in 'Rolling Steel', a 1992 exhibition of railroad art and artefacts in New Rochelle, New York, she wrote that 'the shot most likely to stop the nostalgic in their tracks is that of a freight train in full cry, taken at night from a fully-occupied drive-in in West Virginia'.[89] By then, the nostalgia included the drive-in as well as the steam train.

Robert Frank's 'Drive-in movie – Detroit' did not attempt a carefully staged statement. In 1955, Frank, having emigrated from Switzerland, was awarded a Guggenheim Fellowship to take photographs across the United States. In 1958, eighty-three of those photographs were published in Paris in *Les Américains*, alongside details of American history and culture and quotations from writers including Alexis de Tocqueville, Ralph Waldo Emerson and Langston Hughes.[90] An American edition, *The Americans*, followed in 1959, with the text stripped down to titles for the photographs and an introduction in which Jack Kerouac wrote of how, 'with his little camera', Robert Frank 'sucked a sad poem right out of America onto film, taking rank among the tragic poets of the world'.[91]

'Drive-in movie – Detroit' was one of the eighty-three. Like the *Life* photograph published in 1958, the top of Frank's photograph shows the sky at dusk, but it is a white, partly cloudy sky rather than a glowing sunset. Taken at the Gratiot Drive-In, from among the cars rather than a high angle, the expanse of the sky takes up much of the picture. The image on the off-centred screen is of two dimly lit figures from *The Looters* (1955), a black-and-white morality tale as forgotten as *Battle Taxi*. Frank must have taken the photograph between Wednesday 29 June and Saturday 2 July 1955, which is when *The Looters* played at the Gratiot, on a double bill with *The Purple Plain* (1954).[92] The image is from around six minutes into the film: there has been no attempt

FIGURE 14 *Robert Frank, 'Drive-In Movie – Detroit', © June Leaf and Robert Frank Foundation, from* The Americans.

here to insert another image with a stronger statement. We see a moment caught rather than elaborately staged. To the bottom left we can see a couple sitting separately in an open-top car (Figure 14). Another photograph Frank took not far away, 'Public park – Ann Arbor, Michigan', shows couples embracing on the grass beside their parked cars, but that intimacy is absent from his drive-in photograph. The grandeur of the Oak Hills Drive-In photograph is also absent from 'Drive-in movie – Detroit', though the Gratiot was the grander drive-in.[93] The Gratiot's cascading waterfall behind the drive-in tower cannot be seen in Frank's photograph, only the half-hidden back of the Gratiot sign above the shadowy figures of Rory Calhoun and Ray Danton in *The Looters*.

Each of these three photographs shows the drive-in as a living and functioning place but in contrasting ways. *Life* used Eyerman's photograph to emphasize the power and size of the American film industry: the drive-in has come to stand in for Hollywood. Power in the Link photograph (which at least when first published rested in the train rather than the screen) is juxtaposed against the small-town setting and the romantic couple. Frank's photograph avoids grand spectacle to show a side of America that often went unseen rather than America as it was meant to be seen.

The photographs reached different audiences. Eyerman's originally appeared as a two-page spread in a mass-market general-interest magazine each issue of which had, after the Second World War, been reaching more than 20 per cent of the US population.[94] Link's photographs only became widely known from the 1980s, when the drive-in was becoming, like the steam train and small-town America, a subject for nostalgia. When Frank's collection was published in the United States it was initially in an edition of 2,600 of which less than half were sold.[95] It appeared alongside other photographs showing different aspects of America, from the clear segregation of passengers in 'Trolley – New Orleans' to the shot of two children in 'Motorama – Los Angeles' and others that reveal Frank's fascination with the car.

The Americans tends to be contrasted with the 1955 'Family of Man' exhibition of photographs at New York's Museum of Modern Art (to which Frank contributed), which over the next eight years went on to tour the world, attracting more than nine million visitors. For Miles Orvell, while the 1955 'exhibition was establishing an optimistic vision of the American future, joined to a future of global harmony', Frank was 'capturing scenes that revealed an America riven by racial conflict, loneliness, boredom, religious enthusiasm, and histrionic politics . . . where teens congregated around juke boxes, parked in drive-in movies'.[96] Link's photographs, when they were exhibited in 1983, were also contrasted with Frank's. For Carolyn Carr, the photographers were stylistically and iconographically antithetical: 'Frank's photographs are about spiritual desolation and psychic isolation; Link's are about community and ordered existence. The one, an ode to chaos; the other, a homage to tradition. Juxtaposed, they speak of the polarity of the American experience.'[97] According to Rupert Martin, 'Link gives us a vernacular portrait of rural American life in the late 'fifties, whose charm and optimism contrasts with Robert Frank's bleak vision of urban alienation in *The Americans* made at the same time.'[98]

Even when its importance came to be acknowledged, *The Americans* was often seen as a negative portrayal. Alfred Appel's study of 'American popular culture from World War II to the present' through 'photographs, movie stills, and other images from the past five decades' reproduces Frank's 'Drive-in – Detroit' photograph on its cover (beneath the preceding quote) but suggests that 'Moviegoing is just another dead end in Robert Frank's *The Americans*': for Appel, his photograph shows 'a sunset blocked by a drive-in screen, a movie compromised by twilight'.[99] But Appel condemns the drive-in general. Thus, the Auto-View Drive-In in Utah photographed by Dorothea Lange is 'a wretched patchwork quilt' where we ought to pity the audience sitting in their isolation booth cars at 'a sad substitute for a theater', the speaker poles in a 1966 Bruce Davidson photograph of a San Francisco drive-in evoke 'the new neighborhood as a graveyard, its residents done in by the bleak tonalities and thick, heavy airs of an exhaust fumes and A-bomb culture' and the drive-in seen in Robert Adams' 'Outdoor Theater and Cheyenne Mountain' (1968) obscures the natural beauty of the Colorado landscape.[100]

Later commentary moved away from the idea that the drive-in blocked, compromised or obscured, linking it instead to fascination and pleasure. For Goldberg and Silberman the bleakness of Frank's images is offset by his fascination with 'drive-in movies and diners before they became nostalgic icons'.[101] For Han-Chih Wang, Frank 'consciously contrasted the pleasures and perils of the open road – jukeboxes, drive-in theaters, highway accidents, and roadside crosses'.[102] In 1974, introducing a collection of Robert Adams' photographs, John Szarkowski wrote that in photographs (including 'Outdoor Theater and Cheyenne Mountain') Adams has 'done a strange and unsettling thing. He has, without actually lying, discovered in these dumb and artless agglomerations of boring buildings the suggestion of redeeming virtue. He has made them look not beautiful but important, as relics of an ancient civilization look important. He has even made them look, in an unsparing way, natural'.[103]

William Eggleston photographed the recently closed Sky-Vue Drive-In, Memphis, Tennessee, in his 1970–3 'The Outlands' series: photographs of drive-ins abandoned, sometimes being reclaimed by nature, become more evident and nostalgic (but still ambivalent) from the 1980s.[104] Functioning, German drive-ins appear in Wim Wenders' films, short (*3 American LPs* (1969)) and feature length (*Wrong Movement* (1975)), but his American photographs include 'Abandoned Drive-In' (1983) and (the also abandoned) 'Drive-In, Marfa, Texas' (1983).[105] A 1987 guide to landscape photography advised that there was 'a bittersweet beauty to be found in the shredded skins of a maturing society: The nostalgic romance of the abandoned drive-in theatres, the fading glory of boom town streets'.[106] Reviewing the 1998 Yancey Richardson exhibition in New York, 'Drive-Ins: Disappearing Summer Cinema', Ken Johnson noted that the drive-in had 'been an enduring popular subject for photographers . . . Today's photographers view it through nostalgic lenses . . . the deserted theater remains an elegiac symbol of some unaccountable loss'.[107] The photographers exhibited included Dick Arentz, Jeff Brouws and Sandy Skogland. Arentz's 'Starland Drive-In' platinum and palladium photographs were taken at an abandoned West Virginia drive-in: they show not just the still-intact screen but also a herd of plastic ponies freed from their carousel and seemingly roaming the empty field that once accommodated the audience.[108] Brouws photographed a series of drive-ins flat on, some intact, others decaying, in front of deserted spaces, part of his wider concern with 'exploring the historical, contemporary, everyday aspects of the American cultural landscape'.[109] Skogland's installation photograph, 'Squirrels at the Drive-in', shows a drive-in screen behind which the sun is setting and in front of which there are only two vehicles: a battered pick-up truck and an open-top convertible containing the almost obligatory necking couple. The people are outnumbered by squirrels, clambering over a decaying speaker stand, perched on the pick-up truck, uncannily dominating the foreground as if part of an eco-horror film.[110]

As drive-ins closed, different photographers set off on individual journeys to document those that survived or the traces of those that had not, sometimes as rescue operations. In 2001 Iona Cruickshank started to photograph Canadian drive-ins, setting out 'to document a social and cultural phenomenon before the iconic screens disappeared from the landscape forever'.[111] Looking back on the project nine years later she concluded, 'The reality in 2010 is that the drive-in still lives.'[112] Joan Liftin's *Drive-ins* (2004) is as much about the audience as the place: she photographed drive-ins as living places and her response to its predicted demise was 'I say let baseball go first'.[113] Craig Deman's 'Endangered Icons: The Drive-In Project' took him to eleven states in 2011–12.[114] In 2014, Lindsey Rickert spent sixty-five days on the road photographing twenty-eight drive-ins, abandoned and operational, in partnership with Honda's project drive-in, a scheme designed to raise funds allowing existing drive-ins to purchase digital projection equipment.[115] In 2018 Carl Weese posted that he had photographed over 250 drive-ins in forty-four states over the past twenty years, documenting them as 'an iconic feature of the American landscape'.[116]

Pointing out that most drive-ins he photographed were fully operational when he shot them, Weese insisted that his interest was in the contemporary drive-in, noting that he had:

> never referred to this project as being about 'Abandoned Drive-in Theaters' (or Dead, or Derelict, or Dark, etc). Yet, people almost always use one of those terms to refer to it. . . . Despite the fact that quite a few pictures in the project show evening activities, and a lot of the theaters shown in their daytime landscape are gleaming white and in perfect repair, a lot of viewers just skip over these – maybe, 'they don't fit in' – and say something like 'I used to love the drive-in, too bad they're all gone'.[117]

Working drive-ins can still be presented as nostalgic, while the abandoned drive-in can be pictured for different reasons. The artist Don Stinson told Elizabeth Heilman Brooke that he was not nostalgic about the seemingly forlorn gas stations and drive-ins that reappear in his work.[118] In his diptych, *The Necessity for Ruins* (1998), the larger, 'wide-screen' format of the two panels shows a white drive-in screen looking out over grasslands, in front of mountains in the distance and below the expanse of blue sky. The second, narrower rectangle shows the drive-in's abandoned ticket booth. The title is taken from John Brinkerhoff Jackson's essay, 'The Necessity for Ruins', in which Jackson distinguished between monuments designed to remind us of great leaders or events, or religious and political obligations, and monuments to 'a vernacular past, a golden age where there are no dates or names, simply a sense of the way it *used to be*, history as the chronicle of everyday existence'.[119] Elsewhere Jackson had wondered about America's response to the decay of the modern: 'how will we take the abandoned, more or less modern high school with monster gymnasium? The abandoned drive-in movie theater with rows of empty stanchions emerging from the weeds?'[120] The future tense was unnecessary when these comments were made at the end of the twentieth century but the uncertainty remained indicative of alternative perspectives.

In contrast to the tendency to picture the drive-in abandoned to nature or still surviving, an alternative approach has been to uproot and transform it. The picture of the drive-in could be a monument to an idea of the way things were or a reflection on that idea or the idea could be turned on its head to become what it had not been. In 1980 the Downtown branch of the Whitney Museum in New York presented its 'third annual drive-in', 'Desert Nights', with screenings of experimental films such as Jon Jost's *Canyon* (1970), Kenneth Anger's *Lucifer Rising* (1974) as well as Hollywood's *The Petrified Forest* (1936) and *Son of the Sheik* (1926).[121] Beyond the United States, in 2006, Fire Station Artists' Studios in Dublin organized *12 Angry Films*, 'an outdoor season of films tracing the history of labour and social justice issues in cinema' at a temporary drive-in cinema in Dublin's docklands.[122] In the words of Jesse Jones, the event set out to reclaim the drive-in as 'a kind of lost tapestry that could be rewoven to create new meanings and . . . a social space for a different kind of spectatorship'.[123] For Jones, the drive-in was not only 'symbolic of McCarthyite paranoia' but also 'a space for a burgeoning youth culture', a public and private space that allowed a diverse audience to talk over, reinterpret or ignore the films it screened.[124] The programme opened with *Salt of the Earth*, presented as 'the antithesis of what a 1950s drive-in would have been . . . yet its bad sound quality and grainy black and white colour seemed to fit naturally into the atmosphere of a drive-in'.[125] Ironically, by staging the antithesis of the drive-in, the event returned to a film that had been shown at the Silver Sky-Vue Drive-In in 1954.

Another temporary drive-in arts event, *Auto-Kino!*, took place in Berlin in 2010. Those attending could watch experimental films such as *24-Hour Psycho* (1993), *Dottie Gets Spanked* (1993) and *Kustom Kar Kommandos* (1965), sitting in one of fifteen second-hand cars. In the book accompanying the event, Angela Rosenberg noted that 'the vehicles don't exude the glamour we've learnt to expect from popular representations of the drive-in' but are true to the drive-in experience in that 'the onscreen action is filtered through the windshield, creating a distance *vis-à-vis* the narrative and isolating the viewer'.[126] 'The drive-in cinema is one of the oddest cultural hybrids the culture industry has given rise to', added Bert Rebhandl, pointing out that while in other cinemas the reverse of the screen was invisible this was not the case at the drive-in.[127] However, looking at the back of the screen is not necessarily a distanciation effect. It could mean looking at the spectacle invisible in Robert Frank's 'Drive-in – Detroit', the 115-foot tower and illuminated, cascading waterfall of the Gratiot Drive which caught the eye of those who went to the drive-in and even those who did not.

Drive-ins, grindhouses and postage stamps

Illustrating Adam Gaines' somewhat nebulous 'What means one thing to one person may not mean the same to the person he is talking to', the drive-in has meant quite different, even contradictory things to different people, at different times and in different contexts. Its reinvention as an urban art event followed (but also paralleled) its association with unsophisticated rural films and audiences. It has shifted from a sign of contemporary modernity towards a relic of the past. From songs about 'kissin' at the drive-in' and carefully lit photographs of embracing couples to literary characterizations of the drive-in as a sea of fornication or a scene of mating frenzy, the dominant image has often been of the drive-in as a venue for young couples on a date (though this could mean sitting in uncomfortable cars among rowdy people and could end with one of the couple walking out of the drive-in). Films that depict the family drive-in outing have played a minor role in fictional representation but remain part of popular discourse. Increasingly but not universally associated with the past, films and novels have also repeatedly linked the drive-in to the horror film while photographs of abandoned drive-ins appeal to ambivalent nostalgia. Drive-ins have been imagined not only as disreputable places but also as representative of an earlier 'golden age', as part of America's roadside heritage or akin to wildlife in need of preservation. Their connection with the 1950s sits alongside other period associations, as different generations have brought their own memories and as 'drive-in movie' came to take on new connotations in and after the 1970s in response to changes in programming policies, audiences and film culture. For individual critics and a 1960s/1970s new generation of filmmakers they could represent what was wrong with the contemporary American film industry or contemporary America. They were subsequently celebrated by the 'redneck' persona of Joe Bob Briggs but also adopted as a counter-cultural form, for their liminal, hybrid and unruly status and because they offered a different form (or model) of cinema spectatorship.

They have lived on outside the cinema, not just in the examples of films, songs, novels and photographs mentioned here but also through cult 'drive-in movie' celebration.

This overlaps with what Church discusses as 'a drive-in theatre of the mind': the shift from theatrical to non-theatrical exhibition of exploitation films, as drive-ins become increasingly obsolete as lived places while exploitation films are marketed and viewed as 'drive-in movies' on different home video formats.[128] For Church, the 'selective nostalgia' for an imagined, 'relatively innocent past [in essence, an imagined 1950s], overlaps with another popular (if less prevalent) mythology of the drive-in: as a notorious site for the exhibition of exploitation films'.[129] His focus is on the latter as a variant of the 'grindhouse nostalgia' that not only looks back to a time (up to the early 1980s, before the closure of cinemas specializing in exploitation and adult films) and place (such as New York's 42nd Street, home to a cluster of such cinemas) but also functions as a generic label and transmedia concept.[130] Church argues that the progressive disappearance of drive-ins 'as lived places has allowed the drive-in as generic place to become all the more abstracted into a polysemic *lieu de mémoire* that fans can uphold as an apparent reflection of their own values', while the extinction of grindhouse cinemas has encouraged 'a cultural forgetting that has allowed the lost site's recent reappraisal to take on a wider range of contemporary meanings in the absence of prevailing counter-evidence'.[131]

The overlap with my own account is most evident where Church discusses drive-ins as lived places, measuring the mythology against surviving evidence and counter-evidence. In this chapter I have moved away from the drive-in as it existed in a particular time and in particular locations, and away from history from below, examining the range of meanings available through different media and across time and different forms of drive-in representation and nostalgia. That also points to distinct concerns. Church discusses the drive-in in relation to film fandom, which has not been a particular element of my discussion of how filmmakers, writers, performers and photographers have pictured the drive-in, or in this study as a whole. As he acknowledges, the mythology of the drive-in as notorious site for exploitation exhibition is not the drive-in's only or even dominant image, at least outside film studies. As he also acknowledges, the fact that some drive-ins survived past the eras with which they are primarily associated, beyond the 1950s or the 1970s, complicates the movement towards cultural amnesia. The narrative that sees the drive-in beginning to decline after the 1950s might explain its increased on-screen presence from the late 1960s as a case of the absence of functional drive-ins leaving greater space for their fictional portrayal. Films that used recently closed cinemas fit that argument but it is complicated by the number of drive-ins that continued to function during the 1970s and the films that continued to picture the drive-in as part of the American landscape. Even *Grease* (following in the tradition of *He's a Cockeyed Wonder* and *Kiss of the Tarantula*) used the Pickwick Drive-In in Burbank as a set when it was still a functioning drive-in. The myth of the 1950s drive-in was in part a 1970s construct but it was also developed, through song, slang and other creative forms, in the 1950s. The postal service poll cited at the beginning of this book, which placed the drive-in movie as the image that represented the American 1950s more than any other, indicates a wider resonance, though that resonance took different and contradictory forms.

Conclusion

The drive-in and cinema history

In the 'Afterword' to his *Decoding the Movies*, Richard Maltby defends New Cinema History against the charge that its methods 'involve too much promiscuous extra-cinematic research'.[1] It is a charge that could also be made about the present study. In examining one form of 1950s cinema I have paid more attention to the film programme than other studies of the drive-in but I have also drawn on studies of post-war urban and suburban development, Senate hearings, newspaper advice columns, Harlequin Romances and other extra-cinematic sources. I have examined individual drive-ins in their local contexts but unlike a dedicated New Cinema micro-history have also looked across the nation. In doing this, I have inevitably been selective and ultimately have only been able to scratch the surface. I have compared the different implications of different forms of evidence. Having started with two contradictory images of the drive-in, as a safe space for families with young children or as a disreputable place for amorous teenagers, this project has unearthed other contradictions and in places raised more questions than answers.

An evidence-based approach based on a range of sources can still revise existing accounts, assertions and assumptions. While writing on 1950s drive-ins, from contemporary trade press reports to more recent scholarly articles, has tended to discuss them as independent enterprises, at odds with Hollywood, the records of Interstate Theatres, combined with trade press reports, reveal that many belonged, fully or in part, to larger circuits. Even if they were independent, drive-in owners often also owned indoor cinemas. The distinction between small- and large-scale exhibitors remained, as did, despite the Paramount Decrees, the distinction between Major chains and small-scale exhibitors. Distinctions between ownership of indoor and outdoor cinemas were often subsidiary to those larger differences. The common perception that the drive-in programme was different from, and inferior to, that of other cinemas has some basis. Drive-ins did show films months, even years after their original release, including poor prints and low-budget films in conditions that were themselves poor. However, examining the programmes of individual drive-ins reveals that while they did often get films late, how late varied significantly between drive-ins, and by the 1960s those close to larger urban centres could screen films at the same time as neighbouring indoor cinemas. The films they showed, from the latest Oscar winner to older westerns, were essentially the films shown at indoor cinemas.

The drive-in never was a monolithic entity but it could seem to be, viewed from above. Because of the ways in which drive-ins differed from what were often known as conventional theatres they could be presented as more uniform than they were. Where accounts acknowledge variations, these have often been framed chronologically or in terms of binary oppositions, as the family drive-in made way for the teenage 'passion pit', or vice versa. The reality was more complex.

There are ways in which drive-ins challenge the conventions. The American film industry developed on a centralized model and histories of it have tended to follow suit, devoting most attention to production at the Major studios and when looking at exhibition emphasizing the metropolitan first run. This is complicated by the subsequent-run status and off-centred location of the drive-in. Researching this topic demands looking at the edges, not just beyond films but at the inside pages of local newspapers rather than just the national headlines, at local histories as well as established sources. However, drive-ins remained part of the industrial network that covered the United States, from the Arkansas Amusement Corporation Pines Drive-In in Little Rock opening *The Ten Commandments* on Thursday 14 August 1958 to the Hi-Way 17 outside Edenton, North Carolina, on the same date playing a western double bill of Randolph Scott in *The Stranger Wore a Gun* (1953) and Glenn Ford in *The Sheepman* (1958). In summer months, they could constitute the majority of the US cinema audience and across the 1950s they made up a significant minority.

There are aspects of 1950s drive-in programming, such as dusk-to-dawn screenings and exploitation roadshows, which fit their unruly reputation, though this also highlights the range of films they screened. The short cartoon was a standard part of the drive-in programme, after which they could play horror and science-fiction films, including AIP double bills, as well as other teenpics, though (like many indoor neighbourhood cinemas) they were far more likely to play westerns. Hollywood Major films ranged from that year's Oscar winners to new and not-so-new action melodramas. The occasional American exploitation film or non-American film open to similar exploitation could attract their largest audiences. Feature-length cartoons and other Disney films were also important to the drive-in when they could obtain them on an affordable basis. The main exceptions to this were the drive-ins showing

CONCLUSION

Spanish-language films as part or the whole of their programme. Otherwise, there were differences between indoor and outdoor cinemas, for instance in the extent to which drive-ins relied on the double bill (and subsequently the triple bill). However, in the 1950s the drive-in programme often resembled the film programme of other subsequent-run cinemas. Their owners, after all, often also owned indoor cinemas.

Perhaps it is not surprising that accounts of the drive-in have tended to emphasize their difference. In the 1950s, drive-ins needed to counter accusations that they were taking audiences away from other cinemas: one way of doing this was to argue that those who went to the drive-in would not otherwise have gone to the cinema. Subsequently, writers who have paid attention to the drive-in have tended to do so because of its distinctive features, referring to the small number of drive-ins that provided a laundry service rather than the larger number that played Major studio films a month or more after their first run, as subsequent-run indoor and outdoor cinemas did across the United States. Examining drive-in programming in the 1950s can provide a broader picture of 1950s American cinemagoing outside the first run, illustrating a world where audiences could watch (to take a few days from the programme of the MacArthur Drive-In in Texas) the swashbuckler *The Brigand* (1952) on Monday 12 January 1953, the sex hygiene film *The Story of Bob and Sally* (1948) on the following Tuesday or Wednesday and on Thursday a double bill of the Bill Elliot western *Waco* (1952) and the MGM crime drama, *The Unknown Man* (1951), all at the same cinema. It can draw attention to a broader range of films watched in the 1950s as well as to the fact that the better-known films of the decade played outdoors as well as indoors.

Of course, the fact that drive-ins often showed the same films as indoor cinemas did not mean that going to the drive-in was the same as going to an indoor cinema. The outdoor/indoor distinction was itself important, as drive-in owners liked to remind their customers. In the 1950s there were at least 182 drive-ins called Starlight, Starlite or Star-Lite. There were also variations such as Big Sky, Blue Sky, Moon-Glo, Moonlight, Moonlite, Skylark, Skyline, Skyview, Sky-vue, Skyway, Stardust, Starview, Sunset, Twilight and Twilite. The drive-in audience abandoned the seat beneath the cinema roof for the evening under the night sky or, put another way, replaced the space of the auditorium with the confines of the car. Unlike the indoor cinema, the drive-in combined the open and the enclosed, the public and the private, the cinema and the park, the car park and the amusement park. It could provide an impoverished cinema experience in terms of clarity of image and sound. The climate (above all in the summer) could be an invitation or (along with the mosquitoes) a problem.

While drive-ins programmed (within the limits possible in 1950s America) a range of films, they also differed and therefore offered different experiences even to those watching the same film. The experience of watching Elvis Presley in *King Creole*, alongside the teen crime drama *Stake Out on Dope Street*, on a warm Thursday at the Razorback in Little Rock, 21 August 1958, would have been different for different members of the audience and would not have been the same as that double bill at the same drive-in on the Saturday that followed when the weather had turned cloudy but the audience was almost twice the size of Thursday's. It would have been different again for those watching *King Creole* when it played a full week from 20 August 1958 at the Acres Drive-In in Phoenix, double billed with the Andy Griffith comedy *No Time for Sergeants*, and for those watching the film, single billed, Thursday to Saturday, 4–6 September 1958, at the Hi-Way 17 drive-in North Carolina. *King Creole* was different for different viewers when it played at the Starlight Drive-In in Chipley, Florida ('small town and rural patronage' and space for 150 cars), on a warm Sunday in March 1959, proprietor I. Roche writing that it was 'Strictly for the Presley fans of our drive-in, for a mediocre crowd. Mixed comments'.[2] It would have been different again for those who saw it at the Dubuque Drive-In, where it played Thursday to Saturday, 30 April–2 May 1959, in a Southern-teen themed triple bill alongside Pat Boone in *Mardi Gras* (1958) and Sal Mineo in *The Young Don't Cry* (1957).

It would be possible to use that glance at some drive-ins that played *King Creole* as the basis for a story about the drive-in as a 1950s, teenage, rock 'n' roll inflected space. After 'That's All Right, Mama' became a hit in 1954, writes Peter Guralnick, Presley and Dixie Locke 'continued to go out to Leonard's for hamburgers and go to the drive-in movies and sit on the front porch and spoon'.[3] On 15 July 1955 Presley played a gig at the Joy Drive-In, in Minden, Louisiana, while the night before he joined the army he went to the drive-in to see Tommy Sands in *Sing, Boy, Sing* (1958).[4] A Presley-inflected account of the drive-in should also make space for sixteen-year-old 'SO IN LOVE' who wrote to Ann Landers about her love for her eighteen-year-old boyfriend who worked as a mechanic in a garage and enjoyed the same things: 'roller-skating, swimming, Elvis Presley and drive-in movies', to which Landers curtly replied, 'You can't build a life on drive-in movies and Elvis Presley.'[5]

In its post-1950s afterlife, it could include *G.I. Blues* (1960), the first film Presley made after he left the army, in which, in 'Didja' Ever', he echoed a familiar joke by asking if at a drive-in movie date you ever got 'one of them girls, who just wants to watch the show'. It could move on to the 1970s drive-in exhibitor who told William Price Fox, 'Out under the stars . . . *Citizen Kane* [1941], with a personal appearance by Mr Welles himself, would languish, but anything that Elvis touches will run forever.'[6] It could include the film *Heart-*

CONCLUSION

break Hotel (1988), in which a young man kidnaps the rock 'n' roll star for his Presley-obsessed mother and which begins at a 1972 Elvis Presley drive-in movie marathon. It could end up at the centrepiece of the Elvis Presley Automobile Museum in Graceland Plaza: the Highway 51 Drive-In, where 1957 Chevrolets are bolted to the floor in front of a movie screen, with drive-in speakers next to each car seat and a neon 'Hwy 51 Drive-In' sign to add to the 1950s automobile, movie look.[7]

That is one story, one that reveals aspects of the drive-in as lived and imagined experience. The drive-in was part of youth culture before, during and after the 1950s. It has been correctly pointed out that in the 1950s this audience did not dominate the drive-in as has sometimes been suggested or implied. In the popular imagination the drive-in has often been a teenage space but though drive-ins were associated with teenagers in the 1950s, newspaper and trade press reports (and the proliferation of children's playgrounds) stressed the drive-in's family appeal. However, evidence from surveys to newspaper reports also indicates that there was still a significant 1950s teenage drive-in audience. To set the family audience against the teenage audience is also to set up another oversimplified opposition. The word 'teenager' can have different meanings and covers different life stages. Teenagers went to the drive-in not only on dates, on double or even triple dates, but also in larger, mixed or same-sex groups. The date itself was both public and private, and the fact that at the drive-in the car provided a degree of privacy fostered anxiety, frustration, danger, companionship and pleasure as well as myth.

Even the fictional drive-in is more varied than might have been assumed. Just as there is not a simple contrast between a family-friendly drive-in of the 1950s and the 1970s drive-ins devoted to adult and horror films, the drive-in of the popular imagination cannot be reduced to nostalgia for either 1950s innocence or 1970s exploitation. These alternatives overlap in childhood memories of being taken to see *Star Wars* (1977) at the drive-in, the discussion of *Cat Women of the Moon* (1953) alongside *The Texas Chainsaw Massacre* as examples of *Horror at the Drive-In* and the trailer for *The Blob* as part of the 1950s nostalgia of *Grease*.[8] The nostalgia takes different forms across different media. The 1950s has played a central but not exclusive role in drive-in nostalgia, for the drive-in has come to be viewed also through its subsequent development, decline and reputation. Nostalgia in its different forms has not been the only way in which the drive-in has been viewed, though it has become increasingly evident. In songs, novels, still and moving images, the drive-in has been imagined as contemporary as well as past, as urban and suburban as well as rural, as romantic as well as bleak, as adult, adolescent and as a childhood adventure. Individual versions of the drive-in, from Robert Frank's 'Drive-in movie – Detroit' to *Grease*, have taken on different and ambivalent connotations in their different versions and contexts. All in their own way testify to the hold that the drive-in maintains on the popular imagination.

There were other drive-in audiences besides families and teenagers though not all have made an equal mark on the popular imagination. The drive-in audience of adults without children did not receive particular analysis in the 1950s and has not done so subsequently, again for understandable reasons: it was not a distinctive feature of the drive-in, even if it did account for a considerable proportion of the drive-in audience. Other audiences linked to the drive-in are difficult to quantify. The argument that Richard Hollingshead made in 1933 about the drive-in appealing to people with disabilities has repeatedly been echoed. One problem is that Hollingshead and others were promoting the drive-in rather than reporting on evidence about its audience. Those who claimed that drive-ins attracted a forgotten or lost audience were seeking to allay fears that the drive-in was taking away customers from other cinemas and to counter criticism that the drive-in was a place of immorality and licentiousness. Claims about the drive-in's different audiences are easy to find but evidence to support such claims is more difficult to locate and tends to exist in the form of individual anecdotes. Surveys in the 1950s did not ask questions about disabilities (just as they did not ask about ethnicity), and subsequent research has tended to focus on the representation of disability rather than the experiences of historical, disabled audiences.

There were limits to mixing at the drive-in, and there are limits to what I have revealed about going to the drive-in. The black audience has been largely excluded from drive-in history even when they were not excluded from the drive-in. That exclusion or segregation tended to be enforced silently prior to the 1960s, their voice heard in Doris Crump Rainey's insistence that 'we could hear them, and they could hear us' from opposite sides of the concession stand.[9] More generally, while box-office figures when they are available can allow us to compare the number of people who went to different shows, they do not tell us about the individual experiences of those who made up those numbers. As others have repeatedly pointed out, those who went to the drive-in did not necessarily even watch the film; it is possible to identify instances when they did as well as to indicate what they might also have done but a challenge to do more than that. The accounts that exist about going to the drive-in in the 1950s tend to come from or at least be filtered through journalists, industry insiders or self-styled moral guardians, each with their own agenda. Individual viewing experiences are rarely recorded or recoverable.

Traces remain. Drive-ins were neither simply passion pits for teenagers, nor limited to a low-cost place to watch old movies while the children were asleep at the back of the station wagon, nor simply a combination of those alternatives. It is possible to trace the physical and cultural circumstances in which individuals went to the drive-in (or were prevented from doing so). Even the drive-in myths, the alarm and the nostalgia can tell us about what the drive-in has meant and how this has changed. Acknowledging the drive-in's other attractions can itself help us understand cinema history as not just a history of major films, or a history of film in general, but a history that includes where films played, who watched them, what else they did before, after and while they were at the drive-in and the place of this experience and the cinema within their lives. Examining that history benefits from attention to national distribution and communication networks, cultural trends and differences as well as the local and the personal and how the imagined and experienced drive-in are intertwined.

Notes

Introduction

1 Associated Press, 'What Do Americans Want to Remember: Drive in Movies, Moonwalk, Swing and Zoot Suits . . .', *St. George Daily Spectrum* (UT), 23 July 1998, D2.
2 See '33c Drive-in Movies Single', National Postal Museum, *Smithsonian*, https://www.si.edu/object/33c-drive-movies-single%3Anpm_2000.2020.116 (accessed 20 March 2023).
3 *Mom, The Flag & Apple Pie: Great American Writers on Great American Things*, compiled by the editors of *Esquire* (Garden City, NY: Doubleday, 1975).
4 William Price Fox, 'The Drive-in Movie', in *Mom, The Flag & Apple Pie*, 216.
5 David Church, *Grindhouse Nostalgia: Memory, Home Video and Exploitation Film Fandom* (Edinburgh: Edinburgh University Press, 2015), 31. Church refers to 'a polysemic *lieu de mémoire*', which I discuss further in Chapter 4.
6 See *Weekend with the Baby Sitter*, Internet Movie Database, https://www.imdb.com/title/tt0064055/ (accessed 11 November 2022).
7 Don and Susan Sanders, *Drive-In Movies Memories: Popcorn and Romance under the Stars* (Middleton, NH: Carriage House, 2000), 6–7.
8 Hunter S. Thompson, *Generation of Swine: Tales of Shame and Degradation in the '80s* (New York: Summit Books, 1988), 136.
9 Kerry Segrave, *Drive-In Theaters: A History from their Inception in 1933* (Jefferson, NC: McFarland, 1992), 202.
10 Gary D. Rhodes, 'Introduction', in *Horror at the Drive-In: Essays in Popular Americana*, ed. Gary D. Rhodes (Jefferson, NC: McFarland, 2003), 2.
11 Segrave, *Drive-In Theaters*, 198.
12 Kristin Thompson and David Bordwell, *Film History: An Introduction*, 4th edn (New York: McGraw Hill, 2019), 427.
13 Kenneth T. Jackson, *Crabgrass Frontier: The Suburbanization of the United States* (New York: Oxford University Press, 1985), 255.
14 David L. Lewis, 'Sex and the Automobile: From Rumble Seat to Rockin' Vans', in *The Automobile and American Culture*, ed. David L. Lewis and Laurance Goldstein (Ann Arbor, MI: University of Michigan Press, 1983), 130; James Flink writes of how drive-ins 'quickly gained reputations as "passion pits"

where the show in the cars was usually better than the one on the screen': *The Automobile Age* (Cambridge, MA: MIT Press, 1988), 162.

15 See in particular the Cinema Treasures website, www.cinematreasures.org.

16 In the *History of American Cinema* series see: Thomas Schatz, *Boom and Bust: American Cinema in the 1940s* (Berkeley, CA: University of California Press, 1999), 293–4; Peter Lev, *The Fifties: Transforming the Screen 1950-1959* (Berkeley, CA: University of California Press, 2003), 212, 215; Paul Monaco, 'Drive-Ins', in *The Sixties: 1960-1969* (Berkeley, CA: University of California Press, 2001), 46–7. Mark Fox and Grant Black thus slightly exaggerate when they write that the series does not mention the drive-in before the volume on the 1960s but their broad point about the lack of published research holds: see, Mark Fox and Grant Black, 'The Rise and Decline of Drive-in Cinemas in the United States', in *Handbook on the Economics of Leisure*, ed. Samuel Cameron (Cheltenham: Edward Elgar, 2011), 272. As they note, Bruce Austin has made the same point: his writing on the drive-in and its audience includes 'The Development and the Decline of the Drive-In Movie Theater', in *Current Research in Film: Audiences, Economics and Law, Vol. 1*, ed. Bruce A. Austin (Norwood, NJ: Ablex, 1985), 59–91.

17 Mary Morley Cohen, 'Forgotten Audiences in the Passion Pits: Drive-in Theatres and Changing Spectator Practices in Post-war America', *Film History* 6, no. 4 (1994): 470–86; David Church, 'Drive-In and Grindhouse Theatres', in *The Routledge Companion to Cult Cinema*, ed. Ernest Mathijs and Jamie Sexton (London and New York: Routledge, 2020), 215-22; Thomas Doherty, 'Teenpic Double-Bills', in *Teenagers and Teenpics: The Juvenilization of American Movies in the 1950s* (Philadelphia, PA: Temple University Press, 2002), 91–3; Blair Davis, 'Drive-In Theatres', in *The Battle for the Bs: 1950s Hollywood and the Rebirth of Low-Budget Cinema* (Piscataway, NJ: Rutgers University Press, 2012), 36–8; Peter Stanfield, 'Intent to Speed; Hot Rod Movies', in *The Cool and the Crazy: Pop Fifties Cinema* (New Brunswick, NJ: Rutgers University Press, 2015), 112–34; Yannis Tzioumakis, 'The Era of the Drive-in Theatres', in *American Independent Cinema*, 2nd edn (Cambridge: Cambridge University Press, 2017), 129–31; Douglas Gomery, 'The Drive-In Theatre', in *Shared Pleasures: A History of Movie Presentation in the US* (London: BFI Publishing, 1992), 91–3; Sheldon Hall, 'Ozoners, Roadshows and Blitz Exhibitionism: Postwar Developments in Distribution and Exhibition', in *The Classical Hollywood Reader*, ed. Steve Neale (Abingdon: Routledge, 2012), 343–54; James Russell and Jim Whalley, 'Drive-Ins', in *Hollywood and the Baby Boom: A Social History* (New York: Bloomsbury Academic, 2018), 47–51; W. D. Phillips, 'A Cinema Under the Stars (and Stripes): David Milgram's Boulevard Drive-In Theatre and the Political-Economic Landscape of America's Post-War Drive-In Boom', *Historical Journal of Film, Radio and Television* 40, no. 2 (2020): 275–96.

18 Joe Bob Briggs, 'Why God Created Drive-Ins', in *Joe Bob Goes to the Drive-In* (Harmondsworth: Penguin, 1989), 5–12.

19 John Hinckley and Jon G. Robinson, *The Big Book of Car Culture: The Armchair Guide to Automotive Americana* (St Paul, MN: Motorbooks, 2005), 214.

20 See, for instance, 'Drive-In Anniversary', *Pittsburgh Press*, 6 June 1958, 26.
21 Segrave includes the patent as an appendix to *Drive-In Theaters*, 203–14.
22 'Drive-in Theatre to be Opened Here', Camden *Courier-Post* [*CP*], 17 May 1933, 4.
23 Segrave, *Drive-In Theaters*, 7.
24 David Bruce Reddick, 'Movies under the Stars: A History of the Drive-in Theatre Industry, 1933-1983' (PhD diss., Michigan State University, East Lansing, 1984), 6.
25 Segrave, *Drive-In Theaters*, 237.
26 See, for instance, '353 Million Concession Market', *Motion Picture Exhibitor*, 2 November 1960, PE-5. This reported on a survey which suggested that concession sales accounted for 24 per cent of the gross of US indoor cinemas but 51 per cent of the drive-in gross.
27 Segrave, *Drive-in Theaters*, 78–88.
28 James P. Cunningham, 'The Drive-In Theater', in *Film Daily Year Book of Motion Pictures*, ed. Jack Alicoate (New York: Wid's Film and Film Folk, 1950) [hereafter *Film Daily Year Book*], 801.
29 Segrave, *Drive-in Theaters*, 78.
30 Gomery, *Shared Pleasures*, 92.
31 'Private Approach Speeds Traffic at Detroit Drive-In', *Boxoffice*, 17 July 1949, BT-28.
32 Don and Susan Sanders, *The American Drive-In Movie Theatre*, (1997) (New York: Crestline, 2013), 54.
33 'Private Approach Speeds Traffic at Detroit Drive-In'.
34 Church, 'Drive-In and Grindhouse Theaters', 217.
35 Segrave, *Drive-In Theaters*, 83.
36 Ibid., 56.
37 Eric Mark Kramer, 'Who's Afraid of the Virgin Wolf Man? Or, the Other Meaning of Auto-Eroticism', in *Horror at the Drive-In*, 20.
38 Accounts that emphasize the 1950s teenage audience include Doherty, *Teenagers and Teenpics*.
39 Segrave, *Drive-In Theaters*, 198.
40 Examples of nostalgic celebration of the drive-in include Sanders, *Drive-In Movie Memories*; Sanders, *The American Drive-In Movie Theatre*; and Elizabeth McKeon and Linda Everett, *Cinema under the Stars: America's Love Affair with the Drive-In Movie Theater* (Nashville, TN: Cumberland House, 1998). See Church, 'A Drive-in Theatre of the Mind: Nostalgic Populism and the Déclassé Video Object', in *Grindhouse Nostalgia*, 20–72, for an analysis of cult nostalgia and the drive-in.
41 Segrave, *Drive-In Theaters*, 197.
42 Church, 'Drive-In and Grindhouse Theaters', 220.

43 See Mark Fox, 'Drive-in Theatres and Audience Rules of Conduct: Before and During the COVID-19 Pandemic', *Participations: Journal of Audience & Reception Studies* 17, no. 2 (2020): 66–94.

44 'Open Air Drive-In Theatre for Cars', *Variety*, 13 June 1933, 5.

45 *CP*, 8 June 1933, 15; *CP*, 9 June 1933, 11; *CP*, 10 June 1933, 11.

46 Donald McGraw, 'Drive-In Movies Began in Camden', *Philadelphia Inquirer*, 6 June 1965, NJ1.

47 *Variety*'s brief review was published on 23 May 1933, 15.

48 Sanders, *The American Drive-In Movie Theatre*, 17.

49 *CP*, 21 June 1933, 5; *CP*, 28 June 1933, 6; *CP*, 24 July 1933, 13.

50 *CP*, 21 August 1933, 11; *CP*, 28 August 1933, 11; *CP*, 16 September, 5.

51 *CP*, 8 July 1935, 4; *CP*, 27 July 1935, 5; *CP*, 12 June 1935, 16.

52 *CP*, 24 June 1936, 20; *CP*, 19 September 1936, 8. See Sanders, *The American Drive-In Movie Theatre*, 17, for the Camden Drive-In's advertisement for the latter.

53 Eric Schaefer, *'Bold! Daring! Shocking! True!': A History of Exploitation Films, 1919-1959* (Durham, NC: Duke University Press, 1999), 181–2.

54 For example, the Fox Beyer, Excelsior Springs, Missouri, *Lathrop Optimist* (MO), 12 April 1934, 3.

55 'Delicate Subject Filmed at Drive-In', *CP*, 1 June 1935, 4.

56 'Film Shown Here Seized as Indecent', *CP*, 24 June 1942, 3.

57 'Nudism Ideal Seen in Elysia: New Drive-In Picture Gives Clear Idea of Latest Fad', *CP*, 17 August 1935, 14.

58 McGraw, 'Drive-In Movies Began in Camden', NJ9.

59 The *Philadelphia Public Ledger* advertisement is reproduced, along with the advertisement for the opening night, in Segrave, *Drive-In Theaters*, 6.

60 'New Jersey Drive-In Theatre Holds 400 Cars, and Doing Biz', *Variety*, 24 October 1933, 1.

61 'Those Drive-In Theatres, or Movies through a Windshield', *Motion Picture Herald* [*MPH*], 27 June 1936, BT-8.

62 Bernard M. Sleeth, 'Indiana's First Drive-In Movie', *Indianapolis Star Magazine*, 15 November 1964, 18.

63 Ibid.

64 *Cyclopedia of Motion Picture Work*, prepared by David S. Hulfish, Vol. 2 (Chicago, IL: American School of Correspondence, 1911), 195.

65 Ibid., 210.

66 David G. Thomas, *Screen with a Voice: A History of Motion Pictures in Las Cruces, New Mexico* (Las Cruces, NM: Doc45 Publishing, 2016), 35.

67 Ibid., 109.

68 See Church, *Grindhouse Nostalgia*, 33.

69 Segrave, *Drive-In Theaters*, 235.

70 Ibid. The figures for car capacity are provided in Christopher H. Sterling and Timothy R. Haight, *The Mass Media: Aspen Institute Guide to Communication Industry Trends* (New York: Praeger, 1978), 34.
71 Sterling and Haight, *The Mass Media*, 35.
72 Ibid.
73 'A Study of Influences on Drive-in Theatres in 1952', prepared by Jack H. Levin Associates, cited in 'US Drive-Ins Up 25-fold', *MPH*, 7 June 1952, 30.
74 'Justice Department Denies Leniency towards Film Companies under Decree', *Film Bulletin*, 25 June 1956, 26; 'Play for Play', *MPH*, 25 May 1955, 3.
75 'Good Year Coming Up in '62; Upbeat on Grosses, Product', *Boxoffice*, 1 January 1962, 11.
76 Dennis Giles, 'The Outdoor Economy: A Study of the Contemporary Drive-In', *Journal of the University Film and Video Association* 35, no. 2 (1983): 67.
77 Segrave, *Drive-in Theaters*, 233.
78 Jim Paulin, 'The Demise of the Drive-In Movie, Part One', in *Millers River Reader*, ed. Allen Young (Athol, MA: Millers River Publishers, 1987), 102.
79 Church, *Grindhouse Nostalgia*, 37–8.
80 Church, 'Drive-In and Grindhouse Theaters', 217.
81 Segrave, *Drive-in Theaters*, xiii; Davis, *The Battle for the Bs*', 38.
82 'Theatres closed in the United States from 1947 to 1952', Hoblitzelle Interstate Theatre Circuit Collection, Box 8, 1a, Harry Ransom Center, University of Texas at Austin, no page numbers. Some of those listed did not actually close but changed their name. Others still appear in the list of drive-ins published in the 1955 edition of the *Film Daily Year Book*, which could mean they did not actually close or that the yearbook had not been updated.
83 *CP*, 6 June 1983, 11.
84 *CP*, 6 June 1973, 72.
85 *CP*, 6 June 1973, E4-5.
86 Cohen, 'Forgotten Audiences in the Passion Pits', 484.
87 Church, *Grindhouse Nostalgia*, 37.
88 Philip K. Scheuer, 'Shocker Pioneers Tell How to Make a Monster', *Los Angeles Times*, 21 September 1958, E1.
89 'Film Company Seeks a New Locale for Its Teen-Age Movies', *New York Times* [*NYT*], 6 November 1965, 18; Aljean Harmetz, 'Museum Celebrates "Drive-In" Movies', *NYT*, 27 July 1979, C1.
90 Tony Scott, 'Romero', *Cinefantastique* 3, no. 2 (1973): 13.
91 Segrave, *Drive-In Theaters*, viii.
92 Ben Goldsmith, '"The Comfort Lies in All the Things You Can Do": The Australian Drive-in – Cinema of Distraction', *Journal of Popular Culture* 33, no. 1 (1999): 154.

93 Segrave, *Drive-In Theaters*, 104–14. For an example of a recent discussion of the drive-in outside the United States and Australia, see Roald Maliangkay, 'Sheltering from Streaming Clouds: Nostalgia, Authenticity, and Drive-in Cinema in Korea', *Journal of Korean and Asian Arts* 3 (2021): 31–53.

94 See David Church, 'They Are Risen: Drive-in Distractions and Hallowed Ground under Lockdown', *Flow*, 16 April 2020, https://www.flowjournal.org/2020/04/they-are-risen/ (accessed 20 March 2023).

95 The project was carried out by James Russell and Jim Whalley, who use it in their *Hollywood and the Baby Boom: A Social History* (New York: Bloomsbury Academic, 2018).

96 See Richard Maltby et al. (eds), *Explorations in New Cinema History: Approaches and Case Studies* (Oxford: Blackwell, 2011).

Chapter 1

1 'Fayetteville Traffic Jammed by "Stromboli"', *Charlotte Observer*, 14 March 1950, 11.

2 For an account of the Peoria screening, see Randy Palmer, *Herschell Gordon Lewis, Godfather of Gore: The Films* (Jefferson, NC: MacFarland, 2000), 60–5.

3 'Herb', 'Stromboli', *Variety*, 15 February 1950, 1.

4 See Tag Gallagher, *The Adventures of Roberto Rossellini: His Life and Films* (New York: Da Capo Press, 1998), 346–7.

5 ''50 End of Era for Stars and System: Swanson Cues Comeback Potentials', *Variety*, 3 January 1951, 59.

6 For a discussion of differences between the versions of *Stromboli*, see Peter Brunette, *Roberto Rossellini* (Berkeley, CA: University of California Press, 1997), 114–15.

7 Jeffrey Klenotic, 'Putting Cinema History on the Map: Using GIS to Explore the Spatiality of Cinema', in *Explorations in New Cinema History*, 61.

8 Giuliana Bruno, 'Site-Seeing: Architecture and the Moving Image', *Wide Angle* 19, no. 4 (1997): 11. Bruno's quotation is from Paul Virilo, *Lost Dimension*, trans. Daniel Moshenberg (New York: Semiotext(e), 1991), 25.

9 Karen Lury and Doreen Massey, 'Making Connections', *Screen* 40, no. 3 (1999): 231.

10 Klenotic, 'Putting Cinema History on the Map', 66.

11 Jeffrey Klenotic, 'Mapping Movies', https://www.mappingmovies.com (accessed 6 November 2022).

12 'Drive-in Theatres in the United States', *Film Daily Year Book* (1950), 1024.

13 *Hill's Fayetteville (Cumberland County, NC) City Directory* (Richmond, VA: Hill Directory, 1951), xiii and 4.

14 'News of the Territory', *Exhibitor*, 16 September 1953, NT1.
15 Cohen, 'Forgotten Audiences in the Passion Pits', 474.
16 James Morris, 'Is the Drive-In Here to Stay?' *International Projectionist* 31, no. 4 (1946): 19.
17 James P. Cunningham, 'The Drive-In Theater', *Film Daily Year Book* (1954), 801.
18 'Drive-In Business Burns up the Prairies', *Life*, 24 September 1951, 104–8.
19 John Durant, 'The Movies Take to the Pastures', *Saturday Evening Post*, 14 October 1950, 24–5, 85, 89–90.
20 Wilfred P. Smith, 'Claims – And Problems of Drive-Ins in 1951', *MPH*, 3 February 1951, 53.
21 Gomery, *Shared Pleasures*, 91.
22 Russell and Whalley, *Hollywood and the Baby Boom*, 48.
23 Maggie Valentine, *The Show Starts on the Sidewalk: An Architectural History of the Movie Theatre, starring S. Charles Lee* (New Haven, CT: Yale University Press, 1994), 160; Cohen, 'Forgotten Audiences in the Passion Pits', 483.
24 Jackson, *Crabgrass Frontier*, 255; Neil Brenner and Nikos Katsikis, 'Operational Landscapes: Hinterlands of the Capitaloscene', *Architectural Design* 90, no. 1 (2020): 22–31.
25 'Now it's Portable Drive-Ins, a New Idea in the Carolinas', *Showmen's Trade Review*, 17 July 1948, 6.
26 Ibid.
27 Ibid.
28 Morris, 'Is the Drive-In Here to Stay?' 18.
29 Ibid.
30 The Cinema Treasures website does include an entry on the Fort McCoy Drive-In in a cow pasture in Ocala National Park, Florida, where in 1956 the screen was apparently a sheet nailed to a pair of palmetto trees, there was a single speaker in front of a screen, the projector ran off a car battery and there were breaks between reel changes during which drinks were served: 'Fort McCoy Drive-In', Cinema Treasures, http://cinematreasures.org/theaters/33200 (accessed 13 November 2022).
31 'Elaborate Stands Not Always Necessary, Operator Declares', *Motion Picture Exhibitor*, 30 June 1954, EP3.
32 Ibid.
33 'Exhibitor Has His Say' (EHHS), *Boxoffice*, 6 December 1952, 2.
34 Ibid., 25 July 1953, 1.
35 Karen Dybis, *The Ford-Wyoming Drive-In: Cars, Candy & Canoodling in the Motor City* (Charleston, SC: History Press, 2014).
36 'Laguna Honda Area Rezoning Plan Fought, Residents Protest Proposal for Drive-In Theater', *San Francisco Examiner*, 10 February 1950, 3.

37 'Rezoning for Negro Theatre is Delayed', *Tampa Tribune* (FL), 22 November 1952, 7.
38 Ibid.
39 Dybis, *The Ford-Wyoming Drive-In*, 39.
40 United States Census Bureau, '1960 Census: Population', Part 1–57. Volume 1. Characteristics of the Population. 'Part 1 - Population of Cities in the United States and the Commonwealth of Puerto Rico having, in 1960, 100,000 Inhabitants or More: 1790-1960', 66.
41 Dybis, *The Ford-Wyoming Drive-In*, 85. At the time of writing, the Ford-Wyoming remains open, with five screens.
42 Harrison Kinney and Brendon Gill, 'Moon-Washed', *New Yorker*, 1 October 1949, 20–1; Segrave, *Drive-In Theaters*, 66.
43 'Service for Shoppers by Day, Outdoor Theatre by Night', *MPH*, 8 November 1958, 28–9; United States Census Bureau, '1960 Census: Population', Volume 1. Characteristics of the Population, Part 1–57, Part 32-Number of Inhabitants, New Jersey, 16.
44 'Georgel', 'Dover Drive-In', 'Cinema Treasures', 21 August 2008, http://cinematreasures.org/theaters/12143/comments (accessed 29 November 2022).
45 Robert C. Allen, 'Relocating American Film History: The "Problem" of the Empirical', *Cultural Studies* 20, no. 1 (2006): 64.
46 Alice Hughes, 'A Woman's New York', *Dayton Journal Herald* (OH), 18 January 1950, 16. The article was published in the *Munchie Star Press* (IN), 29 January 1950, under the heading 'New Yorkers Yearn for Drive-In Theaters', 20.
47 Rodney Luther, 'Marketing Aspects of Drive-In Theaters', *Journal of Marketing* 15, no. 1 (1950): 45.
48 Rodney Luther, 'Drive-in Theaters: Rags to Riches in Five Years', *Hollywood Quarterly* 5, no. 4 (1951): 409. In his 'Second Annual Drive-In Audience Survey', in *Theatre Catalog 1950-51*, ed. Andrew W. Shearer (Philadelphia, PA: Jay Emanuel, 1951), 130, he reported the figures of an average of 8.8 miles to get to the drive-in, up from a 7.4 average for the first survey.
49 Smith, 'Claims – And Problems of Drive-Ins in 1951', 14.
50 Arthur Steel to Marvin Mirisch, 4 February 1956, Steve Broidy Collection, Folder 2 Elmsford Drive-In Theatre, Margaret Herrick Library, Los Angeles.
51 'The Eagle and the Hawk', 'EHHS', *Boxoffice*, 23 December 1950, 3.
52 *Policy on Drive-In Theaters* (Washington, DC: American Association of State Highway Officials, 1949), 3.
53 Flink, *The Automobile Age*, 250.
54 *Economic Report of the President, Transmitted to the Congress*, 10 January 1960, 137, https://fraser.stlouisfed.org/files/docs/publications/ERP/1960/ERP_1960.pdf (accessed 5 November 2022).
55 Flink, *The Automobile Age*, 372.

NOTES

56 See Mark H. Rose and Raymond A. Mohl, *Interstate: Highway Politics and Policy since 1939*, 3rd edn (Knoxville, TN: University of Tennessee Press, 2012), 55–67.
57 See 'Drive-Ins Zoom Nationally', *Variety*, 4 June 1952, 7, 22. In its list of drive-ins, *Film Daily Year Book* (1953) includes the Sunset Drive-In under Washington, DC (1066), but this is probably the Sunset Drive-In that Cinema Treasures lists as 5500 Leesburg Pike, Baileys Crossroads, Virginia, http://cinematreasures.org/theaters/11798 (accessed 17 November 2022).
58 'Drive-Ins Zoom Nationally', 22.
59 Ibid.
60 Arnold Farber, 'Survey Proves Drive-Ins Just Grow, Grow, Grow', *Motion Picture Exhibitor*, 28 February 1956, PT 6.
61 Ibid.
62 Richard Egerton, *American Film Exhibition and an Analysis of the Motion Picture Industry's Market Structure* (London: Routledge, 1983).
63 Ibid., 285–6.
64 Segrave, *Drive-In Theaters*, 233–4.
65 'Drive-Ins: Their Relation to Car Registration', *Boxoffice*, 7 June 1952, 19.
66 Egerton, *American Film Exhibition*, 283–4.
67 Giles, 'The Outdoor Economy', 69.
68 Ibid.
69 Ibid.
70 'Drive-ins Zoom Nationally', 22.
71 Segrave, *Drive-in Theaters*, 234.
72 *Texas Theatre Guide* (1955), Hoblitzelle Interstate Theatre Circuit Collection, Box 9, 1af.
73 'San Antonio', *Motion Picture Exhibitor*, 8 April 1959, 21–2.
74 Cited by MichaelKilgore, 'Chief Drive-In', 'Cinema Treasures', http://cinematreasures.org/theaters/58229. This site states that the drive-in opened on 1 November 1951 and closed on 29 October 1956.
75 Randolph B. Campbell, *Gone to Texas: A History of the Lone Star State* (New York: Oxford University Press, 2003), 405; Census Bureau, 'Census of Population 1960, Part 45: Texas', 22.
76 Census Bureau, 'Census of Population 1960, Part 45: Texas', 38.
77 'Drive-In Theatres in the United States', 1096.
78 'Yellow Jacket Drive-In', 'Cinema Treasures', http://cinematreasures.org/theaters/58840 (accessed 29 November 2022).
79 '$20,000,000 in New Cinerama Theatres', *Boxoffice*, 20 November 1961, NT10.
80 'Theatre Circuits', *Film Daily Year Book* (1950), 1201.
81 'Ezell's 42 Ozoners', *Variety*, 11 March 1959, 3. As will become clear, other exhibitors were identified as owning the largest number of drive-ins.

82 'Claude Ezell, Industry Veteran, Dead at 79', *Boxoffice*, 28 August 1961, 8.

83 Ibid., for a brief biography.

84 José Carlos Lozano, 'Exhibiting Films in a Predominantly Mexican American Market: The Case of Laredo, Texas, a Small USA-Mexico Border Town, 1896-1960', in *Routledge Companion to New Cinema History*, ed. Daniel Biltereyst, Richard Maltby and Philippe Meers (London: Routledge, 2019), 257.

85 Javier Ramirez, 'Vamos Al Cine: Film Exhibition and Moviegoing in El Paso, Texas, 1935-55' (PhD diss., Indiana University, Bloomington, 2019), 236.

86 'Minutes of 1st meeting', 9 January 1948, Buckner Boulevard Drive-In Corporation, 1948, MA-77-1, Interstate Theatre Collection (ITC), Dallas History & Archives Division, Dallas Public Library, Box 4b, Folder 8.

87 'Minutes of a special meeting of the Board of Directors, held on 3 March 1952, ITC, Box 4b, Folder 8; 'Drivin' Round the Drive-ins', *Billboard*, 25 December 1954, 52.

88 'Interstate. Drive-In Theatre Companies. Second Income Tax 1951', ITC, Box 88, Folder 2.

89 'Ezell's Texas Theatres Sold to E. L. Pack', *Motion Picture Daily*, 22 July 1955, 1, 8.

90 'End Inappropriate Name; Bordertown Theatres Now Lone Stars under Ezell', *Variety*, 26 April 1961, 15.

91 John Q. Adams to R. J. O'Donnell and W. E. Mitchell, Inter-Office Communication, 12 March 1958, ITC, Box 192, Folder 6, Co-Ed Drive-In, Dallas Public Library.

92 Ibid.

93 Census Bureau, 'Census of Population 1960, Part 45: Texas', 40.

94 Ibid., 38.

95 *Texas Almanac 1956-57* (Dallas, TX: A.H. Belo, 1955), 637.

96 Ibid., 678.

97 'New Palace Theatre Will Open in Seminole, Wednesday July 22', *Seminole Sentinel* [SS], 16 July 1936, 1.

98 See Leo Copeland, 'A Night at the Picture Show, the Tower Theatre', *SS*, 28 April 2013, 8A.

99 'Chief Drive-In Has Capacity Crowd For Opening Night', *Seminole Sentinel*, 8 June 1950, 1.

100 'Theatre Circuits', *Film Daily Year Book* (1963), 1098.

101 Advertisement, *SS*, 5 June 1952, 12.

102 'Fronia Cox 1917-2006', *SS*, 14 June 2006, 3.

103 'Local Business Buildings Undergoing Extensive Remodelling and Repairing,' *SS*, 10 June 1954, 1.

104 'Tower Appliance Observes 5th Anniversary, May 1-2', *SS*, 30 April 1953, 9; 'Exhibitions Will Signal Opening of Indian Lanes', *SS*, 11 June 1959, 20.

105 'W.E. Cox Jr. Manager of Local Palace Theatre', *SS*, 13 June 1940, 51.

106 *Film Daily Year Book* (1961), 635.
107 'Fronia Cox 1917-2006', 3.
108 'Owners of Theaters in Lamesa and Seminole Ban "Stromboli"', *Lubbock Morning Avalanche* (TX), 18 February 1950, 4.
109 'Jennings to Close Long Theatre Career', *Hondo Anvil Herald* [*HAH*], 17 December 1973, 1, 3; 'Headlines and Footnotes of Yesteryear', *HAH*, 12 December 1952, 17; 'Remodeled Raye Theatre, Nostalgic, Contemporary', *HAH*, 28 August 1986, 5.
110 'Jennings to Close Long Theatre Career', 1.
111 'Jennings will Build Drive-In', *HAH*, 1 September 1950, 1.
112 'Drive In Theatre Opens in Hondo', *HAH*, 17 August 1951, 1. The advertisement on page 8 lists the schedule for the opening week.
113 Mary Ann Noonan, 'Life of Hondo Business Man Reads Like a Two-Fisted Adventure Story', *HAH*, 2 October 1953, 11.
114 'H.A. Hammill of Hondo Buys Both Talley Theaters in Mathis: IT Theater Featuring New Wide-Screen', *Mathis News* (TX), 29 October 1954, 1.
115 'dallasmovietheaters', 'Teatro Casino', 'Cinema Treasures', http://cinematreasures.org/theaters/59498 (accessed 29 November 2022).
116 'Drive In Theatre Opens in Hondo'; 'Park Theatre Shows Life of Christ on Tuesday, Aug. 21', *HAH*, 17 August 1951, 2.
117 Schaefer, *'Bold! Daring! Shocking! True!'* 201–2.
118 Advertisement, *HAH*, 1 October 1954, 2.
119 'New Manager Named at Local Drive-in Theater', *HAH*, 8 February 1957, 3.
120 Robert C. Allen, 'Reimagining the History of the Experience of Cinema in a Post-Moviegoing Age', in *Explorations in New Cinema History*, 50.
121 Census Bureau, 'Census of Population 1960, Part 45: Texas', 23; ibid., 26.
122 'Motion Picture Theaters in the United States', *Film Daily Year Book* (1951), 1080. Part of the balcony at the Strand was reserved for black customers, who had a separate entrance: Margaret Toal, 'Orange Once had Six Theaters', *KOGT*, 20 June 2018, https://kogt.com/orange-once-had-six-theaters/ (accessed 7 February 2023).
123 'Theatre Circuits in the United States Operating Four or More Houses', *Film Daily Yearbook* (1949), 1122.
124 *1955 Texas Theatre Guide*, Hoblitzelle Interstate Theatre Circuit Collection, Box 9.
125 Mike Louviere, 'And Now You Know: New "Picture Show" Opens in Orange', *Orange Leader*, 4 August 2018, https://www.orangeleader.com/2018/08/04/and-now-you-know-new-picture-show-opens-in-orange/ (accessed 4 December 2022).
126 'Macarthur Drive-In Opens Here Tonight', *Orange Leader*, 18 August 1950, 1.
127 'Youth Presents Views on Needs of Area Teenagers', *Orange Leader*, 11 February 1958, 7.

128 Ibid.
129 'City Map of Abilene, Texas', Abilene Chamber of Commerce, 1930, https://texashistory.unt.edu/ark:/67531/metapth493448/m1/2/?q=%22abilene%20chamber%20of%20commerce%22 (accessed 6 November 2022).
130 Ibid.
131 Census Bureau, 'Census of Population 1960, Part 45: Texas', 21.
132 Warren Burkett, 'Loop 322 Right-of-Way Cleared for Bid Letting', *Abilene Reporter-News* [*ARN*], 9 September 1958, 1B.
133 'Abilene's Oldest Movie Theater to Reopen Saturday Morning', *ARN*, 2 September 1938, 5.
134 'Tom Griffing Buys Texas Theater', *ARN*, 26 August 1945, 14.
135 'Isley Builds in Mineral Wells and Brownwood', *Boxoffice*, 8 February 1941, 67; Gita Bumpass, '"Show Goes On" but the Man with a Ringside Seat Rarely Gets to See it', *ARN*, 29 June 1945, 2.
136 'Movie House for Negroes Scene of Formal Opening', *ARN*, 8 May 1942, 15. For an advertisement for 'El Teatro Grande', see *ARN*, 6 July 1945, 5.
137 See Bert Babero's complaint about this to Truman Gibson, 13 February 1944, Letters, African-Americans, *The Perilous Fight: America's World War II in Color* (PBS, 2003), http://www.pbs.org/perilousfight/social/african_americans/letters/ (accessed 6 November 2022).
138 'Star Theater Reopened. Family-type Movie House is Beautified', *ARN*, 27 June 1943, 6.
139 Bumpass, '"Show Goes On"', 2.
140 'Tom Griffing Buys Texas Theater', 14; 'Metro Opens Under Griffing Saturday', *ARN*, 8 October 1947, 12; 'First Suburban Theater to Open Doors Here Thursday', *ARN*, 13 October 1946, 12.
141 'Texas and Linda Theaters Sold', *ARN*, 9 July 1948, 13.
142 'Theater to Reopen', *ARN*, 18 September 1948, 7.
143 'Odessa Man Buys 3 Theatres Here', *ARN*, 26 November 1950, 14.
144 'United Par's $10,000,000 Payoff for 50% Stock in Interstate, Texas Cons', *Variety*, 28 February 1951, 7, 17.
145 'Trans Texas Theaters Buys Majestic From Interstate', *ARN*, 25 February 1954, 2A.
146 Advertisement, *ARN*, 2 October 1960, 11-B.
147 'Ex-Teacher, Play Director Now Abilene Theater Owner', *ARN*, 4 December 1949, 16; Dan Streible, 'The Harlem Theater: Black Film Exhibition in Austin, Texas: 1920-1973', in *Black American Cinema*, ed. Manthia Diawara (New York: Routledge, 1993), 231.
148 'Charity Outpatient Clinic Approved', *ARN*, 27 February 1958, 12B.
149 'First Suburban Theater to Open Doors Here Thursday', 12.
150 Patrick Bennett, 'Mrs Likins Leaves Show Biz. "Slow Fade" to Europe Next Scene', *ARN*, 12 February 1965, 1.

NOTES

151 'New Drive-in Theatre to Open Tonight' ARN, 16 August 1947, 3.
152 Details of the campaign supporting the opening of the Park Drive-In can be found in the 'Scrapbook for Park Drive-In', Abilene Texas, 16 December 1949, ITC, Box 407 Folder 1.
153 'Drive-Ins to Be Converted Into 'Twins'', *ARN*, 13 April 1952, 7B.
154 'Permits for Drive-In Theater and Housing Projects Granted', *ARN*, 20 May 1952, B1; 'All States Buys Theater Here', *ARN*, 3 August 1953, 1.
155 'Drive-In Movie Opens Tonight', *ARN*, 21 July 1955, 10-B.
156 'Big Drive-In Theatre To Be Built Here', *ARN*, 19 February 1956, 1A.
157 Ibid.
158 'S. 14th Drive-In To Resume Work', *ARN*, 29 February 1956, 9B.
159 *Polk's Abilene (Taylor County, Texas) City Directory 1960* (Dallas, TX: R.L. Polk, 1960), 219, lists six drive-ins. Abilene City Directories never listed the Chief or the New Chief, but it was advertised in the *Reporter-News*: see, for example, 22 August 1958, *ARN*, 7B.
160 'New Drive-In Theater to Open Tonight', 3.
161 'Scrapbook for Park Drive-In'.
162 'Trans Texas Theaters Buys Majestic From Interstate', *ARN*, 2A.
163 'Big Drive-In Theatre To Be Built Here', *ARN*, 1A.
164 'Theatre Circuits', *Film Daily Year Book* (1963), 1086; 'Metro Opens Under Griffing Saturday', *ARN*, 8 October 1947, 12; 'All States Buys Theater Here', *ARN*, 3 August 1953, 1; 'Drive-In Theater to Open Under New Owner Tonight', *ARN*, 8 March 1957, 2B.
165 'RKO General Buys Out Video Independent', *Boxoffice*, 24 April 1961, 8.
166 'Drive-In Movie Builds on 158', *ARN*, 20 September 1946, 2.
167 'Ex-Teacher, Play Director Now Abilene Theater Owner', 16; Bennett, 'Mrs Likins Leaves Show Biz.', 3.
168 'George Likins, Showman, Dies', *ARN*, 24 June 1959.
169 'Tom Griffing Buys Texas Theater', 14.
170 'Outcome of 'Vumore's' Test Case Awaited', *ARN*, 21 June 1957, B1; Patrick R. Parsons, 'Horizontal Integration in the Cable Television Industry', *Journal of Media Economics* 16, no. 1 (2003): 23–40.
171 'Drive-In Movie Opens Tonight'.
172 'Texas and Linda Theaters Sold', *ARN*, 9 July 1948, 13; 'Odessa Man Buys 3 Theatres Here', *ARN*, 26 July 1950, 14.
173 'Scrapbook for Park Drive-In'.
174 '"Stromboli" Stands Little Chance Here', *ARN*, 8 February 1950, 14.
175 Advertisement, *ARN*, 14 March 1950 (and the following two days), 2.
176 'Movie Delayed; Fuss Unsettle', *ARN*, 9 May 1958, 4A.
177 'That Bardot Film Slated Here Again', *ARN*, 7 November 1958, 2B.

178 'Turn-Away Crowds for Bardot Film', *ARN*, 12 November 1958, 1B.
179 'Once Upon a Time', *ARN*, 14 February 1965, 2B.
180 Bennett, 'Mrs Likins Leaves Show Biz', 1.
181 Ibid.
182 Census Bureau, 'Census of Population 1960, Part 45: Texas', 22; ibid., 25.
183 See James Hay, 'Locating the Televisual', *Television and New Media* 2, no. 3 (2001): 219.
184 Erik Slotboom, *Houston Freeways: A Historical and Visual Journey* (Cincinnati, OH: C. J. Oscar F. Slotboom, 2003), 167.
185 Ibid., 168–70. Slotboom writes (169) that only about 6,800 single family homes were ultimately constructed.
186 'Houston to Open Theater in May', *NYT*, 26 January 1966, 24.
187 David Welling, *Cinema Houston: From Nickleodeon to Megaplex* (Austin, TX: University of Texas Press, 2007), passim.
188 Al Lever to Raymond Willie, 27 January 1956, ITC, Box 93, Folder 8.
189 'Loew Asks for Okay for Houston', *Variety*, 25 January 1956, 7, 19.
190 'Okay Loew's 4th Ozoner', *Variety*, 21 March 1956, 18.
191 'The Emphasis is on the Playground', *Boxoffice*, 7 April 1958, BT7.
192 Ibid.
193 Ibid., BT6-7.
194 Ibid., BT8.
195 Ibid.
196 'Tonite's the Night for Loew's Opening', *Bellaire Texan*, 26 February 1958, 1.
197 'The Emphasis is on the Playground', BT6.
198 David W. Dunlop, 'John J. McNamara, an Architect and Theater Designer, Dies Age 90', *NYT*, 9 May 1998, D11.
199 'Newspaper Tie-ins, Radio Jingles Herald Loew's New Texas Drive-In', *Motion Picture Daily*, 11 March 1958, 4.
200 Ibid.
201 Ibid.
202 Ibid. The Jerry Lewis apology appeared in *Houston Post*, 26 February 1958: see the Sharpstown's Cinema Treasures page, http://cinematreasures.org/theaters/21993/photos/392711 (accessed 22 November 2022).
203 'Ezell Associates Lease Loew's Texas Drive-In', *Motion Picture Daily*, 2 December 1958, 1.
204 'Dallas', *MPH*, 26 February 1964, 17.
205 According to 'Loew's Sharpstown Drive-In', 'Cinema Treasures', http://cinematreasures.org/theaters/21993 (accessed 29 November 2022). The last trade press mention I have seen dates from 1975: 'Houston', *Boxoffice*, 13 October 1975, SW-2.

206 Nancy Sarnof, 'Sharpstown Mall Gets a New Name – Plazamericas', *Houston Chronicle*, 19 December 2009, https://www.chron.com/business/real-estate/article/Sharpstown-mall-getting-a-new-name-1534020.php (accessed 6 November 2022).
207 John Belton, *Widescreen Cinema* (Cambridge, MA: Harvard University Press, 1992), 78.
208 Ibid.
209 John Hannigan, *Fantasy City: Pleasure and Profit in the Post-Modern Metropolis* (London: Routledge, 1998), 37.
210 Ibid., 36–7.
211 Ibid., 37.
212 Hay, 'Locating the Televisual', 75, 82.
213 Belton, *Widescreen Cinema*, 80.
214 Examples taken from *Billboard*, 29 September 1951 issue.
215 Segrave, *Drive-In Theaters*, 75; Nevin I. Gage, 'Average Drive-in Gross is Nearly Fifty Per Cent of the Ticket Dollar', *Boxoffice*, 2 February 1952, 30–2.
216 Ibid., 31.
217 Ibid.
218 'Big Hard Top Chains Still Shy of Drive-Ins', *International Projectionist* 31, no. 8 (1956): 14.
219 W. T. Lhamon Jr, *Deliberate Speed: The Origins of a Cultural Style in the American 1950s* (Cambridge, MA: Harvard University Press, 2002), 22.
220 Church, *Grindhouse Nostalgia*, 46.
221 Cohen, 'Forgotten Audiences in the Passion Pits', 477.
222 Raymond Williams, *Television: Technology and Cultural Form*, 1975, ed. Ederyn Williams, 2nd edn (London and New York: Routledge, 2003), 19.
223 Raymond Williams, *Towards 2000* (London: Chatto and Windus, 1983), 188.
224 Ibid.
225 'Scrapbook for Park Drive-In'.
226 Kevin M. Kruse and Thomas J. Sugrue, 'Introduction', in *The New Suburban History*, ed. Kevin M. Kruse and Thomas J. Sugrue (Chicago, IL: University of Chicago Press, 2006), 1.
227 Lewis Mumford, *The City in History* (1961) (Harmondsworth: Pelican, 1966), 553.
228 See the different contributions to Kruse and Sugrue, *The New Suburban History*.
229 Jordan Bauer, 'Urban Village or '*Burb of the Future?:* The Racial and Economic Politics of a Houston Neighborhood', *Houston History* 6, no. 3 (2009): 40.
230 Ibid.
231 Ibid.

232 Robert Fishman, 'The Post-War American Suburb: A New Form, A New City', in *Two Centuries of American Planning*, ed. Daniel Schaefer (Baltimore: John Hopkins, 1988), 266.

233 Ibid., 273.

234 See in particular Segrave's chapter, 'Drive-ins Battle the Industry', in *Drive-in Theaters*, 52–9.

235 '"Stromboli" Socko in Drive-in Theatres', *Variety*, 18 October 1950, 3, 20.

236 Bosley Crowther, '"Stromboli," Bergman-Rossellini Movie, is Unveiled at 120 Theatres in This Area', *NYT*, 16 February 1950, 28; 'Ingrid's "Stromboli" Set for Showing at Tower', *Rocky Mountain Telegram* (NC), 19 November 1950, 8B.

Chapter 2

1 Segrave, *Drive-In Theaters*, 199.

2 Ibid., 198.

3 Karin Fleck, '"If You Say You Watch the Movie You're a Couple of Liars": In Search of the Missing Audience at the Drive-In', in *Pandemic Media: Preliminary Notes Towards an Inventory*, ed. Philipp Dominik Keidl et al. (Lüneburg: Meson Press, 2021), 71.

4 Durant, 'The Movies Take to the Pastures', 85.

5 Ibid.

6 Sam Arkoff, with Richard Trubo, *Flying through Hollywood by the Seat of My Pants* (New York: Birch Lane Press, 1992), 58.

7 Ibid., 41.

8 Roger Corman, with Jim Jerome, *How I Made a Hundred Movies in Hollywood and Never Lost a Dime* (New York: Da Capo Press, 1998), 31.

9 For a discussion of the young drive-in audience of a genre other than horror, see Stanfield, 'Intent to Speed; Hot Rod Movies'.

10 Phil Hardy, 'The Science Fiction Film in Perspective', in *Science Fiction*, ed. Phil Hardy (London: Aurum, 1983), xiv.

11 Peter Lev cites Hardy to support his statement that 'More science fiction films were shown in drive-in theaters than any other genre', in *The Fifties*, 173, though he also writes that 'drive-in programming ranged from Westerns and comedies to the more youth-orientated horror, science fiction, and teen films' (215). Russell and Whalley also cite Hardy's claim in *Hollywood and the Baby Boom*, 50.

12 Mike Walsh, Richard Maltby and Dylan Walker, 'Three Moments of Cinema Exhibition', in *Routledge Companion to New Cinema History*, 223.

13 Douglas Gomery, *The Hollywood Studio System: A History* (London: British Film Institute, 2005), 74.

14 Ibid., 75.
15 See Phillips, 'Under the Stars (and Stripes)'.
16 Segrave, *Drive-In Theaters*, 57.
17 'The TOA Midcentury Convention', *Harrison's Reports*, 3 November 1950, 176.
18 'Bidding Needs an Overhaul', *Exhibitor*, 26 May 1965, 4.
19 Ibid.
20 Arthur J. Steel to Harold Mirisch, 24 August 1949, 'Elmsford Drive-In Theatre', Steve Broidy Collection, Folder 2, Margaret Herrick Library, Motion Picture Arts and Sciences.
21 Steel to Steve Broidy, 24 March 1961, Steve Broidy Collection, Folder 2.
22 Steel to Broidy, 3 September 1963, Steve Broidy Collection, Folder 2.
23 *CP*, 6 June 1963, 54.
24 *CP*, 6 June 1953, 5.
25 'Testimony of Guy William Meek, Owner, Palo-Alto Drive-In Theatre, Palo Alto, California', US Congress, Senate, Select Committee on Small Business, *Hearings on Motion-Picture Distribution Trade Practices - 1953*, 84th Cong., 1st Sess., 1953, 223.
26 'Drive-Ins Organise New National Unit', *Motion Picture Daily*, 12 September 1949, 4.
27 'Senate Prober of Complaints To Coast Soon', *Motion Picture Daily*, 22 August 1952, 1.
28 'Testimony of Guy William Meek', 224–39.
29 Ibid., 237.
30 Benjamin Melniker to Newell A. Clapp, Exhibit C, Appendix 49A, US Congress, Senate, Select Committee on Small Business, *Hearings on Motion-Picture Distribution Trade Practices - 1953*, 84th Cong., 1st Sess., 1953, 876–7.
31 'Drive-In Owners Want Per Person Admission Earlier Product Runs', *MPH*, 30 June 1951, 13.
32 Ibid., 14.
33 Ibid.
34 Ibid., 13.
35 US Congress, Senate, Select Committee on Small Business, *Hearings on Motion-Picture Distribution Trade Practices – 1956*, 84th Cong., 2nd Sess., 1956, 1.
36 'Affidavit of David C. Forbes', *Hearings on Motion-Picture Distribution Trade Practices - 195*, 506–7.
37 Harry Hynes, *Hearings on Motion-Picture Distribution Trade Practices - 195*, 607.
38 Ibid.
39 Harry Haas, *Hearings on Motion-Picture Distribution Trade Practices - 195*, 683.

40 Ibid., 683–4.
41 'Affidavit of W. E. Horsefield', *Hearings on Motion-Picture Distribution Trade Practices - 195*, 513–15.
42 Samuel Oshrey, *Hearings on Motion-Picture Distribution Trade Practices - 195*, 612.
43 Ibid.
44 John F. Kirby, *Hearings on Motion-Picture Distribution Trade Practices - 195*, 345–6.
45 Census Bureau, 'Census of Population 1960, Part 19: Kentucky', 16.
46 Statement of Adam F. Myers, *Hearings on Motion-Picture Distribution Trade Practices - 195*, 5.
47 Sterling and Haight, *The Mass Media*, 30.
48 The 1951 survey of 3,000 drive-ins reported that 'the majority of replies (40.8 per cent) said 30 to 40 per cent of the total theatre gross came from the sale of food and drink', 'Drive-In Owners Want Per Person Admission Earlier Product Runs', 14.
49 Arkoff, *Flying through Hollywood*, 59.
50 Lev, *The Fifties*, 214–15.
51 Ibid., 214.
52 'MacArthur Opens Here Tonight', *Orange Leader*, 18 October 1950, 1. All screening details in this section are taken from the *Orange Leader*.
53 The films listed here are all included in the 'Selected Filmography' for Thomas Doherty's *Teenagers and Teenpics*, 237–50. Doherty (237) uses the following subgenres: juvenile delinquent, clean teenpic, mainstream, motor-mad, rock 'n' roll, vice and weirdie.
54 I have used the genre given in the AFI Catalog: https://aficatalog.afi.com/. For films that this does not include I have used the Internet Movie Data Base: https://www.imdb.com/.
55 Anthony Downs, 'Where the Drive-in Fits into the Movie Industry' (1953), in *Exhibition: The Film Reader*, ed. Ina Rae Hark (London and New York: Routledge, 2002), 124.
56 Figures for the number of films released are taken from Sterling and Haight, *The Mass Media*, 30.
57 On 23 May 1956 *Motion Picture Exhibitor* reported that Melvin Wilson had been named manager of the Strand, the Royal and the MacArthur: 'San Antonio', 44.
58 James C. O'Connell, *The Hub's Metropolis: Greater Boston's Development from Railroad Suburb to Smart Growth* (Cambridge, MA: MIT Press, 2013), 136.
59 'Drive-In Theatre in North Reading', *Andover Townsman*, 29 June 1910, 10. Subsequent programme details for the North Reading are taken from the *Andover Townsman*.
60 'Boston', *MPH*, 31 December 1955, 43.

NOTES

61 'M & P Theatre Split Set for January 1', *Showmen's Trade Review*, 25 December 1948, 10.
62 'News of the Territory', *Exhibitor*, 24 February 1954, NT1.
63 See, for example, *Andover Townsman*, 31 July 1958, 8.
64 'News of the Territory', *Motion Picture Exhibitor*, 11 May 1955, NT1.
65 'Edenton: Cradle of the Colony', *Hill's Edenton (Chowan County, N.C.) City Directory 1959* (Richmond, VA: Hill, 1959), 11.
66 Ibid.
67 Ibid., 13, 15.
68 'Drive-in Theatre Will Open May 22', *Chowan Herald*, 27 April 1950, 12. Subsequent programme details at the Hi-Way 17 and neighbouring cinemas are taken from the *Chowan Herald*.
69 See Frank Roberts, 'Frankly Speaking', *Chowan Herald*, 16 February 1961, 3-B.
70 'Buy Two Theatres', *Motion Picture Daily*, 20 September 1957, 6.
71 J. B. Harren, 'N.C. NAACP Asks "What Are We Doing?"' *Carolinian*, 24 February 1962, 1.
72 Schaefer, *Bold! Daring! Shocking! True!*, 360. Schaefer dates *I Want a Baby* as '1950s?' The earlier screening I have come across was at the JO cinema, St Joseph, Missouri, advertised in *St. Joseph News Press* (MO), 13 March 1954, 13.
73 Census Bureau, 'Census of Population 1960, Part 17: Iowa', 17–24; Joe R. Feagin and Hernán Vera, *White Racism: The Basics* (New York: Routledge, 1995), 27; John D. Hull, 'Race Relations: A White Person's Town?' *Time*, 23 December 1991, 39.
74 '"Balcony" at Dubuque Drive-In', *Boxoffice*, 3 September 1949, 63. The drive-in's opening advertisement also described it as 'the nation's first drive-in movie with a balcony!': see 'Dubuque Drive-In', 'Cinema Treasures', http://cinematreasures.org/theaters/33660/photos/405691 (accessed 12 February 2023).
75 'High Rider?' *Billboard*, 18 February 1950, 53.
76 A report noted that 'Gene Cramm has been named manager of the Zephyr at Burlington. Cramm, a native of Clinton, has been managing a drive-in at Dubuque for Central States': 'Des Moines', *MPH*, 29 November 1952, 32.
77 'Blanks, Braton, Paramount Set Deal', *Exhibitor*, 21 June 1950, 9.
78 'Blank – Myron N. (Mike)', *NYT*, 13 March 2005, 46.
79 'Sign of Spring: Drive-In Theater To Open Friday', *Dubuque Telegraph Herald*, 25 February 1954, 10. Subsequent programme details are taken from the *Dubuque Telegraph Herald*.
80 *Dubuque Herald Telegraph*, 13 May 1957, no page number.
81 Philip VanderMeer, *Desert Visions and the Making of Phoenix, 1860-2009* (Albuquerque, NM: University of New Mexico Press, 2010), 171.

82 Andrew Needham, *Power Lines: Phoenix and the Making of the Modern Southwest* (Princeton, NJ: Princeton University Press, 2014), 83.
83 Ibid., 84.
84 Ibid., 84–5, citing Andrew Kopkind, 'Modern Times in Phoenix: A City at the Mercy of its Myths', *New Republic* (November 1965), 15.
85 Ibid., 85.
86 Douglas Towne, 'Phoenix's Street of Dreams: The Visual Extravaganza that was Van Buren', 'Modern Phoenix', 2011, https://modernphoenix.net/van-buren/vanburensigns.htm (accessed 15 February 2023).
87 'Grand Opening Tonight' advertisement, *Arizona Republic*, 29 February 1940, 10; 'First Quarter Construction Check Shows Gain; 81 Planned, 65 in Work, 69 Open', *Boxoffice*, 4 May 1940, 18. Subsequent references to Phoenix screenings are taken from the *Arizona Republic* and Phoenix's Spanish-language newspaper, *El Sol*.
88 'Phoenix', *Exhibitor*, 17 January 1951, 17.
89 Advertisement, *Arizona Republic*, 16 February 1951, 29.
90 Advertisement, *Arizona Republic*, 29 June 1951, 29. I do not have an exact date for *Maid in the Hay*. The *Arizona Republic* advertisement claimed it to be 'first run Arizona's premiere show' (as such advertisements tended to claim).
91 'Charges Studied in Film Seizure', *Arizona Republic*, 4 July 1951, 3; 'Novelty', *Exhibitor*, 9 September 1953, Servisection 3602–3.
92 'Phoenix Twin Screener Closes, First in State', *Boxoffice*, 16 February 1952, 66.
93 'Phoenix', *Exhibitor*, 7 May 1952, NT-3.
94 'Phoenix', *Exhibitor*, 6 August 1952, NT-2.
95 '5 Phoenix Drive-ins to Southwest Corp.', *Boxoffice*, 16 June 1956, 35.
96 'Veteran Showman Harry Nace Ends Own Life in Home Here', *Arizona Republic*, 1 July 1953, 2.
97 Ibid.
98 'Theater Circuits in the United States and Canada Operating Four or More Houses', *Film Daily Year Book* (1949), 997; 'Nace Paramount Split Due Oct. 1', *Showmen's Trade Review*, 1 October 1949, 8.
99 'Nace Paramount Split Due Oct. 1'.
100 Arkoff, *Flying through Hollywood*, 59.
101 '5 Phoenix Drive-ins to Southwest Corp', 35.
102 Al Hine, 'The Drive-ins', *Holiday*, July 1952, 9.
103 All these films were released in the year they were screened at the Acres.
104 Schaefer, *Bold! Daring! Shocking! True!* 346–80.
105 Rogelio Agrasánchez, Jr., *Mexican Movies in the United States: A History of the Films, Theaters and Audiences, 1920–1960* (Jefferson, NC: McFarland, 2006), 102.

NOTES **209**

106 The *Arizona Republic* advertisement for the Indian Drive-In and the Strand claimed it was 'direct from the world premier engagement at the Palms Theatre here in Phoenix!', 28 July 1954, 9.
107 'Los Angeles', *Exhibitor*, 28 March 1951, NT2.
108 Ibid.
109 Burt A. Folkart, 'Sherrill Corwin, Magnate of Movie Palaces, Dies', *Los Angeles Times*, 10 May 1980, OC20.
110 'Cinemascope Installation, June 1954', Airport Drive-in (Goleta CA) maintenance costs, Tom B'Hend and Preston Kaufman Collection, File 4265, Margaret Herrick Library, Motion Picture Arts and Sciences.
111 Figures for the Airport are taken from 'Grosses, films played at Granada as well as Airport Drive-In, State and California houses', Tom B'Hend and Preston Kaufman Collection, File 1385.
112 Census Bureau, 'Census of Population 1960, Part 5: Arkansas', 5–20.
113 John A. Kirk, *Beyond Little Rock: The Origins and Legacies of the Central High Crisis* (Fayetteville, NC: University of Arkansas Press, 2007), 69.
114 'Little Rock Theatres Integrate Quietly', *Boxoffice*, 15 July 1963, 11.
115 'Theater Circuits in the United States', *Film Daily Year Book* (1950), 116.
116 'District of Columbia', *Exhibitor*, 11 July 1951, NT-1.
117 'Major Circuits in Texas Climbing on Drive-in Theatre Bandwagon', *Boxoffice*, 6 November 1948, 80; 'News of the Territory', *Exhibitor*, 8 August 1951, NT-1.
118 'Drive-In Opening Announced', *MPH*, 4 October 1952, 30.
119 'About People of the Theatre', *MPH*, 30 October 1954, 10; 'Little Rock to Get a New Twin Drive-In', *Boxoffice*, 7 May 1962, 28.
120 Arkansas Amusement Corporation Papers, Center for Arkansas History and Culture, University of Arkansas at Little Rock, Box 5, Folders 2–5.
121 *Film Daily Year Book* (1955) provides figures (credited to Sindlinger & Company) for monthly drive-in attendance for 1952, 1953 and 1954: 'Division of US Theater Attendance by Type of Operation', 143. For each of these years the drive-in attendance increased month by month, from 300,000 in January 1952 and 1953 and 400,000 in January 1954 to 40,900,000, 33,800,000 and 39,200,000 in August 1952, 1953 and 1954 before declining each month, reaching 400,000, 200,000 and 300,000 in December 1952, 1953 and 1954. Attendance for indoor cinemas peaked each year in September but with a less acute difference between months.
122 See Peter Krämer's 'Annual Top Five, 1949-66', in *The New Hollywood* (London: Wallflower, 2005), 113.
123 Krämer, 'Annual Top Five, 1949-66', lists *Peyton Place* as having the second highest gross for 1957.
124 'Controversy of Famed Novel: A natural for SEXploitation', *Independent Film Bulletin*, 26 May 1958, 19.

125 According to Steve Neale, Columbia set up Kingsley International in order to distribute *And God Created Woman* in the United States without having to submit the film to the PCA for approval, which, as a MPAA member, they would have had to do if they had distributed the film themselves: 'Artists and Imports, Exports and Runaways, Adult Films and Exploitation', in *The Classical Hollywood Reader*, 406. However Kingsley was already importing films: see, for example, 'People in the News', *MPH*, 22 May 1954, 37.

126 Arkansas Amusement Corporation Papers, Box 1, Folders 5–7.

127 Advertisement, *Arkansas Democrat*, 13 August 1958, unknown page number.

128 Sheldon Hall and Steve Neale, *Epics, Spectacles and Blockbusters: A Hollywood History* (Detroit, MI: Wayne State University Press), 159–60. See also Zoë Wallin, *Classical Hollywood Film Cycles* (New York: Routledge, 2019), 229–37. Wallin notes that *The Ten Commandments* played eleven months at the McVickers in Chicago, with a maximum ticket price of $3.30 and specially priced 90c morning screenings for group bookings of children (232), while when it played at the Palace in Corsicana, Texas, in March 1958 the adult charge was $1.20, that is, slightly less than at the Pines for an earlier screening (235).

129 'Bardot Vs. Hierarchy C', *Variety*, 4 December 1957, 14.

130 '"BB" Vs. "C": New Boxoffice Algebra', *Variety*, 16 July 1958, 15.

131 'Arkansas', *Exhibitor*, 7 April 1954, NT-4.

132 Charles Drazin, *The Faber Book of French Cinema* (London: Faber, 2011), 299.

133 *Chicago Herald Tribune*, 19 April 1958, B7.

134 Advertisement, *Dubuque Telegraph Herald*, 13 August 1959, 9.

135 Advertisement, *Arkansas Democrat*, 7 August 1958.

136 Hall, 'Ozoners, Roadshows and Blitz Exhibitionism', 345.

137 Ibid., 348.

138 'New England's Drive-ins Unhappy with "Commandments"', *Harrison's Reports*, 26 July 1958, 118.

139 Ibid.

140 Ibid.

141 Ibid.

142 Testimony of Ruben Shor, theater operator, Cincinnati, Ohio, *Hearings on Motion-Picture Distribution Trade Practices – 1956*, 455–66.

143 Testimony of William Zimmerman, Assistant to the Domestic Sales Manager, RKO Radio Pictures Inc. New York, NY, *Hearings on Motion-Picture Distribution Trade Practices – 1956*, 568.

144 Advertisement, *Chowan Herald*, 6 August 1959, section 2, 6.

145 'Paramount Retreats', *Harrison's Reports*, 18 July 1959, 113: italics in the trade press report.

146 Kathryn H. Fuller-Seeley, '"What the Picture did for Me": Small-town Exhibitors' Strategies for Surviving the Great Depression', in *Hollywood in the Neighborhood: Historical Case Studies of Local Moviemaking*, ed. Kathryn H. Fuller-Seeley (Berkeley, CA: University of California Press, 2008), 191.
147 James H. Hamilton, '*Outcasts of the Islands*', *Boxoffice*, 4 July 1953, BT-2.
148 Robert B. Tuttle, '*Back to Bataan*', *Boxoffice*, 25 November 1950, BT-3.
149 Tuttle, 'Action! Action! Action! Needed for Drive-Ins', *Boxoffice*, 27 August 1955, BT-2.
150 George R. Armstrong, '*Torpedo Alley*', *Boxoffice*, 5 September 1953, BT-1.
151 D. H. Haymans, '*Son of Belle Starr*', *Boxoffice*, 1 May 1954, BT-1.
152 Hamilton, '*Jesse James' Women*', *Boxoffice*, 5 February 1955, BT-1.
153 Olin Evans, '*Beneath the 12 Mile Reef*', *Boxoffice*, 27 October 1956, BT-11.
154 Hamilton, '*Francis Covers the Big Town*', *Boxoffice*, 22 May 1955, BT-2; George R. Cobern, '*Ma and Pa Kettle Go to Town*', *Boxoffice*, 30 December 1950, BT-4; Rene L. Garneau, '*Twilight in the Sierras*', *Boxoffice*, 18 August 1951, BT-3.
155 Charles Townsend, '*Timberjack*', *Boxoffice*, 30 July 1955, 2.
156 O. M. Shannon, '*Funny Face*', *Boxoffice*, 6 January 1958, 113.
157 Arden Richards, '*The Red Shoes*', *Boxoffice*, 26 September 1953, BT-1.
158 W. E. Seaver Jr., '*The Girl Most Likely*', *Boxoffice*, 15 June 1959, 78.
159 Hamilton, '*Singin' in the Rain*', *Boxoffice*, 25 July 1953, BT-1; Hamilton, '*Calamity Jane*', *Boxoffice*, 22 May 1955, BT-2.
160 Pearce Parkhurst, '*The Mummy's Hand*', *Boxoffice*, 28 June 1952, BT-1. For a discussion of Parkhurst approach to promoting the 'sex hygiene' film, *Mom and Dad*, see Schaefer, *Bold! Daring! Shocking! True!*, 134.
161 George Tatar, '*This Island Earth*', *MPH*, 12 October 1955, 31.
162 Billy W. Wright, '*County Fair*', *Boxoffice*, 21 October 1950, BT-3.
163 John C. Coffrin Jr., '*Bend of the River*', *Boxoffice*, 11 July 1953, BT-2; Major I. Jay Sadow, '*Wild Blue Yonder*', *Boxoffice*, 28 June 1952, BT-1.
164 Armstrong, '*Flat Top*', *Boxoffice*, 13 August 1955, BT-1.
165 Hamilton, '*Gentleman's Agreement*', *Boxoffice*, 4 July 1953, BT-1.
166 Armstrong, '*High Noon*', *Boxoffice*, 22 August 1953, BT-1.
167 Armstrong, '*Fort Apache*', *Boxoffice*, 22 August 1953, BT-1.
168 Tuttle, '*Cleopatra*', *MPH*, 18 July 1953, 35.
169 Hamilton, '*Uncle Tom's Cabin*', *Boxoffice*, 24 July 1954, BT-1.
170 Hamilton, '*Singin' in the Rain*', BT-1; Hamilton, '*Pat and Mike*', *Boxoffice*, 15 August 1953, BT-1.
171 Hamilton, '*Actors and Sin*', *Boxoffice*, 22 August 1953, BT-1.
172 O. M. Shannon, '*Stations West*', *Boxoffice*, 6 January 1958, 113.

173 Arden Richards, 'Can You Beat This – Or Even Tie It?', *Boxoffice*, 6 October 1954, BT-1.
174 George Yarborough, '*Horizons West*', *Boxoffice*, 26 September 1953, BT-1.
175 Tuttle, '*Son of Paleface*', *MPH*, 18 July 1953, 35.
176 Tuttle, '*Little Tough Guys*', *MPH*, 18 July 1953, 35.
177 Tuttle, '*Sands of Iwo Jima*', *Boxoffice*, 23 September 1950, BT-3.
178 Tuttle, '*Open City*', *Boxoffice*, 14 October 1950, BT-4.
179 Bentley B. Davis, '*Take Care of My Little Girl*', *Boxoffice*, 16 February 1952, BT-2; Tuttle, 'Karamoja Causes Jams at Michigan Drive-In', *Boxoffice*, 2 October 1954, BT-1.
180 Hamilton, '*Call of the Wild*', *Boxoffice*, 22 August 1953, BT-1.
181 *Movie Market Trends*, issue 39, weekending 27 October 1956, Margaret Herrick Library, Academy of Motion Picture Arts and Sciences, no page number.
182 Kenneth Clem, '*Fancy Pants*', *Boxoffice*, 15 November 1952, BT-1.
183 Parkhurst, '*Elephant Stampede*', *MPH*, 21 June 1952, 48.
184 Hamilton, '*The Clown*', *Boxoffice*, 29 August 1953, BT-1.
185 Paul Wood, '*Sitting Pretty*', *Boxoffice*, 24 June 1950, BT-4; Coffrin, '*Greatest Show on Earth*', *Boxoffice*, 25 June 1953, BT-1.
186 Hamilton, '*The City of Bad Men*', *Boxoffice*, 11 September 1954, BT-1; J. Files, '*Invaders from Mars*', *Boxoffice*, 19 June 1954, BT-2.
187 J. Bye Coverston, '*What Price Glory?*' *Boxoffice*, 8 August 1953, BT-2.
188 Coffrin, '*The Marrying Kind*', *Boxoffice*, 5 September 1953, BT-1.
189 Hamilton, '*Pat and Mike*', BT-1.
190 Fuller-Seeley, '"What the Picture Did For Me"', 192.
191 Harry Ziegler, '*Shane*', *Boxoffice*, 26 June 1954, BT-1.
192 Bill Shaw, 'The Lasting Picture Show', *Indianapolis News*, 7 July 1998, D1-2.
193 'M.E.L.S. at the Starlight Drive-In', 'Cinema Treasures', http://cinematreasures.org/theaters/45641 (accessed 4 December 2022).
194 Gary R. Boye, 'The Sky-Vu Drive-In: 1950-1967', 'Film Exhibition in Watauga County NC', https://sites.google.com/appstate.edu/nwnc-theaters-1/watauga/boone-skyvu-drive-in-theatre (accessed 30 November 2022).
195 Ibid.
196 Michael P. Thomason, *Starlight Memories: 50 Years of Entertainment at the Mesa Drive-In Theater, Pueblo, Colorado, 1951-2001* (Pueblo, CO: Copies in a Flash, 2002), no page numbers.
197 Ibid.
198 See '"Passion Pits With Pix" in Danger of Revival Via All-Nite Drive-Ins', *Variety*, 4 November 1953, 1.
199 Edward Buscombe (ed.), *The BFI Companion to the Western* (London: Museum of the Moving Image, 1991), 427.

200 Ibid.; Sterling and Haight, *The Mass Media*, 294.
201 Ann Carroll, 'Bad Girl Pictures Repel Patrons of Film Drive-ins', *El Paso Herald Post*, 23 July 1952, 54.
202 Tommy Boggs, 'Ad Reveals Drive-In Shows Other than Trashy Pictures', *El Paso Herald Post*, 8 August 1955, 19.
203 'Even though AIP's pictures continued to play in as many indoor theaters as drive-ins, the drive-ins remained crucial to our success', wrote Arkoff in *Flying through Hollywood*, 59.
204 Lev, *The Fifties*, 214–15.
205 Ibid., 215.
206 'Albany', *Motion Picture Exhibitor*, 20 July 1960, 13; 'Cinerama's Now Showing at Drive-in', *Los Angeles Times*, 18 April 1964, 18; see the *Philadelphia Inquirer* listings, 14 March 1964, 7, which shows *South Pacific* playing at the MacDade Drive-In, alongside sixteen indoor cinemas.
207 *Philadelphia Inquirer*, 12 September 1958, 13.
208 Lev, *The Fifties*, 15.
209 Schaefer, *Bold! Daring! Shocking! True!*, 290.
210 See James J. Lorence, *The Suppression of Salt of the Earth* (Albuquerque, NM: University of New Mexico Press, 1999), 137–40.
211 Dean Jensen, *The Lives and Loves of Daisy and Violet Hilton: A True Story of Conjoined Twins* (Berkeley, CA: Ten Speed Press, 2006), 362–4. Jensen writes that, unknown to the twins, the New Monroe Drive-In regularly screened X-rated films, but this confuses different eras: for the drive-in's screening of X-rated films in the 1970s and 1980s and how this led to a jail sentence for the owners, see Segrave, *Drive-In Theaters*, 166.
212 David W. Johnson, *Lonesome Melodies: The Lives and Music of the Stanley Brothers* (Jackson, MS: University Press of Mississippi, 2013), 62.
213 Penny Parsons, *Foggy Mountain Troubadour: The Life and Music of Curly Seckler* (Urbana, IL: University of Illinois, 2016), 87.
214 Warren R. Hofsta and Mike Foreman, 'Legacy and Legend: The Cultural World of Patsy Cline's Winchester', in *Sweet Dreams: The World of Patsy Cline*, ed. Warren R. Hofsta (Urbana, IL: University of Illinois Press, 2014), 22.
215 See Lev, 'Case Study: *The Ten Commandments* as International Epic', in *The Fifties*, 162–8.
216 Ginette Vincendeau, *Stars and Stardom in French Cinema* (London and New York: Continuum, 2000), 104.

Chapter 3

1 'Summer Theatre Attendance Called Best in Decade; Continuance Seen', *Film Daily*, 21 August 1959, 2.

NOTES

2 'Summary of 1959 Theatre Attendance', *Film Daily Year Book* (1960), 107.
3 'The Drive-in Theatre: A Motor-age Experiment', *MPH*, 1 July 1933, 15. See page 3 for the 'better in the cars' story.
4 'News North of 6', *Vidette-Messenger of Porter County* (IN), 27 September 1958, 8; 'Tower Tickler', *Chicago Tribune*, 24 May 1950, 18.
5 The cover is reproduced in Sanders, *Drive-in Movie Memories*, 82, and 'June 6, 1933: America Goes Out to the Movies', 'The Saturday Evening Post', 30 May 2009, https://www.saturdayeveningpost.com/2009/05/america-drive-in-movies/ (accessed 9 February 2023).
6 '365 Club, San Francisco', *Variety*, 4 February 1959, 69.
7 Ian Christie, 'Introduction: In Search of Audiences', in *Audiences: Defining and Researching Screen Entertainment Reception*, ed. Ian Christie (Amsterdam: University of Amsterdam Press, 2012), 12–13.
8 Thompson and Bordwell, *Film History*, 427; Doherty, *Teenagers and Teenpics*, 92.
9 Ellen Meloy, 'Passion Pit', in *Northern Lights: A Selection of New Writing from the American West*, ed. Deborah Clow and Donald Snow (New York: Vintage, 1994), 294.
10 Ibid.
11 Don Iddon, 'Don Iddon's Diary', *Daily Mail* (UK), 28 July 1948, 2.
12 Francis Russell, 'Passion Pit', *Observer* (UK), 19 January 1958, 19.
13 'Claim Drive-In Theaters Turned into Passion Pits', *Panama City News* (FL), 18 April 1957, 2.
14 Loy Warwick, 'Exposing! The Drive-In Passion Pits', *Crime Exposé*, October 1957, 28–9, 54.
15 Arthur Mayer, 'Hollywood: Save the Flowers', *Film Bulletin*, 14 April 1958, 14, reprinted from *The Saturday Review*, 29 March 1958.
16 'All This and the Movies Too: Drive-Ins as Seen by "Time"', *International Projectionist* 24, no. 9 (1949): 29.
17 'Family Goes for the Drive (in)', *Variety*, 26 August 1959, 7.
18 'Hungry Kids vs. Passion Pits', *Variety*, 11 June 1958, 7.
19 'The Flavor of the Drive-in Biz', *Variety*, 6 February 1957, 7; 'Ozoners No More Stepchildren', *Variety*, 7 May 1952, 5.
20 'Ozoners Reverse Current B.O. Dip: Drive-ins Up 10% Over '48 Revenue', *Variety*, 8 June 1949, 5.
21 'National Affairs', *Time*, 26 July 1948, 7.
22 Maureen Daly, 'Fads and Fancies', in *Profile of Youth, by Members of Staff of* The Ladies Home Journal (Philadelphia, PA: Lippincott, 1951), 232. First published in the August 1949 edition of *Ladies Home Journal*.
23 'Jelly Tot, Square Bear-Man', *Newsweek*, 8 October 1951, 28.
24 Louis M. Ackerman, 'Outdoor Movie Talk', *American Speech* 32, no. 3 (1957): 239.

25 'Teenagers Speak for Themselves on Morals and Behavior', *Ladies Home Journal*, May 1960, 192.
26 'Add Drive-in News', *MPH*, 9 March 1940, BT-5.
27 '$1,000 Fee for Drive-Ins: Residents Register Protests', *Film Daily*, 18 December 1947, 2.
28 'The Brass Tacks of Efficient Theatre Management: The Hazards of Drive-in Operation', *Showmen's Trade Review*, 1 May 1948, 23.
29 See Gary D. Rhodes, *The Perils of Moviegoing in America 1896-1950* (New York: Continuum, 2012), for a discussion of sex in the cinema auditorium. See also Lewis, 'Sex and the Automobile', 123–33.
30 Evelyn Millis Duvall, 'III. Course on Adolescence, Adolescence and the Automobile. Points for Study and Discussion. All in a Child's Lifetime Study Discussion Program', *National-Parent Teacher*, October 1959, 36.
31 'Burb and Bottle Crowd Unseats Woo Gang', *Washington Post*, 28 September 1947, L1.
32 Durant, 'The Movies Take to the Pastures', 25.
33 'Baby-Sitters "Picket" Drive-In', *MPH*, 6 December 1947, 47.
34 Durant, 'The Movies Take to the Pastures', 89.
35 'Selig Nixes Drive-In Doomcriers', *Variety*, 22 June 1983, 23.
36 'Moon-Washed', *New Yorker*, 1 October 1949, 20.
37 'Capitol Drive-In', *Exhibitor*, 1 April 1953, PT-8; 'MGM Workshop Hits Mound City', *Motion Picture Exhibitor*, 15 June 1955, NT-4. The report refers to Southwest 14th Street Drive-In but this appears to be an error.
38 'Playgrounds and Family Appeal to Drive-Ins', *Los Angeles Times*, 30 November 1951, 15.
39 'Playgrounds: What Makes Them an Asset', *MPH*, 6 February 1954, 16; 'Playgrounds for Extra Lure', *MPH*, 9 June 1956, 10.
40 'Playgrounds: What Makes Them an Asset', 16–17.
41 'Santa in Park Got 200 Yule Requests', *Sunbury Daily Item* (PA), 28 December 1959, 6.
42 *Movieland Drive In Theater Toy with Patty Duke* (1959), https://archive.org/details/1959RemcoMovielandDriveInTheaterWithPattyDuke (accessed 30 November 2022).
43 See 'Some Tips to Help Select Toys with Care', *Bellaire & Southwestern Texan*, 10 December 1975, Triangle section, 2.
44 Luther discussed his first survey in 'Marketing Aspects of Drive-In Theaters'. He examined the results of his second survey, and their relationship to the first, in 'Second Annual Drive-In Audience Survey' and 'Drive-In Theaters: Rags to Riches in Five Years'.
45 Luther's comments to exhibitors at the National Allied convention were reported on in 'Drive-Ins Nab "Lost" Audience', *Variety*, 24 October 1949, 3, 20, with the note (20) that Luther 'blasted popular concept that drive-

ins are "Passion Pits with Pix," since only 10% of those interviewed were under 20'.

46 Luther, 'Marketing Aspects of Drive-In Theaters', 42.
47 Ibid.
48 Ibid., 46.
49 'Drive-ins Nab "Lost" Audience', 3.
50 Luther, 'Second Annual Drive-In Audience Survey', 128.
51 Ibid., 129.
52 Ibid.
53 Ibid., 130.
54 Ibid., 129.
55 Ibid., 128; Luther, 'Drive-In Theaters', 409; Luther, 'Marketing Aspects of Drive-In Theaters', 45.
56 'Drive-In Attendance One Eighth in July', *Exhibitor*, 6 September 1950, 13.
57 Frank Hobbs and Nicole Stoops, *Demographic Trends in the Twentieth Century: Census 2000 Special Reports* (Washington D.C.: Bureau of the Census, 2002), Table 5, Population by Age and Sex for the United States: 1900-2000, Part A. Number, 163.
58 Ibid.
59 Ibid., Table 5, Population by Age and Sex for the United States: 1900-2000, Part B. Percent Distribution, 163.
60 Ibid.
61 Landon Y. Jones, *Great Expectations: America and the Baby Boom Generation* (New York: Coward, McCann & Geoghegan, 1980), 23.
62 Ibid., 24.
63 Opinion Research Corporation, *The Public Appraises Movies: A Survey for Motion Picture Association of America, Inc.* (Princeton, NJ: Opinion Research Corporation, 1957), National Association of Theatre Owners Collection, MSS 1446 Box 9 Folder 10, L. Tom Perry Special Collections Library, Harold B. Lee Library, Brigham Young University, Provo, Utah, 3. References to *The Public Appraises Movies* (*PAM*) are to the full survey report. I identify below where I cite the report highlights.
64 Ibid., 13.
65 Opinion Research Corporation, *The Public Appraises Movies, Highlights of a Survey Conducted in June and July 1957 for Motion Picture Association of America, Inc.*, 4.
66 Ibid.
67 *PAM*, 104.
68 Ibid., 13.
69 Opinion Research Corporation, *The Public Appraises Movies, Highlights*, 7. The full report gives a '0' figure for men who went alone and '-' for women

who went alone, presumably on the basis that any figure below half a per cent was rounded down while the even smaller figure for lone women attenders was judged to be statistically insignificant: *PAM*, 13.

70 *PAM*, 11.
71 Ibid.
72 Luther, 'Second Annual Drive-In Audience Survey', 128.
73 Ibid., 130.
74 Leo C. Handel, *Hollywood Looks at Its Audience: A Report of Film Audience Research* (Urbana, IL: University of Illinois Press, 1950), 211.
75 'Predict 21,000 Weekly Attendance at Drive-in Theatres This Summer', *Motion Picture Daily*, 5 June 1958, 2.
76 Ibid. In fact, the *Motion Picture Daily* report refers to a fifteen to twenty-five age band but as the next band they use is twenty-five to thirty-four. I assume that the younger age band was actually fifteen to twenty-four.
77 Steuart Henderson Britt, 'What is the Nature of the Drive-in Theater Audience?' *Media/Scope* 4 (June 1960): 100–3.
78 Ibid., 102.
79 'Meet the Drive-In Patron', *Harrison's Reports*, 26 March 1960, 52.
80 Britt, 'What is the Nature of the Drive-in Audience?' 103.
81 Ibid.
82 *PAM*, 5.
83 Sindlinger & Company, *Motion Picture Activity*, Issue 139, week ending 29 November 1958, 10, ITC, Box 122 Folder 1.
84 Britt, 'What is the Nature of the Drive-in Audience?' 103.
85 Ibid.
86 Downs, 'Where the Drive-in Fits into the Movie Industry', 123; Britt, 'What is the Nature of the Drive-in Audience?' 102.
87 Dick Wommack, 'What my Patrons Taught Me about My Business', *Boxoffice*, 22 May 1961, 18.
88 Ibid., 18–19.
89 Ibid., 19.
90 Ibid.
91 Ibid.
92 Dick Wommack, 'Fun for All, Young and Old, at the Drive-in', *Boxoffice*, 20 November 1961, 46.
93 Ibid., 47.
94 'Joe Fiegel Loves His Flying Career – Next to his Home, Wife, 2 Children', *Rochdale Democrat and Chronicle* (NY), 11 February 1950, 15.
95 'Wife of Police Officer Killed by Gunblast', *Marshfield News Herald* (WI), 4 October 1951, 16.

96 'May Stop Late Drive-In Shows If Rowdyism Continues', *Carroll Daily Times Herald* (IO), 5 June 1953, 7.

97 'Rowdy Tulsa Youths Seized', *Miami Daily News Record* (OK), 12 July 1956, 3.

98 'Youth Gives Self Up as Gang Sniper', *Arizona Republic*, 21 July 1959, 1.

99 'Youth Denies Girl's Charge of Assault', *Johnson City Press Chronicle* (TN), 19 September 1950, 19.

100 'Denied Use of Car, Youth Kills Mother, Sister, Brother', *Princeton Daily Clarion* (IN), 11 February 1952, 1.

101 See, for example, 'Student, 18, Strangles His Girl Friend', *Kenosha Evening News* (WI), 4 April 1958, 5.

102 'Girl, 14, Held in Killing of Newport Newsboy, 16', *Petersburg Progress-Index* (VI), 26 July 1954, 1.

103 Ibid.

104 'Violent Deaths Climb in Texas', *Sulphur Springs Daily New Telegram* (TX), 16 July 1956, 6.

105 Ibid.

106 'Carter Bus Driver, Charged with Rape. Pleads Not Guilty', *Johnson City Press Chronicle* (TN), 10 December 1950, 5.

107 'Carter Countian Convicted on Morals Count', *Johnson City Press Chronicle*, 17 February 1951, 1.

108 'Librarian, 35, Accused Here as Molester', *Miami News* (FL), 2 February 1957, 4B.

109 'Convention Time in Full Tilt at Blowing Rock's Mayview Manor: Other News from Resort Town', *Watauga Democrat* (NC), 18 June 1953, second section 1.

110 Ibid.

111 Claudia Poutra, 'Teen-Talk', *Orange Leader*, 27 August 1950, 10.

112 Ibid., 3 December 1950, 3; ibid., 8 July 1951, 10.

113 Ibid., 19 October 1952, 8.

114 Judy Frantz, 'Town Teen Talk', *Indiana Evening Gazette* (PA), 30 April 1958, 16.

115 Marisa White and Marilyn Eyler, 'Teen Talk', *Salina Journal* (KS), 27 August 1953, 16.

116 Connie Taylor and Jere Glover, 'Teen Talk', *Salina Journal*, 1 July 1954, 8.

117 Ibid., 8 July 1954, 7.

118 Sherry Meitler and Rosie Austin, 'Teen Talk', *Indiana Evening Gazette*, 19 April 1956, 11.

119 Caroline Forsyth and Sandy Sloop, 'Teen Talk', *Indiana Evening Gazette*, 27 August 1959, 6.

120 Patty Mathews, 'Snooper', *Rusk Cherokeean* (TX), 20 March 1952, 10. Later 'Snooper' columns do not identify the writer.

121 Ibid., 8 November 1954, 3; ibid., 9 December 1954, 17; ibid., 5 May 1955, 18; ibid., 29 March 1956, 3; ibid., 24 May 1956, 9; ibid., 25 October 1956, 3; ibid., 1 November 1956, section 2, 1; ibid., 3 October 1957, 6; ibid., 10 October 1957, section 2, 1.

122 US Congress, Senate, 'Subcommittee to Investigate Juvenile Delinquency', *Juvenile Delinquency (Motion Pictures)*, 84th Congress, 1st session, 1955, 82.

123 Kirkwood vs. McFarland, Court of Appeal of Louisiana, First Circuit, 29 June 1950, 47 So. 2d 74 (La, Ct App. 1950), https://casetext.com/case/kirkwood-v-mcfarland-1 (accessed 30 November 2022).

124 Wini Breines, *Young, White, and Miserable: Growing Up Female in the Fifties* (Chicago, IL: University of Chicago Press, 2001), 105.

125 Beth L. Bailey, *From Front Porch to Back Seat: Courtship in Twentieth Century America* (Baltimore, MD: John Hopkins University Press, 1988), 13.

126 Ibid., 20.

127 'Hopeful Jill', 'Dear Miss Mayfield', *Tucson Daily Citizen* (AZ), 13 June 1955, 12.

128 'Also Stuck at Home', 'I Feel Like my Life is Already Over', *Miami Herald* (FL), 5 May 1959, B1.

129 'Burned-Up Wife', 'Dear Molly Mayfield', *Davenport Quad City Times* (IO), 20 August 1954, 8.

130 'Husband of Burned-Up Wife', ibid.

131 Dorothy Ricker, 'Dear Miss Ricker', *Miami Herald*, 9 July 1957, 2B.

132 Ibid.

133 Ann Landers, 'Running with Married Man Brings Only Grief', *Janesville Daily Gazette* (WI), 17 March 1955, section 2, 1.

134 Sheila John Daly, 'Necking is Suspected by her Mama', *St Louis Globe Democrat* (MO), 18 August 1955, 1C.

135 Ibid.

136 'Confused', 'Doesn't Mum Trust Me? She Objects to Drive-In Movies', *Miami Herald*, 9 October 1956, 4B.

137 Eleanor Hart, 'Doesn't Mum Trust Me? She Objects to Drive-In Movies', ibid.

138 Sheila John Daly, 'Tips for Teenagers', *Hartford Courant* (CT), 23 July 1950, 'Parade of Youth' section, 2.

139 Sheila John Daily, 'Girl's Dad Can Be Friendly', *Detroit Free Press*, 26 May 1953, 34.

140 Ibid.

141 'Miss B', 'Most Sincerely, Jane Palmer', *Los Angeles Mirror News*, 27 September 1955, 11.

142 'Disgusted', 'Ball Fan Strikes Out', *Knoxville News Sentinel* (TN), 6 July 1958, D7.

143 Sheila John Daly, 'For Shy Boy: Every Date Becomes Easier', *Chicago Tribune*, 30 June 1957, part 7, 2.

144 Ibid.

145 'Beatrice Fairfax', 'Your Heart and Home Problems', *Massillon Evening Independent* (OH), 22 May 1952, 21.

146 'Hal', 'To Maintain High Moral Standards through Teens is Difficult but Always Best Attitude', *Lexington Leader* (KS), 31 July 1956, 10.

147 Ibid.

148 'Drive-In Cats', 'Teen's Girl Shows Too Much Affection in Public', *Davenport Quad City Times* (IO), 23 February 1957, 12.

149 Ibid.

150 Ann Carroll, 'Bad Girl Pictures Repel Patrons of Film Drive-ins', 16.

151 Ibid.

152 George W. Crane, 'The Worry Clinic', *Altoona Tribune* (PA), 2 August 1955, 4.

153 Annette Kuhn, 'What to do with Cinema Memory?', in *Explorations in New Cinema History*, 85.

154 Lauren Stefforia, 'The Gratiot Drive-In: A Memoir', https://www.youtube.com/watch?v=oUu0jj8xcUs (accessed 30 November 2022).

155 Sanders, *Drive-In Movies Memories*, combines information, photographs and memories as do the Cinema Treasures website, http://cinematreasures.org/theaters?q=drive-in&status=all and sites such as the 'Traces of Texas' Facebook group, https://www.facebook.com/profile.php?id=100064332053430.

156 Nancy Manning, '"In the Good ol' Summertime . . ."', *Penny Record* [Bridge City, TX], 25 June 1997, 17; 'Remembering the MacArthur Drive-In Theatre in Orange, Texas', https://www.facebook.com/profile.php?id=100054277789673 (accessed 6 December 2022).

157 Russell and Whalley, *Hollywood and the Baby Boom*, 49.

158 Ibid.

159 Ibid.

160 Jillian Forstadt, 'Oscars: Read Brad Pitt's Acceptance Speech for Best Supporting Actor', *Hollywood Reporter*, 9 February 2020, https://www.hollywoodreporter.com/movies/movie-news/oscars-read-brad-pitts-acceptance-speech-best-supporting-actor-1277805/ (accessed 17 February 2023).

161 'Hollywood and the Baby Boom' survey, respondents 71, 163, 768.

162 Ibid., respondents 79, 108, 208.

163 Ibid., respondent 577.

164 Ibid., respondent 41.

165 Annette Kuhn, *An Everyday Magic: Cinema and Cultural Memory* (London: I.B. Tauris, 2002), 100–1.

166 Ibid., 138.

167 'Hollywood and the Baby Boom' survey, respondent 715.

168 Joseph MacBride, *Steven Spielberg: A Biography* (Jackson, MS: University Press of Mississippi, 2010), 78.

169 Glenna Rogers interview for a Wright State University History Course, Interviewer Cynthia Spangler, Dayton and Miami Valley Oral History Project, 6 July 2011, https://corescholar.libraries.wright.edu/history_oral_history/28/ (accessed 30 November 2022).

170 José Carlos Lozano, 'Film at the Border: Memories of Cinemagoing in Laredo, Texas', *Memory Studies* 10, no. 1 (2017): 43.

171 Miriam Caldwell, 'Diary of Vilma, the Unconquerable', https://www.diaryofvilma.com/ (accessed 30 November 2022).

172 'Vilma and the Fire of Desire', 'Diary of Vilma, the Unconquerable', 3 March 2015, https://www.diaryofvilma.com/diaryblog/previous/5.

173 'Vilma's Secret Sins **Racy Content**', 'Diary of Vilma, the Unconquerable', 17 January 2016, https://www.diaryofvilma.com/diaryblog/previous/2.

174 'Vilma's Fickle Heart & the Glass Factory', 'Diary of Vilma, the Unconquerable', 14 February 2016, https://www.diaryofvilma.com/diaryblog/previous/2.

175 Ibid.

176 'Vilma and Bill. . . Is it Love?', 'Diary of Vilma, the Unconquerable', 2 April 2016, https://www.diaryofvilma.com/diaryblog/previous/2.

177 'Vilma Daydreams in the Shadows of the Sixth Street Bridge', 'Diary of Vilma, the Unconquerable', 30 August 2016, https://www.diaryofvilma.com/diaryblog.

178 'Billie Jean's Screams in the Night', 'Diary of Vilma, the Unconquerable', 8 March 2017, https://www.diaryofvilma.com/diaryblog.

179 'Vilma Goes Ker-PLUNK! Plus: Big Jay and the Final Rub', 'Diary of Vilma, the Unconquerable', 21 February 2018, https://www.diaryofvilma.com/diaryblog.

180 Cohen, 'Forgotten Audiences in the Passion Pits', 475.

181 Dudley Andrew, 'Film and Society: Public Ritual and Private Space', in *Exhibition: The Film Reader*, 165–6.

182 Cohen, 'Forgotten Audiences in the Passion Pits', 478.

183 Ibid. Cohen's source is Charles R. Underhill Jr., 'The Trend in Drive-In Theaters', *Journal of the Society of Motion Picture and Television Engineers* 54, no. 2 (1950): 162.

184 Underhill, 'The Trend in Drive-In Theaters', 161.

185 *The Drive-In Theatre*, Radio Corporation of America, Camden NJ, circa 1943, Tom B'Hend and Preston Kaufman Collection, file 4781. I do not know if Underwood wrote this account, though he may have.

186 Cohen, 'Forgotten Audiences in the Passion Pits', 478.

187 McGraw, 'Drive-In Movies Began in Camden', NJ1.

188 'Special Telephone Service Enables Polio-Victim to Talk with Friends', *Suffolk News Herald* (VA), 30 September 1951, 2.

189 'Paralysed Victim of Accident Earns Own Living', *Ohio Daily Advocate*, 10 January 1952, 8; 'Cancer Victim, 14, is Released from Hospital', *Decatur Daily Review* (IL), 28 July 1952, 16.

190 W. W. Smith, 'Drive-In Theatres and Their Construction', in *Theatre Catalog* (Philadelphia: Jay Emanuel, 1945), 431.

191 'More than 75 Standard Drive-Ins are Now Being Operated in Texas', *Boxoffice*, 28 August 1948, 87.

192 Advertisement, *Orange Leader*, 18 August 1950, 8.

193 'Alden Smith will Host Invalids at Drive-in', *Boxoffice*, 6 August 1938, 67.

194 'Shows for Shut-Ins', *Motion Picture Daily*, 6 August 1942, 4; 'Omaha', *Showmen's Trade Review*, 9 October 1948, 23.

195 'Sick and Infirm Hear Sermon at Drive-In', *MPH*, 14 June 1952, 57.

196 Bill Kirkpatrick, '"A Blessed Boon": Radio, Disability, Governability, and the Discourse of the "Shut-In", 1920-1930', *Critical Studies in Media Communication* 29, no. 3 (2012): 169.

197 Ibid., 171.

198 Ibid., 172.

199 Ibid., 167–8.

200 Ibid., 180.

201 Advertisement, *Jasper Daily Herald* (IN), 26 April 1958, 10.

202 'National Spotlight', *MPH*, 31 May 1952, 35–6.

203 'Ozoners' Big Negro Draw', *Variety*, 3 August 1949, 4.

204 Luther, 'Marketing Aspects of Drive-In Theaters', 42.

205 Cohen, 'Forgotten Audiences in the Passion Pits', 478.

206 Thomas Doherty, 'Race Houses, Jim Crow Roosts, and Lily White Palaces: Desegregating the Motion Picture Theater', in *Going to the Movies: Hollywood and the Social Experience of Cinema*, ed. Richard Maltby, Melvyn Stokes and Robert C. Allen (Exeter: Exeter University Press, 2007), 204.

207 Marcia G. Synott, 'The African-American Women Most Influential in Desegregating Higher Education', *Journal of Blacks in Higher Education* 59 (2008): 48.

208 Pauli Murray, *States' Laws on Race and Color* (Cincinnati, OH: Women's Division of Christian Service, 1950), 17.

209 Ibid., 380.

210 Ibid., 17.

211 Ibid., 270–1.

212 Ibid., 17.

213 Ibid., 615.

214 'Bombings are Listed by League', *Charlotte Observer* (NC), 4 May 1958, 2.
215 'No Brakes on Drive-In Lures', *Variety*, 13 July 1949, 18.
216 'Negro Theaters in the United States', *Film Daily Year Book* (1950), 1031–5.
217 *Film Daily Year Book* (1952), 947–52; *Film Daily Year Book* (1953), 1090–3.
218 Richard Maltby and Philippe Meers, 'Connections, Intermediality and the Anti-Archive: A Conversation with Robert C. Allen', in *Routledge Companion to New Cinema History*, 23.
219 Tower Drive-In Theatre Advertisement, *Carolinian*, 14 April 1956, 5.
220 'Tower Drive-in Theater Opens Doors to Negroes', *Carolinian*, 14 April 1956, 5.
221 'Twin City Theaters, 1843-2017 . . .', 'North Carolina Collection', 4 March 2017, https://northcarolinaroom.wordpress.com/2017/03/04/twin-city-theaters-1843-2017/ (accessed 6 November 2022).
222 Ibid.
223 '61 of Drive-In Theaters In State Admit Negroes', *Louisville Courier-Journal* (KY), 24 September 1961, 33.
224 Ibid.
225 '"Park-In" Program Seeks D-I integration', *Exhibitor*, 17 June 1962, 14.
226 'Pressure Building for Integration', *Exhibitor*, 26 June 1963, 21.
227 Gomery, *Shared Pleasures*, 157.
228 Shannon Bell, 'From Ticket Booth to Screen Tower: An Architectural Study of Drive-In Theaters in the Baltimore -Washington DC-Richmond Corridor', *Perspectives in Vernacular Architecture* 9 (2003): 223.
229 'Round Table Has Twins!' *MPH*, 10 October 1953, 43.
230 'Drive-In Theater Ready', *Tampa Tribune*, 20 January 1950, 10; Arthur Knight, 'Searching for the Apollo: Black Moviegoing and Its Contexts in the Small-Town US South', in *Explorations in New Cinema History*, 235–6.
231 'Negro Fined for Date with White Girl', *Indiana Evening Gazette* (PA), 5 September 1959, 7.
232 Ibid.
233 Ibid.
234 George D. Brantley, 'Present State of Integration in Public Schools of Missouri', *Journal of Negro Education* 24, no. 3 (1955): 299.
235 Bill Maxwell, 'Sad Goodbye to 28th Street Drive-In", *Tampa Bay Times* (FL), 21 June 2000, 11A.
236 Ibid. There is another version of Maxwell's account in Sanders, *Drive-In Movie Memories*, 27.
237 Segrave, *Drive-In Theaters*, 198.
238 Corman, *How I Made a Hundred Movies in Hollywood*, 31.
239 'Teen-Age Drivers Talk Back', in *Profile of Youth*, 45.

240 Student Government Association of Mary Washington College of the University of Virginia, *Student Handbook 1959-1960*, 38; Student Government Association of Mary Washington College of the University of Virginia, *Student Handbook 1960-1961*, 37. Italics added.

241 Eric Ledell Smith, *African American Theater Buildings: An Illustrated Historical Directory, 1900-1955* (Jefferson, NC and London: McFarland, 2003), 4.

Chapter 4

1 Vincent Canby, 'Adam at 6. A.M. Sneers at Mid-America', *NYT*, 1 December 1970, 58.

2 Vincent Canby, 'Why "Smokey and the Bandit" is Making a Killing', *NYT*, 18 December 1977, 109.

3 Derek Nystrom, *Hard Hats, Rednecks, and Macho Men: Class in 1970s American Cinema* (Oxford: Oxford University Press, 2009), 90.

4 Church, *Grindhouse Nostalgia*, 47.

5 For a discussion of the film and its production and reception see Nicholas Godfrey's chapter on it in his *The Limits of Auteurism: Case Studies in the Critically Constructed New Hollywood* (New Brunswick: Rutgers University Press, 2017), 114–23.

6 Quoted in Thomas J. Harris, *Bogdanovich's Picture Shows* (Metuchen, NJ and London: Scarecrow Press, 1990), 53–4.

7 Church, *Grindhouse Nostalgia*, 38.

8 In his *Teenagers and Teenpics*, Thomas Doherty does refer to *The Amazing Colossal Man* and *The Attack of the Puppet People* as 'elastic expressions of the ebb and flow of pubescent development', going on to write of how a 'necking couple' in the latter watch the colossal man in the former tear apart a Las Vegas drive-in: 119, 124. However, the necking couple in the 1958 film were played by actors born in 1933 (June Kenney) and 1921 (John Agar), and I think Doherty is referring to the destruction of the Danny Thomas Sun Resort in *The Amazing Colossal Man*.

9 'The Delinquents', *Motion Picture Exhibitor*, 6 March 1957, Service Section 2; '"The Delinquents" with Tommy Laughlin, Peter Miller and Dick Bakalyn', *Harrison's Reports*, 23 February 1957, 32.

10 I am drawing here on Jeffrey Sconce's notion of 'paracinema' as 'a particular reading protocol, a counter-aesthetic turned subcultural sensibility devoted to all manner of cultural detritus': '"Trashing" the Academy: Tastes, Excess and an Emerging Politics of Cinematic Style', *Screen* 36, no. 4 (1995): 372.

NOTES

11 'Drive-In' Director Praises Terrell, Tex', *Boxoffice*, 22 December 1974, in '*Drive-In* Clipping File', Margaret Herrick Library, Academy of Motion Picture Arts and Sciences.

12 See Michael D. Dwyer, *Back to the Fifties: Nostalgia, Hollywood Film, and Popular Music of the Seventies and Eighties* (Oxford: Oxford University Press, 2015), Daniel Marcus, *Happy Days and Wonder Years: The Fifties and Sixties in Contemporary Cultural Politics* (New Brunswick, NJ: Rutgers University Press, 2009) and Christine Sprengler, *Screening Nostalgia: Populuxe Props and Technicolor Aesthetics in Contemporary American Film* (New York: Berghahn, 2009).

13 Vera Dika, *Recycled Culture in Contemporary Art and Film: The Uses of Nostalgia* (Cambridge: Cambridge University Press, 2003), 125.

14 Oliver Gruner and Peter Krämer, 'Introduction', in *Grease is the Word*, ed. Oliver Gruner and Peter Krämer (London: Anthem Press, 2020), 29.

15 Ibid., 48.

16 Harris Green, '"Grease"? Groovy', *New York Times*, 4 June 1972, D1.

17 Jan Dawson, '*Grease*', *Monthly Film Bulletin* 45 (1978): 176. For *Grease*'s position at the top of 1978 box-office rentals, see David A. Cook, *Lost Illusions: American Cinema in the Shadow of Watergate and Vietnam* (Berkeley, CA: University of California Press, 2000), 501.

18 Michael Ryan and Douglas Kellner, *Camera Politica: The Politics and Ideology of Contemporary Hollywood Film* (Bloomington, IN: Indiana University Press, 1988), 86.

19 The sort of cartoons seen behind Danny in *Grease* have developed cult status, and McKeon and Everett include an 'At the Snack Bar' chapter in *Cinema Under the Stars*, illustrated with Filmack snack bar advertisements: 38–51.

20 Church, *Grindhouse Nostalgia*, 31.

21 'u/Actual_Caregiver', 'The Drive-in Version of Dominion Doesn't Even Have the Drive-in Scene', Reddit, https://www.reddit.com/r/JurassicPark/comments/vzdp50/the_drivein_version_of_dominion_doesnt_even_have/ (accessed 9 November 2022).

22 Uib Cao, 'An Interview with Passion Pit's Nate Donmoyer and Ian Hultquist', *California Aggie*, 8 August 2012, https://web.archive.org/web/20120808002721/http://www.theaggie.org/2010/04/19/an-interview-with-passion-pits-nate-donmoyer-and-ian-hultquist/ (accessed 11 December 2022).

23 John Cheever, 'The Cure', *New Yorker*, 27 June 1952, https://www.newyorker.com/magazine/1952/07/05/the-cure (accessed 5 November 2022).

24 Walker Percy, *The Moviegoer* (1961) (London: Paladin, 1987), 106.

25 Ibid., 107.

26 Ian Fleming, *Diamonds are Forever* (1956) (London: Penguin, 2004), 154.

27 Ibid.

28 Ibid., 155.
29 R. C. Gold, *Drive-In Girl* (New York: Midwood, 1961).
30 Ibid., 67–8.
31 Ibid., 77.
32 John D. MacDonald, *The Crossroads* (Greenwich, CT: Fawcett, 1959), 86.
33 John McPartland, *No Down Payment* (New York: Simon & Schuster, 1957), 113.
34 John Cheever, *The Wapshot Chronicle, The Wapshot Scandal* (1957 and 1964) (New York: Harper & Row, 1979), 391.
35 John Updike, 'The Deacon', *New Yorker*, 12 February 1970, https://www.newyorker.com/magazine/1970/02/21/the-deacon (accessed 30 November 2022).
36 Philip Roth, *I Married a Communist* (New York: Vintage, 1998), 192.
37 John Irving, *The Cider House Rules* (1985) (London: Black Swan, 1986), 319.
38 Ibid., 316.
39 Ibid., 330.
40 Allen Hannay, *Love and Other Natural Disasters* (Boston and Toronto: Little Brown, 1982), 94–5.
41 Oliver Bleeck (Ross Thomas), *The Procane Chronicle* (1972) (New York: Perennial, 1983), 177.
42 Ibid., 178.
43 Thomas McGuane, 'Hazardous Life in a Meat Bucket', *Sports Illustrated*, 15 May 1972, 30.
44 Thomas McGuane, *Something to be Desired* (New York: Random House, 1984), 82.
45 Ibid., 83.
46 Ruth Doan McDougall, *The Cheerleader* (1973) (Center Sandwich, NH: Frigate, 1998), 198–203.
47 Lisa Alther, *Kinflicks* (1976) (London: Virago, 1999), 52–3, 72.
48 Ibid., 72.
49 S. E. Hinton, *The Outsiders* (1967) (Basingstoke: Macmillan Education, 1979), 20.
50 S. E. Hinton, 'Teen-Agers Are for Real', *NYT*, 27 August 1967, BR14.
51 Ibid.
52 Alice Hoffman, 'At the Drive-In', *Fiction* 3, no. 1 (1974): 27–8; Alice Hoffman, *Property Of* (1977) (London: Vintage, 2002).
53 Alice Hoffman, 'The Drive-In, at Twilight', *NYT*, 4 September 1988, H18.
54 I have only seen the 'play version': Joe R. Lansdale, 'Drive-In Date', *Cemetery Dance* (Winter 1991), 33–9.

NOTES

55 Joe R. Lansdale, *The Drive-In: A B-Movie with Blood and Popcorn, Made in Texas*, in *The Complete Drive-In* (1988) (Chandler, TX: BookVoice, 2020), 21–116.
56 Norman Partridge and Martin H, Greenberg (eds), *It Came from the Drive-In* (New York: Daw Books, 1996).
57 Suzanne Simms, *Dream Within a Dream* (New York: Silhouette, 1984), 52–7.
58 Peg Sutherland, *Queen of the Dixie Drive-In* (New York: Harlequin, 1996), 18.
59 Ibid., 128.
60 Roseanne Williams, *Seeing Red* (New York: Harlequin, 1993), 156.
61 Ibid., 156–7.
62 Ibid., 218.
63 Larry Baker, *The Flamingo Rising* (1997) (London: Abacus, 1999); Marjorie Reynolds, *The Starlite Drive-in* (1997) (New York: Harper, 2011).
64 Marty M. Engle, *Strange Matter: Creature Features* (San Diego: Montage, 1996).
65 Caroline Keene, *Fatal Attraction* (New York: Pocket Books, 1988), 9.
66 Brad Strickland and Thomas E. Strickland, *Drive-in of Doom* (New York: Scholastic Inc, 1998).
67 Ibid., 46.
68 Gertrude Chandler Warner, *The Ghost at the Drive-In Movie* (Morton Grove, IL: Albert Whitman, 2008), 2.
69 Lesley Livingston and Jonathan Llyr, *How to Curse in Hieroglyphics* (Toronto and Ontario: Penguin, 2013), 3, 35.
70 Lesley Livingston and Jonathan Llyr, *The Haunting of Heck House* (Toronto and Ontario: Penguin, 2014), 4.
71 Ibid., 5.
72 Garrison Keillor and Jenny Lind Nilsson, *The Sandy Bottom Orchestra* (New York: Hyperion, 1996), 230.
73 Ibid., 236.
74 Stephen King (writing as Richard Bachman), *The Long Walk* (New York: Gallery Books, 1979), 162.
75 Stephen King, 'This Guy is *Really* Scary!' in 'Briggs', *Joe Bob Goes to the Drive-In*, 1–2.
76 Stephen King, *The Stand: The Complete & Uncut Version* (New York: Signet, 1991), 524, 874.
77 Ibid., 874–5.
78 Stephen King, *11/22/63* (London: Hodder, 2011), 218–19.
79 Eric Shade, 'Eyesores', in *Eyesores: Stories by Eric Shade* (Athens and London: University of Georgia Press, 2003), 3.

80 As well as the 1958 photograph, Ben Cosgrove's 'Let's Go to the Drive-in Movies!' *Life*, includes two Eyerman photographs from 1949: see https://www.life.com/lifestyle/drive-in-theaters-photos-of-a-vanishing-american-pastime/ (accessed 30 November 2022).

81 'A Two in One Issue Devoted to the Fun and Excitement of US Entertainment', *Life*, 22 December 1958, 3. For the drive-in photograph, see 'Great American Midway', *Life*, 22 December 1958, 16–17. The issue can be found at https://books.google.co.uk/books?id=Yj8EAAAAMBAJ&p (accessed 2 February 2023).

82 'A Two in One Issue Devoted to the Fun and Excitement of US Entertainment', 8.

83 Ibid., 16.

84 The photographer's daughter, Kathryn Marshall, is credited for this story by Annie Knox in 'Drive-ins Go Digital, But Some Things Never Change', *Salt Lake Tribune*, 27 August 2013, available at https://archive.sltrib.com/article.php?id=56764268&itype=cmsid (accessed 6 November 2022).

85 Christine Dell'Amore, 'The Big Picture: A Well-planned Single Image Yells the Story of 20th-century Transportation', *Smithsonian* 36, no. 9 (2005): 16, https://www.smithsonianmag.com/arts-culture/the-big-picture-2-110497282/ (accessed 30 November 2022). See also Rupert Martin (ed.), *Night Trick by O. Winston Link: Photographs of The Norfolk & Western Railway, 1955-60* (London: Photographers' Gallery, 1983), 23.

86 The pamphlet is reproduced (in miniature) and discussed in Martin Parr and Gerry Badger, *The Photobook: A History*, Volume II (London and New York: Phaidon, 2006), 188–9. The Photographers' Gallery published the better-known version of the photograph (23).

87 Parr and Badger, *The Photobook*, 188.

88 Dell'Amore, 'The Big Picture', 16.

89 Vivian Raynor, 'A Show's Star is the Steam Locomotive', *NYT*, 15 March 1992, WC22.

90 Alain Bosquet, *Les Américains* (Paris: Robert Delpire, 1958).

91 Jack Kerouac, 'Introduction', in *The Americans: Photographs by Robert Frank* (1959) (Göttingen: Steidl, 2008), no page numbers.

92 'Today's Program at Your Favorite Theater', *Detroit Free Press*, 29 June 1955, 14; ibid. 30 June 1955, 16; ibid. 1 July 1955, 29; ibid. 2 July 1955, 4.

93 See Introduction.

94 A. J. van Zuilen, *The Life Cycle of Magazines: A Historical Study of the Decline and Fall of the General Interest Mass Audience Magazine in the United States in the Period 1946-1972* (Uithoorn: Graduate Press, 1977), 87.

95 Joshua Chuang, 'When the Messenger is the Medium: The Making of Walker Evans' "American Photographs" and Robert Frank's "The Americans"', *Yale University Art Gallery Bulletin* (2006): 120.

NOTES

96 Miles Orvell, *American Photography* (Oxford: Oxford University Press, 2003), 120.
97 Carolyn Carr, 'Rite of Passage: O. Winston Link's Railroad Photographs of the 1950s', in *Ghost Trains: Railroad Photographs of the 1950s by O. Winston Link* (Norfolk, VA: Chrysler Museum, 1983), 7.
98 Rupert Martin, 'Introduction', *Night Trick by O. Winston Link*, 3.
99 Alfred Appel, *Signs of Life* (New York: Alfred A. Knopf, 1983), 64, 67.
100 Ibid., 62–3, 67, 64.
101 Vicky Goldberg and Robert Silberman, *American Photography: A Century of Images* (San Francisco, CA: Chronicle Book, 1999), 84.
102 Han-Chih Wang, 'The Profane and the Profound: American Road Photography from 1930 to the Present' (PhD diss., Temple University, Philadelphia, 2017), xlii.
103 John Szarkowski, 'Foreword', in *The New West: Landscapes Along the Colorado Front Range* (Boulder, CO: Colorado Associated University Press, 1974), viii.
104 Mee-Lai Stone, 'Cars, Bars and Burger Joints: Eggleston's Iconic America – In Pictures', *Guardian*, 22 November 2022, https://www.theguardian.com/artanddesign/gallery/2022/nov/22/cars-bars-and-burger-joints-william-egglestons-iconic-america-in-pictures (accessed 12 December 2022). The Sky-Vue closed in 1972: 'Sky-Vue Drive-In', 'Cinema Treasures', http://cinematreasures.org/theaters/33646 (accessed 12 December 2022).
105 Wim Wenders, 'Abandoned Drive-In' (1983), Artnet, http://www.artnet.com/artists/wim-wenders/abandoned-drive-in-1983-a-bx5pGtuSYVuICNcIU0GYA2 (accessed 30 November 2022); Skye Sherwin, 'Wim Wenders' Drive-In, Marfa, Texas: Romantic Fascination with Decay', *Guardian*, 13 April 2018, https://www.theguardian.com/artanddesign/2018/apr/13/wim-wenders-drive-in-marfa-texas-romantic-fascination-with-decay (accessed 30 November 2022).
106 Jeff Wignal, *Landscape Photography* (New York: McGraw Hill, 1987), 105.
107 Ken Johnson, 'Drive-Ins: Disappearing Summer', *NYT*, 31 July 1998, E35.
108 See Dick Arentz, 'Outside the Mainstream', 'Platinum and Palladium Printing', 22 November 2018, https://www.dickarentz.com/archive-gallery/outside-the-mainstream (accessed 30 November 2022).
109 See Jeff Brouws, 'Abandoned Drive-ins', in *Readymades: American Roadside Artifacts* (San Francisco, CA: Chronicle Books, 2003), 59–77. The section includes an essay by Luc Sante on the drive-in, 'Enormous Bodies in the Night', 60–2. The 'exploring the historical' quote is taken from the home page of Brouws' website: http://www.jeffbrouws.com/ (accessed 4 December 2022).
110 See 'Images 1996-2003', Sandy Skoglund, http://www.sandyskoglund.com/pages/imagelist/1280_960/96_03/index.html (accessed 30 November 2022).
111 Iona Cruickshank, 'Mapping the Fading Light: A Photographic Documentation of Canadian Drive-in Movie Theatres, 2001-2009',

unpublished project book, 2010, Special Collections, Kimberlin Library, De Montfort University, 18.

112 Ibid.
113 Joan Liftin, *Drive-Ins* (London: Trolley Books, 2004), no page numbers.
114 See Francesca Street, 'Drive-in Days: America's Abandoned Movie Theaters', *CNN Travel*, updated 2 January 2018, https://edition.cnn.com/travel/article/abandoned-drive-in-movie-theaters/index.html (accessed 30 November 2022) and 'Deman Imagery', https://www.demanimagery.com/portfolio/G0000WOHqo00FWD0 (accessed 30 November 2022).
115 See Don Bartletti, '5(ish) Questions: Photographer Lindsay Rickert and "Drive-In America"', *Nieman News*, 21 September, https://nieman.harvard.edu/stories/5ish-questions-photographer-lindsay-rickert-and-drive-in-america/ (accessed 30 November 2022) and Lindsay Rickert, 'Drive-in America', 'Lindsay Rickert, Imagery, Elevated', https://lindsey-rickert.squarespace.com/drive-in-theaters (accessed 30 November 2022).
116 Carl Weese, 'Drive-In Theater Photography Presentation in Two Weeks', 'Working Pictures', http://workingpictures.blogspot.com/2018/10/drive-in-theater-photography.html (accessed 30 November 2022).
117 Carl Weese, 'Documentary Photography, Emotion, and Projection', 'Working Pictures', 7 May 2014, http://workingpictures.blogspot.com/2014/05/ (accessed 30 November 2022).
118 Elizabeth Heilman Brooke, 'Home on the Range, With Drive-Ins and Gas Stations', *NYT*, 26 January 2000, E2.
119 See Ann Scarlett Daley, 'The Necessity for Ruins', in *Elevating Western American Art: Developing an Institute in the Cultural Capital of the Rockies*, ed. Thomas Brent Smith (Denver, CO: Petrie Institute of Western American Art, 2012), 156–9; John Brinckerhoff Jackson, 'The Necessity for Ruins', in *The Necessity for Ruins and Other Topics* (Amherst, MA: University of Massachusetts Press, 1980), 94–5.
120 John Brinckerhoff Jackson, *Landscape in Sight: Looking at America* (New Haven, CT and London: Yale University Press, 1997), 228.
121 'Downtown Branch', *Bulletin of the Whitney Museum of American Art, 1980-81*, no. 3 (Fall 1981): 29.
122 Liz Burns, 'Intro', in *12 Angry Films* (Dublin: Fire Station Artists' Studios, 2007), 1.
123 Jesse Jones, 'Ideas Catch Fire in Dialogue', in *12 Angry Films*, 10.
124 Ibid.
125 Ibid., 11.
126 Angela Rosenberg, 'In the Car – With You', in *Auto-Kino!* (Berlin: Temporäre Kunsthalle, 2010), 5, 6.
127 Bert Rebhandl, 'The Living Room in the Car Park: Films You Can Drive in to – A Brief Phenomenology of the Drive-in Cinema', in *Auto-Kino!*, 9.

128 Church, *Grindhouse Nostalgia*, 23. See also the chapter 'A Drive-In Theatre of the Mind: Nostalgic Populism and the Déclassé Video Object', 29–72.
129 Ibid., 30.
130 Ibid., 24.
131 Ibid., 31, 74. Quoting Pierre Nora, 'Between Memory and History: *Les Lieux de Mémoire*', 24, Church defines *lieux de mémoire* as 'material sites to which collective memory attaches and condenses, "invest[ing] [them] with a symbolic aura"', *Grindhouse Nostalgia*, 5.

Conclusion

1 Richard Maltby, *Decoding the Movies: Hollywood in the 1930s* (Exeter: University of Exeter Press, 2021), 334.
2 Roche, 'King Creole', *Boxoffice*, 23 March 1959, 80.
3 Peter Guralnick, *Last Train to Memphis: The Rise of Elvis Presley* (Boston, MA: Little Brown, 1994), 115.
4 'Joy Drive-In Theatre, Minden, LA', 'Scotty Moore: The Official Website', http://scottymoore.net/minden.html (accessed 1 December 2022); Guralnick, *Last Train to Memphis*, 460.
5 Ann Landers, 'Youthful Marriage Regretted', *Nashville Banner* (TN), 28 September 1959, 23.
6 Fox, 'The Drive-In Movie', 213.
7 Phil Serafino, 'Elvis's Cars on Display at Museum', 'UPI Archives', 10 June 1989, https://www.upi.com/Archives/1989/06/10/Elviss-cars-on-display-at-museum/2663613454400/ (accessed 1 December 2022).
8 See Mark Bould, 'Apocalypse Here and Now: Making Sense of *The Texas Chain Saw Massacre*' and Tony Williams, 'In the Science Fiction Name of National Security: *Cat Women of the Moon*', both in *Horror at the Drive*, 97–112 and 113–25.
9 See Chapter 3, 142.

Archive collections and databases consulted

Archive collections

Arkansas Amusement Corporation Papers, Center for Arkansas History and Culture, University of Arkansas, Little Rock

Hoblitzelle Interstate Theatre Circuit Collection, Harry Ransom Center, the University of Texas at Austin

Interstate Theatre Collection, Dallas History & Archives Division, Dallas Public Library

National Association of Theatre Owners Collection, L. Tom Perry Special Collections Library, Harold B. Lee Library, Brigham Young University, Provo, Utah

Samuel Z. Arkoff Papers, Department of Archives and Special Collections, William H. Hannon Library, Loyola Marymount University

Steve Broidy Collection, Margaret Herrick Library, Academy of Motion Pictures, Arts and Sciences

Tom B'hend and Preston Kaufman Collection, Margaret Herrick Library, Academy of Motion Pictures, Arts and Sciences

Databases

Arizona Memory Project, https://azmemory.azlibrary.gov/

Chronicling America, Historical American Newspapers, https://chroniclingamerica.loc.gov/

Internet Archive, https://archive.org/

Media History Digital Library, https://mediahist.org/

Memorial Hall Library, Historical Newspaper Collection, https://mhl.org/historical-newspapers

NewspaperArchive, Newspaperarchive.com

Newspapers.com, https://www.newspapers.com/

North Carolina Digital Collections, https://digital.ncdcr.gov/

Portal to Texas History, https://texashistory.unt.edu/

Proquest Historical Newspapers, https://about.proquest.com/en/products-services/pq-hist-news/

Select bibliography

Ackerman, Louis M. 'Outdoor Movie Talk'. *American Speech* 32, no. 3 (1957): 239.
Adams, Robert. *The New West: Landscapes along the Colorado Front Range*. Boulder: Colorado Associated University Press, 1974.
Agrasánchez, Jr, Rogelio. *Mexican Movies in the United States: A History of the Films, Theaters and Audiences, 1920–1960*. Jefferson: McFarland, 2006.
Allen, Robert C. 'Reimagining the History of the Experience of Cinema in a Post-Moviegoing Age'. In *Explorations in New Cinema History: Approaches and Case Studies*, edited by Richard Maltby, Daniel Biltereyst and Philippe Meers, 41–57. Oxford: Blackwell, 2011.
Allen, Robert C. 'Relocating American Film History: The "Problem" of the Empirical'. *Cultural Studies* 20, no. 1 (2006): 48–88.
Alther, Lisa. *Kinflicks*. 1976. London: Virago, 1999.
American Association of State Highway Officials. *Policy on Drive-In Theaters*. Washington, DC: American Association of State Highway Officials, 1949.
Andrew, Dudley. 'Film and Society: Public Ritual and Private Space'. 1986. In *Exhibition: The Film Reader*, edited by Ina Rae Hark, 161–71. London: Routledge, 2002.
Appel, Alfred. *Signs of Life*. New York: Alfred A. Knopf, 1983.
Arkoff, Sam with Richard Trubo. *Flying through Hollywood by the Seat of My Pants*. New York: Birch Lane Press, 1992.
Austin, Bruce A. 'The Development and the Decline of the Drive-In Movie Theater'. In *Current Research in Film: Audiences, Economics and Law, Vol. 1*, edited by Bruce A. Austin, 59–91. Norwood: Ablex, 1985.
Bailey, Beth L. *From Front Porch to Back Seat: Courtship in Twentieth Century America*. Baltimore: John Hopkins University Press, 1988.
Baker, Larry. *The Flamingo Rising*. 1997. London: Abacus, 1999.
Bauer, Jordan. 'Urban Village or '*Burb of the Future?*: The Racial and Economic Politics of a Houston Neighborhood'. *Houston History* 6, no. 3 (2009): 39–45.
Bell, Shannon. 'From Ticket Booth to Screen Tower: An Architectural Study of Drive-In Theaters in the Baltimore -Washington DC-Richmond Corridor'. *Perspectives in Vernacular Architecture* 9 (2003): 215–27.
Belton, John. *Widescreen Cinema*. Cambridge, MA: Harvard University Press, 1992.
Bennett, Patrick. 'Mrs Likins Leaves Show Biz. "Slow Fade" to Europe Next Scene'. *Abilene Reporter-News*, 12 February 1965, 1.
Bleeck, Oliver [Ross Thomas]. *The Procane Chronicle*. 1972. New York: Perennial, 1983.

Bosquet, Alain. *Les Américains*. Paris: Robert Delpire, 1958.
Bould, Mark. 'Apocalypse Here and Now: Making Sense of *The Texas Chain Saw Massacre*'. In *Horror at the Drive-In*, edited by Gary D. Rhodes, 97–112. Jefferson: McFarland, 2003.
Boye, Gary R. 'The Sky-Vu Drive-In: 1950–1967', 'Film Exhibition in Watauga County NC', https://sites.google.com/appstate.edu/nwnc-theaters-1/watauga/boone-skyvu-drive-in-theatre (accessed 30 November 2022).
Brantley, George D. 'Present State of Integration in Public Schools of Missouri'. *Journal of Negro Education* 24, no. 3 (1955): 293–309.
Breines, Wini. *Young, White, and Miserable: Growing Up Female in the Fifties*. Chicago: University of Chicago Press, 2001.
Brenner, Neil and Nikos Katsikis. 'Operational Landscapes: Hinterlands of the Capitaloscene'. *Architectural Design* 90, no. 1 (2020): 22–31.
Briggs, Joe Bob [John Irving Bloom]. *Joe Bob Goes to the Drive-In*. 1987. London: Penguin, 1989.
Britt, Steuart Henderson. 'What is the Nature of the Drive-in Theater Audience?' *Media/Scope* 4 (June 1960): 100–3.
Brooke, Elizabeth Heilman. 'Home on the Range, With Drive-ins and Gas Stations'. *New York Times*, 26 January 2000, E2.
Brouws, Jeff. 'Abandoned Drive-ins'. In *Readymades: American Roadside Artifacts*, 59–77. San Francisco: Chronicle Books, 2003.
Brunette, Peter. *Roberto Rossellini*. Berkeley: University of California Press, 1997.
Bruno, Giuliana. 'Site-Seeing: Architecture and the Moving Image'. *Wide Angle* 19, no. 4 (1997): 8–24.
Bumpass, Gita. '"Show Goes On" but the Man with a Ringside Seat Rarely Gets to See it'. *Abilene Reporter-News*, 29 June 1945, 2.
Burkett, Warren. 'Loop 322 Right-of-Way Cleared for Bid Letting'. *Abilene Reporter-News*, 9 September 1958, 1B.
Burns, Liz. 'Intro'. *12 Angry Films*, 1–2. Dublin: Fire Station Artists' Studios, 2007.
Buscombe, Edward, ed. *The BFI Companion to the Western*. London: Museum of the Moving Image, 1991.
Caldwell, Miriam. 'Diary of Vilma, the Unconquerable', https://www.diaryofvilma.com/ (accessed 30 November 2022).
Campbell, Randolph B. *Gone to Texas: A History of the Lone Star State*. New York: Oxford University Press, 2003.
Canby, Vincent. 'Adam at 6. A.M. Sneers at Mid-America'. *New York Times*, 1 December 1970, 58.
Canby, Vincent. 'Why "Smokey and the Bandit" is Making a Killing'. *New York Times*, 18 December 1977, 109.
Cao, Uib. 'An Interview with Passion Pit's Nate Donmoyer and Ian Hultquist'. *California Aggie*, 8 August 2012, https://web.archive.org/web/20120808002721/http://www.theaggie.org/2010/04/19/an-interview-with-passion-pits-nate-donmoyer-and-ian-hultquist/ (accessed 11 December 2022).
Carr, Carolyn. 'Rite of Passage: O. Winston Link's Railroad Photographs of the 1950s'. In *Ghost Trains: Railroad Photographs of the 1950s by O. Winston Link*, 6–8. Norfolk: Chrysler Museum, 1983.
Cheever, John. 'The Cure'. *New Yorker*, 27 June 1952, https://www.newyorker.com/magazine/1952/07/05/the-cure (accessed 5 November 2022).

Cheever, John. *The Wapshot Chronicle, The Wapshot Scandal*. 1957 and 1964. New York: Harper & Row, 1979.
Christie, Ian. 'Introduction: In Search of Audiences'. In *Audiences: Defining and Researching Screen Entertainment Reception*, edited by Ian Christie, 11–22. Amsterdam: University of Amsterdam Press, 2012.
Chuang, Joshua. 'When the Messenger is the Medium: The Making of Walker Evans' "American Photographs" and Robert Frank's "The Americans"'. *Yale University Art Gallery Bulletin* (2006): 108–23.
Church, David. 'Drive-In and Grindhouse Theatres'. In *The Routledge Companion to Cult Cinema*, edited by Ernest Mathijs and Jamie Sexton, 215–22. London: Routledge, 2020.
Church, David. *Grindhouse Nostalgia: Memory, Home Video and Exploitation Film Fandom*. Edinburgh: Edinburgh University Press, 2015.
Church, David. 'They Are Risen: Drive-in Distractions and Hallowed Ground Under Lockdown'. *Flow*, 16 April 2020, https://www.flowjournal.org/2020/04/they-are-risen/ (accessed 20 March 2023).
Cohen, Mary Morley. 'Forgotten Audiences in the Passion Pits: Drive-in Theatres and Changing Spectator Practices in Post-War America'. *Film History* 6, no. 4 (1994): 470–86.
Cook, David A. *Lost Illusions: American Cinema in the Shadow of Watergate and Vietnam*. Berkeley: University of California Press, 2000.
Copeland, Leo. 'A Night at the Picture Show, the Tower Theatre'. *Seminole Sentinel*, 28 April 2013, 8A.
Corman, Roger, with Jim Jerome. *How I Made a Hundred Movies in Hollywood and Never Lost a Dime*. New York: Da Capo Press, 1998.
Cosgrove, Ben. 'Let's Go to the Drive-in Movies!' *Life*, https://www.life.com/lifestyle/drive-in-theaters-photos-of-a-vanishing-american-pastime/ (accessed 30 November 2022).
Crowther, Bosley. '"Stromboli", Bergman-Rossellini Movie, is Unveiled at 120 Theatres in This Area'. *New York Times*, 16 February 1950, 28.
Cruickshank, Iona. 'Mapping the Fading Light: A Photographic Documentation of Canadian Drive-in Movie Theatres, 2001–2009'. Unpublished project book, 2010. Special Collections, Kimberlin Library, De Montfort University.
Cunningham, James P. 'The Drive-In Theater'. In *Film Daily Year Book of Motion Pictures*, edited by Jack Alicoate, 799–803. New York: Wid's Film and Film Folk, 1950.
Daley, Ann Scarlett. 'The Necessity for Ruins'. In *Elevating Western American Art: Developing an Institute in the Cultural Capital of the Rockies*, edited by Thomas Brent Smith, 156–9. Denver: Petrie Institute of Western American Art, 2012.
Daly, Maureen (ed.). *Profile of Youth, by Members of Staff of The Ladies Home Journal*. Philadelphia and New York: Lippincott, 1951.
Davis, Blair. *The Battle for the Bs: 1950s Hollywood and the Rebirth of Low-Budget Cinema*. Piscataway: Rutgers University Press, 2012.
Dawson, Jan. 'Grease'. *Monthly Film Bulletin* 45 (1978): 175–6.
Dell'Amore, Christine. 'The Big Picture: A Well-Planned Single Image Yells the Story of 20th-Century Transportation'. *Smithsonian* 36 no. 9 (2005): 16, https://www.smithsonianmag.com/arts-culture/the-big-picture-2-110497282/ (accessed 5 November 2022).

Dika, Vera. *Recycled Culture in Contemporary Art and Film: The Uses of Nostalgia*. Cambridge: Cambridge University Press, 2003.
Doherty, Thomas. 'Race Houses, Jim Crow Roosts, and Lily White Palaces: Desegregating the Motion Picture Theater'. In *Going to the Movies: Hollywood and the Social Experience of Cinema*, edited by Richard Maltby, Melvyn Stokes and Richard Allen, 196–214. Exeter: Exeter University Press, 2007.
Doherty, Thomas. *Teenagers and Teenpics: The Juvenilization of American Movies*. Revised edition. Philadelphia: Temple University Press, 2002.
Downs, Anthony. 'Where the Drive-in Fits into the Movie Industry'. 1953. In *Exhibition: The Film Reader*, edited by Ina Rae Hark, 123–5. London and New York: Routledge, 2002.
Drazin, Charles. *The Faber Book of French Cinema*. London: Faber, 2011.
Dunlop, David W. 'John J. McNamara, An Architect and Theater Designer, Dies Age 90'. *New York Times*, 9 May 1998, D11.
Durant, John. 'The Movies Take to the Pastures'. *Saturday Evening Post*, 14 October 1950, 24–5, 85, 89–90.
Duvall, Evelyn Millis. 'III. Course on Adolescence, Adolescence and the Automobile. Points for Study and Discussion. All in a Child's Lifetime Study Discussion Program'. *National-Parent Teacher*, October 1959, 36.
Dwyer, Michael D. *Back to the Fifties: Nostalgia, Hollywood Film, and Popular Music of the Seventies and Eighties*. Oxford: Oxford University Press, 2015.
Dybis, Karen. *The Ford-Wyoming Drive-In: Cars, Candy & Canoodling in the Motor City*. Charleston: History Press, 2014.
Egerton, Richard. *American Film Exhibition and an Analysis of the Motion Picture Industry's Market Structure*. London: Routledge, 1983.
Engle, Marty M. *Strange Matter: Creature Features*. San Diego: Montage, 1996.
Farber, Arnold. 'Survey Proves Drive-Ins Just Grow, Grow, Grow'. *Motion Picture Exhibitor*, 28 February 1956, PT 5-6.
Feagin, Joe R. and Hernán Vera. *White Racism: The Basics*. New York: Routledge, 1995.
Fishman, Robert. 'The Post-War American Suburb: A New Form, A New City'. In *Two Centuries of American Planning*, edited by Daniel Schaeffer, 265–78. Baltimore: John Hopkins, 1988.
Fleck, Karin. '"If You Say You Watch the Movie You're a Couple of Liars": In Search of the Missing Audience at the Drive-In'. In *Pandemic Media: Preliminary Notes Towards an Inventory*, edited by Philipp Dominik Keidl, Laliv Melamed, Vincenz Hediger and Antonio Somaini, 69–77. Lüneburg: Meson Press, 2000.
Fleming, Ian. *Diamonds are Forever*. 1956. London: Penguin, 2004.
Flink, James. *The Automobile Age*. Cambridge, MA: MIT Press, 1988.
Folkart, Burt A. 'Sherrill Corwin, Magnate of Movie Palaces, Dies'. *Los Angeles Times*, 10 May 1980, OC20.
Forstadt, Jillian. 'Oscars: Read Brad Pitt's Acceptance Speech for Best Supporting Actor'. *Hollywood Reporter*, 9 February 2020, https://www.hollywoodreporter.com/movies/movie-news/oscars-read-brad-pitts-acceptance-speech-best-supporting-actor-1277805/ (accessed 17 February 2023).

Fox, Mark. 'Drive-in Theatres and Audience Rules of Conduct: Before and During the COVID-19 Pandemic'. *Participations: Journal of Audience & Reception Studies* 17, no. 2 (2020): 66–94.

Fox, Mark and Grant Black. 'The Rise and Decline of Drive-in Cinemas in the United States'. In *Handbook on the Economics of Leisure*, edited by Samuel Cameron, 271–98. Cheltenham: Edward Elgar, 2011.

Fox, William Price. 'The Drive-in Movie.' In *Mom, The Flag & Apple Pie: Great American Writers on Great American Things*, compiled by the editors of *Esquire*, 211–18. Garden City: Doubleday, 1975.

Frank, Robert. *The Americans: Photographs by Robert Frank*. 1959. Göttingen: Steidl, 2008.

Fuller-Seeley, Kathryn H. '"What the Picture Did for Me": Small-Town Exhibitors' Strategies for Surviving the Great Depression'. In *Hollywood in the Neighborhood: Historical Case Studies of Local Moviemaking*, edited by Kathryn H. Fuller-Seeley, 186–207. Berkeley: University of California Press, 2008.

Gage, Nevin I. 'Average Drive-in Gross is Nearly Fifty Per Cent of the Ticket Dollar'. *Boxoffice*, 2 February 1952, 30–2.

Gallagher, Tag. *The Adventures of Roberto Rossellini: His Life and Films*. New York: Da Capo Press, 1998.

Giles, Dennis. 'The Outdoor Economy: A Study of the Contemporary Drive-in'. *Journal of the University Film and Video Association* 35, no. 2 (1983): 66–76.

Godfrey, Nicholas. *The Limits of Auteurism: Case Studies in the Critically Constructed New Hollywood*. New Brunswick: Rutgers University Press, 2017.

Gold, R. C. *Drive-In Girl*. New York: Midwood, 1961.

Goldberg, Vicky and Robert Silberman. *American Photography: A Century of Images*. San Francisco: Chronicle Book, 1999.

Goldsmith, Ben. '"The Comfort Lies in all the Things You Can Do": The Australian Drive-in – Cinema of Distraction'. *Journal of Popular Culture* 33, no. 1 (1999): 153–64.

Gomery, Douglas. *The Hollywood Studio System: A History*. London: British Film Institute, 2005.

Gomery, Douglas. *Shared Pleasures: A History of Movie Presentation in the US*. London: BFI Publishing, 1992.

Green, Harris. '"Grease"? Groovy'. *New York Times*, 4 June 1972, D1.

Gruner, Oliver and Peter Krämer (eds). *Grease is the Word*. London: Anthem Press, 2020.

Guralnick, Peter. *Last Train to Memphis: The Rise of Elvis Presley*. Boston: Little Brown, 1994.

Hall, Sheldon. 'Ozoners, Roadshows and Blitz Exhibitionism: Postwar Developments in Distribution and Exhibition'. In *The Classical Hollywood Reader*, edited by Steve Neale, 343–54. Abingdon: Routledge, 2012.

Hall, Sheldon and Steve Neale. *Epics, Spectacles and Blockbusters: A Hollywood History*. Detroit: Wayne State University Press, 2010.

Handel, Leo C. *Hollywood Looks at Its Audience: A Report of Film Audience Research*. Urbana: University of Illinois Press, 1950.

Hannay, Allen. *Love and Other Natural Disasters*. Boston and Toronto: Little Brown, 1982.

Hannigan, John. *Fantasy City: Pleasure and Profit in the Post-Modern Metropolis*. London: Routledge, 1998.
Hardy, Phil. 'The Science Fiction Film in Perspective'. In *Science Fiction*, edited by Phil Hardy, ix–xv. London: Aurum, 1983.
Harmetz, Aljean. 'Museum Celebrates "Drive-In" Movies'. *New York Times*, 27 July 1979, C1.
Harren, J. B. 'N.C. NAACP Asks "What Are We Doing?"' *Carolinian*, 24 February 1962, 1.
Harris, Thomas J. *Bogdanovich's Picture Shows*. Metuchen: Scarecrow Press, 1990.
Hay, James, 'Locating the Televisual'. *Television and New Media* 2, no. 3 (2001): 205–34.
Hinckley, John and Jon G. Robinson. *The Big Book of Car Culture: The Armchair Guide to Automotive Americana*. St Paul: Motorbooks, 2005.
Hinton, S. E. *The Outsiders*. 1967. Basingstoke: Macmillan Education, 1979.
Hinton, S. E. 'Teen-agers Are for Real'. *New York Times*, 27 August 1967, BR14.
Hobbs, Frank and Nicole Stoops. *Demographic Trends in the Twentieth Century: Census 2000 Special Reports*. Washington, DC: Bureau of the Census, 2002.
Hoffman, Alice. 'At the Drive-In'. *Fiction* 3, no. 1 (1974): 27–8.
Hoffman, Alice. 'The Drive-In, At Twilight'. *New York Times*, 4 September 1988, H18.
Hoffman, Alice. *Property Of*. 1977. London: Vintage, 2002.
Hofsta, Warren R. and Mike Foreman. 'Legacy and Legend: The Cultural World of Patsy Cline's Winchester'. In *Sweet Dreams: The World of Patsy Cline*, edited by Warren R. Hofsta, 22–66. Urbana: University of Illinois Press, 2014.
Hull, John D. 'Race Relations: A White Person's Town?' *Time*, 23 December 1991, 39–40.
Irving, John. *The Cider House Rules*. 1985. London: Black Swan, 1986.
Jackson, John Brinckerhoff. *Landscape in Sight: Looking at America*. New Haven and London: Yale University Press, 1997.
Jackson, John Brinckerhoff. 'The Necessity for Ruins'. In John Brinckerhoff Jackson, *The Necessity for Ruins and Other Topics*, 89–102. Amherst: University of Massachusetts Press, 1980.
Jackson, Kenneth T. *Crabgrass Frontier: The Suburbanization of the United States*. New York: Oxford University Press, 1985.
Jensen, Dean. *The Lives and Loves of Daisy and Violet Hilton: A True Story of Conjoined Twins*. Berkeley: Ten Speed Press, 2006.
Jewell, Richard. *Slow Fade to Black: The Decline of RKO Pictures*. Berkeley: University of California Press, 2016.
Johnson, David W. *Lonesome Melodies: The Lives and Music of the Stanley Brothers*. Jackson: University Press of Mississippi, 2013.
Johnson, Ken. 'Drive-Ins: Disappearing Summer'. *New York Times*, 31 July 1998, E35.
Jones, Jesse. 'Ideas Catch Fire in Dialogue'. *12 Angry Films*, 5–14. Dublin: Fire Station Artists' Studios, 2007.
Jones, Landon Y. *Great Expectations: America and the Baby Boom Generation*. New York: Coward, McCann & Geoghegan, 1980.
Keene, Caroline. *Fatal Attraction*. New York: Pocket Books, 1988.

Keillor, Garrison and Jenny Lind Nilsson. *The Sandy Bottom Orchestra*. New York: Hyperion, 1996.
Kerouac, Jack. 'Introduction'. In *The Americans: Photographs by Robert Frank*. 1959, no page numbers. Göttingen: Steidl, 2008.
King, Stephen. *11/22/63*. London: Hodder, 2011.
King, Stephen (writing as Richard Bachman). *The Long Walk*. New York: Gallery Books, 1979.
King, Stephen. *The Stand: The Complete & Uncut Version*. New York: Signet, 1991.
King, Stephen. 'This Guy is *Really* Scary!' In Joe Bob Briggs, *Joe Bob Goes to the Drive-In*. 1987, 1–2. Harmondsworth: Penguin, 1989.
Kinney, Harrison and Brendon Gill. 'Moon-Washed'. *New Yorker*, 1 October 1949, 20–1.
Kirk, John A. *Beyond Little Rock: The Origins and Legacies of the Central High Crisis*. Fayetteville: University of Arkansas Press, 2007.
Kirkpatrick, Bill. '"A Blessed Boon": Radio, Disability, Governability, and the Discourse of the "Shut-In", 1920–1930'. *Critical Studies in Media Communication* 29, no. 3 (2012): 165–84.
Klenotic, Jeffrey. 'Mapping Movies', https://www.mappingmovies.com (accessed 6 November 2022).
Klenotic, Jeffrey. 'Putting Cinema History on the Map: Using GIS to Explore the Spatiality of Cinema'. In *Explorations in New Cinema History: Approaches and Case Studies*, edited by Richard Maltby, Daniel Biltereyst and Philippe Meers, 58–84. Oxford: Wiley-Blackwell, 2011.
Knight, Arthur. 'Searching for the Apollo: Black Moviegoing and its Contexts in the Small-Town US South'. In *Explorations in New Cinema History: Approaches and Case Studies*, edited by Richard Maltby, Daniel Biltereyst and Philippe Meers, 226–42. Oxford: Wiley-Blackwell, 2011.
Knox, Annie. 'Drive-ins Go Digital, But Some Things Never Change'. *Salt Lake Tribune*, 27 August 2013, available at https://archive.sltrib.com/article.php?id=56764268&itype=cmsid (accessed 6 November 2022).
Kramer, Eric Mark. 'Who's Afraid of the Virgin Wolf Man? Or, the Other Meaning of Auto-Eroticism'. In *Horror at the Drive-In*, edited by Gary D. Rhodes, 9–23. Jefferson: McFarland, 2003.
Krämer, Peter. *The New Hollywood*. London: Wallflower, 2005.
Kruse, Kevin M. and Thomas J. Sugrue. 'Introduction'. In *The New Suburban History*, edited by Kevin M. Kruse and Thomas J. Sugrue, 1–10. Chicago: University of Chicago Press, 2006.
Kuhn, Annette. *An Everyday Magic: Cinema and Cultural Memory*. London: I.B. Tauris, 2002.
Kuhn, Annette. 'What To Do with Cinema Memory?' In *Explorations in New Cinema History: Approaches and Case Studies*, edited by Richard Maltby, Daniel Biltereyst and Philippe Meers, 85–97. Oxford: Wiley-Blackwell, 2011.
Lansdale, Joe R. 'The Drive-In: A B-Movie with Blood and Popcorn, Made in Texas'. 1988. In *The Complete Drive-In*, 21–116. Chandler: BookVoice, 2020.
Lansdale, Joe R. 'Drive-In Date'. *Cemetery Dance* 3, no. 1 (Winter 1991): 33–9.
Levy, Peter. *The Fifties: Transforming the Screen 1950–1959*. Berkeley: University of California Press, 2003.

Lewis, David L. 'Sex and the Automobile: From Rumble Seat to Rockin' Vans.' In *The Automobile and American Culture*, edited by David L. Lewis and Laurance Goldstein, 12–33. Ann Arbor: University of Michigan Press, 1983.

Lhamon Jr, W. T. *Deliberate Speed: The Origins of a Cultural Style in the American 1950s*. Cambridge, MA: Harvard University Press, 2002.

Liftin, Joan. *Drive-Ins*. London: Trolley Books, 2004.

Link, O. Winston. *Night Trick by O. Winston Link: Photographs of The Norfolk & Western Railway, 1955–60*, edited with an introduction by Rupert Martin. London: Photographers' Gallery, 1983.

Livingston, Lesley and Jonathan Llyr. *The Haunting of Heck House*. Toronto: Penguin, 2014.

Livingston, Lesley, and Jonathan Llyr. *How to Curse in Hieroglyphics*. Toronto: Penguin, 2013.

Lorence, James J. *The Suppression of* Salt of the Earth. Albuquerque: University of New Mexico Press, 1999.

Louviere, Mike. 'And Now You Know: New "Picture Show" Opens in Orange'. *Orange Leader*, 4 August 2018, https://www.orangeleader.com/2018/08/04/and-now-you-know-new-picture-show-opens-in-orange/ (accessed 4 December 2022).

Lozano, José Carlos. 'Exhibiting Films in a Predominantly Mexican American Market: The Case of Laredo, Texas, a Small USA-Mexico Border Town, 1896–1960'. In *Routledge Companion to New Cinema History*, edited by Daniel Biltereyst, Richard Maltby and Phillipe Meers, 254–67. London: Routledge, 2019.

Lozano, José Carlos. 'Film at the Border: Memories of Cinemagoing in Laredo, Texas'. *Memory Studies* 10, no. 1 (2017): 35–48.

Lury, Karen and Doreen Massey. 'Making Connections'. *Screen* 40, no. 3 (1999): 229–38.

Luther, Rodney. 'Drive-in Theaters: Rags to Riches in Five Years'. *Hollywood Quarterly* 5, no. 4 (1951): 401–11.

Luther, Rodney. 'Marketing Aspects of Drive-In Theaters'. *Journal of Marketing* 15, no. 1 (1950): 41–7.

Luther, Rodney. 'Second Annual Drive-In Audience Survey'. In *Theatre Catalog 1950–51*, edited by Andrew W. Shearer, 128–34. Philadelphia: Jay Emanuel, 1951.

MacBride, Joseph. *Steven Spielberg: A Biography*. Jackson: University Press of Mississippi, 2010.

MacDonald, John D. *The Crossroads*. Greenwich: Fawcett, 1959.

Maliangkay, Roald. 'Sheltering from Streaming Clouds: Nostalgia, Authenticity, and Drive-in Cinema in Korea'. *Journal of Korean and Asian Arts* 3 (2021): 31–53.

Maltby, Richard. *Decoding the Movies: Hollywood in the 1930s*. Exeter: University of Exeter Press, 2021.

Maltby, Richard, Daniel Biltereyst and Philippe Meers (eds). *Explorations in New Cinema History: Approaches and Case Studies*. Oxford: Blackwell, 2011.

Maltby, Richard and Philippe Meers. 'Connections, Intermediality and the Anti-Archive: A Conversation with Robert C. Allen'. In *Routledge Companion to*

New Cinema History, edited by Daniel Biltereyst, Richard Maltby and Philippe Meers, 16–27. London: Routledge, 2019.

Marcus, Daniel. *Happy Days and Wonder Years: The Fifties and Sixties in Contemporary Cultural Politics*. New Brunswick: Rutgers University Press, 2004.

Maxwell, Bill. 'Sad Goodbye to 28th Street Drive-In'. *Tampa Bay Times* (FL), 21 June 2000, 11A.

Mayer, Arthur. 'Hollywood: Save the Flowers'. *Film Bulletin*, 14 April 1958, 12–15.

McDougall, Ruth Doan. *The Cheerleader*. 1973. Sandwich: Frigate, 1998.

McGraw, Donald. 'Drive-In Movies Began in Camden'. *Philadelphia Inquirer*, 6 June 1965, NJ1.

McGuane, Thomas. 'Hazardous Life in a Meat Bucket'. *Sports Illustrated*, 15 May 1952, 28–37.

McGuane, Thomas. *Something to be Desired*. New York: Random House, 1984.

McKeon, Elizabeth and Linda Everett. *Cinema Under the Stars: America's Love Affair with the Drive-In Movie Theater*. Nashville: Cumberland House, 1998.

McPartland, John. *No Down Payment*. New York: Simon & Schuster, 1957.

Meloy, Ellen. 'Passion Pit'. In *Northern Lights: A Selection of New Writing from the American West*, edited by Deborah Clow and Donald Snow, 293–4. New York: Vintage, 1994.

Monaco, Paul. *The Sixties: 1960–1969*. Berkeley: University of California Press, 2001.

Morris, James. 'Is the Drive-In Here to Stay?' *International Projectionist* 31, no. 4 (1946): 18–19, 32.

Mumford, Lewis. *The City in History*. 1961. Harmondsworth: Pelican, 1966.

Murray, Pauli. *States' Laws on Race and Color*. Cincinnati: Women's Division of Christian Service, 1950.

Neale, Steve. 'Artists and Imports, Exports and Runaways, Adult Films and Exploitation'. In *The Classical Hollywood Reader*, edited by Steve Neale, 399–411. Abingdon: Routledge, 2012.

Needham, Andrew. *Power Lines: Phoenix and the Making of the Modern Southwest*. Princeton: Princeton University Press, 2014.

Noonan, Mary Ann. 'Life of Hondo Business Man Reads Like a Two-Fisted Adventure Story'. *Hondo Anvil Herald*, 2 October 1953, 11.

Nystrom, Derek. *Hard Hats, Rednecks, and Macho Men: Class in 1970s American Cinema*. Oxford; Oxford University Press, 2009.

O'Connell, James C. *The Hub's Metropolis: Greater Boston's Development from Railroad Suburb to Smart Growth*. Cambridge, MA: MIT Press, 2013.

Opinion Research Corporation. *Public Appraises Movies, The: Highlights of a Survey for Motion Picture Association of America, Inc*. Princeton: Opinion Research Corporation, 1957. National Association of Theatre Owners Collection, MSS 1446 Box 9 Folder 10, L. Tom Perry Special Collections Library, Harold B. Lee Library, Brigham Young University, Provo, Utah.

Opinion Research Corporation. *Public Appraises Movies, The: A Survey for Motion Picture Association of America, Inc*. Princeton: Opinion Research Corporation, 1957. National Association of Theatre Owners Collection, MSS 1446 Box 9 Folder 10, L. Tom Perry Special Collections Library, Harold B. Lee Library, Brigham Young University, Provo, Utah.

Orvell, Miles. *American Photography*. Oxford: Oxford University Press, 2003.
Palmer, Randy. *Herschell Gordon Lewis, Godfather of Gore: The Films*. Jefferson: MacFarland, 2000.
Parr, Martin and Gerry Badger. *The Photobook: A History*, Vol. II. London and New York: Phaidon, 2006.
Parsons, Patrick R. 'Horizontal Integration in the Cable Television Industry'. *Journal of Media Economics* 16, no. 1 (2003): 23–40.
Parsons, Penny. *Foggy Mountain Troubadour: The Life and Music of Curly Seckler*. Urbana: University of Illinois, 2016.
Partridge, Norman and Martin H. Greenberg (eds). *It Came from the Drive-In*. New York: Daw Books, 1996.
Paulin, Jim. 'The Demise of the Drive-In Movie, Part One'. In *Millers River Reader*, edited by Allen Young. Athol: Millers River Publishers, 1987.
Percy, Walker. *The Moviegoer*. 1961. London: Paladin, 1987.
Phillips, W. D. 'A Cinema Under the Stars (and Stripes): David Milgram's Boulevard Drive-In Theatre and the Political-Economic Landscape of America's Post-War Drive-In Boom'. *Historical Journal of Film, Radio and Television* 40, no. 2 (2020): 275–96.
Ramirez, Javier. 'Vamos Al Cine: Film Exhibition and Moviegoing in El Paso, Texas, 1935–55'. PhD diss., Indiana University, 2019.
Raynor, Vivian. 'A Show's Star is the Steam Locomotive'. *New York Times*, 15 March 1992, WC22.
Rebhandl, Bert. 'The Living Room in the Car Park: Films You Can Drive in to – A Brief Phenomenology of the Drive-in Cinema'. In *Auto-Kino!*, 9–16. Berlin: Temporäre Kunsthalle, 2010.
Reddick, David Bruce. 'Movies Under the Stars: A History of the Drive-in Theatre Industry, 1933–1983'. PhD diss. Michigan State University, 1984.
Reynolds, Marjorie. *The Starlite Drive-in*. 1997. New York: Harper, 2011.
Rhodes, Gary D. 'Introduction'. In *Horror at the Drive-In: Essays in Popular Americana*, edited by Gary D. Rhodes, 1–6. Jefferson: McFarland, 2003.
Rhodes, Gary D. *The Perils of Moviegoing in America 1896–1950*. New York: Continuum, 2012.
Rose, Mark H. and Raymond A. Mohl. *Interstate: Highway Politics and Policy Since 1939*. 3rd edn. Knoxville: University of Tennessee Press, 2012.
Rosenberg, Angela. 'In the Car – With You'. In *Auto-Kino!*, 5–8. Berlin: Temporäre Kunsthalle, 2010.
Roth, Philip. *I Married a Communist*. New York: Vintage, 1998.
Russell, Francis. 'Passion Pit'. *Observer* (UK), 19 January 1958, 19.
Russell, James and Jim Whalley. *Hollywood and the Baby Boom: A Social History*. New York: Bloomsbury Academic, 2018.
Ryan, Michael and Douglas Kellner. *Camera Politica: The Politics and Ideology of Contemporary Hollywood Film*. Bloomington: Indiana University Press, 1988.
Sanders, Don and Susan Sanders. *The American Drive-In Movie Theatre*. 1997. New York: Crestline, 2013.
Sanders, Don and Susan Sanders. *Drive-In Movies Memories: Popcorn and Romance Under the Stars*. Middleton: Carriage House, 2000.
Schaefer, Eric. *'Bold! Daring! Shocking! True!': A History of Exploitation Films, 1919–1959*. Durham: Duke University Press, 1999.

Schatz, Thomas. *Boom and Bust: American Cinema in the 1940s*. Berkeley: University of California Press, 1999.
Scheuer, Philip K. 'Shocker Pioneers Tell How to Make a Monster'. *Los Angeles Times*, 21 September 1958, E1.
Sconce, Jeffrey. '"Trashing" the Academy: Tastes, Excess and an Emerging Politics of Cinematic Style'. *Screen* 36, no. 4 (1995): 371–93.
Scott, Tony. 'Romero'. *Cinefantastique* 3, no. 2 (1973): 8–15.
Segrave, Kerry. *Drive-In Theaters: A History from their Inception in 1933*. Jefferson: McFarland, 1992.
Serafino, Phil. 'Elvis's Cars on Display at Museum'. 'UPI Archives', 10 June 1989, https://www.upi.com/Archives/1989/06/10/Elviss-cars-on-display-at-museum/2663613454400/ (accessed 1 December 2022).
Shade, Eric. 'Eyesores'. In *Eyesores: Stories by Eric Shade*, 1–14. Athens and London: University of Georgia Press, 2003.
Sherwin, Skye. 'Wim Wenders's Drive-In, Marfa, Texas: Romantic Fascination with Decay'. *Guardian*, 13 April 2018, https://www.theguardian.com/artanddesign/2018/apr/13/wim-wenders-drive-in-marfa-texas-romantic-fascination-with-decay (accessed 30 November 2022).
Simms, Suzanne. *Dream Within a Dream*. New York: Silhouette, 1984.
Sindlinger & Company. *An Analysis of the Motion Picture Industry*. Vol. 1. Ridley Park: Sindlinger & Company, 1953.
Sleeth, Bernard M. 'Indiana's First Drive-In Movie'. *Indianapolis Star Magazine*, 15 November 1964, 16, 18.
Slotboom, Eric. *Houston Freeways: A Historical and Visual Journey*. Cincinnati: C. J. Oscar F. Slotboom, 2003.
Smith, Eric Ledell. *African American Theater Buildings: An Illustrated Historical Directory, 1900–1955*. Jefferson: McFarland, 2003.
Smith, W. W. 'Drive-In Theatres and Their Construction'. In *Theatre Catalog*, edited by Herbert M. Miller, 431. Philadelphia: Jay Emanuel, 1945.
Smith, Wilfred P. 'Claims – And Problems of Drive-Ins in 1951'. *Motion Picture Herald*, 3 February 1951, 13–14, 27–8, 52–4.
Sprengler, Christine. *Screening Nostalgia: Populuxe Props and Technicolor Aesthetics in Contemporary American Film*. New York: Berghahn, 2009.
Stanfield, Peter. *The Cool and the Crazy: Pop Fifties Cinema*. New Brunswick: Rutgers University Press, 2015.
Sterling, Christopher H. and Timothy R. Haight. *The Mass Media: Aspen Institute Guide to Communication Industry Trends*. New York: Praeger, 1978.
Stone, Mee-Lai. 'Cars, Bars and Burger Joints: Eggleston's Iconic America – In Pictures'. *Guardian*, 22 November 2022, https://www.theguardian.com/artanddesign/gallery/2022/nov/22/cars-bars-and-burger-joints-william-egglestons-iconic-america-in-pictures (accessed 12 December 2022).
Street, Francesca. 'Drive-in Days: America's Abandoned Movie Theaters". *CNN Travel*, updated 2 January 2018, https://edition.cnn.com/travel/article/abandoned-drive-in-movie-theaters/index.html (accessed 30 November 2022).
Streible, Dan. 'The Harlem Theater: Black Film Exhibition in Austin, Texas: 1920–1973'. In *Black American Cinema*, edited by Manthia Diawara, 221–36. New York: Routledge, 1993.

Strickland, Brad and Thomas E. Fuller. *Drive-in of Doom*. New York: Scholastic Inc, 1998.
Sutherland, Peg. *Queen of the Dixie Drive-In*. New York: Harlequin, 1996.
Synott, Marcia G. 'The African-American Women Most Influential in Desegregating Higher Education'. *Journal of Blacks in Higher Education*, no. 59 (2008): 44–52.
Szarkowski, John. 'Foreword'. In *The New West: Landscapes Along the Colorado Front Range*, by Robert Adams, v–xi. Boulder: Colorado Associated University Press, 1974.
Thomas, David G. *Screen with a Voice: A History of Motion Pictures in Las Cruces, New Mexico*. Las Cruces: Doc45 Publishing, 2016.
Thomason, Michael P., *Starlight Memories: 50 Years of Entertainment at the Mesa Drive-In Theater, Pueblo, Colorado, 1951-2001*. Pueblo: Copies in a Flash, 2002.
Thompson, Hunter S. *Generation of Swine: Tales of Shame and Degradation in the '80s*. New York: Summit Books, 1988.
Thompson, Kristin and David Bordwell. *Film History: An Introduction*. 4th edn. New York: McGraw Hill, 2019.
Toal, Margaret. 'Orange Once had Six Theaters'. *KOGT*, 20 June 2018, https://kogt.com/orange-once-had-six-theaters/ (accessed 7 February 2023).
Towne, Douglas. 'Phoenix's Street of Dreams: The Visual Extravaganza that was Van Buren'. 'Modern Phoenix', 2011, https://modernphoenix.net/vanburen/vanburensigns.htm (accessed 15 February 2023).
Tzioumakis, Yannis. *American Independent Cinema*. 2nd edn. Cambridge: Cambridge University Press, 2017.
Underhill, Charles R. 'The Trend in Drive-In Theaters'. *Journal of the Society of Motion Picture and Television Engineers* 54, no. 2 (1950): 161–70.
United States Census Bureau. '1960 Census: Population, Volume 1. Characteristics of the Population, Part 1–57', https://www.census.gov/library/publications/1961/dec/population-vol-01.html (accessed 1 December 2022).
Updike, John. 'The Deacon'. *New Yorker*, 12 February 1970, https://www.newyorker.com/magazine/1970/02/21/the-deacon (accessed 6 November 2022).
Valentine, Maggie. *The Show Starts on the Sidewalk: An Architectural History of the Movie Theatre, starring S. Charles Lee*. New Haven: Yale University Press, 1994.
van Zuilen, A. J. *The Life Cycle of Magazines: A Historical Study of the Decline and Fall of the General Interest Mass Audience Magazine in the United States in the Period 1946–1972*. Uithoorn: Graduate Press, 1977.
VanderMeer, Philip. *Desert Visions and the Making of Phoenix, 1860-2009*. Albuquerque: University of New Mexico Press, 2010.
Vincendeau, Ginette. *Stars and Stardom in French Cinema*. London and New York: Continuum, 2000.
Wallin, Zoë. *Classical Hollywood Film Cycles*. New York: Routledge, 2019.
Walsh, Mike, Richard Maltby and Dylan Walker. 'Three Moments of Cinema Exhibition'. In *Routledge Companion to New Cinema History*, edited by Daniel Biltereyst, Richard Maltby and Philippe Meers, 217–31. London: Routledge, 2019.

Wang, Han-Chih. 'The Profane and the Profound: American Road Photography from 1930 to the Present'. PhD diss., Temple University, Philadelphia, 2017.
Warner, Gertrude Chandler. *The Ghost at the Drive-In Movie*. Morton Grove: Albert Whitman, 2008.
Warwick, Loy. 'Exposing! The Drive-In Passion Pits'. *Crime Exposé*, October 1957, 28–9, 54.
Weese, Carl. 'Documentary Photography, Emotion, and Projection', 'Working Pictures', 7 May 2014, http://workingpictures.blogspot.com/2014/05/ (accessed 30 November 2022).
Welling, David. *Cinema Houston: From Nickleodeon to Megaplex*. Austin: University of Texas Press, 2007.
Wignal, Jeff. *Landscape Photography*. New York: McGraw Hill, 1987.
Williams, Raymond. *Television: Technology and Cultural Form*. 2nd edn, edited by Ederyn Williams. London and New York: Routledge, 2003.
Williams, Raymond. *Towards 2000*. London: Chatto and Windus, 1983.
Williams, Roseanne. *Seeing Red*. New York: Harlequin, 1993.
Williams, Tony. 'In the Science Fiction Name of National Security: *Cat Women of the Moon*'. In *Horror at the Drive-In*, edited by Gary D. Rhodes, 113–25. Jefferson: McFarland, 2003.
Wommack, Dick. 'Fun For All, Young and Old, at the Drive-in'. *Boxoffice*, 20 November 1961, 46–8.
Wommack, Dick. 'What My Patrons Taught Me about My Business'. *Boxoffice*, 22 May 1961, 18–19.

Index

Acres of Fun Drive-In (Phoenix, AZ) 59, 79–83, 86, 92, 93, 101, 103–5, 184. *See also* Twin Drive-In
Adam and Eve (1956) 83, 84
Adam at Six A.M. (1970) 147–9, 177
Adams, Robert 173, 174
Agrasánchez, Jr., Rogelio 84
airdomes 12, 36
Airport Drive-In (Goleta, CA) 59, 84–6, 101, 103
Akin, Wally 40, 44
All About Eve (1950) 67, 71
Allen, Robert 38, 141
Allied Artists 61, 65, 76, 89
All States Theatres 41, 43
All That Heaven Allows (1955) 63, 69, 87
American Association of State Highway Officials 28
American in Paris, An (1951) 67, 70, 106
American International Films (AIP) 8, 15, 57–8, 65, 67, 75, 82, 89, 100, 103, 104, 144, 151, 155, 182
American Theatres Corporation 71
amusement parks 6, 46–7, 49–50, 183
And God Created Woman (1956) 44, 89, 91–3, 106, 107, 170
Andrew, Dudley 135–6
Angels in Stardust (2014) 157
Appel, Alfred 173
Arentz, Dick 174
Arkansas Amusement Corporation 87, 182
Arkoff, Samuel Z. 57, 65, 80, 104
Armored Attack! (1943) 90, 92, 103
Around the World in 80 Days (1956) 71, 81, 105

Arroyo Drive-In (Cortez, CO) 96
Asher Drive-In (Little Rock, AR) 86, 90–1, 95, 101, 103
ATCO Drive-In (Atco, NJ) 14, 15
Attack of the 50 Ft. Woman (1958 and 1993) 66, 155
Attack of the Puppet People (1958) 151
At the Drive-In (band) 161
'At the Drive-In' (Alice Hoffman) 165
Audience Research Corp. 118, 119
audiences 14, 17, 18, 22, 26, 31, 57, 99, 105, 107, 110–46, 148, 177, 182, 183
  African American 12, 26, 40, 139–43, 145, 186
  class 8, 12, 65, 123, 124, 136, 144, 148, 159
  cult 8, 57, 158–9, 178
  with disabilities 4, 117, 136–9, 145, 186
  families with children 1–4, 6, 8, 11, 14–15, 17, 46, 57, 58, 65, 71–2, 75, 104, 110, 111, 114–25, 129, 132–3, 136–8, 143, 161, 177, 181, 185, 186
  gender 118, 122, 127, 129
  group 119–21, 127, 185
  Hispanic 12, 34, 40, 134, 141, 145
  older 4, 117, 122, 134, 136–8
  segregated 12, 35, 36, 40–1, 73, 86, 110, 139–43, 145–6, 186
  small-town and rural 59, 95, 148
  surveys 116–24, 186
  teenage 1–3, 8, 9, 15, 57–8, 110–14, 117–20, 122–36, 143–4, 146, 152, 155, 181, 185, 186

Aurora Motor-Inn Theatre (Seattle, WA)   114
Auto-Kino! event   176–7
Auto-Mates (1978)   157
Aventuras de Robinson Crusoe, Las (1954)   84

Babb, Kroger   37
babysitting costs   1, 8, 114, 133
Bailey, Beth L.   129
Bambi (1942)   72, 83
Bardot, Brigitte   44, 92–3, 107, 170
Battle Stripe (1950)   90, 92, 103
Battle Taxi (1955)   86, 170, 171
Beacon Drive-In (Bristol, TN)   96
Bellwood Drive-In (Richmond, VA)   142
Belton, John   49
Bergman, Ingrid   21, 55, 70
Bewildered Youth (1958)   83
Big Circus, The (1959)   82, 104
Big Sombero Drive-In (Sulphur Springs, AR)   100
Bikini Drive-In (1995)   158
Black Fist, The (1976)   153, 158
Black Horse Drive-In (Camden, NJ)   15
Blood Rage (1987)   158
Bogdanovich, Peter   149–50
Bordertown Theatres   32, 33
bottle-warming services   57, 114–15, 139
Boulevard Drive-In (Allentown, PA)   60, 61
boxing fight screenings   66, 72
'Boy Back Home, The' (Linda Davis)   160
Breines, Wini   129
Bridge on the River Kwai, The (1957)   71, 88–9, 103, 105
Briggs, Joe Bob   4, 8, 15–16, 159, 165, 168, 177
Britt, Steuart Henderson   121–2
Brooksville Drive-In (Brooksville, FL)   142
Brouws, Jeff   174
Bruno, Giuliana   22

Buckner Boulevard Drive-In (Dallas, TX)   32
Buena Vista. *See* Disney
Buñuel, Luis   84
Buscombe, Edward   103
Buster and Billie (1974)   153

Cake (2014)   156
Calamity Jane (1953)   97
Caldwell, Vilma   134–5, 144–5
California   13, 29, 30, 155, 160
Camden, New Jersey   4, 10, 11, 14–15, 62
Camden Drive-In (Pennsauken, NJ)   4, 9–12, 113
Camera Politica (Michael Ryan and Douglas Kellner)   155
Canby, Vincent   148
Candler Drive-In (Metter, GA)   96
Capitol Drive-In (Des Moines, IA)   115
Carr, Caroline   173
Carroll, Ann   104, 131–2
Carroll, Beth   155
cars   4–5, 9, 12, 28–9, 45, 50–2, 113, 130–1, 144, 156, 159, 173, 185
  car journeys   27–8, 46, 52, 130–1, 134
Cars (2006)   159
Casablanca (1943)   70, 156, 160
'Casablanca' (Bertie Higgins)   160
Cell (2016)   157
censorship and regulation   10, 19, 23, 44, 60, 92, 96
census population figures   26, 27, 31, 34, 38, 39, 45, 72, 75, 78, 86, 118–19
Central States Theatres   75
Century Drive-In (Los Angeles, CA)   105, 151
Chained for Life (1952)   66, 106
Cheerleader, The (Ruth Doan MacDougall)   164
Chief Drive-In (Abilene, TX)   41, 43
Chief Drive-In (Jacksonville, TX)   128
Chief Drive-In (Paducah, TX)   31
Chief Drive-In (Seminole, TX)   34–8, 49, 51, 73, 102
Christie, Ian   110

INDEX

Christine (1983) 156
Church, David 1, 13–15, 51, 148, 159, 178
Cider House Rules, The, (1999) 156
Cider House Rules, The (John Irving) 163
cinema history 3–4, 17, 19–20, 22, 181–7
Cinema Treasures website 19, 132
'Circle of Love' (Steve Miller Band) 160
cities and urban areas 9, 22–31, 54–5, 59, 181, 182, 185
City of Bad Men (1953) 81, 99–100
Cleopatra (1934) 97
climate 28–9, 85, 87, 88, 92, 99
Cobweb, The (1955) 85, 86
Co-Ed Drive-In (Denton, TX) 33
Cohen, Mary Morley 15, 23, 51, 135, 136, 140
Cold in July (2014) 156, 158
Columbia 88, 89, 102
Corman, Roger 57–8, 67, 69, 144
Corwin, Sherrill C. 85
Cowboy Bebop: The Movie (2001) 158
Cox, W. E. and family 34–6, 51
Craigsville Drive-In (Craigsville, WV) 95
Crane, George W. 132
Crazies, The (1973) 16
Creature Features (Marty M. Engle) 167
Crescent Drive-In (Abilene, TX) 41, 43, 44
Crime of Passion (1956) 151
Crossroads, The (John D. MacDonald) 163
Cruikshank, Iona 175
'Cure, The' (John Cheever) 161
Curse of Frankenstein, The (1957) 72, 83

Daly, Maureen 130
Daly, Sheila John 130–1
Damn Citizen (1958) 87, 92
dates and sex 1, 109–14, 119, 121, 123–35, 143–4, 147, 150–5, 157, 159–60, 162–6, 168–70, 172, 174, 177, 184, 185
Dauphin, Edouard 15
Davidson, Bruce 173
Davis, Blair 14
Dawson, Jan 155
Day the World Ended, The (1955) 57, 90
'Deacon, The' (John Updike) 163
Deadhead Miles (1972) 157–8
Delinquents, The (1957) 152
Deman, Craig 175
Detective, The (1954) 86
Detroit, Michigan 6, 26, 27, 132, 138, 171–2, 177
Diamonds Are Forever (Ian Fleming) 162
Dika, Vera 154
Dino (1957) 66, 77
Disney 49–50, 66, 71, 72, 77, 83, 89, 94–5, 103, 104, 115, 124, 150, 182
Doherty, Thomas 111, 140
Don't Knock the Rock (1957) 75, 77
Dover Drive-In (Dover, NJ) 27
Downs, Anthony 67, 102, 123
Drazin, Charles 92
Dream within a Dream (Suzanne Simms) 165–6
Drive-In (1975) 153, 157
'Drive-in, The' (The Beach Boys) 159, 160
Drive-In, The: A B-Movie with Blood and Popcorn, Made in Texas (Joe Lansdale) 165, 167
'Drive-In Date' (Joe Lansdale) 165
Drive-In Girl (R. C. Gold) 162
Drive-In Horror Show (2009) 159
Drive-In Massacre (1976) 153
'Drive-in Movie Picture Show' (Jim Henry) 161
'Drive-in movies' 1, 15–16, 159, 177–8
Drive-In of Doom (Brad Strickland and Thomas E. Strickland) 167
drive-ins
  abandoned 156–7, 174–6
  admissions 5, 12, 14, 109

INDEX

architecture 6, 22, 47–8
box-office 84–98, 106–7
closures 8–9, 12–15, 156–7, 159, 165, 169, 175, 178
dressing as you want at 79, 123, 136, 138
jokes 109–10, 128, 145, 184
laundry services 49, 57, 183
location 13, 15–19, 21–55
in novels and short stories 150, 161–9, 177, 181, 185
number of 2, 5, 9, 12–15, 19, 29–30
outside the US 16, 24, 32, 58, 155, 157
ownership 5, 11, 17, 23, 31–2, 43–5, 49–50, 55
as passion pit 8, 17, 110–15, 117, 123, 130, 182, 186
photographs of 150, 169–75, 177–8, 185
portable 22–5, 54
property value of 9, 14, 44, 48
publicity 42, 48, 93, 98–9
on screen 2, 147–59, 179, 184–5
seasonal closures 5, 29–31, 35, 36, 71, 73, 76
seating areas 28, 39
sleeping at 1, 20, 115, 125, 129, 133, 186
in songs 150, 159–61, 177, 178, 184, 185
talking at 131, 136
ticket prices 91, 94–5, 114–15
toys 116, 159
violence at 125–6, 129, 152, 164–5
'Drive-Ins: Disappearing Summer Cinema' exhibition 174
Drive-In Theatre (Thorntown, IN) 100
Dubuque, Iowa 75
Dubuque Drive-In (Dubuque, IA) 59, 75–7, 82, 88, 93, 101, 105, 184
Durant, John 57, 114, 116
'Dyess, Arkansas' (Buddy Jewell) 161

Egerton, Richard 29, 30
Eggleston, William 174
Electric Dreams (1984) 156
Elephant Stampede (1951) 99
El Monte Drive-In (El Monte, CA) 135
Elmsford Drive-In (Elmsford, NY) 27, 61–2
Elmwood Skyline Drive-In (Abilene, TX) 41, 43–6, 54
Elysia (*The Valley of the Nude*) (1934) 10, 11
Erickson, Rudy and Mrs 41, 44, 45
Escambia Drive-In (Century, FL) 99
Eternal Sunshine of the Spotless Mind (2004) 156
'Everything's Changed' (Lonestar) 161
exhibition
 arthouse 65, 105
 chains and circuits 31–4, 38–42, 46, 48, 50–1, 54, 55, 60, 62–3, 71, 75, 79–80, 85–7, 92, 95, 101, 181
 double bill 3, 57, 60, 65–7, 70, 71, 73, 76, 80–5, 98, 103–4, 182–3
 dusk-to-dawn and midnight screenings 66, 67, 77, 79, 90, 103, 125, 182
 grindhouse 60, 178
 independent 5, 31, 34–41, 50, 59–64, 72–5, 94–102, 113, 181
 live performances 66, 100, 106, 184
 multi-screen 12, 26, 41, 78–9
 programme changes 36, 66, 71, 76, 80–1, 87, 102
 road-show 37, 65, 93, 105
'Exhibitor Has His Say' column 25, 28, 59, 95–100, 103
Eyerman, J. R. 169–70, 172
'Eyesores' (Eric Shade) 169
Ezell, Claude 31–3, 48

Facts of Life, The (1960) 151, 158
Fairfax, Beatrice 131
Family Drive-In (Jasper, IN) 139
Fatal Attraction (Caroline Keene) 167

INDEX

Film History (Kristin Thompson and David Bordwell) 3, 110–11
films 3, 6, 8–11, 14–15, 17, 18, 57–107
   action 67, 71, 78, 81, 95–6
   adult 1, 8, 14–15, 69, 75, 91, 150, 178
   art 70, 105
   B- and low-budget 3, 8, 57, 60, 65, 102, 104, 155, 181
   biker 158
   cartoon 77, 89, 103–4, 182
   comedy 58, 65, 90, 95, 96, 105, 155, 158
   coming of age 156
   crime 158
   Disney 66, 71, 72, 77, 83, 94–5, 103, 104, 150, 182
   documentaries 150
   exploitation 8, 10, 11, 15, 37, 38, 58, 60, 76, 78–9, 83, 97, 106, 150, 152, 159, 178, 182, 185
   first- and subsequent-run 3, 4, 6, 8–11, 19, 23, 27, 33, 46, 48, 57–65, 67, 70, 81, 105, 182, 183
   horror 3, 58, 66, 72, 75–7, 82, 97, 102–3, 177, 182, 185
   imported 10, 65, 69–70, 72, 75, 83, 98, 107, 182
   musical 96–7, 158
   old 8, 9, 39, 70, 73, 77, 83–4, 97–8, 100, 162, 167, 168, 186
   Oscar-winning 67, 103, 182
   science-fiction 58, 67, 72, 75–7, 82, 97, 100, 102, 155, 182
   short 77, 89
   Spanish-language 37, 59, 78, 79, 83–4, 106, 182
   teenpic 3, 58, 65–7, 72, 75, 76, 82, 154, 182–3
   war 88, 103
   western 1, 11, 36, 37, 58, 66, 67, 71, 72, 76–8, 81, 83, 86, 90–1, 96, 97, 102–3, 105, 123, 155, 158, 182
First Time, The (1952) 151, 158
Fisher, Terence 69
Fishman, Robert 54
Five Gates to Hell (1959) 82
Flamingo Rising (Larry Baker) 166–7
Flamingo Rising (2001) 158, 166
Flink, James 3, 28, 189 n.14
food and drink 1, 4, 8, 57, 104, 141, 143
   concession sales 6, 25, 35, 39, 46, 65, 85, 94–5, 100, 104
Forbidden Planet (1956) 67, 75
Ford-Wyoming Drive-In (Dearborn, MI) 25–6
Foreman, W. R. 80
Fort Dobbs (1958) 87, 161–2
Fox, William Price 1, 184
Francis film series 81, 86, 96
Frank, Robert 169, 171–3, 177, 185
Frankenstein and Me (1996) 156, 158
French Line, The (1953) 90, 92
From Hell It Came (1957) 81, 82
From Here to Eternity (1953) 66, 67, 72, 103, 150, 153–4
From the Terrace (1960) 151
Frontier Theatres 31
Fuller-Seeley, Kathryn 95, 100
Funny Face (1957) 96

Gentleman's Agreement (1947) 97
Ghost at the Drive-In Movie (Gertrude Chandler Warner) 167–8
Giant Gila Monster, The (1959) 67–8, 104
G. I. Blues (1960) 184
Gidget (1959) 71, 166
Giles, Denis 30
Girl Can't Help It, The (1956) 76, 77, 155
Go, Johnny, Go (1959) 67
God's Little Acre (1958) 89
Gomery, Douglas 59, 142
Gordon, Bert I. 151
Graham, Billy 138
Gratiot Drive-In (Roseville, MI) 6–7, 132, 171–2, 177
Grayslake Outdoor Theater (Grayslake IL.) 15
Grease (1978) 16, 154–5, 157, 158, 179, 185

INDEX

Grease (stage musical) 154
Grease is the Word (Oliver Gruner and Peter Krämer) 154
Greatest Show on Earth, The (1952) 63, 71, 73, 99
Griffing, Tom 40, 41, 43, 44
Gross, Jerry 152
Gun Glory (1957) 77, 92
Gunslinger, The (1955) 90, 91

Half Way to Hell (1953) 76
Hall, Sheldon 93
Hamilton, James H. 95–100
Hammill, Harry 36, 37
Hannigan, John 49, 50, 54
Happy Ending, The (1969) 150
Hardy, Phil 58
Hart, Eleanor 130
Hay, James 49, 51
Heartbreak Hotel (1988) 184–5
Hellstrom Chronicle, The (1971) 150, 153
Herbie Rides Again (1974) 150, 153
He's a Cockeyed Wonder (1950) 151, 179
heterotopia 135
High Noon (1952) 25, 71, 97, 158
'High School Heart' (John Michael Montgomery) 160
High School Hellcats (1958) 66, 82
Hilton, Daisy and Violet 66, 106
Hine, Al 81
hinterlands 24
Hinton, S. E. 164–5
Hitler's Strange Love Life (1948) 70
Hi-Way 17 Drive-In (Edenton, NC) 58, 73–5, 86, 88, 93, 95, 101, 105, 141, 182, 184
Hoblitzelle, Karl 39, 40, 44
Hoffman, Alice 165
Hollingshead Jr., Richard 4–5, 8–10, 11, 114, 135, 137, 186
Hollywood and the Baby Boom (James Russell and Jim Whalley) 52, 132–3
Hollywood Boulevard (1976) 150, 158

Homestead Drive-In (East Montpelier, VT) 25, 97
Hondo Drive-In (Hondo, TX) 34, 36–8
Horsefield, W. E. 64
Horse Soldiers, The (1959) 67
Hot Rod Gang (1958) 66, 82
Hound of the Baskervilles, The (1959) 69, 104
House on Haunted Hill, The (1959) 81, 82
HOWCO 65, 89
Hughes, George 109

Iaeger Drive-In (Iaeger, WV) 170–1
I Led Two Lives (1953) 73
I Married a Communist (Phillip Roth) 163
Imitation of Life (1959) 71, 105
in-car heaters 6, 52, 53
Infante, Pedro 84
International Drive-In Theatre Owners' Association 32
Interstate Theatres 32–4, 39–42, 44, 46, 50–1, 181
Invaders from Mars (1953) 100
Invasion of the Saucer Men (1957) 67, 82, 167
It Came From the Drive-In (anthology) 165
I Walk the Line (1970) 153
I Want a Baby (1949) 75
I Was a Teenage Werewolf (1957) 82, 155

Jackson, John Brinkerhoff 175–6
Jackson, Kenneth T. 3, 24
Japanese science fiction films 72
Jawbreaker (1999) 157
Jaws (1975) 133
Jefferson Amusement Company 32, 38–9, 66, 70
Jennings, Ray 36
Jesse James' Women (1954) 96
Jones, Carroll 41, 43
Jones, Jesse 176
Joy Drive-In (Minden, LA) 184
Julius Caesar (1953) 86
Jumping Jacks (1952) 87, 135

INDEX

Jurassic World Dominion (2022)   159
juvenile delinquency   128, 152

Karamoja (1954)   76, 99
Kentucky drive-ins   141–2
Key City Drive-In (Abilene TX)   41, 43
Killer Shrews (1959)   67–8, 104
Kinflicks (Lisa Alther)   164
King, Stephen   168–9
King Creole (1958)   89, 184
Kingsley International   89, 210 n.125
Kirk, John A.   86
Kirkeby, Katherine and Owen   41, 44
Kirkpatrick, Bill   138–9
Kiss of the Tarantula (1976)   158, 179
Klenotic, Jeffrey   22
Kramer, Eric Mark   8
Kuhn, Annette   133

Ladies Home Journal   112–13, 144
Landers, Ann   130, 184
Lange, Dorothea   173
Lansing Drive-In (Lansing, MI)   97
'Last Drive-in, The' (Chris LeDoux)   160
Last Picture Show, The (1971)   150, 153
LeCrone, Harold B.   111
'Lee Van Cleef' (Primus)   161
Legion of Decency   92, 107
Leon Enterprises   41, 43
Lev, Peter   58, 65, 105
Levin Associates, Jack H.   29, 30
Lewis, David L.   3
Lharmon, W. T.   51
Liane, the Jungle Goddess (1958)   83, 91, 93
Liftin, Joan   175
Likins, Ruth and George   40, 43–5
Link, O. Winston   169–73
Lippert Pictures   65, 69, 76
Little Rock, Arkansas   59, 84, 86
Lockport Drive-In (Gasport, NY)   97
Loew's Incorporated   46
Loew's Sharpstown Drive-In (Houston, TX)   45–9, 53–5
Lone Star (1995)   156–7
Lone Star Theatres   33, 48

Looters, The (1955)   171–2
Lords of Flatbush, The (1974)   153
Love and Other Natural Disasters (Allen Hannay)   163
Love in Limbo (1993)   155
Love Me Tender (1956)   72, 76
Lozano, José Carlos   32, 134
Luther, Rodney   27, 117–22, 140, 145

Ma and Pa Kettle film series   72, 79, 86, 96, 101
MacArthur Drive-In (Orange TX)   18, 38–9, 46, 54, 58, 66–71, 73, 82, 86, 92, 93, 101, 104, 105, 126–7, 132, 138, 183
McGuane, Thomas   164
McNamara, John J.   48
McNeil, Clarence   41, 43
Magnificent Obsession (1954)   69, 72
Maid in the Hay (date not known)   79
Maltby, Richard   181
Manning, Nancy   132
Marrying Kind, The (1952)   100, 151
Martin, Rupert   173
Mary Washington College (Fredericksburg, VA)   145
Massey, Doreen   22
mass transit. *See* public transport
Maxwell, Bill   143
Mayfield, Molly   129, 131
Medford Twin Drive-in (Medford, MA)   94, 101
Meek, Guy William   62–3
Melody Drive-In (Thompson, GA)   142
Meloy, Ellen   111
Meloy, J. Henry   11
memory   22, 132–4, 143, 156, 177–8, 185
Mesa Drive-In (Pueblo, CO)   102
MGM   63, 73, 89, 98, 102, 115
Midnight Cowboy (1969)   149
Midway Drive-In (Ascutney, VT)   96
Mid-Way Drive-In (Winston-Salem, NC)   141
Milgram, David E.   60–1
Mischief (1985)   155
Missouri drive-ins   143

Mister Roberts (1955)   85, 86, 103
'mobile privatisation'   49, 51–2
Modern Marriage, A (1950)   78, 83
'Moments to Remember' (The Four Lads)   160
Monocacy Drive-In (Taneytown, MD)   25, 99
Monster Squad (1987)   158
Moon is Blue, The (1953)   36, 75, 97–8
Mooring, William   128
mosquitoes   6, 163, 183
Motion Picture Association of America   60, 119
Motorcycle Gang (1957)   66, 82
Moviegoer, The (Walker Percy)   161–3
Mumford, Lewis   52
Murray, Pauli   140
My Darling Clementine (1946)   66

Nace, Harry, Jr.   79–80
Nace, Harry, Sr.   79
Needham, Andrew   78
New Hollywood   148–50, 177
New Monroe Drive-In (Monroe, NC)   106, 213 n.211
New York City   27, 92, 96, 105, 173, 174, 176, 178
Night of the Living Dead (1968)   16, 158, 165
Night of the Quarter Moon (1959)   75
No Down Payment (John McPartland)   163
North Carolina   24–5, 29, 38, 55, 59, 84, 102, 106, 140–2
    Edenton   72–3, 93, 182, 184
    Fayetteville   21–3
North Reading Drive-In (North Reading, MA)   58, 70–2, 81, 82, 88, 92, 93, 101, 104, 105
nostalgia   1–3, 8, 150, 153–7, 159, 160, 171, 174, 177–8, 185, 187
No Time for Sergeants (1958)   73, 184
Nystrom, Derek   148

Oak Hills Drive-In (Salt Lake City, UT)   169–70
'Old Coyote Town' (Don Williams)   160
'Old Days' (Chicago)   160
Old Yeller (1958)   83, 88
One Potato, Two Potato (1964)   157
One Summer of Happiness (1951)   69–70
On the Waterfront (1954)   66, 85
Operation Dames (1959)   82, 103
Orvell, Miles   173
Other Side of the Wind, The (2018)   158
Our Man Flint (1966)   153
Our Winning Season (1977)   156, 157
Outsiders, The (1983)   156
Outsiders (S. E. Hinton)   164–5
Ozark Drive-In (Crocker, MO)   63

Pacific Drive-In Corp.   80, 114
Paramount Decrees   5, 33, 42, 46, 49, 50, 52, 60, 79, 181
Paramount Pictures   33, 63, 89, 94, 102
Parisienne, La (1957)   93, 105
Park Drive-In (Abilene, TX)   33, 34, 41, 42, 44, 48, 55, 114–15
Park Drive-In (Phoenix, AZ)   81, 82
Parkhurst, Pearce   97, 99
Passion Pit (band)   161
Passion's Payment (1946)   70
Pat and Mike (1952)   98
Pelican Drive-In (Jennings, LA)   98
Pennsauken Drive-In (Pennsauken, NJ)   14
Peso Drive-In (Phoenix, AZ)   59, 79, 80, 82–4, 101. *See also* Twin Drive-In
Peter Pan (1953)   94
Peyton Place (1957)   71, 87–9, 91
Phoenix, AZ   78
Pickwick Drive-In (Burbank, CA)   151, 179
Pine-Hill Drive-In (Picayune, MS)   95
Pines Drive-In (Little Rock, AR)   86, 91–3, 95, 101, 103–4, 182
Pitt, Brad   133

playgrounds 1, 6, 8, 35, 41, 46–50, 75, 93, 116, 124, 133, 143, 154, 185
'Popcorn Box' (Edwin McCain) 161
'Popsicles and Icicles' (The Murmaids) 160
popular imagination, the 17, 185–6
Pork Chop Hill (1959) 81, 103
Portland Drive-In (Portland, TX) 96
Possum Pearl (1957) 92, 103
Poutra, Claudia 126–7
Pratt-Mont Drive-In (Prattville, AL) 28, 96
Presley, Elvis 89, 184–5
Prince of Peace, The (1949) 37
Procane Chronicle, The (Oliver Bleek) 163–4
projection 8, 25
   CinemaScope 6, 81, 85
   CineMiracle and Cinerama 105
   colour 97
   digital 9, 157
   image quality 6, 97–8, 181–3
Property Of (Alice Hoffman) 165
Public Appraises Movies survey 119–22, 143–4
public transport 5, 28, 52

Queen of the Dixie Drive-In (Peg Sutherland) 166

Racing Strain (1932) 9–10
radio 25, 51, 131, 138–9
Rainey, Doris Crump 142, 186
Rancho Drive-In (Phoenix, AZ) 125
Razorback Drive-In (Little Rock, AR) 87–90, 95, 101, 103, 105, 184
Reading, Massachusetts 70–1
'Real Country Song, A' (Dale Watson) 161
Rebel without a Cause (1955) 2, 76, 77, 85, 105, 155
Rebhandl, Bert 177
Red Dawn (1984) 156
Red Shoes, The (1948) 96
Republic Pictures 76, 89
Reseda Drive-In (Reseda, CA) 149
Rhodes, Gary D. 2
Ricker, Dorothy 130, 131

Rickert, Lindsey 175
Rio Bravo (1959) 66, 81
Riverdale (2017–) 2, 8
RKO 21–2, 55, 94–5, 115
roads and roadbuilding 5, 23, 28, 39, 41, 45, 46, 52, 54
Road to Ruin, The (1934) 10, 11
Robb and Rowley United 31, 32, 50, 59, 86–7, 93
Rock All Night (1957) 69, 72, 76
Rock Around the Clock (1956) 67, 75, 76, 86
rock 'n' roll 1, 67, 76–7, 111, 155, 184–5
Rock Pretty Baby (1956) 72, 76
Roman Holiday (1953) 72, 81
Rome, Open City (1945) 22, 98
Room at the Top (1959) 69
Roper Drive-In (Fallon, NV) 156
Rosenberg, Angela 176–7
Rossellini, Roberto 21–2, 44
Ruby (1977) 153, 158
Runaway Daughters (1956 and 1994) 77, 155

Sad Sack, The (1957) 90, 91
Salt of the Earth (1954) 106, 176
Sanders, Don and Susan 1, 6, 10
Sandy Bottom Orchestra, The (Garson Keilor and Jenny Lind Nilsson) 168
Satellite Boy (2012) 157
Seeing Red (Roseanne Williams) 166
Segrave, Kerry 2, 3, 6, 8, 9, 12–14, 16, 26, 50, 57, 61, 144
Senate Hearings 62–5, 94–5, 128, 181
Sepulveda Drive-In (Van Nuys, CA) 125, 158
71 Drive-In (Fayetteville, AR) 123–4
Sex Kittens Go To College (1960) 113
Shaggy Dog, The (1959) 66, 81, 95
Shake, Rattle and Rock (1955) 75, 77
ShaNaNa 154
Shane (1953) 71, 100
Sharp, Frank 45, 46, 48
'She's Never Coming Back' (Mark Collie) 160
She's Working Her Way Through College (1952) 135, 144–5
Shor, Ruben 94–5

INDEX

'shut-ins' 138–9
Silver Chalice, The (1954) 104, 164
Silver Sky-Vue Drive-In (Silver City, NM) 106
Sindlinger & Company 87, 109, 122
Singin' in the Rain (1952) 96–8
Sirk, Douglas 69
Sklogland, Sandy 174–5
Sky Drive-In (Adrian, MI) 96
Sky-Vue Drive-In (Rockingham, NC) 102
slang 110–13, 162, 179
small-town and rural locations 24–5, 30, 31, 34–8, 59, 72–3, 95–100, 171, 172, 185
'Small World' (Andrew Belew) 160
Smith, Eric Ledell 145
Smith, Willie Warren 5
Smoky Canyon (1952) 135, 144
Snowfire (1957) 67–8, 89
Snow White and the Seven Dwarfs (1937) 72, 125
Some Like It Hot (1959) 71, 105
Something to be Desired (Thomas McGuane) 164
Sonomarin Adult Drive-In (Petaluma, CA) 1
Sore Loosers, The (1997) 156
sound 4, 6, 8, 25, 97, 183
Southeast 14th Street Drive-In (Des Moines, IA) 115
South Pacific (1958) 82, 105
Southwest Drive-In Theatres 79
spectatorship 3, 176–7
Spielberg, Steven 133
Spies Like Us (1985) 156
Spy 77 (1936) 10
Stake Out on Dope Street (1958) 89, 184
Starlight Drive-In (Chipley, FL) 184
Starlite Drive-In, The (Marjorie Reynolds) 166, 167
Starlite Drive-In (Florala, AL) 96
Starlite Drive-In (Gloucester, NJ) 15
Starlite Drive-In (Grand Junction, CO) 100
Starlite Drive-In (Rossville, GA) 97
Star Wars (1977) 133, 185
Statler Brothers, The 153

Steel, Arthur J. 61
Stinson, Don 175
Stock Auto-Torium (Williamsburg, VA) 142
Story of Bob and Sally, The (1948) 37, 70, 105, 183
Strategic Air Command (1955) 97, 103
Street Corner (1948) 78, 83
Stromboli (1950) 21–2, 36, 44, 55
Stuart Little 2 (2002) 157
Studio Drive-In (Culver City, CA) 151
suburbia 5, 12, 24, 31, 41, 45–6, 49, 52–4, 59, 70–1, 181, 185
'Summer Means Fun' (The Fantastic Baggies) 160
'Summer of '69' (Bryan Adams) 160
Summer Place, A (1959) 105
'Summertime' (Josh Rouse) 161
Super 50 Drive-In (Ballston Lake, NY) 105
Szarkowski, John 174

Tacony-Palmyra Bridge Drive-In (Palmyra, NJ) 14, 15
Take Care of My Little Girl (1951) 98–9
'Talk Dirty to Me' (Poison) 161
Talley, Gidney 36, 37
Tank Commandos (1959) 82, 103
Targets (1968) 149, 150, 153, 158
Teaserama (1955) 106
Teenage Bad Girl (1956) 83, 104
Teenage Cave Man (1958) 66, 69, 82
Teenage Wolfpack (1956) 83, 104
television 51, 52, 60, 85, 99, 137, 139, 149, 156
Ten Commandments, The (1956) 71, 91–5, 101, 103, 106–7, 164, 170, 182
Texas 13, 17, 18, 23, 29–55, 153, 156–7
  Abilene 23, 38–45, 92
  Hondo 34, 36–8
  Houston 30, 31, 33, 45–8, 53–4
  Orange 23, 38–9, 82, 126–7
  Seminole 23, 34–6, 38
Texas Chainsaw Massacre, The (1974) 165, 185
Texas Consolidated 33, 39, 40

Texas Drive-In Theatre Owners' Association 32, 36
Theatre-screen Advertising Bureau 121
This is Cinerama (1952) 105
This Island Earth (1955) 97
Thompson, Hunter S. 1
'Those Lazy, Hazy, Crazy Days of Summer' (Nat King Cole) 160
1000 Islands Drive-In (Alexandria Bay, NY) 25
To Catch a Thief (1955) 88, 167
Too Soon to Love (1960) 152
tourism 25, 73, 78
Tower Drive-In (Abilene, TX) 41, 43, 44
Tower Drive-In (Raleigh, NC) 141
Tower Drive-In (Rocky Mount, NC) 55
Town and Country Drive-In (Abilene, TX) 41, 43
traffic congestion 21, 26, 28
Trail Drive-In (El Paso, TX) 104
Trail Drive-In (Houston, TX) 138
Trans Texas Theatres 32, 40
Tri-States Theatres 75
12 Angry Films event 176
20th Century Fox 61, 89, 98, 102
20,000 Leagues Under the Sea (1954) 72, 104
Twin Drive-In (Phoenix, AZ) 59, 78–81

Uncle Tom's Cabin (1918) 97
Underhill, Charles R. 136–7
Underwood, W. B. 32
Unholy Wife, The (1957) 83, 92
United Artists 65, 73, 75, 89, 98, 102
Universal 63, 64, 89, 98, 102, 152
Up Periscope (1959) 81–2

'Vacation' (Connie Francis) 159
Valentine, Maggie 24
Varietease (1954) 106
Vertigo (1958) 87, 169
video 1, 8, 159, 178
Video Independent Theatres 43
Vikings, The (1958) 67, 68

Wagon Wheel Drive-In (Spearman, TX) 96
Wang, Han-Chih 174
Wapshot Scandal (John Cheever) 163
Warner Bros. 64, 89, 98, 102
Washington Shores Drive-In (Orlando, FL) 95
Wayward Girl, The (1957) 88, 92
Weekend with the Babysitter (1970) 1
Weese, Carl 175
Weirdsville (2006) 157
Wenders, Wim 174
West Dodge Drive-In (Omaha, NE) 138
What Price Glory? (1952) 100
'What the Picture Did For Me' column 25, 59, 95–100, 103
White Heat (1949) 151
Whitestone Bridge Drive-In (Bronx, NY) 26, 115, 116
Whitney Museum 176
Wiggins Weird novels (Lester Livingston and Jonathan Llyr) 168
'Wild Ride' (The Doobie Brothers) 161
Wilkinson, E. L. 41, 43
Williams, Chuck 41, 43
Williams, Raymond 49, 51
Winchester Drive-In (Winchester, VA) 106
Windjammer (105) 105
Wives Beware! (1932) 4, 9
Wizard, The (1989) 156
Wizard of Oz, The (1939) 99
Wommack, Dick 123–4
Wright, Frank Lloyd 54

X . . . The Unknown (1957) 72, 83

'You Bug Me, Baby' (Larry Williams) 159

Ziegler, Harry 100, 101
zoning regulations 26, 45, 54

www.ingramcontent.com/pod-product-compliance
Lightning Source LLC
Chambersburg PA
CBHW070027010526
44117CB00011B/1731